Wendy —
May your ministries
prosper, + your
spirit soar.

Fond regards,
— Carl Gohlman

Soul
and
Silicon

Spirits in a High-Tech World

Carl A. Goldman

Rising Star Press
Los Altos, California

Soul
and
Silicon

Spirits in a High-Tech World

Carl A. Goldman

Rising Star Press
Los Altos, California

Rising Star Press
Los Altos, California

Library of Congress Catalog Card Number: 97-69777

Interior design by Joanne Shwed, Backspace Ink
Jacket design by Detta Penna
Jacket photos by Ginger Smith Bate

Manufactured in the United States of America

Publisher's Cataloging-in-Publication
(Provided by Quality Books, Inc.)

Goldman, Carl A.
    Soul and silicon : spirits in a high-tech world / by Carl A.
Goldman. -- 1st ed.
    p. cm.
    Includes bibliographical references.
    ISBN: 0-933670-01-X

    1. Santa Clara County (Calif.)--Religious life and customs.
2. Santa Clara County (Calif.)--Religion--20th century. 3.
Technology--Religious aspects. I. Title.

BL2527.C2G65 1998   291'.09794'73
                                      QBI97-41033

For *M*
Path starter, life partner

Contents

Acknowledgements

Spiritual matters are deeply personal, and people are understandably hesitant to bare their souls for public review. Those who agreed to be interviewed for this book earned my profound admiration and respect as well as my gratitude. I hope that readers will find them good companions for their own journeys.

My sincere thanks also to those who contributed to the mind- and eyeball-taxing task of reading drafts and providing editorial feedback: Ginger Bate, Kit Goldman, Joan Passarelli, Joanne Shwed, Jackie Vaccarello, and Michole Nicholson, Editorial Director of Rising Star Press.

And finally, thanks to Diane Wood Middlebrook for her many helpful suggestions and comments throughout the project.

Interviewees' names and other identifying details in this book have been changed to protect privacy.

Introduction

This book is about spiritual journeys in the computer technology capital of the world: Silicon Valley, California. It's about people here, and how the unique local culture—future-oriented, engineering-driven, fast-moving, intensely competitive—interacts with and influences the search for meaning in life.

The Valley has been a particularly fertile environment for the growth of independent, iconoclastic minds. It hums to the energy of people pushing the boundary of what *is* in search of what is even better—faster, more powerful, more ingenious. Stakes are high, both in money and ego, fueling the passion to create something new. In this environment, "conventional wisdom" is an oxymoron. All ideas must be tested. New information is constantly being gathered and examined to find some new wrinkle, some new piece of data from which the next "killer app" will be developed.

These traits are not confined to practical matters; they carry over to the philosophical. For those who have participated, even indirectly, in the creation of technological wonders inconceivable 10 years ago, it is a short leap to ask what truths elsewhere in life are yet to be fully understood. Inquirers into this conceptual realm

often find themselves questioning, in the true Valley style, the va-
lidity of old assumptions and traditional approaches.

This is largely a book of stories about individuals' paths and
the adventures behind them. It is an anecdotal account, not a sociological or theological study.

At its heart are the voices of the people who shared with me
their experiences and thoughts about the human spirit and life in
the Valley. For research, I conducted over 80 formal interviews and
a like number of informal ones. The people in these pages represent widely diverse beliefs, backgrounds, ages and professions—
corporate CEOs and community volunteers; homemakers and engineers; clergy and laity; believers, agnostics and confirmed atheists; all emerging from a multiplicity of ethnic and religious backgrounds. Some have chosen spiritual paths, some haven't. Some
have given names to their life philosophy, some haven't. Practically
everyone has strong opinions, even when those opinions are in
transition. All shared the sense that their view of life has been influenced by Valley culture.

Interview questions were open-ended, designed to encourage
free association. I asked people:

❖   about the events and processes they felt had shaped their spiri-
    tual lives and beliefs

❖   how spiritual life in Silicon Valley compared with spiritual
    life where they came from (and practically everyone comes
    from somewhere else)

❖   what changes they've experienced in their spiritual life or views
    since coming here

❖   whether or not they had done any exploration of alternative
    belief systems and, if so, whether they had found anything of
    value

❖ what they want from their spiritual lives, and how that compares to what they actually get

Next, I asked them to define what some of the core concepts of religion and spirituality mean to them. Questions included:

❖ what their vision of God was, how they communicate with God, and how or whether they get communication back

❖ whether one can be spiritual, even if one does not believe in a defined deity or practice a religion

❖ how they think about the soul, and whether they believe everyone has one, even those who never experience any spiritual awakening

Then we turned to the dynamics of spiritual life in a material, high-tech world. I asked people:

❖ what conflicts, dilemmas or problems they've had to deal with in living their beliefs in the real world

❖ if any specific job-related experiences caused them spiritual conflict

❖ whether their code of morals and ethics comes primarily from their spiritual beliefs, or from some other source—their upbringing, or just being a law-abiding citizen

❖ whether they thought that those with spiritual lives or beliefs were likely to hold different moral and ethical codes from those without a spiritual life

Then I asked interviewees to think about those who reject any spiritual life or beliefs:

❖   what factors lead to that rejection

❖   do people stay with that decision once made, or do they revisit it

I also asked them to describe situations they knew where one person in a marriage or relationship had a spiritual life but the other did not, and how that tended to work out.

Then I switched the focus from where they started and where they are to where they're going: the trends and future directions they see for their personal spiritual lives, and for the Valley in general.

Clergy were asked to provide a somewhat different perspective, commenting on their observations about their parishioners' views more than their own. However, I did ask clergy to talk about how their role as a spiritual leader in Silicon Valley differed from being a spiritual leader elsewhere.

The interview process itself produced unexpected reactions. Many interviewees remarked that this was the first time they had occasion to talk about these matters to anyone—even the people closest to them. It was striking to hear the comment repeated, "I wish I could be a fly on the wall when you interview my _____ [spouse, adult child, colleague, friend, neighbor, pastor]."

Some found the process of answering the questions to be an act of self-discovery: they had not previously put their beliefs into words. They came away intrigued, and considered their answers to be the starting point for further reflection.

Many expressed surprised appreciation at being listened to by an interested, nonjudgmental party. It is often said that there is a great spiritual hunger in the world today. Based on the experience of writing this book, I would add that part of that hunger is a great need to be *heard*.

Many of the dynamics and characteristics of modern times reflected in these pages are found elsewhere. But Silicon Valley culture is unique. It is a primordial soup out of which the new and unpredictable constantly emerge. Questions about the meaning of life are ingredients in the soup pot, and the fire is lit. Spiritual life in the next millenium will be influenced by the forces already at work in the lives presented here.

CHAPTER ONE

✣

Silicon Valley Overture

In the past decade, the dynamic work environments of so-called baby boomer companies, most notably the high-stakes, high-tech firms of Silicon Valley and Route 128 outside of Boston, provided a perfect breeding ground for such ("every man for himself") attitudes. ...Each new success generated more work and more of a sense that the pace of the job had taken on a life of its own.

Amy Saltzman, *Downshifting—*
Reinventing Success on a Slower Track

There is no formal "Silicon Valley" designation on most maps.

Driving in from the south along U.S. Highway 101, you pass the lettuce and artichoke farms of Salinas, the garlic fields of Gilroy, and the low, rolling, summer-brown, winter-green hills of south San Jose.

Coming in from the east, terrain is spare and dusty along Highway 580 from Tracy to Pleasanton. A few cows and the wind farms of the Altamont Pass, reaping stored energy to be sold to PG&E, provide landscape variety. On one flank grow the affluent bedroom communities of east Contra Costa County.

Heading in from the north takes you through the area's heavy civilization: Marin County, The City (San Francisco), the suburban upper Peninsula communities.

Finally, you can vector in from the west: here are the beaches, funk, college ambience and '60s counterculture remnants of Santa Cruz; and the more prosaic settings of Half Moon Bay, fog-shrouded Aptos, and the blue-collar-and-folk-arts persona of Pacifica.

Wherever your trip started, when you get here you've arrived at one of the world's most unconventional locations. Think of it as one-third geography, one-third history, and one-third state of mind.

❖ The geography includes, roughly, the northern two-thirds of Santa Clara County, the southern half of San Mateo County and the southwestern quadrant of Alameda County.

The two million people within this 30-mile radius have played a part in crafting a lifestyle richly, if hotly, spiced by the area's unique culture and economy.

❖ The history is an amalgam of top-notch educational institutions, inspired inventors, entrepreneurial energy and a synergistic business climate.

Seeds dropped into this soil have produced blooms beyond anyone's expectation. The stories of the fabled founders—Hewlett and Packard, Noyce and Moore, Jobs and Wozniak, Treybig and Perkins, and many, many others—are the warp and woof of the Valley fabric. They helped create a singular, ongoing success story. Some of the new generation of Valley companies have attained billion-dollar market valuations and revenue levels in incredibly short periods.

They also pioneered innovative views of how business organizations ought to work. Maximize employee creativity. Minimize bureaucracy. Simplify decision making. Put authority where the knowledge is. Ability outranks seniority. Speed is essential. Growth is king. Missions are stated. Involvement should be high. Profits should be shared.

Most of this was not unique in a rhetorical sense: these buzzwords were afloat elsewhere. The difference was that in Silicon Valley they passed the talk stage and became reality. Not in every company, not in all situations and departments, not all the time. But enough to say a new industrial culture had been born.

That culture was a magnet. People wanted to be where the action was, where they could push back technical frontiers, move up fast, make big money. The bright, the creative, the aggressive, the impatient, the first nerds flocked to the area. The race was on.

❖ The state of mind revolves around the predominant economic activity: producing the tools of information technology that will shape much of 21st century life.

Some people are directly involved with this effort because they're the ones making the technology happen. Others are close, but not directly involved. Still others are neither involved nor close, but they know it's going on. It's in the air, the water, the wires. Osmosis happens. Everyone gets affected by the technology chase, one way or another.

OPTIONS AND STARTUPS

Valley companies have trailblazed some radical compensation notions. These notions helped define the economy, and the economy has helped define the culture. One notion was dramatic expansion of the use of stock options. Traditionally, in American industry, options were an executive perk. Many companies in the Valley have had a policy of awarding options to *every* employee. Some haven't gone quite that far, but use guidelines which include the majority of employees. Most companies grant additional options to eligible employees every year.

"Stock options" and "incentive compensation" have become part of the working vocabulary of most Silicon Valley profession-als. Companies which don't offer them may have a hard time keep-ing their work force in place. Annual turnover rates of 30 to 40 percent are a fact of life for many organizations in any case. A substantial portion of this turnover consists of people leaving es-tablished companies for the wilderness of a new, small company: either a startup, or one still in its formative stages.

The lure is not just financial. There's an excitement and an involvement level in new companies that established companies just can't match.

Rules are nonexistent.

Everyone gets into everything.

Jeans and tennies are OK every day, not just on dress-down Fridays.

Massive amounts of pizza get ordered in for 10 PM debugging sessions which run until 3 AM or until everyone is too loony to continue.

Cots for overnighters populate the cubicles.

To keep costs down and avoid running through the venture capital too fast, computer parts and office supplies are bought with personal credit cards.

Offices leased to house 20 people now contain 56.

Fascinating, cryptic notes fill the whiteboards: thoughts of ultimate profoundness when first written; now smudged, incom-prehensible scrawls.

Hobbies, families and love lives are put on hold until FCS (first customer shipment) of whatever the new product is.

People *commit*: to the schedule, to the success, to the team.

Listen to someone who's done this talk about it. Watch the eyes glow. Many who have been there regard the new-company experience as the high point of their career, and wonder if they'll ever match it for exhilaration and sheer fun.

There is, however, another side to the dynamics of fast wealth and new-company romance. The area is rife with stories of three years of 80-hour weeks poured into startups which didn't make it, leaving behind exhausted, deprived shells instead of new millionaires. It's part of the drama.

No, the money's not the only thing. But it is by no means a rare story for employees of technology companies to find that their stock options have vested with a value that exceeds a year's salary. Some strike it big: early option grants (particularly "pre-IPO"—grants awarded prior to a company's initial public stock offering) from a successful company might catapult even nonmanagerial recipients into full financial independence. It's not unusual. This potential carrot helps keep many people working very long and very hard.

RESIDENCE ROULETTE

When a substantial increase in personal net worth arrives, what happens next is often a real estate tradeup. Micro-moves (15 miles or so) to larger houses as salaries increase or options vest keep the ambience transitory in many neighborhoods. They contribute to the pervasive atmosphere of restless rootlessness. The concept of the generation-to-generation family home is not well known in the Valley. The concept of the amazing runup in property values is.

Forty years ago, the out-of-the-ordinary demographics and economics of Silicon Valley were nascent; no more than a hazy outline, visible only to the most farsighted among the fruit tree orchards, Eichler tract homes, suburban shopping strips ... and the first electronics facilities. A typical middle-class house sold for $16,000.

Real estate agents who have been in the business long enough still recall the profession's disbelief when a typical ranch-style home in the area was first listed for over $100,000 in the '70s—and sold. Now, a 1,200-square-foot bungalow in a prime spot might cost half a million, and might sell within 24 hours with several backup offers waiting in the wings in case the first buyer can't swing the mortgage.

Absent a stock option windfall, these high-overhead households often run on two high-tech incomes, both with 70-hour work weeks. A few years of hard work might permit the luxury of migrating to one salary and one 70-hour week. It can't be counted on. Predictability isn't one of the Valley's strong points.

OUT WITH THE OLD

Deep local roots are rare: most residents are from somewhere else.

Tradition is even rarer, unless it is redefined to mean one-tenth the time span "tradition" implies elsewhere. The contrast with other parts of the country is stark. People in most areas develop affection, respect, even reverence for time-honored ways and things. In Silicon Valley, the frantic pursuit of the latest feature in the newest product seems to osmose through individual nervous systems and collective consciousness, and generate a ceaseless whirl of change. Anything tagged as tradition is a ripe target for suspicion of obsolescence, assumption it needs an update, or the same flavor of contempt given to "down-rev" software.

This pace is driven by the fact that product life cycles in the technology business are often only three to five years from "womb to tomb." The products making up an entire revenue stream today may not be generating a nickel in 36 months, and this puts enormous pressure on the tempo at which companies operate and change.

Product death tends to reverberate. People know this. The tension keeps them focused. That focus does not make it easy to find time to participate in the community. It does not make it easy to pursue intangible, nonmortgage-payment-related esoterica such as spiritual paths.

New work paradigms are emerging, and some of the historic fellowship, contact, and community offered by the office is fading:

❖ Telecommuting allows workers to get the job done from home via electronic communication.

❖ "Virtual" work groups are formed to accomplish a task. When it's done, everyone is reassigned. Group members may never see each other's faces except via videoconference.

❖ Meet the project gypsy. This person carries a laptop computer and a portfolio of technical skills from project to project, company to company, location to location. He or she is the Information Age Lone Ranger—a contractor, not an employee, galloping into the sunset once the new system successfully boots up. Life for this gypsy is a one-task stand, with no commitments or promises on either side, and no time to make friends.

THE 'HOOD

Silicon Valley is a working definition of the term "multiculturally diverse." The emphasis on technological achievement and business success has meant open doors for anyone from anywhere who can perform. People with these skills have come to the Valley from every part of the world. Cultural differences are not just tolerated, they are welcomed. This is not to say that culture clashes don't happen in the Valley, but the insatiable demand for highly competent workers makes intolerance a liability no organization can afford.

Many towns face the challenge and opportunity of building a cohesive and functional community from a widely diverse population. Neighborhoods change rapidly, and people can suddenly feel like outsiders, nonmembers of the community, when they step outside their doors. A few years ago California schools, which routinely offer classes in English as a second language, reported that they were faced with the challenge of teaching students who speak 74 different first languages. A recent *San Jose Mercury News* article reported that the number is now over 100.

STRESSES AND STRAINS

A substantial price tag comes with the affluence and sense of achievement that shaping technology and pushing back its frontiers have brought to the area. The price includes several varieties of stress, difficult or impossible time demands, conflicting priorities, family identity crises, career triumphs turning to heartbreak (and vice versa), and recurring "who am I really?" angst.

Some people end up concluding that the price is too high, and depart for Oregon, Washington, New Mexico, or "back home," wherever that might be. Others find soothing relief just thinking they might split some day. A few can thrive in this stew indefinitely. Most stay put and cope, and eventually have to deal with some form of burnout or emotional fatigue.

These secular dynamics add up to a fine formula for relegating thoughts of spiritual values or quests to a very low spot on the priority list—if for no other reason than personal energy stores are sucked dry by the pace and demands of daily life. They are also, arguably, a fine formula for molding people who may need a spiritual life more than most.

In much of the country, places of worship over a hundred years old are common, and families have been attending them for generations. It's a hard-coded part of life, a given. There's comfort to the continuity, to the certainty of community, to the existence of some spiritual component in life's pattern, even for those who experience it mostly on automatic pilot. They can be effective parts of a strategy for coping with tough times. Transplants to the Valley often find that structure difficult to duplicate.

DUELING DYNAMICS

A January 12, 1996 *Wall Street Journal* article entitled "The Spirit in Technology," by Tom Mahon, starts by saying, "Coincidentally or not, our nation's spiritual crisis has paralleled a remarkable explosion in technological prowess." Part of this book's thesis is that Mahon's observation is no coincidence, and it's clear he doesn't think so either. Since the technological explosion booms loudest in Silicon Valley, here is where we would expect to see its impact strongest. Why is there any inherent incompatibility between technology and spirituality?

The reasons fall into two categories. Let's call them the *cultural* and the *intellectual*.

Some of the factors relating to the cultural category have been alluded to above. Getting in touch with the inner person requires time for reflection, energy for exploration. Serious pursuit of answers to meaning-of-life questions needs space in which to take form. Consideration of matters spiritual benefits from having a foundation on which to build. Structuring a lifestyle which includes active participation in the community flows most easily when that tradition exists and the community is known.

Spare time, energy, space, foundations and traditions are not in long supply in the Valley.

The intellectual category contains the orientation that must, by nature, accompany technological endeavors. It requires a focus on analysis, not faith. Unlike pure science, it's not heavy on theory, demanding instead expedient pragmatism. Demonstrability often buries the conceptual when they collide. "Vaporware," a term referring to a software product which is not yet ready to use, is one of the Valley's most scathing pejoratives.

The dictum of constant change and short product life cycles creates a mindset that does not often encourage—or more importantly, reward—ongoing contemplation of recurring themes. These terms are chosen advisedly. This is not a *contemplative* environment. And it's generally considered better for thoughts to keep moving rather than recur.

Being regarded as a traditional thinker, or one whose rate of mental change doesn't keep up with the Valley beat, can equal the playing of taps to a career.

But it's not human nature to turn on a dime, or slip into different mindsets and personae two or three times a day as if they were clean shirts. The person at work is pretty much the person who comes home, the same one who makes decisions about whether or not there's room and support and need for philosophical bricklaying.

When that person leaves for the office at 6:45 AM and comes home at 7:30 PM, the odds against engaging in metaphorical masonry are long. If the arrival typically includes a full briefcase and a terse comment that, for example, Microsoft announced a competing product today, the smart money drives the betting off the board.

There are those who are gifted with the ability to put it down at the end of the day, pick it up in the morning, and have a free mind in the interim. They are rare.

(NOT) GETTING AWAY

An indicative trend in the Valley is that many companies have had to establish a maximum number of accrued vacation hours employees can carry. You might ask why. It's particularly surprising since the combination of brisk turnover and relatively new companies means that few employees have been on the payroll long enough to get up to the hallowed realm of earning five weeks or more of annual vacation.

The answer is that people are taking fewer and shorter vacations. The job demand level and the business crisis frequency level make it difficult to get away. The two-job household has double the problem: when one can make it, the other can't. Even if they manage to schedule it, there's a good chance something will come up and one of them will be asked to reschedule. A vacation alone is not much fun, so they both cancel. By the time the dust has cleared, the end of another year is approaching. They've accrued another 80 hours of vacation apiece, which they have no idea when they'll be able to take.

So the vacation has mutated to bite size. A day here. A three-day weekend there. An extra day slipped in with a holiday. If the stars line up right and no one has been kicking the cat, things might come together to allow a full week. More than that can be tough.

It's particularly tough for those whose internal operating systems don't slip into relax mode quickly. If you've got a four-day vacation and it usually takes you three just to get unwound enough to be able to start to play, the actual relaxation you get from the break might fit in a thimble.

As if time pressure isn't enough of a roadblock to recreational intervals, a new round of technological invasion is in full force. Say howdy to your cellular phone, worldwide pager, notebook computer with extra-long-lasting lithium ion batteries, remote e-mail package, wireless modem, and car fax. You're IN TOUCH, and you can't get out.

That's fine most of the time. But it can certainly take a toll on the mood when you're lying on the beach with your main muffin, sipping long-awaited mai tais, letting the warmth of the sun and the gentle sound of the surf do their magic, fingertips ready to jolt each other with a megawatt of marvelous magnetism, and three of the above devices clatter into action.

More and more people are being issued these tools. And it's often considered bad form to leave them behind, no matter where you're heading.

AND YET ...

No, it's not a conducive environment for pursuing deeper meaning. And yet ...

Against the background of semiconductors, networks, bandwidth, peripherals, clock speed, baud rates, Web surfing, source code, motherboards, stress, rush and uncertainty, some people find themselves (sometimes to their surprise) on a reconnaissance mission to find spiritual significance or something akin to it. Let's meet some of them.

CHAPTER TWO

❦

Enter the Spirit

What we call "the spiritual life" and "the spiritual quest" are simply the ways we discover to transcend our delusions of our own separateness, superiority, or inferiority and gradually feel our identity with our fellow beings and compassion for them.

Sam Keen, *Hymns To An Unknown God*

What causes people to embark on a spiritual path and stay on it?

Sam Keen's view of spirituality as a manifestation of the inherent connection between humans is certainly not universal. But even the casual observer can't miss the fact that members of spiritual "search parties" often form powerful links.

TWO VIEWS

Justin and Walter are both ministers to vigorous, medium-sized Protestant churches in the heart of Silicon Valley. Their theological outlooks and personal observations have led them to different perspectives on the question of what gets people started on a path.

Walter sees the momentum to commence a spiritual journey stemming primarily from the life experiences and conditions of the individual. Some of the contributory variables he identifies are:

❖ curiosity (fed, in part, by the Valley's "inquiring minds" culture)

❖ success, money and power, once achieved, being a less filling dish than had been expected, leaving a puzzling, inner hunger for something else

❖ dissatisfaction with the obvious or pat answers offered to questions about deeper life meaning

❖ gratitude or appreciation for good things swelling past the ability of the usual mechanisms to adequately express it

❖ problems that can't be solved by attacking them with the usual tools—or at all

This last item captures an important part of Valley culture. A frequently used term here is "Silicon Valley cowboy" or "Silicon Valley maverick." These designate individuals who do life and business their own way; disregard rules or values established by others; make things happen through the force of their personalities; and characterize the high-tech version of the American rugged individualist. "Cowboy" and "maverick" are generally considered very complimentary appellations. To these hard-chargers, the idea of a problem that can't be solved is an alien concept, probably originating somewhere in the Centaurus cluster.

However, self-containment, nonconformity, and implacability of vision can add dangerous levels of mass and velocity to a single-minded steeplechase to success. A crash, even a serious bump, is magnified. The individual may be caught between the need for a new kind of intervention and a personal direction which rejects both the intervention, and the very idea that one might ever need it. Show weakness and the sharks will smell it, gather, and devour you: the maverick's ultimate nightmare.

At the very least, unsolvable problems can be good inner conversation starters.

Justin's view on spiritual birth is founded more on theology and less on the pragmatism of circumstances than Walter's. He believes that, ultimately, no external condition *decides* or *causes* the start of a journey. Rather, it is an "awakening," and the result of the work of the Holy Spirit. However, he does see high-impact events such as children, marriage, emergency, grief, economic loss or failure as having the capability to produce an opening in which the Spirit can do its work.

Justin has a guardedly optimistic view of increasing numbers of people finding their way onto spiritual paths. "Silicon Valley is not atheist, it's agnostic," he says. He sees the need for churches and spiritual leaders to take a strongly proactive approach in reaching out to the community, partly because wallflowers don't thrive in this climate, and partly because of the nature of the populace.

Justin's first church was in Pennsylvania. "Denomination was much more important there. Here, we have a lot of young people pursuing high-tech careers who are part of the 'post-Christian' generation. They're growing up without a church." He believes many will sense isolation in their lives, and initiate some kind of spiritual exploration. He does not believe denomination will be the key to their eventual choice. He sees them focusing on people, message, programs, responsiveness, "organizational personality." The free market competition for ideas and products may spill over into spirits.

BAR TALK

At this point, let me pose a question.

You're sitting in your favorite pub, enjoying a bracing mineral water with a twist of fresh lime. A person you know well and like joins you. It's a rare, laid-back moment. Neither of you has to run off at any particular time, so the conversation flows. Let's hypothesize that you have recently had some thoughts about spirituality, religion, God, or maybe just the deep-meaning-of-life brand of philosophy. Or perhaps you've been thinking about what you're reading in this book.

Do you discuss this with your companion?

Statistically, the answer is *probably not*.

Here are some numbers which appear to contain contradictory messages. Sixty percent of Americans are members of churches and synagogues, and 70 percent say they are involved with one even if they're not a member. Yet a recent Gallup poll reported that only 2 percent of men and women talk with even their best friends about religion. And it's reasonable to assume that we share deep issues more freely with best friends than just about anyone else.

So the bottom line appears to be that this is a rare discussion topic. In Silicon Valley, based on anecdotal evidence, it's rare to the point of disappearance. Maybe it's because there's a concern that introducing the topic might drive people away, and no one likes to be lonely. Maybe it's more complicated than that.

Olivia, who moved here from the South, described how spiritual lives in her home area were tightly intertwined with social

---

Spirituality is definitely not a cocktail party topic in this area. People will reveal their sexual orientation sooner than their religious orientation.

Jesse, a Bay Area journalist

activities. As a teenager, she joined a church partly because she enjoyed hanging out with members of their choir and youth group. In sharp contrast, the Valley tends to regard matters of the spirit as private and personal. Not everyone wants tight coupling of the social and the spiritual—but many aren't sure what takes its place.

QUICKENING

Marie and her husband Ray came to Silicon Valley from old-line neighborhoods in East Coast cities. He's chief executive officer of a high-tech services firm. She was a marketing analyst for an electronic communications company. The "gotta-go-whether-you-want-to-or-not" approach of her parents toward church had turned her off to anything smacking of religion: no way was she going to get snared again.

The hard-charging Valley environment kept her mind off spiritual matters until she became pregnant. Then, consciousness of the miracle of new life began to enwrap her. When their first child was born, they made the decision that she would become a full-time homemaker. As the corporate world receded she felt ready to begin an inner dialogue on spirituality, and how it might work for her and her family. "In Boston," she says, "you're either Catholic, Protestant, Goddess or weird. You can be so much more unconnected out here."

Indeed. "Connection," or its lack, is often central to the initial energy flow impelling people to search for meaning or spirit. A faint touch of emptiness appears. A vague sense of dissatisfaction crawls up to a noticeable level. A knock on an inner door behind which something valuable should be found is greeted with a hollow echo. This can be disconcerting enough to jump-start a new process or revive a comatose one.

This process might be subtle, even elusive. Discovering emptiness is one thing; figuring out what to fill it with is another. The
time span from initial gnaw to defined direction can be lengthy
and filled with numerous dialogues: internal, external, to the point,
cloudy, uplifting, confusing. This is the nature of exploration, and
it's not unusual for people dealing with exploration's ambiguity to
envy those who have already made up their minds, one way or
another.

Nagging feelings of missing community and missing pieces of
self can be low level and intermittent in the midst of daily life demands. Some come onto a search path via more intense experience.

MIRIAM

Miriam is a well-qualified observer of the scene. In the early '80s
she left a job at a large bank to join a hot Silicon Valley telecommunications company. They had decided to form a finance subsidiary
to do in-house equipment leasing. As employee number two of
the leasing sub, she experienced the dynamics of both an established Valley stress mill and a startup. The company was subsequently acquired by a larger corporation, leading her to a rotating
set of assignments over the next few years.

Miriam had been raised Roman Catholic, but by age 16 she
had concluded that she wasn't getting anything she needed or
wanted from the Church: "I came to believe that religion was for
people who were weak." She didn't regard herself as weak. For the
next 20 years there was to be no spiritual practice in her life.

The Silicon Valley experience gave her inner person a rough-
ing up it won't soon forget. As the pace and her perceived need to
prove herself increased, she found less and less time for anything
but work. Eventually, she was to separate from her long-time
boyfriend, become almost inaccessible to friends and family, and

discontinue all activities that didn't relate to work. "Work pressures drove me to my knees," she recounted.

Miriam never felt that her spirit had died; more that it was taking a long nap. She felt ungrounded, insecure, afloat. As her anxiety waxed, her dormant belief in a higher power kicked in. She began to do something she hadn't done for a long time, and hadn't expected to do again: pray for help. Her spirit stirred. She hoped it wasn't waking up just in time to be devoured.

On a muggy Wednesday night in a tacky hotel room in North Carolina, Miriam had an epiphany.

She was there on the most mundane of business purposes: a sales call the next day. It would be a tough presentation to a skeptical audience. The pressure was on. The company wanted this business. They expected her to get it. To do that she'd need to absolutely nail the presentation, then have crisp, flawless answers to an unpredictable set of questions.

A good night's sleep would help. But as she lay, apprehensive and alone, in the strange bed in the rundown hotel in the humid, sticky night 3,000 miles from home, she wondered if she'd be able to sleep at all. She drifted. Then, she sensed … she was … being tenderly held … by "a being that I *knew* was the Holy Spirit." It offered her comfort, reassurance. It was "a transforming moment."

The next day she was calm and capable, and aced her sales presentation. Over time, the business transaction faded into the obscure wastebasket of industrial history which is the destiny of somewhere between 95 and 99 percent of all daily business activities. The transforming moment will live in her forever.

Miriam reclaimed her awakened spirit, and will never again leave home without it. Through that process, she came to realize that for her, the demands of the Silicon Valley business environment were inimical to her inner life. She did not have the bandwidth to commit the time, the emotional energy, the mindset required for business success and have anything left with which to sustain the spirit.

Circumstances gave her choices. She quit. She does not expect to return to the corporate world. She also does not expect to forget it.

Miriam now uses her business skills in local community and church work. She has become a certified spiritual director. She will be well qualified to direct those struggling to balance soul and silicon needs in the Valley corporate environment. She has become something she would never have predicted: a Silicon Valley success story. The definition may be new, but that's fine. The Valley likes new ideas.

Miriam found that her spiritual life and her high-pressure professional career could not peacefully coexist. Yet, perhaps she owes her fulfilling current path to the work-related strains. Her spirit may have gone into hibernation because it was not needed or appreciated. If she had not cooked in the Valley crucible for a while, she might never have tenderized up enough to welcome it back.

FRANK

Frank's centrally located, glass-wall office gives him a panoramic view of the bustling office activities around him. He's CEO of a community bank in the heart of the Valley. The bank's mission is to provide financing and business counsel to smaller, local enterprises.

It's a financial services version of the startup story. Frank competes with the giants of his industry. He's comfortable with this. He knows them well.

One of the things he knows is that the climate in large corporations has mutated in some unpleasant ways over the years. "People don't make friends in big companies anymore," he says. "There's the politics. Then, it's become like war. Chances are good friends will get killed off at some point. It's painful, and it's pervasive." He moved to the smaller organization because he wanted more relationships and closer ties to the community.

Frank's parents had no religion or spiritual practice, and neither did Frank for most of his life. He saw no particular need, felt no particular lack.

Seven years ago, in his late teens, Frank's younger son attempted suicide during a period of severe emotional problems. He survived. But the impact of the event caused Frank's wife, Yvonne, to restart her spiritual path. She joined a church and introduced Frank to her minister, Allen.

Over the next few months Allen became both friend and "conduit to spirituality" for Frank. The inner opening, the creation of a space in which a spiritual journey could take initial form, was the product of three things: his son's problems, Yvonne's bringing her journey into the home, and a high-impact realization about himself.

Despite his professional success, Frank saw that he did not have much in the way of meaningful, personal (as opposed to material) resources in his life. He had himself and his considerable abilities; he had his job; and he had his wife. "If any of these went away, I knew I'd be in trouble."

This was not just idle worry. Frank is solidly into midlife; health problems can happen. Today's economic uncertainties probably put anyone who doesn't think he or she can get canned smack-dab in the Pollyanna category. And, in fact, he and Yvonne had worked through a period where they discussed a separation.

Frank needed community: connection with others at a meaningful level, not the wary, let's-couch-all-our-conversation-in-company-clichés-and-accepted-business-code-so-neither-of-us-exposes-too-much-of-ourselves level. He was ready to *explore* spirituality. But he was ready to *commit* to community. He saw the church they were attending as a good place to do both. It proved to be not so simple.

Frank's experience and abilities, and his close relationship with Allen, led to an invitation to join the lay board responsible for church oversight. He accepted. Shortly thereafter, tragedy struck. Allen was diagnosed with cancer.

The original prognosis was that Allen would respond to treatment and enjoy at least partial recovery. He asked Frank to accept responsibility for chairing the lay board during his incapacitation. He felt Frank was the right person to hold the parish together during a tough time, and trusted him to maintain the church's course.

Frank took the responsibility. During this period he was also in the process of moving from a large bank to the top job in the community bank. This wasn't just a full plate. This was a heaping plate, with gravy sloshing over the sides.

Allen's illness meant that the parish had little pastoral support. The decision was made to bring in an interim minister. Frank quickly discovered that political wrangling is not unique to the corporate world.

The interim pastor was a disaster. She moved forcefully to further her own agenda: positioning herself to assume the ministerial mantle upon Allen's death. She was controlling and manipulative. She stimulated the formation of feuding factions. She drove a wedge between the younger and older members of the congregation. "Enemies lists" were drawn up. Machiavelli was alive and moving through the pews.

Frank had never anticipated that his newly started spiritual pursuit would entail such ugliness—or worse, that he would be the point person who had to deal with it. But he's a trained executive and used to taking charge. Allen had entrusted him with the health of the parish; he wasn't going to let his friend and spiritual guide down. "This was not going to happen on my watch," he recalled emphatically.

He threw himself into the muck. How he got things resolved is not the story here. Eventually, he did. But he paid a price.

"Much too early, I got to see the warts on the organizational side of religion," he says. His emerging spirituality was not yet past that critical stage where it could stand alone, unquestioned and strong, without a formal support structure. It had been fed the wrong nourishment at a critical time, and had been stunted.

The battle left dregs and doubts. He decided he couldn't stay there. Too much baggage would have to be carried forward and dealt with.

Spiritually, Frank is now doing what may be the hardest thing in the world for a take-charge executive: *waiting*. "I'm not good at just letting things flow," he says. But he's enough in touch with the inner process to realize that it took a body blow. The spirit entered. The spirit got roughed up. It hasn't left, but it needs an injury time-out.

Frank and Yvonne have acquired a 55-acre farm in Tennessee. ("To her, it's spiritual. To me, it's rural.") Visits there are a voyage to a land as far away from Silicon Valley as Kansas is from Oz. The multitude of contrasts includes the role of spiritual life.

"You're in Church of Christ and Baptist country," Frank says. "The interesting thing is the pervasiveness of the structure church creates in society there. Everyone goes to church. Then everyone goes to brunch. Don't even try to get a table in the local restaurants late Sunday morning.

"We intellectual types tend to look down our noses at the fundamentalist types. Our image of them is Bible-thumping. But there's a lot of positives that come out of that shared spirituality, a lot of community strength.

"I was standing in line at the water company outside Cedar Hill, Tennessee, to get our water turned on. I saw a guy I knew there, and after we talked a bit, he said, 'Let's go to church together sometime.' I was amazed. That just doesn't happen in Silicon Valley."

Frank places a high value on the Valley's dynamic qualities, its warm embrace of change. But he also believes that there are some absolutes and some eternal truths, some things that don't require a design update every two years.

Frank's high-octane personality would almost certainly miss the action if he spent much time in rural Tennessee. But his spirit might find a little rest, a little healing, and the assuring certainty of a community which believes it has found some things worth keeping.

COURSE CORRECTIONS

Over the past few years there has been increasing focus, research and writing on the dynamics of midlife. Not "midlife crisis," which is old hat. The new view might correctly be termed "midlife opportunity," or "it's midlife and the sky's the limit," or "let that pony run." In her book *Roads Home—Seven Pathways to Midlife Wisdom*, Kathryn Cramer offers this insight:

> *Many scholars believe that midlife offers the best*
> *opportunity for a deep conversion of the spirit because it*
> *is during this period that a person experiences a*
> *convergence of life skills, confidence, pain over the*

harsh realities and compelling necessities of life, and a desire to rethink inconsistencies or untenable spiritual beliefs.

OLIVIA

Olivia, the Southern transplant we met earlier, is in the process of sorting out her midlife beliefs. Rethinking inconsistencies is high on her list. The complexities of her journey started long ago. She's been in Silicon Valley for eight years, and this is where she'll try to resolve them. The good news: the Valley is a fine place for asking questions. The bad news: sometimes it's a tough place to find answers.

Olivia was born into a fundamentalist family. "Religion gave no comfort," she says. "It was a behavioral system. God was a watchbird and a rule maker."

Her first spiritual feelings emerged at a campfire service with some friends from another church. She responded to the quiet and the darkness, and felt a touch of something sacred. Their minister "talked thoughtfully," while her minister "harangued." She didn't like harangues. Also, the other church had a better choir and youth group. She joined.

During college she felt increasingly uncertain about religion. She questioned her beliefs. One day, in the middle of a service, she realized it wasn't speaking to her. Olivia was forthright and decisive. She got up and walked out. She didn't go back.

Olivia's first husband practiced no religion when they were married. Five years down the pike, he experienced big-time personal change and joined a charismatic Christian church. She finally told him if he said "Praise the Lord" one more time, she'd leave. He did. And she did.

After her divorce, she wanted to restart her spiritual search, but via a different path. She found a church that had many things she liked: short, philosophical, commonsense sermons; liturgy that moved her; beautiful music. Her fundamentalist memories made her wary of highly emotional worship, and she enjoyed the restrained style of the new church. She joined.

Now she's in midlife, and the midlife mindset has enabled her—maybe *required* her—to gaze more deeply at her path. She's finding some disturbing things.

She feels there's a conservatism in the church that puts it out of touch.

She doesn't see people connecting with each other.

She has serious reservations about the quality of some of the spiritual leadership she's seen.

She doesn't see prayers being answered.

She's looking for a "system of kindness and comfort," and thinks church actions or teachings can sometimes be cruel.

She thinks the virgin birth doctrine is a sexist teaching.

In short, it's not working for her. Olivia is still forthright and decisive. She may walk out. She's done it before; she can do it again. But it will leave her with a problem to solve.

Olivia's spirit is alive and kicking, but it has not found the fulfillment it craves. It is not yet feeding on the peaceful energy which springs from inner truth.

She is not a solitary person. Her spirit wants to commune with others. But she is inherently a person of strong opinions, a person who judges, and it would be almost contrary to her nature to avoid observational criticism of any group to which she belongs.

The Valley's open-ended, freeform environment provides her no particular guidance. On the other hand, a more traditional setting could trigger an iconoclastic rejection of what she might see as presumptuous "ought-to's."

In the meantime she'll read, write, seek daily quiet time, and look for opportunities to do good works. She is attracted to the concept of small groups sharing spiritual quests. It may be that such a group, flexibly and undogmatically accommodating its members' needs, is her best bet for finding her true path.

ARI

An unseasonable warm spell made the early April air smooth and toasty, even though it was only 8:30 in the morning. Ari and I sat on well-seasoned wooden furniture in the beautifully landscaped garden in front of his house. Each shrub looked like it was born to be there. It made a perfect setting for discussing Silicon Valley spirituality with a former large-technology-company manager who had started life in an East Coast Jewish family, and was now a Buddhist monk.

Ari's entire career was spent with a household-word computer company. Early on he became interested in the power of meditation, and the possibility of what might now be called "new paradigms" for workplace interaction. He still remembers being amazed when his employer immediately granted his request for a three-month leave of absence to go to a Zen monastery. "It's an unproved premise," he says, "but on reflection, I think the managers who approved it probably felt the same way I did: that it was a good thing. I think it touched their sense of spirituality."

I started by asking about his parents' reaction to his pursuit of Zen. "I sensed that the formal observation of Judaism wasn't really a big part of their lives," he said. "But they were a little confused by my decision. They saw it as something of a threat. They associated Zen with hippies and drugs, and it wasn't easy for them to sort it out."

Ari's many years in the technology trenches were processed in parallel with his adventurous path of personal enlightenment. I asked him to reflect on the area's spiritual dynamics.

"What often starts people onto a spiritual path is suffering, in the broad sense. A feeling of isolation, aloneness, lack of community. That explains the fascination some people have with cults. It's not what the organization is preaching—it's that it's *an organization*, and fills a need for community.

"My wife's family is from Oklahoma. People there are less sophisticated, but more at peace, and friendlier. They smile. They're courteous. It's wonderful to go back there.

"In the Valley we have a lot of experimentation and exploration, and a willingness to try new things. The 'technology presence' goes with this. In smaller towns, people tend to just stay with the religion of their childhood, and don't seem to feel the same need to experiment.

"What takes people off their path is usually doubt, or alienation from the group, or a more realistic view of their leader. In fact, it's *usually* a leadership issue.

"People here are looking for their spiritual practice to show them how to find equanimity, peace, joy and wisdom in the frantic, stressful, uncertain events of their everyday life. These issues are not unique to Silicon Valley. We just have more stress, more uncertainty, more change.

"I truly believe that everybody recognizes the existence of something greater than themselves. And they recognize that they're a part of it. We give different names to the 'something greater.' Some say God. Some say 'Big Self.' We come up with a word, and because we assign a word, people mistake the word for the thing. Then, because our definitions differ, we fight or go to war. Needless to say, this has nothing to do with true understanding.

"The word is a 'pointing finger,' not the thing. The whole point of spiritual practice is to bring that into view. Spiritual practice should transcend religious strife, and the confusion people feel about God, and ideas relating to beliefs.

"Technological change happens so rapidly in this area. It puts pressure on companies and people. They live with a constant feeling that their survival is threatened. In the effort to feel safe, and cope with the stress, the tendency is to put aside matters of the spirit as not being useful to professional or economic survival. But at the extreme, stress can cause spiritual seeking.

"Work and spiritual pursuits can be integrated. But it's much easier if the spiritual practice is a contemplative one that enables us to explore and accept our own suffering. Having just a belief system, as opposed to a contemplative practice, may not lead to the compassionate, nonjudgmental viewpoint which helps us see ourselves in others.

"Meditation lowers our emotional defenses, and we're more easily touched."

RON

Ron has a goal: he wants to help the spirit grow in his neighbors.

He's been in Silicon Valley for six years. He grew up in a comfortably middle-class family in Connecticut. His "cradle religion" was agnostic: his family had no active religious affiliation.

After receiving a liberal arts degree from Dartmouth, Ron entered the Columbia University architecture program. He put his newly learned expertise about line and structure to good practical use by leaving to become a furniture maker. He got married, had four daughters, moved to Northern California.

Ron always had a gut feeling that there was something sacred, something to be held in awe, somewhere. When making furniture, he enjoyed thoughts of trying to connect the buyer's spirit with the piece. But he felt no drive whatever to take the thoughts further.

One day his wife told him she would like to put the kids in Sunday school. His response was, "Over my dead body." He didn't mind pursuing spiritual ideas, but not Christianity and, in fact, not any formal religion. Religion was hypocrisy. Christianity was a fairy tale. End of discussion.

About three months later he was standing in a doorway of his house. Suddenly, he felt reality blurring, melding into a dream-image hybrid. The air was still and he stood still and felt as if a wind were blowing through the house. He sensed a new presence, very deep inside him. And he *knew*. Improbably, with no thing, no event happening, unexpected, unrequested, Christ had come for him, and to him, in "a whisper and a thunder."

As a matter of fact, Ron knew very little about *Jesus* at the time, which didn't matter. What happened was what he calls "a profound mystical connection with *the Christ*"; a powerful life force to which he had to respond. He had not one shred of question about this.

Shortly thereafter, he began teaching Sunday school.

His new-found faith was not without its practical challenges. The first time he visited a Christian bookstore, he skulked furtively through the storefront shadows, and peered carefully down the street in both directions to make sure no one he knew would see him going in. "It would have been easier to go into a porn shop," he recalls.

Sadly, Ron's new path was not enough to keep his marriage together. After 15 years, the festering of old, unresolved problems and the entry of new problems brought separation. "My heart was split open, in both grief and attendance to spirit," he says.

During the year following his divorce, he walked five miles every day in the low hills near his house. He used these walks for deep contemplation, and maintained an extensive journal of his thoughts while walking. He kept life simple: "I cried, I wrote, I sweated."

One day he walked to the top of the hill and experienced "images of an abyss." He got home, booted up his computer, and keyed in journal entries to record the images. He finished and was ready to power the machine down. Suddenly he felt the pressure of one more paragraph waiting, needing to be written. His fingers hit the keys. On the screen, in italics, were the words:

You have been a stubborn child and you must be stripped naked. I can't promise you'll end up with everything you want, but I can give you the gift of love.

Ron believes he has received a clarion call which he must not deny. He will dedicate his life and professional pursuits to his own spiritual path, and to enabling others to follow theirs. The fact that he'll be trying to do this in Silicon Valley should probably daunt him somewhat. But he's up for the challenge.

He's been ordained as a minister in a mainstream Christian denomination and spent four years as a church pastor. Now he knows it's not the right setting for him. In fact, he doesn't think "mainstream church" is the right setting to make the right things happen in this environment at all. So he's doing the Valley thing. He's planning to establish a center to focus on spiritual formation and "helping people attend to God in their lives": a spiritual startup.

JOSH

I was fortunate to catch Josh. The day after our discussion he was heading out. His mission: a two-year pilgrimage in Syria.

Josh hails from Fort Worth, Texas, and arrived in the Valley before it was under a full head of steam. He sold computers in the prehistoric times when the industry was known as "IBM and the BUNCH," an acronym for IBM's competitors: Burroughs, Univac, NCR, Control Data and Honeywell. He sold these mysterious, new machines to "bare dirt," an affectionate expression for new accounts.

Josh's early entry into computers opened other doors, and he sailed through management positions in timesharing, product development, and application systems. His career was hot, but his inner life during this period was not. He had spent time in a Roman Catholic seminary, and was aware of the role spiritual beliefs can play in lending life meaning. He felt a low-level hunger. But he couldn't muster a commitment.

He thought the problem might be that traditional religion just didn't fit him anymore, so he took a long look at New Age spirituality. That didn't fit either. He decided he needed to change things around, shake them up, "for the sake of my family, myself, and our spiritual lives."

He left the big-company environment and bought a business that would give him more free time. Then he embarked on the search for an answer to a straightforward question: "What does God want from me?" His search included exploration of all the world's major religions, except Islam. "I had too many negative images of Islam," he recalls.

Five years ago, his business took him to a technical publications trade show in Atlanta. A young woman was seated next to him on the plane. Josh regarded airplane time as a valuable opportunity for reading and reflection. He did not like to talk to seat mates. Clearly, however, this woman wanted to talk. Josh relented. "When the coffee and tea came, I reluctantly took my nose out of my book."

She was having family troubles. She needed to unburden herself to a stranger. He listened. He noticed that references to God were interleaved throughout her story. She seemed like a very spiritual person, he told her. They talked throughout the flight. Eventually she told him she was a Muslim.

The way she described Islam shocked him by being such a good fit with what he was searching for, but hadn't found. He was inspired to do research. He read the Koran. He boiled it down: "I concluded this is what I believed."

During his religious exploration, he had come to feel that "... Christianity today has been altered, and in many ways has nothing to do with Jesus' message. I reread the New Testament. Separating out what I read from what I had been told, I concluded that Jesus hadn't said he was God, hadn't really preached the concept of the Trinity.

"I believe that God sends messengers to us from time to time to help us sort things out. But clergy and church organization and power structure, that stuff is human, not divine, and it gets in the way.

"All religions say basically the same thing about God and ethics and walking humbly on the earth. We're here to use what we've been given. We're here to be good to each other. That's what Islam is about, and I discovered that I had inadvertently become a Muslim, and believed exactly what Mohammed preached.

"What I want to accomplish during my two years in Syria is to get back to the sources. Translations don't do justice to sources.

Translators often have their own bias or agenda, and I think that's why there are some problems with the Bible.

"I'm going to study Arabic, then I'm going to dig into the source documents. I'm going to read the originals of the sacred, traditional Islamic texts. The Muslim world is fragmented and fractious because of the differences between sects, but of all the major religions, it has the most complete database."

Commenting on spirituality in the Valley, Josh says, "When I left big business, I got involved in a 12-step program because my son had an alcohol-addiction problem. I got a better understanding of addiction, and I believe Silicon Valley is addicted to its own success. People here seem to be saying, 'I'll do anything to get well except give up my addiction,' and the core addiction is to wealth and success.

"Maybe we won't have real, widespread spiritual life in the Valley until that addiction is cured. Success must flow from spirituality, not the other way around."

ALICIA

Alicia's journey to the Valley started in Arizona, with stops in Texas and the Midwest. She's been here for 12 years. Her household has been a well-entrenched member of the two-careers-in-high-tech bunch. She's the administrative assistant to the chief information officer for a networking company. Her husband, Sean, is a telecommunications engineer for a large semiconductor firm.

There has always been a spiritual component to Alicia's life, but it's taken some twists and turns. Her family was Roman Catholic. As a kid, she thought everyone in the world was Catholic.

When she started having her first serious thoughts about God, she was struck by how much was going on in the world, and the number of people who must be vying for His attention. She concluded that busy as He must be, she'd better plan on figuring life out for herself. This worked for a while.

Shortly after moving to the Valley, Alicia had her first child. The life pattern modifications mandated by the arrival of first children are not news. But during this period Sean was also dealing with increased demands at work, and one of the well-known Silicon Valley dynamics kicked in: families are number two. His employer and his boss were not particularly sensitive to or interested in his new parental role.

In addition to long work hours, it was part of the internal culture of Sean's work group to head out after work and spend time unwinding together at local watering holes. After a stressful day, this was often a more enjoyable prospect than going home to an equally tired spouse and a fretful child. He found himself joining the group more and staying later. His boss approved. His wife did not. She felt he wasn't doing his share at home. She said so, often. It didn't help.

After more than a year of deteriorating domestic relations, Alicia began to comprehend that her husband was dealing with inner demons with big-time fangs and claws. It was good to feel she understood more. But she didn't have a clue about what to do next.

Alicia is skilled at evading reality when she wants to, but she didn't want to in this case. She sensed both of them withdrawing, creating a web of miscommunications and unmet expectations, the

I know my family sometimes feels that work and church "outrank" them. In Silicon Valley it's easy to get caught up in the race for more, and you probably have enough already.

Trent, president of a Valley telecommunications company

marriage falling apart. They had serious disagreements about money. It would have been a good time to draw on her spiritual life. But the internal program that told her God was busy and she'd have to wait for an appointment was still running. Also, she's a strong person; she felt she should be able to fix the problems herself.

But she couldn't, and she didn't know where to go for help. "Living through this just hollowed me out," she says. "I was spiritually bankrupt."

Joining a support group composed of people dealing with similar problems was a major step for Alicia. It may have kept her off a disastrous path. Her inability to return her marriage to health was laying down a psychic topsoil in which the seeds of perceived failure were growing into riotous luxuriance. The group provided a desperately needed herbicide: *look how strong some of us are, and yet look how many of us can't solve these problems.*

After their second child arrived, Alicia felt that her spirit had been revived. Largely through her support group, she had come to terms with what she could and couldn't fix in her marriage. She attended a women's renewal retreat and felt … renewed. Gratitude for her children had reopened her connection with God: she no longer felt she was waiting for the next available teller in a Friday afternoon bank line when she wanted a word.

Alicia also has all the requisite office automation skills an administrative assistant of the '90s needs. Such people are highly valued and well compensated in the Valley. She felt she was economically and internally ready to take a bold step.

She still loved her husband, still felt committed. But it wasn't going to fly without change. The drinking problem, the money issues, the time priorities had to be addressed. Parenting had to be a joint venture. So did household responsibilities.

Words hadn't worked, so she decided on a trial separation. It wouldn't have been her first choice, and she understood the risks. But the status quo had to be shattered if a new life was going to form. She felt guided and supported by rejuvenated faith. An anecdote which was powerful for her told of a circus performer pushing a wagon across a tightrope. Everyone enjoys it from the seats, but faith is being willing to get in the wagon. She felt ready to climb aboard.

Alicia and Sean were separated for a year. She developed the habit of getting up half an hour earlier each morning, while the children slept, "for meditation and quiet before hell breaks loose." She prayed about things that bothered her, and for the success of their marriage. She and Sean engaged in lengthy, meaningful dialogue about their problems, the kind of dialogue that never seemed to happen before.

Her program worked. They're back together, and she thinks they'll stay that way. They have been able to address the forces that were driving them apart.

The challenges in Alicia's journey have led her to frequent inner reflection. She's not sure what the precise relationship is between practice of a religion and true spiritual belief. Maybe not much.

But she is struck by the degree to which both were a greater part of the fabric of life in other places she's lived. Extra stitching, to stop things from tearing while their owners scrambled over sharp obstacles.

MARTY

Marty vividly remembers the morning he took a .357 Magnum to his failing T-shirt shop, and sat there for an hour and a half with the gun in his mouth.

His business was dying. His wife was planning to leave him—his second failed marriage. His electrical engineering degree and former job at a pioneering Valley electronics company had brought him no joy. He was struggling to think of a reason he would want his life to continue.

Suddenly, he heard a noise. The man who worked in the print shop next door had come in early. He was never there that early. Marty had expected complete privacy and solitude as he contemplated ending it all.

"I knew if I shot myself, he'd hear it," Marty recalled. "Then he'd be involved in finding me. It would be a terrible experience for him. It wouldn't have been fair to him. I didn't want that.

"I always wondered if God put that person there. Otherwise, I might have pulled the trigger. Instead, I found myself asking, 'OK, God, what do you want me to do?'

"Three months later I was in a seminary studying to become a minister."

He completed his theological education and became pastor of a large mainline Protestant church in the heart of the Valley. But after many years of ministry, he found himself squaring off with issues which made him question whether he should continue.

A big issue was the impending breakup of his third marriage. "We were married for 18 years," he said, "the last 12 of which we shouldn't have been. But our denomination doesn't really allow divorced ministers, and I agonized over this because I knew it would end my ministry. I finally decided to resign before the issue could cause divisiveness in our church."

So "minister" joined "engineer" and "T-shirt entrepreneur" in Marty's hats-worn collection, and he executed another career change. He now makes his living as a car salesman, adding to an unusually varied set of perspectives. I asked him to reflect on his personal path, and his views on spirituality in the Valley.

"I've only gone to church a few times since leaving the ministry," he said. "As a car salesman I only get every fifth Sunday off, but I don't know if I'd be going anyway. I have a hard time with organized religion now. A lot of people in this area do.

"Organized religion doesn't seem responsive to people's needs. If an engineer is working 70 or 80 hours a week, but the church wants him or her there every time the doors are open, that's a conflict. And often churches don't really want to hear people's problems. They're not showing the unconditional love they're supposed to. When I was going through my struggles, I got more support from the local Rotary Club than I did from my spiritual community.

"Even though I didn't live an exemplary life, my experiences made me a better minister. Some of my parishioners came to me *because* I had been divorced. They could relate. One woman came to me because her former pastor had told her to solve her marital problems by being obedient to her husband. Probably not good advice in the Valley.

"People here are looking for something that gives them hope beyond what they see in their daily lives. They need to feel someone cares for them. We have a lack of concern for each other in this area, a tendency not to care. Most churches fall short. With God in the equation, you would think we would be able to get past our tendencies and reach out to each other more. Churches should feed spirituality, but sometimes they drain it.

"Within every human, implanted by God, there is a spiritual need. But there are a lot of good, spiritual people here who can't or just don't want to go to church on Sunday. Organized religion equates sitting in the pews with spirituality too much. Sometimes one finds more spirituality in people who don't go to church much.

"The relationship most people have with God in Silicon Valley is not as personal as Christian theology would present it. People here have a hard time with heaven, hell, Christ's miracles, the idea of God excluding anyone. Turns people off, and makes them struggle with their vision of God.

"Another turn-off is the pressure people feel to share any spiritual life they might have, to be 'out there,' witnessing or evangelizing. For some people spirituality is too private and personal to do that, so they opt out. I think Christianity has missed the boat by making this an issue. What's important is the way people *live*, not being 'out there.' "

I asked Marty if he saw a difference in the moral and ethical codes of those who had spiritual lives and those who didn't. "Those with spiritual lives do have a different code—mostly toward others," he replied. "They're *less* tolerant! But other than that, there may not be much difference. Sometimes we forget that Christian belief says we get salvation by grace, and we go around judging others. If God were to judge us the way most of us judge others, we probably wouldn't do too well, and that's sad."

MISSION CONTROL

A May 24, 1996 *San Jose Mercury News* article was headlined "Workplace stress and the meaning of life," and subheadlined "Spirituality is a godsend for workers trying to cope." It's noteworthy that this was in the business section, and labeled as a "Management/ Leadership" focus article.

"There's a new trend developing in the workplace," the article starts off. "It's not teamwork, it's not layoffs and it's not retraining. It's spirituality." Author Laurie Beth Jones, interviewed in the article, has a recommendation: people should look inward and determine what their mission is in life. Not work, life. Then use the insight to go through the common business exercise of developing a personal mission statement. What do *you* really want to accomplish in this life?

Her point is that if you don't say it, you don't know it, and if you don't know it, you can't do it. Her conclusion: "You are either living your mission, or you are living someone else's."

Pat, a local pastor, has a similar observation. "You have to discover why you're here," he says. "If you don't, you live a compromised life. You're responsible, but you're not in charge." Many Valley residents would agree. They're pouring substantial energy into efforts to make the mission they're living their own.

CHAPTER THREE

❧

Discoveries Along the Path

A friend ... showed his résumé to ... a corporate headhunter ... who told him crisply that if he was serious about moving ahead in the business world, he should remove from the resume any mention of his involvement with a social welfare organization that was connected with a church, but not one of the genteel mainstream denominations. Otherwise, she explained, a potential employer might think him a religious fanatic.

Stephen L. Carter, *The Culture of Disbelief: How American Law and Politics Trivialize Religious Devotion*

To call competition for technical talent in Silicon Valley "fierce" is like referring to a Lamborghini as "a car": too understated to convey the full picture. Therefore, I was delighted to get the news from the human resources director of the company I worked for that our difficult search for an engineering vice president had finally been successful. She described the new member of

43

the executive team in detail, and concluded by mentioning that he was a serious, practicing Christian. She added that this should not be discussed with others: the new VP felt it would undermine his credibility and acceptance.

He may have been right.

"Technologist with religion" is tough enough contrast for one's image. But in a peculiarly Silicon Valley-flavored twist, the VP's baggage might have been heavier because he *did* belong to a "genteel mainstream denomination." Affiliation with a New Age cyberchurch could be viewed as commendably quirky, at least requiring some computer keystroking expertise to "attend." But mainstream church? Bending the knee to traditional authority is often felt to reflect a deficit in gumption, a lack of creativity, or a null individuality quotient.

There has always been an inherent tension between science and spirit. Much of what goes on in the Valley is more properly called "technology development" than "science." Whatever it's called, it has inherited much of the personality of science. It's from Missouri. It says "show me."

Nothing wrong with that. But some things are hard to show, and not everyone is comfortable doing head-on confrontations with skepticism. Journeys of the spirit, and discoveries along the path, are frequently held close to the vest.

But, sometimes, out they come.

PHIL

Phil is a seemingly rare breed: born and raised in Silicon Valley. As a successful real estate agent in the area's explosive property market, he has been close to the dynamics of "doing the deal," geographical change, and sudden wealth. He has also had to gaze into the mirror and confront a face on the road to hell.

Phil's life got off to a dicey start before he was old enough to recognize the fact. His parents got divorced when he was 3 months old. He was adopted by his paternal grandparents. His grandfather was an urban missionary, working primarily in African-American ghettos and helping black workers form labor unions. Phil went to Sunday school most weeks and liked it.

When Phil was 7 his grandfather had a severe stroke. Incapacitated, he and his wife could no longer care for a small child. Phil went to live with his father and his father's second wife. He did not have a good time.

His father and his stepmother were both alcoholics at the peak of their substance abuse. Phil's life was predictably unpleasant. They practiced no religion, and Phil found himself missing Sunday school. At age 9 he started bicycling himself to a neighborhood church school on Sundays. His father and stepmother were too fuzzy to know or care.

By the time he was 11, conditions at home were intolerable. Phil decided to start a new life for himself. He hopped on his trusty bicycle, vectored to the nearest on ramp, and began pedaling up the Bayshore Freeway. He headed for San Francisco. He had heard good things about the City, and figured it was the right place for a heads-up kid like himself.

There have been immense changes in my spiritual outlook since coming to Silicon Valley. From naiveté to blistering reality. From simplicity to complexity. From invincibility to vulnerability. From altruism to commercialism. We deal with an environment of overwhelming materialism, incredible avarice and self-indulgence, where everything has to have a value, and if you give, you have to get. The Valley has made me a realistic mystic.

Pat, a Valley pastor

He was sailing along at a good clip when the police picked him up. He ended up back with his grandparents, but it wasn't a homecoming. His grandfather had never completely recovered from the stroke, physically or mentally. His grandmother was becoming senile. It wasn't like the abuse he had experienced with his father and stepmother. It was more like being alone, made eerie by the presence of bodies with absentee landlords. He didn't like spending time there, so he didn't. The streets were better.

❧ "No Creator" ❧

Phil's early enjoyment of Sunday school, the initial touch of a spiritual component, faded. Circumstances didn't support it.

He remembers lying in bed one night at age 14 and having a rather advanced thought for a 14-year-old: "The universe is infinite and infinity implies no creator." Therefore, there was no God. He had felt relieved, somehow released from obligation.

He remembered how his father and stepmother had enjoyed drinking. He decided to give it a try. He found he had something in common with his dad: he enjoyed it, too.

One month after they both graduated from high school, when he was 17, Phil's girlfriend became pregnant. He found out on Thursday. On Monday he did what he felt was the responsible thing and married her. He stopped drinking, got a job. They had a baby girl.

When he was 21, the marriage went the way so many do when they start too fast and too young. He and his wife divorced. At that, he gave his daughter a better start than he got. She got three years of living with Mom and Dad.

The divorce gave Phil a feeling of release, somewhat similar to what he experienced from his revelation that there could be no God. He celebrated in a similar but expanded fashion, commencing the use of a panoply of recreational substances.

Phil started college at 22. He wasn't particularly motivated by a desire to learn; mostly he didn't want to carry a 1-A draft classification and get sent to Viet Nam. He did not lack for company. Draft avoidance was a widespread national phenomenon at the time, but in the Bay Area, home of Berkeley and Stanford, it was Unquestionable High Doctrinal Correctness.

His previous experience with illicit substances gave Phil a head start on college life of the late '60s. He settled on "LSD, peyote, grass and cheap red wine" as his mixture of choice. This put him into a receptive, exploratory frame of mind, and he became "New Age, drug-induced spiritual."

Phil did not make blazing progress through the higher educational system. By the time his daughter was 10 and wanted to come and live with Phil, he was still in his junior year. He agreed to take her, dropped out of college, and got a job. A few years later he remarried and had two more children.

❧ Bad to Worse ❧

He and his wife were compatible in that they both enjoyed copious quantities of alcohol and other substances. He started a property management company which quickly folded. Then he landed a job containing both good and bad news. The good news was that it had strong financial potential and involved a product he knew well. The bad news was that it wasn't helpful to his problem. He became a buyer and sales rep for a wine wholesaler.

Silicon Valley is less than a two-hour drive from the premium wine-making areas of Northern California, and wine is a very big part of the area's affluent ambience. Some of the capital invested in the cabernet vineyards of Napa, the chardonnay vineyards of Sonoma, the zinfandel vineyards of Monterey, and the boutique wineries throughout the region originated as technology money. "Palate wars" are a form of friendly competition. Restaurants vie for the most imaginative wine lists. Upscale liquor emporiums run allocations and waiting lists for high-demand vintages. Residential wine tasting parties are frequent fun. Wine-tasting weekends, staying at sumptuous bed-and-breakfast inns, are a signature mini-vacation for the area. Wine is in, and Phil was in with what's in.

It didn't work. "Eventually I couldn't stay sober long enough to make my sales calls," he says. No surprise, not even to Phil.

As he passed his 40th birthday with his life in tatters, Phil thought back to the relief he had felt when, at 14, he concluded there was not, could not be, a God. He had no remaining sense of relief. He did have, rising like a triage supplicant from a battlefield, an emerging sense of discovery: he was thirsty for something besides a big, oaky reserve chardonnay. He needed a connection, an anchor. To survive, he had to touch and revive his core of life, his spirit—if any of it was left.

❧ Making the Bed ❧

He knew what he needed to do; he just didn't know how to start. He didn't think he could go it alone. But since his teenage revelation, he had felt repulsed by discussions of God and thoughts of prayer. "It was like the cross to Dracula." Then he remembered some advice that gave him the boost he was looking for.

An acquaintance had said to him once, "Don't think of God, if that's threatening. Use the word as an acronym: Good, Orderly Direction." Not an earthshaking suggestion, but enough to allow Phil to bypass a long-standing psychic jam-up.

He used the acronym. To give it concrete form, he started making his bed every day. It became an important symbolic act. He got up. He made his bed. It was good. It was orderly. It was the beginning of a new direction.

"That's where my spiritual path started," he says. "Making my bed. It was a ray of light. It removed some darkness."

He got his real estate license and went to work. He stopped drinking. He was poised for good things to happen.

But the universe was not yet done testing Phil, not by a long shot. His wife filed for divorce. His father-in-law killed himself. And Phil was diagnosed with throat cancer.

During this time Phil's spiritual life had slowly, painstakingly inched forward. His good, orderly direction felt established. He did something he would never have expected to do a few years back: he joined a church. It was what might be called an alternative church, one that doesn't mention God, but focuses on inner spirit and harmony. But it was a church. He started saying one prayer, Reinhold Neibuhr's "Serenity Prayer":

God, grant me the serenity
to accept the things I cannot change,
the courage to change the things I can,
and the wisdom to know the difference.
Living one day at a time,
enjoying one moment at a time;
accepting hardship as a pathway to peace ...

It helped. He accepted that his cancer would probably leave him dead or seriously disabled. But he cranked his spirit up as high as it would go and started treatment. During treatment, he says, "I was a frightening apparition. I looked like an Auschwitz survivor."

"Survivor" it was to be. The treatment worked. He lived, and did not need disabling surgery. He met his current wife and reestablished relationships with his children. He sold lots of houses in the hot Silicon Valley market, and joined one of the prestigious real estate firms in the area.

A day came when his alternative church didn't seem quite enough. He needed something more. He saw an interesting article about a small, local church and went there for services a few times.

One Sunday, the associate pastor delivered a sermon in which she referred to God as "she."

"When she said that, I knew I was home," he recalls. He had never associated God with a gender identity. Removal of the masculine representation swept away a barrier.

Phil looks fit and affluent. He believes he is now a counselor of value to people in his life. He reflected on his walk through the valley of the shadow.

"There was a time when I had no ethics, no fidelity, no honor, no life. Somehow that evil went away, and the space feels filled with Good, Orderly Direction.

"I threw away a piece of my inner life puzzle at 14. Without that piece, the puzzle couldn't fit together."

MELIAN

In a way, Silicon Valley is the refuge that Melian has wanted for a long time. That's unusual. The Valley is many things, but rarely a refuge.

Melian was born to a Roman Catholic family and grew up on the East Coast. At 17, she entered a convent hoping it would be a refuge from years of vicious family abuse. "I needed to do the virgin-in-the-volcano thing," she remembers.

The convent ended up being a workable, interim escape mechanism. It was not a long-term refuge from memories, hormonal pressures, and the need to find out who she was. Also, as the youngest and healthiest nun in the convent, she saw her work assignments creep up to 18 hours a day, with no relief in sight. She left the convent at 28, to take her first shot at being an independent adult participating in the adventure of life.

She eventually left the Catholic Church completely, and became an ordained Protestant minister. It proved to be a frustration-filled pursuit, fraught with church politics, problematical acceptance of female clergy, and passive parishioners when she wanted passionate parishioners. "I tried to be flamboyant," she recalls, "and preach sermons that would stimulate energy, thought and challenge. Then people would come up to me and say, 'That was a lovely sermon,' and I wanted to say 'NO! It wasn't *lovely!*' "

Two religious environments having failed to deliver what she wanted, Melian is now adamant that organized religion is not right for her, and that it needs to fix some problems before it's right for others. She has discovered that the freedom to pursue her own spiritual path is a strong Silicon Valley feature, and she's doing that as a counselor and community volunteer. She's even managed to get some Valley maverick language into her vocabulary. "I never said the f-word before I came to California," she said with a mischievous grin.

I asked for her observations on spiritual life in this area.

"People here are less bound by theology and more bound by emotion," she believes. "They're less bound by liturgy, more bound by practice. I see much less denominational commitment here, particularly to what might be called middle-of-the-road denominations. The energy flow seems to be toward either agnostic beliefs and turning away from churches, or passionate involvement in charismatic or missionary activities.

"There's an openness here. More freedom, different ways of looking at things, less judgmental, more live and let live. That freeform environment is probably good, because I have very strong negative feelings about 'self-righteous Christians'—or self-righteous anything, for that matter.

"But there's an anonymity to spiritual life here. You don't see people talking about it in their neighborhoods the way you do back East. It's not part of being a citizen in the community.

"Most church denominations tend to have a legalistic approach, and I don't think that's where God is. To me, God is personal, a partner, not a thundering, Old Testament God of truth and law."

She paused, then concluded, "And it's God that people want a sign from, not a pastor. Ultimately, everyone's walk with God needs to be their own."

KAMAL

Kamal's route to Silicon Valley was roundabout: San Jose via Oklahoma, Pakistan and South Africa (where he was born), with other assorted stops. He is an engineer and technical training curriculum developer for a large, successful software company.

Kamal demonstrated strong multiplexing ability (the gift of doing several complex things at once) when we met at his house for our discussion. He and his family had just moved into their new home that day; his 3-year-old son was in hyperdrive and couldn't get enough of Dad's attention; an urgent computer problem which needed his expertise joined the party via telephone; and I was asking him questions about his journey and philosophy. He proved to be a first-rate juggler, able to keep his train of thought on track while 3-year-old elbows and knees mercilessly marauded his solar plexus.

Coming to the United States nine years ago gave Kamal a strong dose of culture shock. He is a devout Muslim, and understands fully the Islamic code of behavior. He was dismayed to find himself violating it.

"Muslims don't hear God's voice," he explained, "they see His signs. The Muslim is encouraged to look at and ponder what he has been given. What does this mean? What could it mean?" He was to have several experiences that he regards as signs meant to teach him during this period.

Two well-known American customs that he found he enjoyed were casual dates with women, and imbibing alcoholic beverages. These activities are not in accord with Muslim beliefs. One night he was enjoying a few drinks at a party when he met a Hindu woman.

She asked him about his roots, and he told her he was a Muslim from Pakistan. She said, "But Muslims aren't supposed to drink." He was humiliated. "I wanted the ground to swallow me up." But in the depth of the humiliation he felt he had received a sign.

On another occasion he decided to experience the American tradition known as "macho male." A friend wanted some marijuana. He agreed to go score it for him. As he was consummating the transaction, the dealer put a knife to his throat and robbed him. He felt certain that his life being spared, despite his wrong actions and bad judgment, was another sign.

Other signs emerged, and eventually Kamal changed friends, discontinued alcohol and macho, and got back to Islamic basics. His brother convinced him it was time to get married and start a family, which would short-circuit the dating issue. He married a woman he had met in Pakistan. They are spiritual partners, and their faith is the centerpiece of their marriage.

Kamal observes the Muslim practice of ritual prayer five times a day. He and a Muslim co-worker go behind the company tennis courts or onto a path on the company campus for noon prayer.

Occasionally he finds himself in a business meeting when it is time for prayer. He knows it raises questions when he excuses himself.

Kamal received threatening crank calls during the Gulf war. "The war was tough on Muslims living in the United States." However, he is very pleased with the strong response the U.S. Muslim community makes to what it considers unfair attacks. "In Europe, you see a lot of Muslims with their heads down, broken, from being called terrorists."

Comparing Muslim communities in other lands to those he has seen in Silicon Valley, Kamal observes, "Colonized countries tend to have an ongoing slave mentality even after being freed. The fact that many Muslims are well-to-do here gives them respect."

Kamal wants to play a significant role in helping to spread the Islamic faith and the word of Allah. He would particularly like to contribute by working in inner cities with gangs and at-risk youth. "I look up to most American converts to Islam because they have usually learned a lot," he says.

Technology has been harnessed to help do sacred work: Kamal has set up a site on the World Wide Web through which he offers books, tapes, CDs, and information relating to Muslim activities and publications. If this business becomes successful enough, he would love to devote himself full time to his spiritual path.

"I have to speak softly to hear myself thinking," he says, "and what I often think about is, 'what is a human?' The human is not just a seller or buyer in a consumer sense. He finds himself when he finds God. For me, that answers the question."

I asked interviewees and many Silicon Valley spiritual leaders to comment on discoveries along the path. What are people in the area searching for in their spiritual lives? How does this compare with what they need and what they find? Here are some of the answers.

From nonclergy:

I need to believe. I don't want to go around again, not even in heaven. I just want to believe my spirit will become a part of a massive force for good. I want to spend my life feeling that I'm working in tandem with that force.

I'm trying to reach the point where I'm just satisfied to know there's a higher power, and we don't need to live in existential loneliness. Even if the higher power was an abusive father, it would be good just to know He's there.

Peace. Direction.

A sense of having a place and a space which is neither work nor home, but a community I belong to.

A way of understanding life, death, and the way we're supposed to live together.

A feeling that I'm listened to, loved, cared for, and forgiven. To know that I can screw up and it's not a big deal, I can go back again and try not to screw up next time.

To banish fear.

Growth, strength and increased closeness to God.

I'm an engineer and I'm not good at expressing myself with words. I need music and the ritual of services to carry my spiritual emotion.

To connect to everyone I meet from the heart.

To set my inner compass on True North.

… and from clergy:

People want to have their hearts listened to. Every human being carries a deep longing. They want to match up the work and the value system with emerging spirituality. But they find it's tough to do, and the attempt can threaten their inner equilibrium.

For some, spirituality is their center; for others it's "icing on the cake." For some, what they want isn't what they need. Successful churches here need unique offerings for different "ages and stages."

They're looking for a sense of community and a place to belong. If you're spending hour after hour writing programs and starting companies, that's not enough. It's isolating. We try to fill a deep hunger people feel to know God.

People are aware they live in a rat race, and they get to a point where they say, "Let me have peace." But it's scary to go from a hundred miles an hour to a calm and quiet place. The speed gives people juice, and when they slow down they have to look closer.

What people long for is a Savior who will "do it for us."
What they need and what they get is a Messiah who comes
to show us the way. In my more judgmental days I might
have had more to say about what this difference tells us.

This is the cradle of high tech, computer science, and
workaholic creativity. People begin to ask bigger questions
because of that mixture. They want a sense of meaning and
purpose. They need a real connection with the spiritual
reality that's there. Some get what they need, but some try
to do their own thing and get a one-legged stool that has no
chance of providing balance to their lives.

Many want prosperity and a quick fix. The Valley is very
consumption-oriented, and the challenge to afford
everything they want causes people stress. They may embark
on meditation or a spiritual journey to get relief. Some
aren't looking for transcendence, they're looking for a
cosmic Valium.

WHAT IF

In her book, *Roads Home—Seven Pathways to Midlife Wisdom*, Kathryn Cramer says:

> *The trap of fatalism is quite compelling at midlife. By age forty, many of the men and women I counsel have seen, in their companies and their communities, a full range of self-serving, power-hungry, unethical and immoral behavior undertaken in the name of the organization, the city, the state and the nation. They have witnessed the destructive power of human frailty. It is natural for midlifers to become numb, disenfranchised, or themselves corrupted by the influence of evil.*

Let us speculate.

Let's suppose *everyone* stopped in the middle of every day, went out to the tennis courts (or wherever) and communed with their personal vision of a higher power. Let's suppose everyone had been doing that since their careers in their companies and communities began.

Might it be less likely that midlifers would be susceptible to becoming numb, disenfranchised, or themselves corrupted by the influence of evil?

Of course, the fact that Kathryn Cramer says they are doesn't mean they are.

MARJORIE

Perhaps Marjorie's professional destiny was molded by the size of her family. Her parents had 12 children—just the right number to staff a home-grown jury. Marjorie became an attorney.

When she was 23, her mother's death prompted her to begin exploring spiritual groups and philosophies. Ultimately she became a member of the Baha'i faith. "I regard my mother as a Baha'i, even though she never heard of it," Marjorie says. "She lived the kind of life a Baha'i should."

Marjorie has been in Silicon Valley 13 years. She came here from the Midwest to attend Stanford Law School. "When one becomes a Baha'i, one gets tested by difficulties," she says, and law school qualified. It was tough and stressful. Added stress arrived in the form of a setback for her husband, who is also an attorney. Hired by one of the Valley's well-known law firms, he didn't pass the California bar exam on his first try. "When you don't pass on your first attempt," she explained, "you get a dark cloud hanging over your head at the firm.

"These were soul-wrenching times, particularly in an environment where people are very image-conscious and achievement-oriented, and no one seems to be suffering—or lets you see it if they are. To walk around as if life is OK when you're really facing big challenges is very tough. But we regarded this period as a test of faith, an opportunity for what Bahai's call 'deepening.' "

Most evenings, as part of her spiritual practice, Marjorie "calls herself to account" for what she did that day, and reflects on what she wants to accomplish the next day. When she misses her prayer and meditation time, she becomes aware that her spiritual wants and needs are not being met. "This is the essence of the Silicon Valley challenge," she says. "To be calm, centered and spiritual in the midst of the time crunch and the work demands. To be steadfast, and maintain routines, is tangibly important.

"It's a hard row to hoe here. We've been given so much, but there are so many distractions and more is expected of us. Recently I flew into Montana, and immediately felt a sense of peace from the place. But I would not want to be elsewhere, wouldn't want to give up the excitement and diversity we have here.

"I'm very conscious of the Valley's diversity, because the area I grew up in was very racist. My school was almost all white, and as an African-American I would get called names as soon as I got on the bus. But I also got it from the black kids because I wasn't dark enough, so I was getting it from all sides. Just as I now call myself to account at the end of each day, I hope these folks will someday call themselves to account for their actions.

"The greatest challenge to my spiritual values comes from my work. Litigation is subject to so many variables that holding on to ethics can be difficult. I want to uphold standards, but I don't want to be taken advantage of. Spirituality is rewarding, but there are tempting times when one would just like to be selfish. I probably wouldn't struggle as much with this if I weren't a Baha'i. As a Baha'i, it would be tough for me to just suck in profits and not be concerned with where they came from.

"There has been a lot of change in the Valley in the last several years, and I'm very optimistic about the future of spiritual life here. It won't be easy, and there will be many challenges. But social insensitivity may fade, I hope without great social upheaval, and baby boomers are hungry for moral values. This is a very rich area, with tremendous spiritual potential."

THE VIEW FROM THE PULPIT

There is a great deal of commonality in spiritual professionals' view of the Silicon Valley culture. Their outlook is influenced by the makeup of their individual flocks, but key themes and challenges recur. One of them is that spiritual leadership in this high-dynamics arena is no walk in the park. Sam Keen's short recipe for a successful vision quest wasn't written for the Valley, but it captures some of the natural inclination of the collective psyche, and gives a fine hint regarding the challenges faced by local leadership:

> *The path to personal freedom involves two long and terrifying steps across the void. Step one: Question authority. Step two: Overthrow authority.*

Heck, that's not so terrifying for Silicon Valley stalwarts.

Roland, a local pastor, offered an ad hoc statistical analysis. "On the East Coast, most people who go to church either go 10 percent of the time or 90 percent of the time. Anyone midway between the two would be considered a flake. Here, most people who go to church probably go 50 to 60 percent of the time. That's considered normal, and it's the 10 percenters and the 90 percenters who are considered the oddballs."

Pat, also a Valley pastor, pointed out characteristics specific to each geographical region of the country. "In the Sunbelt, people attend church in far greater numbers than anywhere else. Churches are filled to capacity. In the Northeast, the religious experience tends to be *reserved:* smaller churches, more intellectual, less emotional. In the 'great middle plains,' you find the traditional institutional religious experience. Denominations are still important. When people cross the Rockies, they tend to drop their religion on the mountains, and discontinue their practice when they hit the West Coast. If they pick one back up, people here become very *intentional* about their religion."

SAM

The church secretary put me right through to Sam when I called to arrange an interview. He's pastor of a sizable, mainstream Protestant congregation. We shared immediate rapport: he couldn't confirm an appointment time until his computer finished a disk initialization and he could restart his calendar program.

He also mentioned that the office was fully automated, and had been for some time, thanks to a former church member who had been associated with a computer company and donated lots of equipment. He expected to head home shortly because he liked to prepare his sermons on his home computer. We discovered that we both used the same word processing software.

A little tech talk, to get an acquaintanceship off to a good start.

Our meeting took place at a coffee shop he called his "office East." He knew the staff by name. Over chicken Caesar salad and iced tea we discussed life experiences, spiritual paths, and his observations about Silicon Valley.

"My father came to the U.S. from Sweden. When I turned 21 he told me 'Make sure you vote, and make sure your vote counts.' He was a Socialist; he made his vote count for Eugene Debs.

"I was born and raised in Iowa. Our family had a strong belief in a Christianity more of deeds than of words.

"There's a solidity and a history in the heartland which we don't have here, so we experiment. People here want to try new things. It's fun. Matthew Fox would have died in Toledo.

"There's no community pressure here to belong to any spiritual institution. In other parts of the country, corporate officers are expected to belong to churches and community organizations. In the Valley, if you tell people you can't meet them on a Sunday morning because you're going to church, you're likely to get derided. It's close to what it must have been like when St. Paul first started out.

"If people who had never been involved in the community transferred from a job at Hewlett Packard in Silicon Valley to a job at an HP facility in, say, Boise, Idaho, within one year they'd be involved in the PTA.

"The hardest part of becoming a pastor out here is that people have no respect for office or institution. But if spiritual journeys stay purely individualistic, they'll die. You need the continuity of an institution."

❧ Friends and Acquaintances ❧

"A part of the Silicon Valley culture I find terribly sad is that people so often have no real friends. They think people they ski with or bowl with are their friends. But usually they're just doing things together. Doing things together isn't necessarily the same thing as being friends. People sometimes get quite offended if others they're doing activities with suddenly want to talk about personal stuff. That's not my idea of friendship.

"I know of a man who had been bowling with a group for 30 years. *Thirty years.* One night, after bowling, he went home and hung himself. The investigators asked his bowling group if they had noticed anything unusual that night. They said, 'No, he didn't seem any different.'

"I've noticed an interesting thing about weddings. Attendance is always about 20 percent less than confirmed RSVPs. People walk outside on the wedding day, and say, 'It's a nice day, let's go to the beach instead.' There's just not the respect for the importance of rituals and ceremonies. And no one's mother lives in the area to take them to task and tell them to do what's right."

❧ Technical Expertise ❧

"One thing that's great about this place is that a lot of my parish are engineers. They're used to working on projects and schedules. All my committees run well except one: buildings and grounds.

Everyone knows how to use a computer, but no one knows how to use their hands or what to do with tools.

"My prior parish, in another state, was largely doctors and lawyers. If I started a discussion about 'What is truth?' they'd talk and argue about it forever and probably have a great time, but not get anywhere, of course. If I started the discussion here, I wouldn't be surprised if four days later the group came back and said, 'Pastor, we have an interactive program to step you through the "What is truth?" issue. We're going to beta test it in Bakersfield next week, and once it's debugged, everyone can get it on the Internet at "TruthSearch.com."'

"Pastors in some areas may get stale after they've been with their churches awhile. With the speed at which things change in the Valley, there's not much risk of that here.

"The most secular institution in our society is the university, and this is a very university-oriented environment. More advanced degrees seem to lead to rejection of spiritual paths."

❧ Roots ❧

"Because so many people came here from somewhere else, they don't have the rhythmic involvement of an extended family in their daily lives. That can make them feel very lonely. If you have a fight with your spouse, you can't go blow off steam to your sister, and you don't have an uncle around to take you out for a drink, calm you down, and explain how he and your aunt used to fight the same way, and you really shouldn't go call that divorce lawyer just yet.

"As far as taking that first step onto a spiritual path, you either believe there's a God or you don't. There's probably nothing that clergy or anyone else can do if the belief hasn't been born yet. If you have to explain God, people won't get it.

"People need to relearn the art of *welcoming someone back*. Some may stop coming to a church for a while, for any reason, or for no reason. When they come back, they're likely to be greeted with accusatory questions about why they've been away so long, or find parishioners needling them about their absence. This makes it hard to come back, and just encourages people to find another church, or no church, and never return."

✤ Culture and Counselors ✤

"There's a lot of diversity in this area, and spiritual leaders have to have the flexibility and sensitivity to deal with that. Last week I married an Asian couple. I gave the groom my card and said, 'I am your pastor.' He said, 'But we're not Christian.' I said, 'That's OK, I'm your pastor anyway. And I want you to stay in touch, let me know how you and your family are doing, and let me know if there's anything I can do for you.'

"I don't do much counseling. Not because people don't need it, but because they get it elsewhere. They need it so much, and get it so much, that the secular counseling business is a thriving growth industry. There's a lot of counselors in this area.

"In most companies, it seems people have to work 12 hours a day or they're considered shirkers. I started up a class recently, and all but one of the people who attended were retired. You can't schedule anything on weeknights, because everyone works late. Maybe 5:00 AM would work, but I'm not going to get up at 5:00 AM to teach class.

"Eighty percent of the visitors to a church are there because someone in the parish invited them. Of the remaining 20 percent, most are there because of a family crisis, such as an illness. I call them 'foxhole Christians.' They're under fire, and somehow we have to get them through the battlefield safely.

"It's important for clergy to take doses of their own advice, and try the things they advise others to do to make sure they work. A story I like is about the pastor in a traffic jam. He peers around the cars, and sees the problem is a dump truck with a flat tire. The driver has a lane blocked. He's struggling to get the flat tire off, but it won't budge. The pastor pulls over and asks, 'Have you tried prayer?' The driver says, 'No, but at this point, I'll try anything.' He says a quick prayer, and the tire slides right off the wheel. The pastor says, 'Well, I'll be damned!'

"Getting caught up in making money causes many people in the Valley heavy conflict. They say they're doing it for their family. But the stress and the 16-hour days can end up destroying the family. Michael Milken was once asked, 'What do you need all that money for?' and he said, 'To keep score.' I think that applies to some people here. The carrot is always moving.

"There's a dynamic of noncontinuity we have to deal with in this area. People always have their résumé updated, and there's no real trust or commitment anymore between company and employee."

❧ Rejuvenation ❧

"The youth orientation in high-tech companies can be tough on midlifers. Lots of older tech whizzes feel they have to use Grecian Formula 16. In fact, there's even starting to be a youth movement in the clergy world, and most churches won't hire anyone over 50. How sad!

"Everyone needs to have quiet time, peaceful time, in their life pattern, to recharge and permit the spirit to rest and grow. Before I came here I interviewed at a church elsewhere. They asked how I maintained my spiritual life. My answer was, 'First, I take my days off.' I get exhausted from my work, from caring. I need to read and sleep late occasionally like anyone else. They were very uncomfortable with that answer. I think they wanted to hear me say I spend my leisure time memorizing the writings of 16th century clerics. I didn't get the job.

"It's great how the Holy Spirit works. I got turned down for a job in one of the least attractive places in the world, and ended up in Los Altos, one of the nicest."

Many of the people interviewed offered observations about the differences between spiritual life and pursuits in Silicon Valley and other places they knew. Here are some perspectives of local clergy:

In the Southeast, you're expected to belong to a church. It's a sense of duty. But here, people go to church based not so much on expectations, but because they're truly seeking a path. The numbers may be greater there, but perhaps there's more real dedication here. There's more tradition there. Here, we're willing to blend traditions to create something new.

There's an intensity about this area that sometimes I love and sometimes I hate. People here are used to making choices and being proactive. We're in Stanford Country. There's a real tolerance for new ideas and open dialogue.

Some people spend all this money to be in big houses on large, private grounds, and then feel disconnected. Before coming here I worked as an inner city urban minister. In a way, I feel as if I traded one homeless population for another.

Silicon Valley has more diversity, more freedom, more "soul liberty."

Other areas may have a much deeper sense of past and continuity.

This area seems to have a greater awareness of both the threat and the promise of other religious traditions.

People here ask more questions.

… And comparisons from some nonclergy observers:

Everything's bigger in Texas, including the size of churches and the percent of people who attend.

Where you have traditional values and a relatively stable population, you'll find churches playing the strongest roles. That describes the East Coast and the Southwest. It doesn't describe Silicon Valley.

Spiritual diversity here seems to match the cultural diversity. The exposure to different things helps keep my mind open.

When I talk to people from the Midwest, we're not communicating. I used to find much of my spirituality in nature, and spent a lot of time hugging trees. I'm sure they'd think I was nuts.

New Jersey was very homogeneous—lots of whites, Christians and pilots. This area is a melting pot, and the different beliefs require tolerance and bring challenges to conventional thinking. But the diversity, and the "careerism," can make it harder to build community.

Even in spiritual matters, people here are self-starters and wonder how technology can help their journey.

In other areas neighbors were more neighborly. If people are helping and volunteering, they're being spiritual even if they don't go to church.

Lots of New Age stuff here which isn't found elsewhere. There's a lack of the traditional rhythm of life. Spirituality here is a smorgasbord, and people pick whatever seems tasty.

When I was first asked to come out here, I wasn't sure I wanted to leave Illinois and raise my family on the "left coast." But although religion here may not be as "in vogue" as it is back there, many people here are just as committed.

We're an intellectual, science-driven area. Intellectuals often don't take religion seriously. The scientific mind has difficulty accepting the mysterious, and tends to be skeptical.

We have strong pockets of spirituality, but we also have spiritual vacuums where people have no fellowship.

My home area's spiritual practices are more structured, conservative, and punitive. Here, no one knows if you go to church, and no one talks about religion at work.

In Chicago I was in a homogeneous Southside Polish Catholic community. You saw everybody on the streets: friends, neighbors, priests. Community life and spiritual life continued when you went out. Here, you don't see anybody on the street. I've never seen a priest just walking through a neighborhood, and it's difficult to have spiritual continuity once you leave the church premises. People don't just "hang out" together here.

Back East, where you go to church is part of the social pecking order. In Silicon Valley, the social pecking order is one thing: money.

In Oregon and Indiana, spiritual thinking is much more "Western traditional." Here, you can make a religion out of anything. Maybe the intolerance in other areas comes from fear of having their belief systems proved wrong.

CHAPTER FOUR

❧

Visions of Higher Powers

It is ironic but appropriate that science should be the possible path back. Science probably did more than anything else to take away the wonder in nature that we associated with the divine ... In the present age, a religious believer may not want to agree that God has disappeared or that God has died; but he or she can acknowledge, albeit sadly, that the awe has disappeared, or at least diminished dramatically, both among religious and nonreligious persons.

Richard Elliott Friedman,
The Disappearance of God

"I wish you'd quit thinking of me as God," Joe said a bit irritably. "The term is so outdated."

Joan Brady, *God on A Harley—A Spiritual Fable*

*What we're often looking for when we add the extra
overhead of building a computer into our business and
our lives is certainty. We want something to believe in,
something that will take from our shoulders the
burden of knowing when to reorder muffler clamps. In
the twelfth century, before there even were muffler
clamps, such certainty came in the form of a belief in
God, made tangible through the building of
cathedrals—places where God could be accessed. For
lots of us today, the belief is more in the sanctity of
those digital zeros and ones, and our cathedral is the
personal computer. In a way, we're replacing God with
Bill Gates.*

Uh-oh.

Robert X. Cringely, *Accidental Empires—How The Boys
Of Silicon Valley Make Their Millions, Battle Foreign
Competition, and Still Can't Get A Date*

Stop.

I want you to stop reading at your normal speed.

In a minute I'm going to ask you to stop reading, period. Not
for long. Just for a bit. But in preparation for that, I'd like you to
… just … slow … the … pace … and … … let … …your … …
mind … … feel … … … peaceful … … … and … … … … deep.

Now,
      get ready
            to think,
                  to picture
                        and to feel.
Put the picture
            before the words
                      but don't let
                an unclear
            picture
          block
    the words.
Picture
        then emotions
                then words.

If you believe in a God, a Creator, a Higher Power, close your eyes for a moment. Let whatever *picture* you have of your Divinity take shape.

Trace the vision back. Has this always been the picture? Have there been others? Where did they start? What was the progression? What caused the picture to change?

Is He/She in one place? Or in the rocks and waves, trees and malls, people and cats?

Now the emotions.

Who or what *is* God to you? Parent? Teacher? Boss? Bully? Guardian?

Does She/He cause you to feel reverence? Joy? Anger? Resentment? Puzzlement? Unquestioning love?

Any fear in there anywhere?

Now the words.

How do you *think* of God? What role does the Divinity play in your daily life? How about in the world at large? Does He/She let the universe just tick along? Or are events and happenings micro-managed? Or something in between?

How do you communicate with the Higher Power? Do you ever hear His/Her voice coming back to you?

Take a few minutes. Or as long as you like.

If you do not believe in a God, a Creator, a Higher Power, close your eyes and transport your imagination back 15 billion years or so. Picture a point of infinite density and infinite temperature hanging suspended in a roiling bath of colorless, lightless probabilistic foam twisting and convulsing continuously into and out of existence in berserk, mutated obeisance to the Schwarzchild solution to the Einstein field equation, leaving a nebula of unknown and impossible particles performing unknown and impossible physical phenomena, dancing, trailing and contorting back into the 26-

> *I served as an evangelist and high school teacher in Kenya for 17 years. The natives call Mount Kenya "The Hill of Brightness." At its top, 17,000 feet, it's snow and glaciers, shining and radiant, inaccessible. The name and the vision of God many tribes use is "The Great Divider": He divides the heavens above from the earth below. When He comes down to visit the Earth, they believe He lives at the peak of the Hill of Brightness. The vision is part of a powerful metaphor. We want to climb the mountain and be with God. At first it's easy. But then we get to the snow, and then the glaciers, and we can't see how to go any farther.*
>
> *From Kenya, I was transferred to Silicon Valley.*
>
> Michael, a Valley priest

dimensional multiverse where it was spawned a quadrillion years ago by its torturous protrusion from a 39-dimensional hyperverse, exploding outward, suddenly and finally, in a paroxysmal cataclysm of energy, death and birth.

Or, if that's too easy …

The objective is just to get you thinking about whatever *your* vision is of Beginnings and Meanings. This can be a difficult, elusive track to follow. It's probably somewhat easier for those who do believe in a God. For one thing, the belief wraps a lot of complex variables into one entity. For another, there's been so much written, discussed, and sung about God, so much formal and informal religion developed, that there's a rather large set of jumping-off points available.

Of course, the jumping-off points often contradict each other. The advantage may be a little less than first meets the eye.

I asked you to consider the pictures, emotions and words which comprise your vision of Higher Powers and Beginnings and Meanings to give you a foundation for considering the visions of others. Part of the dialogue with people interviewed for this book focused on those visions. They are not the easiest visions to develop. They can be even harder to communicate.

ANNA

Anna is a single parent. Her son is now 21, so in theory, most of the rough parenting spots are behind her. (On the other hand, it's the late '90s, and this particular theory is starting to develop some warts.) Her ex-husband dropped out of their life very soon after the birth of their son. He provided neither participation nor financial support for child rearing.

That was OK with Anna. It was still OK when several years went by and Mr. Right had not appeared. She didn't put much energy into looking for him, anyway. Work and child kept her very busy.

She did get to a point, however, where she was interested in putting energy into something else: her own house. She was tired of living in rented digs. She wanted her own piece of turf. She wanted to be able to have two dogs and a cat; or two cats and a dog; or two cats, three dogs, six hamsters and a macaw without checking in with the landlord. She wanted to plant flowers and tomatoes in her own soil, and paint the walls vermilion if she was in the mood. The basics.

The problem: this was Silicon Valley, with its bloated property values. Getting into a house, unless you've hit it big or inherited big, is often a two-income proposition. She only had one.

A second income was needed. A second job was the obvious solution.

However, she was not able to find another job like the one she had, or that paid as much, or that wouldn't have required her to clone herself so she could be in two different places during normal work hours. She cogitated. She did the logical thing: she took *two* more jobs.

Anna became a female, Silicon Valley version of Clark Kent. By day, she blended in as a mild-mannered customer service representative for a microwave subsystem manufacturer. On weekends,

> *Through prayer and meditation, one is often inspired. This is not a rational process, but more akin to the Aha! experience related by many mathematicians and scientists. Something spiritual is going on in these experiences.*
>
> Neil, a former Silicon Valley programmer

she checked in as an intrepid utility player for a department store chain, taking inventory, running cash registers, balancing accounts receivable payments, helping a customer find a size 8—whatever was needed. And every morning, seven mornings a week, she got up at 4:00 AM to metaphorically don her blue-and-red Superwoman togs, and toss copies of a local newspaper into the dark driveways of houses with still-sleeping occupants on a neighborhood paper delivery route.

That's what she needed to do to save the down payment. That's what she needed to do to meet the mortgage payments. That's what she did. She succeeded. She bought the house and kept it.

For a few years, sick days and vacations were purely theoretical abstractions. She knew they were things other people did. She couldn't. That was OK.

Eventually, raises and promotions happened, the furniture got paid for, and the son graduated from high school and got a job. Anna is now back to living a normally frenetic lifestyle, and working just one job. She's even found time for the pleasure of teaching country-and-western dance classes.

Anna derives a great deal of strength and centering from her spiritual life, which she practices in a totally institution-free manner. She regards herself as a "generic Christian." She is not associated with a church and doesn't expect to be. One reason is her vision of God. Another is her church experience.

> *Everyone defines their own God. Ask a group of 20 people how they think of the Creator and you'll get 25 answers. God loves us, looks out for us, and it's His job to throw curve balls at us. In the past, people saw God primarily as a bookkeeper, maintaining a ledger of what you did right and wrong. Very few think that way anymore, and that represents real growth in people's visions.*
>
> Edward, a Valley priest

Music is what first brought Anna to religion. She loved to sing, and started going to a neighborhood church to do it. The music and the singing brought out her spirituality.

Then she and her mother became involved with another church, and problems came up. Anna saw church leaders doing things she thought were wrong: things she felt were harmful, arbitrary, maybe even a little cruel. She got to a point where she could not continue to accept the spiritual leadership of these individuals, and by extension, the church which had placed them in authority. She left to pursue her own path.

Anna's communications with her God require no intermediary, and no formal faith community. God is with her at all times. She does not have regular prayer times set aside. She carries on an ongoing conversation. It's one-sided in the sense that she doesn't feel she has ever heard God's voice coming back to her—but she feels His presence.

"God is the closest thing I've ever had to a grandfather," she says. "It's a different vision from seeing Him as a father. A father image might be tied up with a very authoritarian relationship. I don't want to picture God as telling me 'do this or don't do that because I'm your father and I said so.' That wouldn't work for me.

"He might still be telling me the same things. But with the grandfather vision, one step removed from the parent, He's doing it as a loving mentor."

COLIN

Colin is a senior product manager for a leading-edge company making specialized computer equipment. He describes himself as cerebral and introverted. He's currently devoting a substantial amount of cerebral effort to developing his vision of a Higher Power.

About six years ago Colin went through a period of strong inner conflict. His introverted nature was acting as a barrier to understanding people he worked with. He couldn't figure out why they didn't think the same way he did. He frustrated others, and they frustrated him back. The barrier became too big to ignore. It had to be torn down, or at least diminished, if he was going to continue to be successful at his work. "I was desperate for personal change," he says. "Despite having a great life on the surface, I was miserable, and knew I had a problem."

He got a couple of unusual suggestions from his manager. The first was to try Vedanta meditation as a way of getting more in touch with his core. You can't share with others what you don't know yourself.

The second suggestion was to consult a psychic. The psychic emphasized the importance of finding solitary, self-awareness-increasing time on a daily basis.

Colin's father was Roman Catholic, his mother's father was a Presbyterian minister, and his parents compromised on Episcopalian. As the Vedanta meditation led him deeper into Hinduism, he pondered the direction his spiritual path had taken.

He realized that following the practices of his childhood had ceased to have any meaning. "I was a 'rote Christian.' My spirituality had no humility, no depth, no real thought."

Sometimes people ask, "Does God know what I'm going through? Doesn't He understand how hard this is?" Usually when this happens it means they've moved away from God, not vice versa. I almost always get an answer to my prayers, but few of the answers are "Damascus Road blinding light" responses.

Trent, president of a Valley telecommunications company

It is through Hinduism that Colin feels he has rediscovered Christianity. A major signpost of inner change has occurred for his cerebral self: he has gotten past being so highly judgmental.

During the season of Lent he banishes computer books from the bedroom and reads Christian mystics for an hour each night. His vision of God contains ingredients from each of the sources that has influenced him, blended together with the product of his personal reflections. A quote from a swami has stuck with him: "Belief in God is not necessary, but it's useful."

His God is unknowable, but close. There is the Trinity; above that is the Godhead, the Transcendent, the quiet-mind Presence, an integral part of everything. Hinduism offers multiple manifestations of God, and Christian mystics provide glimpses into an afterlife tantalizingly tinged with their own inner certainty: the beginnings of a rich, flowing, composite vision.

"We are knives, and life is a whetstone," Colin says. "You have to position yourself to get sharpened, not blunted."

MOLLY

Molly is human resources director for a Valley company that makes computer networking equipment. Her faith has always been unshakably bound to her life, but she described two circumstances in which she felt severely tested.

God is light. Light is healing, soothing, joyful. I have a problem with the "Father" image, and "light" gets me around that. I totally reject the Old Testament view of a vengeful God, although I could wake up one morning and find I'm wrong.

Kate, a Valley church office administrator

The first related to her husband's cancer. They had been married a relatively short time when it struck, and struck hard. They were very much in love. She prayed with everything in her for his healing. When he died after a valiant battle, she felt a surge of bitterness toward her God. "My first thought was, 'I don't have anything more to say to You,'" she recalls.

But she felt her bitterness fade into a realization: her prayer had been answered in a higher sense. Her husband had been freed from the cancer that was choking him. And she had been given the strength to be there for him. "Realizing his *soul* had been healed made me feel God was my counselor again."

The other challenge she described took place in the more prosaic surroundings of her company's offices. It happened in her first month on the job. During a conversation, the CEO, standing in the hall near her office, bellowed "Jesus F__ing Christ." Molly was shocked and dismayed. "I had a great salary and a great job, and I suddenly had to wonder if I was working in a vulgar hellpit."

She thought about it. Ultimately, she decided that her vision of her relationship with God required her to take such statements on in the future: a fairly gutsy decision in iconoclastic Silicon Valley. "Now when I hear someone say that, I say, 'Hey, that's my Lord,' and get them to stop."

"My spiritual life is huge," Molly says. "It's my air. And God is fire. Consuming fire."

GERALD

Gerald considers himself a Christian, but is not affiliated with any church and doesn't think he needs to be. "I go to church occasionally for the sermon," he says, "but I really don't like the 'stand-up, sit-down, fight-fight-fight' stuff."

Gerald is chief financial officer for a laser equipment company. He is turned off by the structure and the politics he usually sees associated with churches. Not being active in a spiritual community makes him aware of the need to weave his spiritual beliefs into other aspects of his life. "I relate to God through the principles I've been taught," he explained.

"I tie my morals and ethics very closely to my spirituality, and everything is a test. What do you do if you see someone drop a buck? Are you honest with customers? With vendors? Do you compete fairly in sports? Do you omit or commit things because it's temporarily expedient, even if it's wrong? Do you disclose fully to investors and analysts? How do you treat people who make mistakes? How should you respond when competitors lie, cheat and steal? How do you report company earnings? Do you cheat Uncle Sam when you can? Do you conceal things from auditors? How do you treat your wife? If someone cuts you off on the road, do you flip him off? Are you the kind of person who can be trusted to do things on a handshake? How do you react when things are not going well, at work and at home?

"None of these are black and white. But they're examples of the kinds of tests we face every day. And how we respond to the tests is between us and God. We have to live it, not preach it."

His vision of God is that of a mentor: providing guidance, direction, hope, and "... a path you can rely on when the chips are

---

One of my favorite stories is about a boy busily drawing on a large sheet of paper. His mother asks him, "What are you drawing?" He answers, "I'm drawing God." His mother says, "But no one's ever seen God. No one knows what He looks like." The boy says, "When I finish my drawing, they will."

Esther, a Valley homemaker

down. My God is loving and forgiving. But some established religions are neither. I can't accept the teaching that whole continents are damned just because they don't have the right religion. On the other hand, I believe missionary types are often very sinful in *pushing* religion rather than *teaching* it. I think that's a crime.

"Because of the way they live, some people who go to church and believe in Him may still not get anywhere near heaven."

MELINDA

"When I was 17, I actually thought of joining a religious order," Melinda recalls, "but then I realized I liked boys and dating too much."

Of such stuff are life decisions made.

Melinda works out several times a week at the Decathlon Club, and that's where we met for our discussion. The Decathlon is *the* upscale fitness facility in Silicon Valley. It's also a fine networking spot, both socially and for business. Conversations are heavily skewed toward sports, startups and cybersurfing.

At 2:00 in the afternoon only one other table besides ours was occupied in the Club's lounge area. When I sat down Melinda said, "You asked how I hear the voice of God. Sometimes it's just in the most improbable things. While you were gone I could hear some of those guys' discussion at the other table. They're talking about spirituality and God and the Bible. Two tables, two spiritual discussions. Got to be a first for the Decathlon Club."

Melinda is a licensed therapist. That profession represents a major midlife career change. Previously she was an administrator at a large Valley biotechnology company. Before that she worked as a sales rep for a telecommunications equipment manufacturer. Eventually, the tech world and the corporate environment became dimensionless: places where she earned a paycheck, period. She needed more. She wanted work that had meaning, work that would allow her spirit to speak and participate. She did her training, got her MFCC license, and started a new adventure.

Melinda was born into a Presbyterian family. Although she didn't join a religious order at 17, she did convert to Roman Catholicism. A tempestuous relationship was thereby launched.

After a few years of church participation, she felt its tug on her declining. She stopped going in her mid-20s, except for a brief period following the divorce from her first husband.

In her 30s, she felt she was back on a search path, but one leading in a completely different direction: philosophical rather than theological; psychological rather than spiritual. She neither needed nor wanted religious institutions during this phase.

About six years ago, in her early 40s, Melinda noticed thoughts about the Church sliding gently into her consciousness again. After a while they dropped the subtle approach, began knocking on the door of her psyche, and demanded admission.

She decided she'd open the door enough to talk, but keep the chain on until she knew the intruder wasn't dangerous. She went to a function for ex-Roman Catholics called the "Give Us Another Chance" retreat. It worked. She's giving it another chance. She expects the relationship to stick this time.

"There are still things I don't like about the Roman Catholic Church," she says. "For example, its position on women clergy. Somehow, though, I'm now at peace with the Church's shortcom-

---

The God of the Bible is a comfortable convenience. But those who have had problems with their fathers might have trouble with the masculine imagery.

Marie, a Valley homemaker and former marketing analyst

ings. I get a feeling of connection with God when I attend Mass, and the Church is the vehicle for that. But it's frustrating that the material world creeps back in so fast. The feeling of grace tends to fade 30 minutes after I leave the service.

"I don't like the God of the Bible that much. But the Bible is metaphor and allegory, not a literal work. I would like to think God is a loving God. It's hard to be sure. It's hard to make peace with the suffering of the innocent. But I understand that human justice is different from divine justice.

"God is cosmic, everywhere, not a robed person or a mountain. The vision of God I would most enjoy would be to see Him in every person I meet—even those I don't like."

CAL

They don't know each other, but Cal and Pete (whom you'll meet next) have something in common. Both of them initiated their first serious foray into religion to get dates with girls they had a crush on.

In Cal's case, the experience was not a keeper. Neither the religion nor the date stuck around for long. He found the religion "formulaic, dogmatic, and in denial." (He offered no further comments about the date. I didn't ask.) He looked into other denominations and found the same thing. He's still looking.

Cal is an accounting professor at a Valley community college. He classifies his parents as atheists. He classifies his own spiritual pursuits as "episodic" ("I look. I stop.") but he firmly believes in a Higher Power. He's just not sure how he should structure their relationship.

For a while, he went with a girlfriend to some meditation-based Eastern services. "Lots of drug addicts there," he says. He might still be going, but he broke up with the girlfriend, and she still goes there, and it would be uncomfortable.

"I'll probably end up practicing some form of Eastern religion. I feel I communicate with a Higher Spirit, but I don't see God as a personal God. My first choice would be to have a personal God. But I just can't buy it now. It's an 'I-know-You-exist-but-I'm-not-sure-in-what-form' thing.

"I do believe in the concept of collective consciousness. A biologist says all living things leave behind a 'spiritual residue' in some dimension, and I think I believe that. Maybe the collective, spiritual consciousness of every human who ever lived is my vision of God right now."

PETE

Unlike Cal's experience, when Pete jumped aboard his spiritual train to pursue romance, he stayed aboard.

Pete is in the thick of the Silicon Valley technology action. He manages an information services group for a large computer manufacturer. In an unusual scenario for the area, he's been there 15 years.

Pete's parents went to Sunday services, but he didn't sense any true spirituality in their lives. "It felt like they never really made the choice of having a life in God, as opposed to just going to church." He recalls being able to negotiate deals with his mother to avoid boring church attendance. Offers to vacuum the house or wash the car were among the more successful ploys.

Then the girl came along.

She wouldn't go out with him until he agreed to meet with her pastor. The pastor made a persuasive case. His mind told him committing to faith would be a rational decision. His hormones told him he *really* wanted to date this girl. He signed up. He's never regretted it.

His initial view was that Christian life was "a piece of cake." He remembers the incredulous responses he got to that perspective. It's an opinion he dropped a long time ago.

Several years ago, Pete made a decision which was good for his spirit but possibly deleterious to his career. There were a few other practicing Christians in his office building. They were interested in spiritual growth, and Pete was knowledgeable. He started a lunchtime Bible study and discussion group. Four or five of them met and talked over sandwiches and sodas, chairs cramped together in his small office, twice a week. If organizational advancement had been his number one priority, this was an error.

Pete is a sensitive, intelligent individual, firmly committed to high standards of professional performance and hard work. It was not the easiest thing in the world for him to hear that he was regarded as a "Jesus freak." It was not easy to deal with obvious disdain from colleagues, and averted gazes in hallways. No one asserted that his beliefs affected his work. But many found his practice to be jarring and inappropriate in that environment. To them, he became a dubiously regarded fringe member of the organization.

Occasionally, Pete would write Scriptural quotes on the whiteboard in his office. They were primarily to provide uplift and inspiration for himself. He hoped they might also be an upper for

---

During a guided meditation, I had a vision of bright, intense light and a sense of warmth and well-being that was absolutely overwhelming. My eyes were closed, but the vision was so intense that I could feel the heat. The feeling stayed with me for a long time, and the vision is burned into my mind.

Stuart, general counsel for a Valley instrumentation company

others, or at least an interesting mental refreshment from the day's travails. He found out later they were regarded by most co-workers who saw them as intrusive, or pretentious, or offensive, or all three. He discontinued the practice.

He also ended the lunchtime meetings and has changed departments. He's had reasonable career success. Was his success less than it might have been because of his spiritual activities in the workplace? Hard to say. Doesn't matter, anyway. He wouldn't have done it differently. At the time, he felt called to bear witness. It wasn't a call he would decline.

To Pete's delight, technology has permitted a workplace spiritual presence to flourish where the old-fashioned personal approach stumbled. Through the ease, ubiquity and comparative anonymity of modern electronic mail systems, believers at his company have a way to find each other and share matters of faith. The system has the capability for users to form "special interest groups," or SIGs, to exchange e-mail on topics of common interest. Some of the users wanted to have an electronic forum to do what Pete was doing at his office lunch meetings: talk about Scriptures. SCRIPT-SIG was born. Those who are interested can join in. Those who aren't can ignore it. No pressure. No offense. No mayonnaise on the carpet.

Pete's vision of God is one of grace and compassion, and very much the God of the Bible. He tries to consciously remember and honor his spiritual beliefs throughout his workday. This gets harder

---

The God of the Bible is the jumping-off point. The Bible gives you pinpoints of data, very tiny. We have to flesh out the full picture ourselves.

Loretta, a Valley homemaker and former corporate professional

when, for example, the system crashes or the network dies, just as critical information to high-ranking recipients is being generated.

But he tries. "God ought to say to me, 'Sorry, Pete, you've failed me too many times. I'm cutting you off.' But He doesn't, and that reminds me to try to treat others the same way."

SARAH

Sarah hails from upstate New York. She grew up in a conservative Jewish home that maintained kosher laws and Sabbath traditions. The family didn't get in the car on the Sabbath; they walked.

A major difference between Silicon Valley and her home town is neighborhood makeup. "I lived in a heavily Jewish neighborhood back East," she says. "Here, there's no concentration of particular religious groups in any area. We're liberal, we're accepting, and there's so much diversity."

Sarah feels that religious activity in the Valley is a much lower-profile part of the culture than it was back East. "A lot of my co-workers are atheists who don't believe in anything," she says.

She sees both goodness and badness in this. "On the one hand, intensity in religious life can have a dangerous side. That intensity can lead to fanaticism, intolerance, and antagonism between members of different faiths. On the other hand, I think a lot of the problems we have today can be traced to the shrinking of spiritual commitment. I see morals getting more questionable, and young people drifting without a course, and I wonder if a deeper and more structured spiritual life wouldn't make a big contribution toward dealing with these issues."

Sarah places herself among those whose religious life has diminished. Her attendance at synagogue has fallen off substantially over the years. She used to go every week; now she goes mostly on the major Jewish holidays.

She attributes this in part to the demands of her work as a pharmacist at a hospital—in part, but not in total. For whatever reason, perhaps many reasons, she hasn't found quite the same comfort level, hasn't been inspired to have the same involvement level, with the temple as she did back home.

Sarah thinks it's important for Jews, as a relatively small group, to pass on the religion to their children. At a personal level, she has found this to be difficult here—perhaps more so than it might have been in a more traditional setting. Her daughter married a Roman Catholic. Her son is still single, but told her he doesn't think he would marry a Jewish woman.

Although she regards herself as a feminist, God, to her, is very definitely a masculine presence. She is not completely comfortable with some of the changes which have been made in her synagogue's worship to eliminate differences between the roles of men and women in the services.

Sarah doesn't practice regular prayer times. She talks to God on an "as-needed" basis. "I don't really have a concrete picture of God," she says. "He's good and wonderful, and watches over us. I believe He does help those who make an attempt to help themselves, but I pray for help for anyone who needs it. When bad things occur I don't say 'How could God let that happen?' I just try to accept it. My parents died young, but I was never angry with God—I just took comfort in my spirituality and my connection with Him."

> *I see God when I see people acting together as a community to accomplish good things.*
>
> Frank, a Valley bank executive

DOREEN

Most of us can cope reasonably well with trauma on the job front if our personal lives are supportive and fulfilling. We can generally make it through upsets and disappointments in the personal sphere if our professional pursuits are hitting on all cylinders. When the personal and the professional both head south at the same time, we're likely to feel emotional quicksand closing over our ears.

Doreen remembers that feeling. She had been having a dicey affair with a man who was separated, but not divorced, from an acquaintance. The relationship was falling apart. At the time, she was working for a small sporting goods company which was being run into the ground by an inept and alcoholic CEO. "I was losing my job at the same time my love life was failing," she recalls. "And I was alone. When you're having the kind of affair I was, you don't tell a lot of people."

With the help of a friend who had a strong spiritual life, she was able to keep a grip. Things took a big-time turn for the better when she got a job at a well-known Valley optical instrumentation company. It proved to be a bastion of sanity and stability compared to the sporting goods fiasco. It also contributed mightily to her personal life: one of the executives there was the man destined to become her husband.

Doreen's path started in the South, with a father who was "jealous and overbearing." He was also a minister. "Mom just loved him, and gave and gave," Doreen recalled. "I would have hit him on the head with a frying pan." She came to California at age 19

God lives in people. He is cheerful, loving, fun-loving, adorable and accepting.

Rochelle, CEO of a Valley counseling group

to work on a youth services project, and stayed. The crisis point of simultaneous bad job and bad love has long passed, and life is good, but Doreen has continued her efforts to define and direct her spirituality. She has always felt the active tug of her spirit. She just hasn't settled on the precise practice and format which will fit it best. She regularly attends a mainline Protestant church, but has not joined. She does foster parenting, and serves on an urban ministry board.

"I need to know God is God," she says. "I wrestle with this fundamental issue. I want to know He's real and who He says He is. I need to have Him be a part of my daily life. I need to have that knowledge as firmly implanted in me as the faith of a Gandhi or Mother Teresa. I need it to be so grounded I'll never question it at the fundamental, down-deep level. I'm positive of my husband's love. I just don't have the same confidence regarding God's love.

"I think there's a difference between people's view of God here and back home. People are more honest here about what they do and don't believe. In the South, more people go to church; it's more of a lifestyle. There, the focus is on the traditional. Here, it's on the new. People are more self-reliant here, and it leads them to believe they don't need God. There's something about admitting you strongly believe in God that's unpopular in this area.

"I don't always get what I want from my spiritual life, and I don't always feel God's presence. But if I devote the time, I get what I need. When I pray I get communication back: thoughts,

---

No one will run away from a life in God if introduced to it properly. It's like getting honey from the hive—you might get stung, but it's worth it.

Hamza, a Valley Sufi Muslim leader

not specific words or an audible voice. I have felt turning points where God was speaking to me."

THERESA

"I'm currently a Catholic Church shopper. I want a church that has an intellectual approach to Roman Catholicism, not a simplistic one. I don't want a bureaucracy, and I don't want a monarchy. I want the focus to be on what Christ made, not what man made."

Theresa is the human resources department manager for the Silicon Valley operation of a very large, foreign-owned technology company. Her road to the Valley started in a Polish Catholic Chicago neighborhood. Her road to finding the right church will be made a little more complex by two facts: she's divorced (although she was granted an annulment after 10 years of marriage); and her current husband is not Roman Catholic. They were not wed in a Roman Catholic ceremony. She is confident that these issues will not be a problem in the right setting.

Theresa remembers that her mother went to church more than her father, yet somehow she felt that her father had the deeper spiritual beliefs. She is definitely not into form over substance. "It makes a lot more sense to fix a wrong than say five Hail Marys about it," she believes.

She remembers her initial vision of God. "When you're a kid, you pray to God and you know if you play by the rules, good things will happen, or at least nothing bad. But eventually you learn praying is not enough; you have to get involved in shaping your life."

Theresa observes that most religions have similar tenets. Most promote ethical behavior. She thinks she could be happy within any of their frameworks, but she'll probably stick with her roots.

During the day she has an ongoing dialogue with God. She likes to use the *Aha!* approach to these interchanges. As thoughts and ideas take form and percolate through, she believes she's hearing God's voice when an *Aha!* kicks in.

An example she gives relates to the Catholic Church's prohibition on birth control. She didn't agree with it. She didn't understand it. She initiated extensive dialogue about it.

An *Aha!* eventually struck. There needs to be an entity on earth that holds life sacred. The Roman Catholic Church is that entity. Birth control represents a form of denial of life. It's part of a package: if life is truly sacred, the steward responsible for upholding that view would be in violation of its charge if it permitted the intentional stoppage of life formation.

She adds a subtle but important clarification. She still doesn't necessarily agree. But she understands why the Church takes the position it does, and she feels she has no further quarrel with it on this issue. "Now I'll deal directly with God on this," she says.

Theresa's adult vision of God is one of energy. "Energy can't be created or destroyed, and that's God, or like God. That energy is a force that attracts goodness. It pushes people to do good things."

"Is God Dead?"

For the past 30-plus years, a recurring question, usually asked by sociologists and mass-market magazine covers, has been, "Is God dead?" There is an ironically-humorous-verging-on-bizarre aspect

---

I know the experience of perceiving a vision of God, but I can't put it into a specific box. The Unnamable One, the Light, the Luminous Consciousness, a powerful universal presence, spacious, the totality of all life and all there is.

Victor, a Silicon Valley teacher

to the way the question is phrased. The issue is usually whether people have entered a stage of widespread disbelief, casting off the traditional faith of their youth. If there is a God, the idea that our disbelief would cause His death is a marvelous example of our egos subconsciously wriggling, coiling and sidewinding us into a position of logical absurdity. (Of course, it could also be no deeper a matter than unimaginative, slogan-oriented, lazy headline writing.) And if there isn't a God, there never was, and the question is infinitely moot.

In *The Disappearance of God*, Richard Elliott Friedman looks at one aspect of this question from the perspective of the professional spiritual leader:

> *But why be a theologian if God is dead? If people stopped wearing shoes, a shoe store owner would have the sense to switch to another line. The same applies for any other product that became unavailable. Only a theologian would stay in business in the absence of the product.*

Aha! There's another possibility.

Much of the traditional vision of a Higher Power, particularly as promulgated by mainstream religions, may be fading. Or perhaps there have always been faded sections, and now they're coming under close scrutiny. This scrutiny does not necessarily imply rampant iconoclasm or naysaying. It may be the reflection of healthy

---

My God is a God of judgment and grace. When I listen, I hear His voice guiding me, reassuring me, setting me in the new direction I need to follow. But more often than not, I'll pray, and then not wait to hear the answer.

Ray, a Valley software company CEO

questioning of assumptions, willingness to adopt new perspectives, slates wiped clean enough to accept fresh insights, a rejuvenated search for workable wisdom.

In the introduction to her book, *A History of God,* Karen Armstrong says:

> *Despite its otherworldliness, religion is highly*
> *pragmatic. ... it is far more important for a*
> *particular idea of God to* work *than for it to be*
> *logically or scientifically sound. As soon as it ceases to*
> *be effective it will be changed—sometimes for*
> *something radically different.*

This is very different from gratuitous rejection of the traditional just because it's the traditional. There is some of that. But I don't think it's the real story. The real story is that people feel motivated and free to find what *works* for them.

It takes energy, emotional focus and mental horsepower to formulate visions of Higher Powers. Occasionally, while discussing this topic, the television warning that says something like, "Don't try this at home, you might get hurt. Proper supervision required" popped into mind.

The fact is, I detected only trace elements of this view. Developing visions in settings which may be unsupervised, trying them on in the privacy of the home, and being willing to exchange them if they don't fit, seem to be common in the Valley.

I have a theory about the recent resurgent interest in angels: they offer a cultural icon of instant, safe spirituality. Angels provide awe-inspiring imagery and do beneficial things for people without the demands and rules of a God.

Loretta, a Valley homemaker and former corporate professional

Sam Keen says:

Authentic spiritual language about God does not confuse the map with the territory, the symbol with the thing. Literalism concentrates on the letter and misses the spirit; it gets the words but never the music, creates a spiritual tone-deafness. You can starve to death trying to eat a cookbook.

A cookbook containing a robust collection of recipes has been created here, from which some tasty dishes have been produced. It's a potluck from which all are free to partake, or not. Some people are advanced spiritual chefs. Some have just opened a can or two. Some like to look at what's on the plates, but aren't inclined to do any cooking themselves at present. Others find it enjoyable and useful to ask for a taste of what's on someone else's plate. Most people know someone who's living on junk food, whom they hope will turn to better nourishment. Few, if any, seem inclined to fruitlessly munch on the pages of the book.

I'm fumbling toward communication with God. I need to get my own words out of the way so I can hear His voice.
Loretta, a Valley homemaker and former corporate professional

Valley clergy had these observations on how people here form their visions of Higher Powers:

People born into a religion start with the Biblical God. Later in life, the vision tends to be much more personal. Then there's a search to find some commonality between the personal vision and the God of the Bible. In California, we're more willing to go with our own feelings and use our own imagery, and share it. We're not as tied to Scriptural references and descriptions.

Most people don't explore visions of God beyond what we teach third graders. The God they encounter is the God of the Bible, the God they hear preached, or more accurately, the God of Sunday school.

One person in our congregation sees God as the Good Mother she never had.

The traditional view of God as patriarchal, bearded, sitting on a throne, has largely been rejected, particularly by women.

The biggest issue people have in their vision of God is dealing with misconceptions. Most people feel God is aloof or angry. We have to convince people there's mercy and grace in the real, living God. We have to peel back the layers of 2,000 years of misconceptions.

We live in a high-tech environment, and we expect change. Because He doesn't change, many people see God as archaic. In their vision, He's covered with cobwebs.

More so here than elsewhere, people want a blessing. They're not necessarily looking for God at all. If they could be one with the Star Wars *"Force," that might work. They want energy and power. They want to enhance themselves. But people who are just looking for energy and power miss God, who offers only Himself.*

The Biblical, anthropomorphic view of God—the elderly man with the white, flowing beard—is fading or gone. God as spirit, God as energy, is in. The Star Wars *trilogy "Force" may represent more people's view of God than theologians ever dreamed.*

Some people use standard prayers, some make up their own. But I don't know if there's much reflection or listening to God. I think there's lots of one-way communication. People in Silicon Valley are so busy and moving so fast. They think they're in a rat race. I think it's more of an ant race. But it's so important that they find the time to listen.

CHAPTER FIVE

❧

Homes for the Spirit

"Meditation was invented as a way for the soul to venture inward, there ultimately to find a supreme identity with Godhead ... Whatever else it does, and it does many beneficial things, meditation is first and foremost a search for the God within."

Consciousness theoretician Ken Wilber, quoted in
What Really Matters—Searching for Wisdom in America,
by Tony Schwartz

Ornish has come to believe that the single most important factor in "opening" the heart— physiologically and otherwise—is the degree to which people are able to find a greater sense of meaning, contentment and connectedness in their lives.

Tony Schwartz discussing internist and mind/body
theoretician Dean Ornish in *What Really Matters—
Searching for Wisdom in America*

"Do you think we should check the prototype?" he asked.

"Let's not risk it. Kevin warned me that it could die at any time. Let's just leave it in the hands of God."

"I'm glad to see you're coping with all this strain by turning to religion."

Jerry Kaplan, *Startup—A Silicon Valley Adventure*

Those of us who use well-known personal computer programs for applications such as word processing and spreadsheets are familiar with a function called "cut and paste." This function allows you to pick pieces from one file and plunk them down into another. You can repetitively pick and plunk, selecting and combining the contents of as many files as you wish, keeping only the portions you want, leaving behind or ruthlessly overwriting the dross until the final creation is precisely to your liking.

Great concept. Just doesn't go far enough.

What we need is a function called "Real Life Cut and Paste," designed to address the fact that everything in life is a package. Anything big enough to really matter is going to be a combination of good and bad: houses, jobs, lovers, friends, cars, religions, communities, racquetball partners—the list could go on indefinitely. Following are some examples of how "Real Life Cut and Paste" modules might work on these complex packages.

Let's suppose you're in the market for a new home. You like the exterior of one house, but prefer the interior of another. "House Cut and Paste" would allow grafting of, say, the better floor plan of house A onto the landscaping of house B.

In the realm of romance, "Lover Cut and Paste" would allow us to combine the body of person C with the personality of person D, saving us from a frequently vexatious selection dilemma.

To manage the complexities of friendship, we introduce "Friend Cut and Paste." This handy reengineering tool permits the overlay of energy and creativity from friend E onto the humor and supportiveness of friend F, thereby crafting the all-purpose, no-compromise friend.

For professional pursuits we have "Job Cut and Paste" ... but I am sure the concept is now clear.

Many Silicon Valley residents have crafted an approach to their spiritual lives which might be called "Spiritual Life Cut and Paste." They have made the personal decision that none of the prefab packages of spirituality fit them well enough to be acceptable. Therefore, they have reached into their inner tool kit, pulled out metaphorical blueprints, hammers and nails, and either constructed custom-designed homes for their spirits, or at least applied for the building permits.

SALLY

"Christianity never did it for me," Sally said. "I just can't accept virgin birth stories. I wanted to know more about what happened to Mary. I finally decided Christianity didn't have much for women."

Sally is a former technical writer. She currently teaches in one of the Valley's most prestigious school systems. She has been a Presbyterian and a Congregationalist. Now she regards herself as a spiritual searcher and leader. She expects to require no institution, no previously defined religion.

"My husband is a fallen-away Mormon, and he's rabidly anti-religious," she says. "My mother is being recruited by the Jehovah's

Witnesses, and I really don't like the Jehovah concept. My best friend is a man who was raised as a Quaker, and now shares my husband's negative view of religion. I've tried to convert them or open up their spirituality, but nothin' doin'. So it's just me and the women now."

She currently leads a small group of seekers. They meet every two weeks. They are trying to create a spiritual practice which includes pieces from many sources they feel have valuable ideas to offer. Their focus is on developing a feminine religious practice, because they sense a predominantly masculine orientation in traditional religions.

The practice Sally and her group are fashioning includes the Goddess religion of eight cycles, and Jungian psychology. Sally has written up rituals and formal celebrations of the eight ancient holidays of the Goddess. Through their practice they honor the environment, the seasons, Mother Earth.

Ultimately, Sally would like to see partnership and balance between feminine and masculine energy in all spiritual pursuits. Her group would be delighted to have men join in their celebration.

She does not believe in one God, whether the Judeo-Christian or any other anthropomorphic vision. She believes there *is* a greater spirit or essence, and that perhaps the American Indian Great Spirit or the Hindu concept of multiple God-spirits might be closer to the truth. The limited minds of humans are not designed to comprehend it, but altered states might allow us to channel into this truth. Sometimes jogging peacefully through the pristine beauty of an old redwood grove can put her into that altered state.

"I believe in something divine, but the term 'God' annoys me. I like Carlos Castaneda's 'web' idea. He says someone will happen into your life who appears human but isn't, and that being will direct you down the right path if you don't miss her or him. I think maybe I missed mine. If I get another chance, I don't want to miss again."

Sally has difficulty finding the right approach to communication with her deity. She was not raised to pray. An early, Michelangelo-inspired image of God as decidedly masculine made her feel uncomfortable in prayer. She tried chanting and Buddhism, but had a problem with what she saw as patriarchal Buddhist priests. She also discovered she was just too nervous and hyper to meditate successfully. It was the Goddess who called her to her rightful path of spiritual growth.

What she tries to do every day ("badly—I fail") is connect from the heart to everyone she meets, and to live in the present. Exercises to strengthen and enhance the ability to connect are a part of her group's spiritual practice. She believes people may manifest spirituality in many ways—some of them strange—and participation in an organized religion has nothing to do with true spirituality.

Sally's decision to redirect her career from a corporate technical writing job to part-time teaching involved substantial financial sacrifice. Occasionally, while engaged in somber consideration of her checkbook balance, she wonders if she did the right thing. But not for long. She is positive that returning to the corporate environment would kill her spirit.

"In the corporate world, I felt surrounded by people who were visually and spiritually blind. They had a lot to learn about how to treat women. There was no place there for my talents and creativity. I was inside. It was dark. I was missing the seasons.

"One day I left to pick up my kids and the trees were blossoming. The season had changed and I hadn't had time to notice it! It threw me into a spiritual crisis. I decided I had to quit the job.

I chose freedom and spirituality. I also knew I might be choosing poverty. But I was going to die if I stayed."

Sally subsequently met the man who was to become her current husband. ("After we had dated for a while, I offered to keep a coffee mug of his own at my apartment. When he accepted, we both knew we were committed.") Although he has elected not to participate in her spiritual life (or any), they're a two-income household and poverty has been avoided.

"Change is coming to Silicon Valley," she says. "The male/linear/math/science orientation must allow sharing with the feminine. The more of us who get involved in spiritual life and bring it into companies, the more the companies will change for the better.

"Women are being bombarded by little snowflakes of change—and so are men, whether they know it or not. It's in the air. Magically, mysteriously, good people are being moved by the spirit, and all of us are being exposed to a new way of doing things.

"We're reaching for the global village. Spiritual life means trying to get past polarities and finding out about people, even if you can't stand them. A spiritual heart will reach out past the forms, past the rules, and connect with the spirit living in the hearts of others."

Can one be spiritual even if one does not believe in God or practice a religion? If spirituality means just recognizing something beyond the body and the physical, yes. But I think I'd answer the question no. What is it if it's not God? The purpose of our being here is to bring light into the darkness of the world. That's done by bringing God to people, and to me, any practice that doesn't include God would not be called spiritual.

Aaron, a Silicon Valley rabbi

MATT

In 1995, the large company which had acquired the small company for which Matt worked threw in the towel on the acquisition.

Matt joined the company in the early '80s. He worked hard and well, and enjoyed a gratifyingly consistent upward organizational path. He attained the chief financial officer title. He even enjoyed it for a while. Then the company's numbers turned bad, and his stomach lining followed suit.

Reductions in force were inevitable. The revenue wasn't there, so some employees had to not be there also. Matt was obliged to terminate people he had known for a long time. He developed a rash which made his skin look like his stomach lining felt.

Ultimately, the day of reckoning arrived. Matt had spent a ghastly year living the lie that the company should be tracking to an impossible financial plan. The parent decreed they would now receive the fate they deserved as a wayward, miscreant child: a new foster home would be found, as quickly as possible, with anyone who would take them. However, the process was to be kept highly confidential. Matt had the additional pressure of not being able to share with most of his employees and co-workers the fact that something was in the works that could have a significant impact on them.

During this period Matt's personal life took a turn that added further drama to his situation.

He had married his high school sweetheart shortly after they graduated. They had two lovely daughters. His wife worked when she wanted, stayed home when she wanted. Matt's career was always successful enough to make a second household income optional. In his view, they had an idyllic existence.

Matt's wife, Lydia, saw it differently. Matt sensed she was drifting away from him and the marriage. He had no idea what to do. They tried counseling; it didn't help. About the only things they still seemed to be sharing were their kids and the sport of racquetball.

They had both taken up racquetball. They got serious, and they got good. Matt was playing three times a week, Lydia as many as eight times a week. Sometimes, even while they were playing doubles together, Matt sensed hostility from his wife/partner. "It seemed like she was hitting me with her racquet a lot," he recalls.

"That's bound to happen occasionally with four players on the court," I responded comfortingly.

"Yeah," he said, "but the last time it happened I was standing by the water fountain."

On Valentine's Day, Matt planned a romantic dinner *à deux* at an intimate restaurant. They were seated at their table. Then Lydia cleared her throat and said she needed to discuss a couple things.

OK, Matt said.

First, she informed him, she had been thinking about the upcoming mixed doubles tournament, and the strategy which would be required to prevail over the competition. The bottom line was, she thought she'd have a better chance of winning if she played with one of the other guys at the club instead of partnering with Matt. She had already made the arrangements with the other player.

Matt was stunned. OK, he said. He didn't know what else to say.

The second thing she needed to discuss, Lydia continued, was that it wasn't just the racquetball partnership that wasn't working for her. It was the whole life partnership. She wanted a divorce. She wanted to start planning the separation immediately. Her mind was made up: no chance of change.

Happy Valentine's Day, Matt.

Eventually, both divorce settlements were agreed on: Matt from his wife, the company from its parent. A buyer was found for the company. Its new CEO proposed restructuring, further lay-offs, and extraordinarily long work hours for those who remained.

For the first few weeks after the sale was complete, Matt worked long and hard to integrate the company's financial operations with those of its new owner. Then one morning he got up and pondered the days stretching into the foreseeable future that awaited him at the office. He considered the twinges in his gut, and the stress rash that made him look like he'd had an overdose of tropical sun. To paraphrase an old folk/rock song, some kind of message shot through.

He tried to make an appointment with his superior, the new CEO. All he needed was five minutes to resign with dignity. He couldn't get it. On a Sunday afternoon, after a week of trying to meet with his boss, Matt's phone rang at home. It was the CEO, calling from his car phone. He only had a minute. What did Matt want to talk about? Through the cellular static, Matt told him.

Within a few days the stress signals from his innards had subsided. The rash was gone. He knew his decision would create new, perhaps unpredictable challenges, but that was fine. He had opened up his life.

After the usual number of dubious dating adventures in the singles world, he met Tanya. Things clicked. They dated, they moved

---

There's lots of spirituality without religion. During a recent TV channel-surf, Deepak Chopra was on one channel, and another had a woman whose spiritual philosophy was "fake it 'til you make it."

Stella, public relations manager for
a Valley networking company

in together, they got married, and they're happily blending together a family with his two daughters and Tanya's son.

On the career front, Matt has decided to become an entrepreneur. He has gone through training, and has hung out his shingle as a financial planner affiliated with a national financial services company.

I was particularly interested in hearing what effect the "opening up" of his life might have on his spiritual views. We met at his comfortable East Bay home, and sat in the breakfast nook of his newly remodeled kitchen. He offered me a choice of several coffee blends, made in any of the five types of coffee makers he owns. Our caffeine levels properly elevated, he talked about his path.

Christians sometimes speak glowingly of new developments that are causing a major new synthesis of science and theology, so that these two disciplines that previously have been quite diverse, now are merging into one new discipline of the future, a new paradigm, a new synthesis of science and faith. Science will bring validation to religion, and religion will bring transcendence to science—a New Age.

It is important to appreciate the great temptation that such New Age thinking poses for modern people immersed in a scientific world but looking for a means of religious expression. We must be prepared to distinguish between appropriate interactions between authentic science and authentic theology and the general tendency to move toward pseudoscience and pseudotheology as the ideal thought patterns.

Unpublished lecture notes from *Putting It All Together: Seven Patterns for Relating Science and Christian Faith*, a 1996 seminar series led by Richard H. Bube, Professor Emeritus of Materials Science and Electrical Engineering, Stanford University

❧ Religion and Spirits ❧

"I'm very spiritual, and my spirituality has increased now that I'm not in the corporate world. I try to do transcendental meditation twice a day. I talk to spirits all the time. From my perspective, they're all over, including the larger variety, which some might call God. Some spirits are dead relatives. I talk to the ones with whom I have interests in common.

"Before Tanya and I met, she befriended a lonely, elderly man whose wife had passed away. He was in poor health. She took care of him, and he told her that when he died he wanted half his ashes scattered in the Bay Area and half in Hamburg, Germany. The first half is done, and the second half is sitting in a jar upstairs. One day we'll go to Hamburg and honor the rest of his request. In the meantime, while the jar with his ashes is upstairs, I talk to his spirit. He doesn't have a body, but he's still a person. Some people have 'hardware' and 'software,' some are just *on the Net*.

"My ex and I didn't connect on spiritual beliefs. She went to church regularly, but she was never a spiritual partner. When she moved out, the spirits in the house had to rebalance themselves. Tanya has been a Mormon and a Roman Catholic, but now she's very much in tune with my spiritual life.

"My parents sent us to Sunday school when we were kids," he remembered, "but it didn't take long to figure out why. They just wanted to have some time to themselves. That seemed a little hypocritical, and gave me a negative attitude toward religion. In fact, it set me on a crusade to never participate in one.

"Then I got to studying history and I learned about all the misuses of religious power to inflict pain, cruelty and genocide, and act out obsessions, and it just reaffirmed my decision."

✤ Lives and Death ✤

"I look to my spiritual path to help me better enjoy life, and to prepare me for death. Someone once said 'death is the biggest kick of all, and that's why they save it for last.' In the long run, most things in life aren't important, particularly in the context of death.

"Death is just the necessary step in the cycle of continuing lives, ongoing learning, and attainment of higher states of consciousness and enlightenment. There's no heaven, unless that's it. It's not a question of *believing in* reincarnation. It's *there to be seen*, a matter of personal experience. If you haven't figured this out yet, you haven't been paying attention.

"It's very sad when people spend a lifetime and never get in touch with their own spirit. They die, but they haven't prepared for it, and their next assignment might be to come back as a snail. This wouldn't represent a very positive evolutionary process.

"Everyone has a soul or a spirit, even if they never experience its awakening. Just because a rock doesn't know it's a rock doesn't mean it's not a rock, although I hope most rocks do.

"The two biggest obstacles which keep people from embarking on spiritual paths are organized religion and television. Organized religion is always placing things like 30-centuries-old dogmatic documents, or a spiritual bureaucrat, in the middle of the path to block it up. And television just empties people's heads out until there's nothing left.

"Since our spirits recycle and are always here, they always have been here. Fifteen billion years ago, everything was in a state of complete harmony of material, energy and spirit. There was perfection. Then we all made a decision to have some fun, and the universe was created. We were all there, and we all made the decision. If you're not having fun, you're not paying attention.

"There's a spectrum of consciousness in all living things. Redwoods must think we're just awful. We're not that important in the scheme of the universe. But when I see some of the things we do, I think if I were an alien looking at earth, I might be tempted to flood the planet with an antitoxin to protect the universe.

"Recently I was feeling a little insecure, and went into a meditative session looking for a spiritual contact. I received a strong thought or direction which said, 'Seek me through my other children.' I was looking for a hug; instead I got a homework assignment."

∾ Doing What's Right ∾

"There may be some connection between people's spiritual beliefs and their moral and ethical codes, but the connection is far from universal. Spiritually and intellectually enlightened people may develop very similar codes of morals and ethics. But some who profess religion don't seem to have the codes I would expect, and some intellectual people don't seem to have a very good understanding of the difference between right and wrong.

"My personal ethics aren't based on laws or government edicts. I will do what I think is right before I obey the government. I would have been willing to smuggle Jews out of Nazi Germany even if it was against German law. I go over 65 miles per hour

Religious practice and spirituality can each exist without the other. In the Christian tradition, spirituality says there's a divine essence. To reach it, you have to touch a sacred dimension beyond yourself. The spirituality is the grace part, and the practice is the human part meeting the grace.

Ron, a Silicon Valley pastor

when I know it's safe. My primary concern is what's healthy for myself and for others.

"One of the toughest parts of living in the Valley is time demands. The challenge for me is to better integrate my spiritual life with life in the material world. My new career direction should make that possible. I want to see helping other people become a priority. I'll keep working on my program, continue finding myself, and stay engaged in daily spiritual life.

"Silicon Valley has always been a breeding ground for new ideas. It's a creative zone for the planet. I hope the tolerance and acceptance we have here will permeate everywhere, maybe even to troubled places like the Mideast and Northern Ireland. Technology like the World Wide Web will allow us to accept and enjoy our differences instead of hurting each other."

MARTA

"When one opens one's self to the life force, when it's got breathing space and is welcome, one can't help but become aware of the sacred," Marta says.

Marta is a tech writer for one of Silicon Valley's icon organizations. She was born in Germany, and moved to Minnesota as a child with her mother. Her mother had her baptized as a Lutheran because she felt that Minnesotans valued membership in institutional religions. Marta has been in Silicon Valley for 28 years, and that's been more than enough time to explore spiritual alternatives.

Several years ago, Marta embarked on a process to expand her inner frontiers. Her childhood religion was uninspiring. Her ex-husband was "a capital-A atheist." She had been in a spiritual stall. It was time to open up. She had previously taken a number of personal growth seminars and programs, and felt she was ready for new enlightenment.

When she opened herself, she expected the Christian spirit to enter her and come to life, but that is not what happened. Christian traditions were high on her exploration list, but she found nothing she could put her arms around. A substantial theological roadblock for her was the doctrine of original sin. She doesn't buy it. She doesn't believe we're "bad and black deep down," and she feels focusing on sin is "getting off the mark" of a true spiritual pursuit. She felt no connection with churches or church communities. "I remember thinking maybe you had to be a nun or a monk to get Christianity," she says.

A friend introduced her to some of the concepts of Zen Buddhism. She found them interesting. She bought a book on the subject and read it carefully. As she went through it, she methodically checked off things with which she resonated. It ended up being a substantial list, and she decided to explore Zen retreats.

The quiet, tranquil ambience of the retreats was a dramatic contrast to the inner maelstrom they brought her. Meditation opened paths to issues and conflicts with which she had never dealt. She found a prayer which she felt was allowing the Creator to flow through her. She cried extensively while meditating. She felt she was being broken open, made vulnerable, being given a road to "inward time" as a medicine for the frantic pace of life.

During one retreat, between meditations, an older woman said something to her which triggered "an emotional storm of terror and catharsis." It didn't have much to do with what was said. It had everything to do with the presence of someone Marta felt was accepting and nonjudgmental, the nature of the retreat, and the process she was going through.

("This woman told me she once spent a whole year crying," she recalls. I asked Marta if she knew why. "I guess it was just her year to cry," she said.)

Marta regards herself as "closest to Buddhist" in terms of applying a label to her spiritual path. "The practice is hanging out with whatever comes up, going through your mind and feelings, letting it go, witnessing, and coming back to your breath. It's the place of quiet." An image she likes is that of the upright toy with the weighted base: life throws punches, and may knock her to the side, but her spirituality helps bring her upright again.

The vision of God which speaks to Marta is closely akin to the Buddhist view of "a web of life with causality." God is the unmanifested potential, the pervasive substance. All creatures are God made manifest. She doesn't see a separation, with "God over there and creation over here." Everything's integrated. What we put out affects the world, and comes back and affects us, too. When we die, we go from the manifested back into the pool of the unmanifested.

A meaningful metaphor for Marta is God as ocean and humans as waves. Waves are differentiated, manifested, temporary. They have birth, fruition, death. They're made from, and always part of, the ocean. "Meditation is about coming to that still, calm place that says 'ocean.'"

An emerging part of Marta's practice is to combine prayer, meditation and exercise during brisk walks. As she passes other

---

Ethical or moral behavior is not so much an arbitrary decree from above as the natural outgrowth of careful attention to the consequences of one's thoughts and emotions.

Tony Schwartz, discussing Buddhism, in *What Really Matters—Searching for Wisdom in America*

people, she has a prayer for them: "May you have peace; may you have no suffering; may you be connected to God." Prayer may not change the color of a wall, she believes, but it can cause the wall to glow with a different light.

Twenty-five years ago, Marta's prayer channel opened up for two-way communication. The message she received was "Risk! Learn to let go of yourself. Learn to love in a larger way." She is trying to follow this direction. She feels confident that God talks to all of us, through our intuition, if we're open and available to it. She doesn't think the obstacle is that God is shy. The obstacle is that this is Silicon Valley, and our incoming lines are busy.

Marta thinks interest in Buddhism in this area is growing. She regards it as a fine foundation for building a custom home for one's spirit—particularly for those who are disenchanted with mainstream Western religions.

"Western civilization thinks man is a special case and doesn't have to obey natural laws," she says. "Not true. We are not exempt from nature. If we're going to survive, we have to find our connection with nature and each other. Our outer manifestation has to spring from inner values. Maybe it takes a spiritual renaissance."

HELENE

Helene, a Silicon Valley minister, was born and raised a Baptist. She has come to believe there are many paths to workable spirituality and connection with deeper meaning.

The diversity of viewpoints and philosophies the area sports and supports led her to establish an organization focusing on interfaith sharing. Its goal is to facilitate communication and understanding among those of disparate beliefs, and encourage pooling of wisdom to assist in the search for truth. She says, "Spirituality is not so much a list of beliefs as a relationship which can't necessarily be defined." She thinks this perspective, combined with the area's frequently negative view of the traditional, will make New Age approaches much more attractive than mainline churches to spiritual newcomers in the Valley.

BRAD

After exchanging a series of messages via each other's answering machines, Brad and I finally connected for an online, real-time, bisynchronous telephone conversation. He's a Roman Catholic priest. I had been told he was doing interesting things and might have some valuable insights on spiritual dynamics in the Valley. We agreed to meet at the Los Altos Peet's for coffee. He said he'd be wearing teal.

A priest wearing teal ... sounded interesting already.

Turns out he's not currently working in his clerical role. His spiritual vision has become tightly woven with a passion for education, and a desire to help teachers teach. He and two colleagues have established a nonprofit foundation to develop courses, training tools, and seminars to make educators more effective. They are particularly interested in working with the area's high-tech companies to "break down the walls between religion/spirituality and science/technology."

The foundation will also develop and offer support programs for educators, with emphasis on showing them how to incorporate the teaching of ethics and wellness into their subjects. Seminars to help people deal with long-term illness are also in the works.

Contributing to the effectiveness of Silicon Valley's educational infrastructure has become a core part of Brad's view of his spiritual journey. There is no legacy he would rather leave than to see people who are better educated, and more spiritually and ethically aware, coming out of the Valley's schools and corporations through his efforts. It's a logical continuation of his life.

Brad was born in upstate New York, and received most of his education in Roman Catholic schools. As he grew up, he developed respect for clergy who took the lead in social issues. Daniel Berrigan was an early hero. Brad entered seminary because he wanted to follow those footsteps, help change society for the better, learn to use religion to pursue the common good. He saw that the Church could be a "critical conscience" in our culture.

After ordination he worked as a parish priest for two years, but discovered what he really enjoyed was working on educational projects. If he'd been a member of an educational order, he believes he might have cheerfully embarked on a career of academic administration. But he wasn't. So he looked for other routes to involve himself with teaching.

One day he woke up and asked himself, "Self, do you really want to spend the rest of your life in Buffalo?" Self responded resoundingly in the negative. He ended up in Silicon Valley, a place he finds intriguing for its leading-edge economy, openness to change, multicultural diversity and strong educational institutions.

Wozniak and Jobs started Apple in a garage. Brad's following the mold, renting rooms and working out of an empty convent while getting his foundation rolling. As we sipped French roast, he shared his observations on the Valley's spiritual scene.

"Everything here is so competitive, so product- and process-driven, that the care of the soul has taken a back seat. Affluence grabs hold and takes over. New product introductions give people such a rush that they've practically become the drug of choice.

"But the work can be draining and exhausting. People sometimes start wondering if 'that's all there is,' and that may open the inner door a little. I've talked to many VPs who have been downsized. These were people who had virtually enslaved themselves to their jobs and their companies, then got flattened. They felt they had done all the right things. Then they went from six-figure jobs to no-figure jobs.

"But those with some spiritual component in their lives dealt with the whole thing so much better. They seemed to be able to transcend the devastating circumstances. They realized they were still good husbands or wives, still good parents, still valued members of a community. They kept their dignity. I believe it's people who bring dignity to work, not work that brings dignity to people.

"Sometimes I start retreats by asking people to think about a scene from the movie *Philadelphia*: the one where Tom Hanks lets an operatic aria just *transport* him to another place while he's in conference with his lawyer. Then I ask them, 'What's the music in your life?' In Silicon Valley, I'm not sure people know what that music is, or are ready to hear it and be touched by it.

"People back East ask me what it's like living in Silicon Valley. I tell them it's like having all 30 NFL teams located between San Francisco, San Jose and Oakland, all competing for the same fans. Competition and survival are the focal points.

"People here have such tremendous aspirations. What happens if they don't achieve them? Bust times may come again. The soul is the one thing we should invest more in. We'll need it if the Valley turns back into prune orchards. I don't know if people are ready to take care of their souls yet. They know they should, and they'll flock to Kepler's or Printer's Ink or East-West Books to buy literature, but they may not be ready to find the music and devote the energy.

"People here know they're making history, and the business is addictive. Andy Grove wrote a book called *Only The Paranoid Survive*. OK. How long do we want to be paranoid? Is that a way to live? Sooner or later everyone takes a kick in a sensitive portion of their anatomy. We have to be able to keep it in perspective. For many, it might take something as big as failed health or failed families to snap the money and the success back into perspective.

"In *Habits of the Heart*, Robert Bellah made the case that we have become a nation of individuals, not a community. That applies even more to Silicon Valley. But when individuals don't have a community to share their spirituality with, the spirituality tends to fade. The most true spiritual expression I've seen in the Valley has been at Alcoholics Anonymous meetings.

"I think the image of God many people in this area have is the one they're most comfortable with for their authority figures: he's the CEO. One thing I still like about the Catholic Church is that they teach a God of compassion, not of wrath. But there are some people in the Valley who are hungry to find simpler, black-and-white things in this incredibly complex environment we live in. There are some fundamentalist churches starting to thrive as some of these people join, and they're hearing about a wrathful CEO.

"People don't have to practice a religion to be spiritual, or even believe in the usual concept of a deity. The inner spirit, the

---

The problem with spirituality without an organization is that it emphasizes an individuality which leads to isolation, renunciation, and self-righteousness. Churches require sharing. "I can be spiritual alone" is a great way to escape responsibility, and promotes a false experience. If I'm a person of faith, I'm also a person reaching out to others.

Pat, a Valley pastor

thing that brings purpose, joy, exultation, may be experiencing God even if the mind isn't at the moment. I believe there are five ways people experience God that involve no formal worship:

- ❖ first, just having self-worth and self-respect;

- ❖ second, having the capacity to give unlimited love;

- ❖ third, dealing with our own mortality;

- ❖ fourth, having hope;

- ❖ and last, raising children, the willingness of every generation to sacrifice for the next.

"The human spirit *soars* during these five situations. It doesn't have to be mystical or magical. The moments of spirituality are in the ordinariness of daily living.

"The people who are the most spiritually grounded are people who like themselves and don't want to be someone else. Spiritual people won't be *users* of others. They see people as creations like themselves, to be reverenced and respected, not as subjects. They don't always have to be playing the trump card and controlling others.

"A key ethical conflict everyone has to work out before taking a job is, 'If I go to work for you, how much of my soul am I gonna have to give you?' Another one is, 'Can this workplace be a place of meaningful conversation, or does it have to be what the boss wants to hear?' A good environment must ensure mutual success, and not end up with a posse of burned-up, burned-out souls.

"I think it's a part of American culture to respect team spirit, and I don't think the Valley is an exception to that. And team spirit is a form of spirituality. Most folks like to see others who show great team spirit succeed. When people demonstrate spirituality in their business relations, no one begrudges them their money or their success.

"In terms of my personal spiritual path, I'm going to keep doin' what I'm doin'. My passion is for education, and for teaching people how to take care of their souls, making it possible for them to teach others the same thing. If I never presided at another Eucharist it wouldn't matter. I didn't get ordained just to wear robes. It was about moving forward with a social vision and making it happen. Heroes are fine, but what we really need are role models.

"I don't know how the Valley will end up blending technology with spirituality—I just know it needs to happen. You can't stay paranoid forever."

STREET SCENE INTERLUDE

As I waited for Victor in a downtown Palo Alto coffee shop, a compelling figure shuffled repeatedly into the shop, then back out. He looked 42 going on 106. His clothes were an unrelated collage of old, tired cotton. His full beard was mostly black, streaked with gray. So was his mane of wildly disheveled hair.

I found some of the same adjectives popping into mind as I looked at his eyes: Black. Streaked with gray. Disheveled. Wild.

The eyes stayed fixed dead ahead as he moved. He left his shopping cart—brim-full of ancient garments, two canteens, and unidentifiable objects wrapped in untraceable pieces of plastic—by the bench in front of the shop. I sipped blueberry Italian soda and watched him come ... through ... the ... door ... at ... a ... painstakingly ... slow ... pace, ... careful ... step ... by ... careful ... step. My inner metronome, used to the manic Silicon Valley clock speed of life, was going nuts.

Eyes straight ahead, he moved glacially past the service counter to the rear of the shop where large burlap bags full of coffee were stacked. His mission was a mystery. From behind the counter, the coffee server/cashier watched, radiating discomfort and indecision. The stranger wasn't hassling anyone. But he also wasn't buying anything, and his bizarre looks and behavior might scare the customers away. What to do?

Outside, a woman crossed the street and sat down on the bench, a few feet from his cart. She was plump and blonde, wearing blue jeans which looked worn and faded enough to have been handmade by Levi Strauss himself. What was left of her boots indicated similar vintage. She looked 34 going on 106. She gazed through the door into the shop for a few moments, then grimaced or smiled (no way to tell which). Her teeth didn't look too good. She closed her eyes in the late afternoon sun.

The bearded man retraced his steps and eventually made it back out the door: his fourth round trip. He looked at his cart, the bench, the woman. He stood statue-still for about 45 seconds. Then, with the same torturously slow tread, he moved toward the woman. If she heard the shuffle of his approaching feet, she gave no sign. Her eyes stayed closed. Her hands were folded in her lap. He finally arrived at her location. He paused. He leaned over. With utmost gentleness, he kissed her. She did not move or open her eyes. He stood up, turned around, headed back toward the shop door with the same timeless rhythm, entered, and began his well-defined return journey to the burlap bags. The woman opened her eyes and stared straight ahead, face completely expressionless. No clues were in evidence to tell whether she knew the man, or that she had been kissed.

I felt an almost overpowering urge to get up, introduce myself to both of them, and request an interview. What would be their thoughts about spirituality in Silicon Valley?

Victor pulled up outside the shop, dismounted from his bicycle, secured it and joined me at my table by the window. The bearded man exited, and this time did not return. I scored a blueberry Italian soda for Victor, and we began our conversation.

VICTOR

Victor was born in Illinois, but has lived in Silicon Valley for over 20 years. His father was Jewish. His mother belonged to a mainline Protestant denomination. He was baptized, but his parents let him make his own call about his spiritual direction. At 13, he decided not to go through with confirmation into his mother's church. "My path will be neither Jewish nor Christian," he says. "It will encompass both, and other things. An image I sometimes use for my spiritual life is a butterfly. The wings are Judaism and Christianity, and the body is the center I'm trying to get to."

While in college, Victor spent summers in Japan, and he lived there for two years after graduating. "Life in Japan made me realize I'm not Japanese," he recalled, "but it gave me some shelter from the spiritual confusion I felt at the time. What I had to realize was that my journey was not geographical, it was *inward*. Once I got to that point, I decided that the Bay Area was the place for me to be. This is an excellent environment for exploration, for quests, for me to find out who I am."

Fluent in Japanese, Victor is now a language instructor. Finding his spiritual destiny is at the top of his priority stack. He includes Quaker meetings, Buddhist meditation and labyrinth walking in his current practice. "I find the Quaker style nurturing in the sense that the silence offers space and balance. Teachings come from within. People speak if they are 'moved to speak.'"

"Connectedness" and "centeredness" are terms Victor used frequently during our discussion. They represent core concepts of his path. "The connectedness has to be with what's authentic in me, not what's superficial," he says. "Mindfulness meditation is a bedrock to my pathway. I'm using it to achieve a sense of wholeness, of completeness, of authenticity. To get to a place where I can say 'Aha! I am this, and I am this.' And sometimes, when I'm meditating, or praying for direction, things will become known, and I'll say 'Aha! It's been made clear! Thank you!' "

Although he values the Valley's freedom to explore and experiment, Victor also has a healthy concern for the area's snares for the unwary. "The overstimulus provides a tremendous challenge to remaining centered and authentic," he says. "We're like fish swimming upstream. We have to constantly keep our eyes out for hooks. One of them is the increasing sense that technology determines your value, and that the faster modem, the better Internet connection, the more advanced program will lead to fulfillment. It's almost as if the servant has become the master.

"One of my biggest spiritual challenges is trying to keep a balanced sense of compassion and understanding when I'm feeling attacked by my boss. It's been a struggle. My boss is a jerk. But maybe his parents were jerks, and maybe all he knows is how to be a jerk. So the challenge is not to grab onto his 'jerkness,' but to see past it, see him as a person, stay centered, but still make my point.

"I'm looking to my spiritual life to lead me to peace within myself, and to allow me to fully express my gifts. I need greater balance between involvement in the outside world and focus on

> *Nature lovers could be closer to God than people realize. Maybe closer than those practicing in churches.*
>
> Rhonda, a network equipment company program manager

the inner world. I may be doing longer periods of silent meditation—perhaps even a 10-day silent retreat. We need to counter the speed of the Valley, and return to a natural human rhythm. We need the spaciousness of quiet."

TRAIL FOR TWO

An issue discussed at greater length in Chapter Nine is what happens when one partner in a marriage or relationship has a spiritual life but the other does not. There's another version of the question: what happens when both spirits are alive and well, but each partner wants to build a different spiritual home?

Additional subtext may arise when the home one or both of them have in mind is very much a build-to-suit project rather than a prefab. Making up the rules as we go along can be liberating, but also confusing. The fact is, it's hard enough to blaze a new trail just for oneself. Making it wide enough for two to stride side by side adds much to the task. And for some, walking the path without a partner is just not their first choice. Things might end up that way, but not by preference.

For many years, Paula and Gavin have been members of an established, mainstream Protestant church in an affluent Valley community. They have come to feel that the relationship with this institution is no longer working well for them, not doing what it's supposed to do. However, this is not a joint decision. It's two individual decisions, for two different sets of reasons.

GAVIN

Gavin is a biology professor at a local community college. He's a tenor in the church choir, and takes great pleasure in making music in that setting. He belongs to the church men's club, and enjoys the social experience. Music and mixing are happening for him there, but not much spirituality.

Part of the drawback to his spiritual experience at the church relates to the idea that familiarity can breed, if not contempt, then at least irreverence. Gavin has come to know the long-time minister almost too well. He knows his foibles, sees his human failings, enjoys the camaraderie. But his acceptance of the man as his spiritual leader has faded. Not by design. It just happened.

In a way, Gavin feels that his religious involvement peaked in his teens. He had a great time in the church youth group, and he went to Mass with a Roman Catholic girl he was dating to show her he cared. After high school, life took over, and he wasn't interested in getting back onto a spiritual path until children came along. Then he and his wife put a great deal of energy into shopping for a church, but he felt it was more for the kids' benefit than his.

A few years ago, Gavin felt his spiritual life had leveled out. Then a guest speaker at the men's club gave a presentation on meditation. He tried it. He liked it. So did some of the other men. They have formed a group which meets every two weeks for meditation. Gavin now meditates three times a week for 30 minutes—or tries to. He says it has made a big difference in his life, made him calmer. He gave an example:

"I was walking through the Price Club parking lot with a shopping cart full of stuff, and two cars honked at me. In the past that would have made me very angry. I was going fast enough. Let them wait! But meditation has mellowed me out, so I didn't get angry. Then I saw they were honking at me because a package of 5,000 napkins had fallen off the bottom of my cart."

At this point Gavin doesn't know exactly what his spiritual life is, or what he wants to get from it. He wants to be more in touch with himself, more in control of himself. "I want to be more the driver than the car," he says.

Mostly what he'd like is to be able to recreate the spiritual feelings he had as a child. He didn't know as much then. Now, his scientific orientation is putting up a real barricade to internalizing some tenets of Christian belief.

"I have a hard time accepting things on faith anymore," he explained. "I want an explanation of the miracles. 'The Red Sea gets shallow at certain times'; 'locust mating patterns support the plague schedule'; that kind of thing. And as a biologist, I just can't handle virgin birth. Mary and Joseph have to have been fooling around.

"But in my men's group, I would have a hard time expressing my doubts. I would get, 'What, you don't believe?!' I wonder how many people in church on Sunday have primal doubts about doctrine and God and life after death. I suspect a lot of prayers are the adult version of 'God, please increase my allowance.' "

Gavin's vision of God is right in sync with the observations of clergypersons Roland and Pat in the prior chapter: something like the "Force" in *Star Wars*. He observes that sometimes things do seem to happen when people pray together, and thinks maybe God functions like a cosmic network server to which everyone connects.

Without the leavening of a creative intellectual focus, the quasi-therapeutic blandness that has afflicted much of mainline Protestant religion at the parish level for over a century cannot effectively withstand the competition of the more vigorous forms of radical religious individualism, with their claims of dramatic self-realization, or the resurgent religious conservatism that spells out clear, if simple, answers in an increasingly bewildering world.

Robert N. Bellah et al., *Habits of the Heart—Individualism and Commitment in American Life*

But he also observes that there are too many people praying to too many Gods for conflicting things, and he's troubled by the inherent contradictions. How can He take sides? How can He not? Why does He let so many bad things happen? If He has the conscious control of His creation which people ascribe to Him, how can you not blame Him for the world's problems?

He doesn't have the answers to his questions and doubts, and he hasn't settled on a well-defined strategy for getting them. He thinks he may focus more on exploring Eastern religions via retreats, mantras and continuing meditation. But he likes the people in his church, and likes the music there, and he's not going to walk away. The current pastor is approaching the end of his reign. Gavin thinks having a new leader will be healthy for the congregation, and might help him refocus his journey.

PAULA

Like her husband, Paula has come to the conclusion that their church no longer meets her needs. She was born into an affluent, mainstream Protestant family in Colorado, and she's fairly certain that her family and old friends would look harshly on the direction her path is taking. She has not yet disengaged: she feels ties to the church community and some aspects of traditional belief. But she is energetically engaged in the pursuit of the right alternative.

"The church is hierarchical, and structured on centuries of patriarchy and male domination," she says. "There's a wound to heal, and issues to deal with. There are a lot of very controlling male ministers, and when you look at what traditional churches have foisted off, it's appalling. It's a power play, backed up by hellfire and damnation.

"The Christian boat is sinking. But if you jump, where do you jump and who do you jump with? I think I'm looking for the Goddess, for the pre-Christian harmony of humankind and earth. 'Christian feminist' may be an oxymoron; some might call me a pagan."

Strong feelings that traditional religion just didn't add up entered Paula's consciousness in her late 30s. She concluded that organizational structure was a big part of religion's problems. She thought she could be a part of the solution by becoming an organizer and activist within her spiritual community. She did research. She prayed for direction.

She made little progress. She remembers sitting in a church committee meeting and being struck by the lack of diversity of thought and perspective in the group. She couldn't restrain herself. "We're inbred and incestuous," she said. Everything stopped. There was silence. Then the discussion continued as if she hadn't spoken. For the first time, the thought came to her that it might be time to leave, time to find something new—or start it.

Then she saw a play that changed her life. It was written and performed by one woman, built around a series of scenes reflecting women's relationship with spirituality over the ages. She took several women to see it. They were all moved. They decided to form a group to discuss its concepts.

Paula put a blurb in her church newsletter to announce the formation of the discussion group. She felt it was a relatively modest undertaking, not requiring the minister's approval. He saw it

> *The more I accept that I can't accept some of the theological details of my Christian faith as truth, the more the Holy Spirit deepens within me.*
>
> Celeste, a Silicon Valley attorney

differently. He called her on the carpet for not going through channels. He told her the whole thing sounded like she was trying to form a new sect.

She told the minister that henceforth she would seek the appropriate clearance. Furthermore, she would commemorate this resolution by having T-shirts printed up saying, "We have safe sects with our minister."

"It'll be a long time before a woman is the senior minister here," she says. "Teaching and healing, yes. Leading and decision making, no.

"I want a numinous connection to the higher spirit. I want to feel connected to the God/dess within. I can understand why people become mystics or hermits—it's a powerful experience, and may be the best way for many to find that connection. But I need to find it with a community, although stepping out of the mainstream makes it harder to find that community. Starhawk [a well-known Bay Area Wiccan practitioner] has written a wonderful 'Tree of Life' meditation, and the image is connection of all through the roots, and strength through the trunk.

One can probably be spiritual without religion or belief in a God, but it might be somewhat superficial: like ordering a cheeseburger, hold the meat and hold the cheese. One can be humanistic, but the question of what's the difference between the humanistic and the spiritual is a tough one, and the answers are full of gray. The commonality seems to revolve around the sense of peace. The humanist is at peace because he has accepted the human condition. The spiritualist is at peace because he has transcended the human condition.

Richard, a Silicon Valley software company executive

"I've been an energy vampire for much of my life, and now I want to stop taking and give. I'll do my part, if I can just figure out what it is. Or if 'someone' will tell me.

"Silicon Valley has a very open culture, and it's easier to explore new directions here than it might be back home. I think I'd have to be cautious, more careful, if I tried to talk about my 'alternative' beliefs there. And if I were accused of witchcraft there, I'm really not sure who would stand by me and who would join in stoning me.

"What I'm looking for is unity between God and Goddess, but since traditionally we get taught more about God, maybe we have to focus harder to find the Goddess. There was a point in my life where I came to feel that, as a woman, I had been dealt a hand with no face cards and no trumps, despite having brains, education and money.

"Men have to focus on being humble. Women have to focus on being equal. Men have to get in touch with their nurturing side, women with their power side. Women are usually the keeper of the spiritual flame, the home, the religion. Western society gives women more permission to be contemplative and spiritual than it gives men. It seems like men have to wait until they retire to get that chance.

"I had a deeply emotional experience while I was walking the labyrinth at Grace Cathedral. I was trying to figure out where my spiritual path should go and what I should do about my relationship with the church. I started to cry. Then I realized I didn't have any tissues. I didn't want to weep. I didn't want to leave all the good parts of Christianity behind. I said to Jesus, 'I don't know where I'm going. Will you walk with me?'

"Yes," He said.

"Then I said, 'Will you carry me?'

"No," He said.

"Then I said, 'Will you hold my hand?'

"Yes," He said.

"My friend was behind me on the labyrinth. Suddenly, she reached out and held my hand. I started to cry again. She started to cry. Her hand touching mine at that moment was the Holy Spirit in her touching the Holy Spirit in me. It felt like lights could have come on and a host of angels lifted us up. Our souls had connected.

"I'm not sure how my search for the Goddess and my Christianity will play together. I believe that if Jesus came back today he would put his head in his hands and weep—and then the male-dominated institutional power structure of religion would crucify him all over again.

"To some extent, the relationship of women to the church is like a wife to an abusive husband. I will not leave Jesus. He personified all that was good. But I will leave the church. And that makes me feel very sad and very tired. It takes a lot of energy to build a new structure."

You can achieve a limited degree of spirituality on your own. But to realize your potential, I think you need some sort of guide. I cannot imagine an Olympic athlete without a coach.

The fact that one ostensibly follows a guide, however, is certainly no guarantee of spiritual enlightenment. I can't remember the exact circumstances or words, but Gandhi was once asked why, since he believed in the teachings of Christ so much, he never became a Christian. He replied that he never found a Christian denomination that followed the teachings of Christ.

Neil, a former Silicon Valley programmer

CHAPTER SIX

❧

Soul Tracks

Many trainers and consultants maintain that the soul belongs at home or in church. But with little understanding of the essential link between the soul life and the creative gifts of their employees, hardheaded businesses listening so carefully to their hardheaded consultants may go the way of the incredibly hardheaded dinosaurs.

David Whyte, *The Heart Aroused—Poetry and the Preservation of the Soul in Corporate America*

"Our nervous system isn't just a fiction; it's a part of our physical body, and our soul exists in space and is inside us, like the teeth in our mouth. It can't be forever violated with impunity."

Boris Pasternak, quoted in *What Really Matters— Searching for Wisdom in America,* by Tony Schwartz

For every man and woman, midlife is a pivotal time of internal rebirth. No matter what we have accomplished or what we command, midlife calls on us to experience it in a new way, to birth ourselves into a new kind of usefulness. Returning from years of work ... we know now the sacredness and soulfulness of belonging once again.

David Whyte, *The Heart Aroused—Poetry and the Preservation of the Soul in Corporate America*

Spiritual matters are inherently nebulous and elusive, a characteristic which provides built-in tension between them and well-defined technical knowledge. That elusiveness doesn't deter some people from expressing their spiritual views with striking certainty. However, of all the topics discussed in this book, none caused as much hesitation, reflection and uncertainty during interviews as the issue of "soul." Even interviewees who sailed through most of the questions with breezy conviction often sputtered a touch here.

THE GREAT DIVIDE

Consideration of soul might be divided into two perspectives: its nature and significance during life, and its nature and significance after life. Almost everyone, even those with no spiritual life at all, felt there is something within humans, somehow different from mind or body, that might be called *soul*. And when asked, "Do you believe a soul is inherent in all people, even if they never experience any spiritual awakening of any kind?," the answer was, almost unanimously, "Yes." Many people added provisos, however: strongly held beliefs that qualitative differences would exist between souls which inhabited people with spiritual lives, and souls which didn't.

The question of the soul's significance after life (if any) is the more abstract and metaphysical issue. Yet, in a way, it's easier to consider than the question of significance during life (if any). Discussion of human afterlife has been around for a long time, and most doctrines about life after death (if any) invoke some form of soul. This is a well-debugged application of the concept.

It's also an application which causes a curious sort of comfort: most people have accepted the fact that they may have *beliefs* about soul's role in an afterlife, but they know they're not going to be able to prove or demonstrate the accuracy of their beliefs until they get there. Therefore, there's no specific action item required at present.

However, if soul plays a role while a life is in progress, then it is during that life that one must figure out what the role is, and how it should be connected with life: a somewhat less theoretical, more immediate issue, requiring somewhat sharper attention. Of the two "significance" perspectives (after life/during life), it's also the one we might conclude we have been given less time to noodle through.

There is increasing recognition, both in literature and, I believe, in the general consciousness, that there is a special part of us which the grindstone of life agitates, abrades, hones and molds. That special part is not related to skills and abilities, likes and dislikes, personality traits or accomplishments. I would characterize it more as *convictions*, as the piece which says, "Here is what I stand

> *A friend once said, "It didn't hurt me to not exist before I was born, and it won't hurt me to not exist after I die."*
>
> Cal, a Valley college instructor

for, here is what I believe is valuable and right, about me and about the world. Here is what I would fight for, and make great sacrifice for, although no one would tell me to do that, and no one has the power to force me to do that."

It takes time for this special part to declare itself and take lasting shape. Perhaps its emergence is a core portion of the midlife experience. When it does emerge, the Pasternak quote at the beginning of this chapter carries a message of importance for all of us: ignore that part at great risk.

A picture which emerged from interviews with clergy is that soul may be a concept which is less defined than other aspects of their theology. Substantially different visions were offered, even from clergy in the same religion or denomination. This is not surprising. The attempt to visualize and describe the soul is that leap into an unknown which has tantalized us for as long as there have been humans to ask deep philosophical questions: what are we *really*?

It's easy to understand the connection between traumatic developments in personal life and the sudden onset of spiritual interest. But a slower, subtler process may take root and grow: an awareness of being *part of*. Part of a group. Part of a community. Part of the universe, a being whose body is made, literally, of stardust. (The very early universe contained only the elements hydrogen and helium. All the heavier elements, of which human bodies are made, were manufactured by the nuclear processes of

> *The soul is the light of the universe coming through our physical manifestation. It's our purpose, our path, our work, our intention, the reason we're here. It's not often seen because it's hidden by many masks. It's like a flame. Some flames have burned low, some are shining like a Roman candle.*
>
> Victor, a Silicon Valley teacher

stars. Then the particles were distributed by stellar explosion for subsequent usage. Crosby, Stills, Nash and Young were exactly right when they sang "We are stardust" in Joni Mitchell's song *Woodstock*, although it is unlikely they were aware of this, or that they would have been particularly interested in the technical correctness they were displaying.)

And finally, perhaps, an awareness grows of being part of a family of human souls. Depending on one's vision, it might be a very large family.

JERRY

Jerry started his career as a lawyer, which proved to be excellent preparation for his current calling: rabbi of a large Silicon Valley synagogue.

As a lawyer, Jerry felt a profound disconnect between the work he was doing and the life he wanted. He was looking for meaning and involvement. He wanted to feel his time was being invested, not wasted.

Jerry sees the interplay of many factors in the spiritual awakening of people in the Valley and in his congregation. Joys and sorrows; existential anxiety; success and failure; pressure to succeed; doubts about the right definition of success; children; the dehumanizing effects of modern existence; pursuit of goals which prove to be vacant and illusory; progressive materialism; workaholism; narcissism; the approach of midlife.

"One thing we learn from Eastern religions," he says, "is that spirituality is not an event, but a product of sustained, disciplined engagement which can open us up and allow us to grow. There's some similarity to the dynamics of joining a health club or going on a diet. The reality of the discipline often means people don't stick with it. Tough commitment is required. Faith is meaningless without faithfulness.

"We live in an agnostic time and place, and people don't know what to believe. Religion has become so tied up with pop culture that spirituality is almost disposable. People want to mix it with water, get instant spirituality, and pour what they don't drink down the drain. They'll get more out of their spiritual pursuits if they see themselves as *partners in creating* a spiritual community, rather than just being *consumers* of community. A journey of faith without a community seems to me like reading sheet music and never hearing it played.

"When some people tell me they're not religious and don't believe in God, I say 'Tell me about the God you don't believe in.' When they do, my response is often, 'Well, I don't believe in that God either.' Then, maybe, we can talk about a God we *do* believe in.

"Soul is that aspect which survives us, the aspect which contains the divine within us. Christianity often differentiates body and soul, with the body being the source of our lusts and our appetites. Jews tend to see body and soul as a united whole, and the body as a source of potential holiness.

"Back East, I was president of the local clergy association, and hosted the annual holiday dinner. We had a scrumptious black forest cake for dessert. A minister came back for seconds and said, 'This is what we Christians call sin.' My wife smiled at him and said, 'This is what we Jews call pleasure.' I don't see the body as

---

Soul is the essence, the flame, the drive that gets us up in the morning. When you're doing the things you were created to do, the soul is like a balloon that keeps expanding until you feel it's going to burst because you feel so good.

Kate, a Valley church office administrator

distinct from soul, and I don't see the body as inherently bad. It's possible for talk about soul to miss the mark on its relationship with the body and the rest of the person."

MELANIE

"I try to approach questions of soul and afterlife scientifically," Melanie says. "Unfortunately, it's hard to get good data."

Melanie is a computer scientist and engineer who spent most of her career at one of the Valley's flagship research installations. Her vision of soul is a mix of ingredients from life observations, multicultural theology and analytical scrutiny.

Melanie's father was Roman Catholic, her mother Protestant, and she ended up with no real interest in either. "All head, no spirit," she remembers. "Also, some people who go to church are very rigid and arrogant and self-righteous. Some of the worst arrogance is spiritual arrogance."

Her upbringing left her in a spiritual vacuum. Years later, as an adult, she felt her spirit beginning to wake for the first time during a trip to Egypt. "The leaders of the trip pointed out that Egyptian art reflected more living spirituality than all our organized religions." She was inclined to agree. "The same kind of thing is also true in India," she observes. "There's a living spirituality that everyone there seems to have. You don't see that when you're out and about here."

Eventually, Melanie joined a relatively small, nonmainstream religious group. Of her current spiritual life, she says, "If I do my part, I'll get what I need. I know that with inner certainty. It is not the certainty of faith or belief. It comes from 25 years of being a research scientist, from the scientific method, which says the data support my conclusions."

Melanie sees God "... primarily as the Divine Mother. Prayer is talking to God. Meditation is listening to God. I try to do both. Sometimes we get divine messages through signs. I ran a stop sign recently and got a ticket. I saw and felt it as a warning: 'You're not stopping. You never stop. Take your foot off the accelerator.'

"Soul is our consciousness, our thoughts, who we are. When I live life in a way that generates good karma, good things happen. If I live as if whatever I do to others will eventually be done to me, everything makes sense. When I'm rude to someone, next time I go into the grocery store the clerk is rude to me. I finally got the data on this! Maybe some of the starving people in Rwanda were Nazis in a former life.

"Believing that people create their own 'soul destiny' saves me the anguish of not being able to control or help what happens to them. It's also empowering, because I can control what happens to me by living a good life. It enables me to accept what is, and not

I believe that the soul becomes associated with the body at the time of conception and survives after death—not to come back into this world, but to progress through many other worlds of God, of which we are only dimly aware. It is the soul which experiences joy and illumination. As such, it is my belief that the soul is essential to consciousness.

Roger Penrose, a mathematician/cosmologist, has investigated the essence of consciousness in two of his books. He allows for the possibility of a spiritual aspect essential to consciousness, but as a scientist does not allow himself to believe it to be necessary. I find it difficult to explain certain discoveries in mathematics and science without a spiritual influence. I have myself 'discovered' things which I have absolutely known to be true, only later to be confirmed by rational thought. I think the soul is definitely involved in this process.

Neil, a former Silicon Valley programmer

hassle myself about what might be, which is a totally new way of thinking for me.

"For most of my career as a scientist, I was the only woman in my work groups. All-male groups, all male supervisors. At one point I was thinking about suing my employer for some rather blatant sex discrimination. I was trying to figure out what was the right thing and the spiritual thing to do. I talked to my spiritual counselor, and she said, 'We never sue for personal gain, but we do fight for principle.' There's strength in that! When you stand up for *principle*, you can't get pushed around. One woman who did end up suing became a basket case because she didn't have that spiritual anchor.

"It's really much easier to believe there is no afterlife. It's scary to realize there are spiritual consequences to our actions. A spiritual life is hard work. But Jung said, 'Unless you achieve a spiritual understanding, you don't make it to the later stages of life.' And that's been my observation.

"Again, I'm a scientist. I'm not looking for a belief system. I'm looking for something that works."

STAN

Until age 17, Stan thought there was a good chance he might become a minister. Then he discovered the world of technology. Engineers 1, clergy 0.

Stan is a highly educated engineer and technology consultant who reveres *intellect*. Intellectually, he's trying to understand the

> *The soul is a little mass of shining energy in our bodies, about the size of a grapefruit.*
>
> Olivia, a Silicon Valley homemaker

relationship between spirituality and the church. And intellectually, he struggles with the concept of a soul that can't be measured despite the fact that it has to be in there somewhere. He has an engineer's view of the reason there must be a form of eternal life: "Every person is a generator and emitter of energy. Those waves go on forever." When asked if those waves—and therefore, perhaps, a soul—are inherent in all people, even those who have had no spiritual awakening, Stan replies, "Absolutely. But the waves may have more desirable characteristics when one is spiritual."

RICHARD

Richard is vice president of strategic planning for an aggressive, acquisitive software company. He tries to balance a strong moral code and ethical values with business necessities when his company acquires another, and decisions must be made about the fates of the acquired company's employees. He works to keep candor and compassion in the forefront, particularly when the headsman's axe must fall.

In much the same way, he tries to strike a balance between the pragmatic reality he knows and the deeper issues he can never really know. In wrestling with the tough topic of soul, he is trying to

Science is not normally interested in nonmaterial, apparently mysterious things ... The soul is not an easy subject to deal with either scientifically or spiritually ... [But] the idea of the soul is perhaps the single, most significant, concept of our time: one that needs a current, scientifically relevant and heart-centered spiritual view.

Fred Alan Wolf, *The Spiritual Universe—
How Quantum Physics Proves the Existence of the Soul*

craft the kind of elegant analysis and supportable thinking he might use for a business problem. He knows he can't get there, but he'll keep trying.

For Richard, soul or spirit is eternal partly through the impact we make on others. He senses communication with those who have died, through their impact on him; but he's pretty sure that afterlife doesn't involve going around saying hello to everyone you once knew. He finds this area a little anxiety-provoking, because he feels there are certain things he's supposed to believe, and he's not sure he does.

STUART

For many years, Stuart has been general counsel for a medium-sized Valley company which makes electronic instrumentation systems. Born into a mainstream Protestant family, he has continued to find comfort and satisfaction in the religion of his birth. That doesn't mean he hasn't had an occasional sag.

"Sometimes I've felt that my spiritual life was getting dry and needed some watering," he says, "but I've never felt it was arid. Doubt happens to everyone. Someone once said, 'If you haven't stopped believing in God at least once, you probably never did.' The idea is, if you've worked long enough and hard enough on your path, you're going to have those moments."

> *Since this is Silicon Valley, I'll use a personal computer analogy for my view of soul. Our bodies are the keyboard, monitor, hard drive, etc. Soul is the electric current which allows them to run, and the "principles of life" program that tells them what to do. Soul is God's way of turning on our switch and booting us up.*
>
> Michael, a Silicon Valley priest

Stuart's view of soul is "the essence of a person's being, the person's core, wrapped up in all the person's beliefs. What some might call 'heart.' It's what's left when you've stripped away the clothes and the body, what prevails when the person is in the highest emotional state. It's what animates us, and what goes on to eternal life.

"We get messages from our soul through dreams and the subconscious. We have to learn how to separate what's coming from our active consciousness from what's coming from deeper within.

"When you die, you continue your spiritual journey in a realm beyond space and time. Given *enough* time, even Hitler's soul could come to God's presence. You continue to have the opportunity to approach God after death, even if you were the most confirmed atheist imaginable during life. There's never permanent estrangement; there's always the chance for reconciliation."

ERIC

Eric is a technical publications editor who has had a whirlwind tour through the technology tangle over the past few years. He spent three years at a high-profile startup, worked like a maniac along with everyone else, then saw the effort crumble into oblivion due to fatal flaws in the company's product and market vision. Bummer.

Then he joined a software megacompany and became one of 18,000 employees, working in a corporate headquarters campus big enough to qualify for nation-state status in selected historical

> *The opportunity [of midlife] is to get on with the real work of your Second Adulthood—the feeding and crafting of the soul.*
>
> Gail Sheehy, *New Passages*

periods. Good pay, interesting enough work. But after sampling the involvement and excitement of the newly born enterprise, it's hard, very hard, to be a blurry face in an army-sized crowd.

He floated his résumé and the right call came. He's back with a startup, and this one looks like it's going to make it. He's a happy camper.

Although Eric and his family have always been active in a church, he senses that his spiritual path is becoming an increasingly important part of his life. "I nurture my soul through worship, reflection and singing," he says. "I don't consciously listen to my soul—it's me, not separate, and I have a hard time prying the two apart.

"I'm a Christian, but I believe in the combined concepts of responsibility and karma. The soul's destiny depends on the quality of actions during life. A person's life, deeds and work produce a legacy that makes up one part of the soul. The other part is God transcendent.

"What you leave behind, based on what you did during your stay, is a form of afterlife. I'm intrigued by the idea that somehow, in some form, we can visit earth after death. The 'web you weave' determines what happens to you in the next life. Maybe we shouldn't risk a bad life!"

DISCOVERY BAY

On a day punctuated by rain squalls interleaved with luminous cloud formations and sudden, unexpected rays of pale sun, I drove 45 miles north and east of Silicon Valley to Discovery Bay: a top-choice residential community for boating buffs. Eastern Contra

When someone feels hurt, it is the soul which is hurt.

Dana, a former Silicon Valley training manager

Costa County, just south of the Sacramento Delta complex of waterways, islands and levees, is a hopscotch blend of the old and the new. Once, it was almost all agricultural. Much of it still is, featuring well-tended orchards, a variety of produce farms, and rotund cows enjoying their brown and green Northern California salad bars.

Increasingly, however, much of it isn't. The sky-high cost of housing in the Valley communities has provided builders with incentive to construct outlying housing developments. It has also provided buyers with incentive to put up with excruciating commutes in exchange for owning a bigger, newer house for $200,000 less than they'd pay for a smaller, older one in the heart of the Valley. There are a lot of those houses, smack in the middle of what was farmland not long ago. More—many more—are on the way.

Sharing the landscape with the new, large housing tracts are old, small towns such as Brentwood and Byron. Driving through them, one feels in touch with years such as 1941, or perhaps 1955. Virtually no building in the older section of Byron, residential or commercial, seems without its very old, very rusty car part or piece of equipment or unidentifiable artifact accenting its lot. Fifteen minutes down the highway, 200 brand new houses snap the observer back to the '90s.

"I had spent my entire life studying science ... only to be met with the wretched realization that science was, not wrong, but brutally limited and narrow in scope. If human beings are composed of matter, body, mind, soul and spirit, then science deals handsomely with matter and body, but poorly with mind and not at all with soul and spirit ..."

Consciousness theoretician Ken Wilber, quoted in *What Really Matters—Searching for Wisdom in America,* by Tony Schwartz

Railroad tracks crisscross the turf, many of them unused for years. The planned community of Discovery Bay is built around waterways, and it's on the water, not the tracks, where the action is now. This is a stellar location for boating enthusiasts. Many of the houses have fingers of the bay gently sloshing right outside their back doors, with private mooring spots allowing residents to step from their boats to their patios. The port of San Francisco is a few leisurely cruising hours away, the exact interval depending on how much horsepower one is cruising with. On this day, multitudes of mallards and gaggles of gulls floated and soared on and above the water made silvery by gray clouds and unpredictable shafts of sunlight. Their quick flash of wings and adventurous plummets from midair to underwater added to the ambiance, and kept the fish honest.

RUTH

Ruth and Mel have lived in Discovery Bay for three years, and like it. Mel is a successful Silicon Valley entrepreneur who has dabbled in an impressive variety of economic endeavors. His early career was as a manufacturing manager and executive, eventually with one of the Valley's seminal technology leaders. Those were heady days. Mel thrived.

But a large pool of restless energy is part of Mel's makeup, and eventually the corporate world seemed too tame and well

> *Soul is the human spirit, the "essence" of the person, but the soul is not eternal. The Hebrews could not conceive of a disembodied soul. The whole person dies, body and soul. Then resurrection is given as a gift of God, and there is a new body of some kind, and a new soul.*
>
> Walter, a Valley minister

known. He quit and went into business for himself. He left the world of high-tech materials manufacturing for the world of—sandwiches. He bought a catering company. After a time, he sold that and bought a vocational school. Now he's a financial consultant, tax planner, accountant-for-hire, and real estate investor. For added excitement, he serves as a county sheriff reserve commander.

Ruth's professional track could not have been more different from Mel's. She balanced out his exploits by bringing an element of predictable stability to their life. She taught elementary school for 35 years in one of the Valley's larger school systems.

Ruth and Mel became interested in boating several years ago. They bought a boat, and grew to love life on the water. Ruth's retirement was coming up. There was no reason they couldn't build their life around the boating activity they enjoyed so much, and the friends with whom they shared it. They sold their house in the Valley, and bought the house in Discovery Bay. A year later, Ruth was diagnosed with cancer.

We are constantly being asked to turn our faces away from our own internal images of what is right, true, and most of all alive for us. The very simplicity of these images may seem to speak against them. They may be images of harmonious relationship, a vital company producing useful things, a new product, a life in the country, a loving family, or clear, simple images of flames, swords, feathers, iridescent birds, or enticing forest paths. We give them away thinking they cannot be reflected by the complex experience of the world in which we have learned to live. But giving them away, we find ourselves strangely empty. Finally, we understand that though the world will never be simple, a life that honors the soul seems to have a kind of radical simplicity at the center of it.

David Whyte, *The Heart Aroused—Poetry and the Preservation of the Soul in Corporate America*

Ruth has always felt there was a spiritual component to her being, but its form and magnitude have varied greatly over time. She is currently putting much energy into deciphering her path and beliefs. She is thinking extensively about soul.

Ruth comes from a Seventh Day Adventist family ("the Puritan version," she says). She didn't like it much. "No dancing, no fun, no meat," she recalls. "Mother wanted us to look like good Christian ladies, but really, we looked weird. And if she'd had to choose between the church and my father, she'd have chosen the church." This made for a household Ruth found critical, unloving and oppressive.

Eventually, Ruth was able to start down her own path. She grew comfortable with the idea that God would not zap her with lightning if she drank a beer or had some ham. She vowed that her childhood environment would never be inflicted on her family, and particularly not her husband, when she married.

It hasn't been. Put off by the early exposure, she has pursued her spiritual life without formal religious association. At the beginning of the interview, when I asked if she belonged to any religion, her answer was, "Absolutely not. Dead set against it."

Ruth's cancer treatment has required surgery, and she is currently undergoing both radiation treatment and chemotherapy. "When the cancer came, that was life saying 'get moving and start growing again.' I don't like the concept of people turning to God just as they start to fear dying; it's kind of like whining. As a matter of fact, this isn't the worst thing I've gone through. My divorce from my first husband was worse than this, but it was also another

---

We tried to set up a spiritual retreat for executives. The topic was 'care of the soul for businesspeople.' Not one soul came.

Brad, a Silicon Valley priest

example of a message: 'get rolling, be independent, take care of yourself.'

"I feel so grateful for all the good things. I owe the world a lot, and I need to give much back. I couldn't dream of saying to God 'Why me?' regarding this cancer. When I think about it, I actually think, 'Well, why *not* me?' I was born an American, given two daughters, an education, so much good life. I wonder if I've done enough with what I've received. Perhaps what I'm supposed to do, what I'm here for, what I can give back, is to walk with this and show it can be done in grace and spirit. When I'm having my chemotherapy, I say, 'Thank you, God, for teaching people how to do chemo.'

"The soul is your spirit, the part that remains. Soul is what comes back. It's what chooses what to learn, and what to teach others. Some souls decide to devote their entire life to helping others. The body gets recycled. The soul gets reincarnated.

"My two daughters are so different that I think the only way to explain it is to think in terms of soul difference. One is a physician, successful and comfortable in just about every aspect of life. There's an old soul there. The other has a very young soul, maybe a special soul. At 17 she married a guy who can't seem to do much in life. They have always lived just one step above poverty, but they've stuck together for 24 years. Their son is autistic. He's 18 years old, 6' 6" tall, good looking, and can't say his own name.

"Some souls come here just to teach us lessons. I think this applies to the handicapped son. He's teaching us patience and humility. But I don't know what *he's* getting out of it. What kind of

---

Soul is spiritual DNA.

Brett, a Valley engineer

wonderful soul would be willing to give up a whole lifetime to teach us?

"I had a session with a 70-year-old woman who channels for an Indian shaman spirit. She went into a trance, and I spent an hour talking to the spirit. I told him I wanted to feel that my soul had done well in this life, that I had done what I was supposed to do, and had given back enough. In a guttural voice, he said, 'You Americans always think you have to be *doing* something. Just be. Our souls chose our parents, and our mission here is to be.'

"I think it's more than that. We're here to learn and grow. All of us, and our souls, keep learning. There's more magic, more miracles, waiting to happen and be discovered.

"Nothing ever disappears or goes away. Form may change, but our atoms are always here. During radiation treatment, I visualize the cancerous cells being broken up, and the molecules freed by the radiation, freed to go out in the atmosphere and become a rainbow, not trapped in cancer cells anymore. And then the molecules go from the rainbow to the clouds and become healing rain and fall on the desert and provide healing and nurture to the lizards and plants and sand—and sometimes the treatment is over before the visualization and the dream ends."

Rest, as we all know, brings perspective, vitality and good humor. But it also brings a relaxation into inner silences and images that are sometimes too difficult to face. We might wonder if this has anything to do with our addiction to being busy. Concerning ourselves with the music of the busy outer world, we might not have to face the inner music that was composed as a score for our future destiny.

David Whyte, *The Heart Aroused—Poetry and the Preservation of the Soul in Corporate America*

HAMZA

Shortly after sending a letter to a relatively new Muslim mosque, I received a response via electronic mail. I had written to describe the research I was doing for this book, and to request an interview. The e-mail message came from a member of the group which founded the mosque. He is an engineer with a large software tools company, and he graciously volunteered to arrange an interview with Hamza, the Sufi Muslim group's spiritual leader.

An evening interview was set up at Hamza's residence. When I arrived, a group of followers offered tea and refreshments. Hamza appeared, invited several of the other people present to join us for the discussion, and led us upstairs to his study.

Hamza has been in Silicon Valley for four years. He believes that every human heart is a mosque, but that spirituality in this area is drowned by the focus on business and material pursuits. "Everyone is a carnivore. We eat each other. We want what each other has."

He observes that many churches are heavily focused on ceremony and social activities, perhaps to the detriment of true spiritual seeking. These are barriers to the success of the churches and the fulfillment of their members. He thinks that Native Americans may have the deepest spirituality among Western belief systems.

Hamza sees Americans eventually migrating away from the dogma of their religions to truer and more direct spiritual paths.

Soul/body dualism is not a helpful way to look at things. What is helpful is to see ourselves as integrated beings, capable of both joy and stupidity. I'm not sure what we'll look like in the afterlife, but it will be the best of us.

Sam, a Silicon Valley pastor

He believes there will be increasing interest in Sufi, Buddhist and Hindu teachings. "Sufism is from the heart."

Asked for his vision of the human soul, he says, "According to Islam, soul is the spirit known only to God. It is the unseen. It cannot be defined. It is out of our knowledge. But we have many signs that soul exists. For example, if we say a person is generous, the statement gives no description of the person's physical makeup. It's a reflection of the nature of his soul.

"Soul is like an inner, frictionless moving object. It keeps people moving. Soul is God-made electricity—the divine version of the electric energy which keeps your heart pumping. Maybe we should focus our technological efforts on developing a 'spirituality chip' for humans, so the electricity would power that also."

DEAN

Just before the outbreak of World War II, Dean's parents moved back to their native Japan, and that's where he was born. His parents had no way of foreseeing the war, nor had they any way of knowing that if they had stayed here they would have ended up, with other Japanese-Americans, in a relocation camp. After the war, when they could, they moved back to the U.S. with Dean.

Dean's parents practiced the traditional Japanese beliefs of Shinto and Buddhism. As a small child in Japan, Dean remembers asking his mother "Who is God?" and getting an answer that made him believe there was a God. At age 12, in California, he recalls

> *Soul is what Jung calls "Self with a capital S." It's that piece of God which we are given and called to reflect into the world.*
>
> Erica, a Valley pastor

going into a Christian church for the first time. Into his 12-year-old mind came the words, "*Aha*, God is here."

It took him eight years to accept the sign he had been given, and, as he put it, "… to figure out who Jesus Christ was. Also, my pride got in the way. I kept wanting to say, 'I don't need these beliefs, I'm capable of living my life without them, thank you.' "

Dean attended a major university in Southern California, earning a master's degree in electrical engineering and computer science. After graduation, he worked for several years as an engineer at two large computer companies. Then, something unexpected happened. He began to feel God calling his name, tugging on his sleeve, insistently, unmistakably, to suggest a career change.

He accepted the suggestion. The computer engineer became a pastor. He currently serves at a church whose congregation comes primarily from the Japanese-American community in the Valley.

"I was the youngest of five children," he recalls. "In my parents' eyes, becoming a Christian minister made me (to use a double metaphor) both the black sheep and the prodigal son of my family.

"I had many concerns about leaving the engineering profession and entering full-time ministry. I did it very gradually. I've seen many ministers suffer and sacrifice for their calling. I've seen too many former pastors selling insurance. But it's worked for me, and I wouldn't want to be cooped up back in the computer world.

"Our church encourages non-Christians to consider the good news of Jesus Christ. Ninety-eight percent of Japanese-Americans are non-Christians. Buddhism is the predominant Japanese-

---

I strongly believe in a woman's right to choose. I also strongly believe unborn babies have souls. This makes abortion a tough issue for me, and it leaves me frustrated and conflicted.

Kate, a Valley church office administrator

American faith. In fact, I've never seen a Japanese Christian funeral. We're a minority of minorities, and we know it.

"I think people have a lot of inner conflict about what they want from religion. San Jose sponsors a festival of lights to celebrate Christmas, but there was pressure on them to remove the manger scenes from the festival. How can you have a celebration of Christmas and censor out the image of Christ?

"I've been to secular events where they ask me to lead a prayer as part of the proceedings, but someone will tell me, 'Do the prayer, but don't pray in the name of Jesus.' After one event, a guy actually came up to me and said he had been offended because I mentioned Jesus in the opening prayer. In general, if you invite a Christian minister to lead a prayer, you're likely to hear Christ's name.

"My view of soul is that we're all made in God's image, but in the way we think, feel, express ourselves, we show that each of our souls is unique. Soul is the totality of who you are.

"Each person has a vacuum in their heart that they try to fill with something. Most try to fill it with material possessions, but it can really be satisfied only with eternal values.

"Many people are hurt, and their souls need healing. They want to be 'all that they can be' in God's army, even if they don't think about it that way, but they need comforting first. My job as pastor is to comfort the souls who are hurt, and discipline the ones

... we eventually come to the realization that it is injurious to the soul to remove portions of our life from exploration, as if, at work, certain parts of experience suddenly lie out of bounds. We simply spend too much time and have too much psychic and emotional energy invested in the workplace for us to declare it a spiritual desert bereft of life-giving water.

David Whyte, *The Heart Aroused—*
Poetry and the Preservation of the Soul in Corporate America

who are complacent. Some will avoid discipline, but some are wise enough to know they need it. People can sharpen each other, and improve each other."

LORETTA

Loretta was born in Memphis, but her family moved to California before she was old enough to develop any Southern drawl to hint at her roots.

She sees her spiritual development in distinct phases. Her family belonged to a mainstream Protestant denomination, but until age 15, Loretta felt no spirit moving in her. At 16, she decided she would be a nun. This inclination lasted until she was 20. Then she realized that marriage and family were calling her more strongly than the cloth.

While attending Stanford she engaged in a certain amount of religious exploration. ("Lots of undergraduate epiphanies," she says.) She's done time in the corporate world, and her husband is in the thick of the high-tech race as a marketing manager for a leading-edge hardware company. For the last few years her focus has been on her home and three children, and on pursuing the right spiritual life for herself and her family.

She has discovered that exercise has a spiritual dimension. While jogging, she's conscious of the discipline it builds, of the way it makes her pay attention to herself. She's aware of taking care of the body she's been given to house her soul. She notices the beauty of the flowers she passes, and rejoices in the way the air smells and feels as she runs through it: moist, opaque, mysterious in midwinter; warm, fragrant, beckoning in early summer. She makes it a point to actively notice, actively be thankful.

Loretta writes when she can. Some of her writing is pure recreation, such as the unfinished murder mystery featuring a properly aged, thoroughly poisoned Napa Valley cabernet sauvignon. Some is pure soul expression, such as her essay on a chapel window she fell in love with while in the choir.

"Soul is the part of your being that touches eternity," Loretta says. "But the body and soul are tightly coupled. We will have bodies after our resurrection. Something will go on, and maybe death is the seed from which it grows.

"There's a soul in everyone, even if they never experience any spiritual awakening. You can keep God at arm's length throughout your life, but you will get one opportunity, one second, at the end of life to choose God.

"I want my spiritual path to play more and more of a role in shaping my daily life. I want to pray, write and exercise every day. I would like to be transformed; to get rid of all the internal grunge; to feel that I've scraped all the barnacles off my soul."

While similar, spirit and soul are different. For now take it that spirit is unmanifested vacuum vibration, while soul is the same thing but reflected back on itself so a pattern within it can be seen. The soul is able to manifest intent through this reflection, while the spirit is not. The spirit desires but knows not what it does nor even what it desires when it spews out matter and energy. The soul desires and knows what it is about and what it craves. The spirit is potentially conscious and potentially unconscious, while the soul is conscious.

Fred Alan Wolf, *The Spiritual Universe— How Quantum Physics Proves the Existence of the Soul*

PERRY

Perry and I had scheduled our meeting downtown, but only the most oblivious would have failed to realize we had been given a perfect park day. We decided to migrate in Perry's van to a nearby park, a move which required shifting a large number of books from the passenger seat. One of them was enormous: they could use it for bench presses at 24-Hour Nautilus. Moving it made my biceps feel buffed.

Perry's a scientist. Most of his career was spent at one of the Valley's premiere research institutions. He assured me the technical importance of the book's contents justified its preposterous size.

Recent heavy rains had given the park's foliage the color of the Emerald City. The grass felt 8" thick. We pulled up at a stone table half in the shadow of a California redwood. The interview was closely supervised by a fearless, inquisitive squirrel. Between trips up the tree to shuttle acorns and other goodies to his cache, he perched on his hind legs a few feet away, and scrutinized us closely. He radiated a no-nonsense attitude: stay sharp, or incur his scorn.

Perry has been in Silicon Valley for 34 years. He's been a member of the same mainline Protestant religion all his life, but it is not that membership per se that is central to his spiritual life. "I could be anything," he says, "as long as there's belief in a deity. Specific format of worship is not important. My current church is

---

One certainly has a soul; but how it came to allow itself to be enclosed in a body is more than I can imagine. I only know if once mine gets out, I'll have a bit of a tussle before I let it get in again ...

Lord Byron, in a letter to the poet Thomas Moore

fine, and I might miss the forms if I left, but I could find God through other paths.

"God is just 'there.' I don't waste my time trying to think about God in terms of a physical form that I could never recognize anyway. God is a real and central part of my life, part of everything. I don't sit down and figure out words to pray. I don't meditate. I'm dyslexic; it's not easy or enjoyable for me to read, so I don't do much spiritual reading. My spirituality is oriented toward action and feeling: trying not to hurt others, trying to see God in everyone I talk to, even avoiding accidents when I'm driving. I *live* my spiritual life and my prayer.

"My vision of soul is similar to my vision of God: transcends everything, no physical form, no relationship to the body. Lots of relationship to attitude toward other people. Our souls were probably here millions of years ago, and will probably be here millions of years from now. Configuration-wise, soul is a miniature of God, a part of the deity. God is an accumulation of an infinite number of people's souls, sort of an Omega Point.

"The way I am today is all God's fault," he smiled. "Through my soul, I am part of Him."

TERITA

Terita arrived in Silicon Valley 17 years ago from her native Iran. Her father was an Iranian Muslim, her mother a French Catholic, and Terita was raised Catholic. It didn't stick. "Roman Catholicism seemed very static," she says. "You stay in the box."

She remained a practicing Catholic until she became 21, but found the religion increasingly unfulfilling and hard to accept. She had no inclination toward another belief system as she left her Roman Catholic upbringing behind. If Roman Catholicism was not of interest, she expected no more appeal from any other religion.

Terita met her husband soon after she became a Silicon Valley resident. He was a Baha'i, a faith with which Terita had not been familiar. She liked much of what she saw in the Baha'i belief system, and decided to learn more. Among the things she learned was that Baha'i is considered an illegal religion, Islamic heresy, in her native country. Members of the faith are frequently imprisoned and killed, and are certainly not granted passports to leave.

Terita became a Baha'i. She appreciates having found her new faith in a location where she enjoys complete legal and social freedom to pursue it.

Among the many things which attracted Terita to Baha'i was the concept of "progressive revelation." Everything is evolving, including mankind's spirit. Baha'is believe all the great prophets of the past—Buddha, Moses, Jesus, Mohammed, among others—were valid and right for their time. The prophet for our time is Baha'u'llah, the founder of the Baha'i religion. In a thousand years, another prophet will emerge for that time. "God sends teachers to guide us, and at different stages in our development we have needed different teachers," Terita says, "just as we have different teachers while we progress through school. Many teachers, many religions, one path, one God."

Terita agrees strongly with other Baha'i tenets: acceptance of all cultures, world unity, equality between men and women, and universal, continuing education and search for truth. The latter is a

Soul is a difficult concept. It's intellect, heart, feelings, innermost thoughts and being. It's hard to articulate in a way that doesn't sound like you're trying to write a Hallmark card.

Trent, president of a Valley telecommunications company

striving she applies with particular vigor to her own spiritual path. "Baha'i has made me see that truth can be looked at from many angles, and is never completely known. You must always struggle to learn truth, although the search is endless."

Most religions depend on clergy to provide spiritual teaching and leadership. There is no Baha'i clergy, no formal place of worship. "In the past, clergy were needed because people weren't educated," she points out. "Now, education is available to everyone."

To help each other achieve enlightenment, groups of Baha'is gather in members' homes every 19 days for sharing, discussion and reading. Terita likes the idea that she can't depend on formally vested authority to chart her path, that the ultimate responsibility for success or failure in finding truth rests firmly in her own hands.

"But we do need the prophets," she says. "God is an unknown essence which we will never fathom. We have different 'kingdoms' on earth: mineral, vegetable, animal. Each is not necessarily aware of the one 'above' it. God is the one above us, and we can't grasp or be fully aware of Him/Her. The only way we can glimpse Him/Her is through the Messengers He/She sends.

"The soul is the person's true identity, the part that continues. Our fundamental nature, or reality, is that we are spiritual beings. Our physical bodies are simply clothes we're given to wear during our stay in this plane. Our purpose in this plane is to develop our spirits.

"When a baby is in the womb, he's developing parts even though he has no idea what the parts are going to be used for. In this world, it's our spiritual qualities that have to be developed. We're going to need them when we're 'born' into the next world, even though we don't know what they'll be used for. Without them, just like a baby who's born without some of his parts, we'll be crippled.

"Baha'u'llah says death is a messenger of joy, taking us to a much better plane than this one. If people knew what was coming next, they'd probably commit suicide to get there faster. People who have had near-death experiences don't want to come back.

"It seems to be the law of this plane that we grow through suffering. Maybe we're like plants, and we have to be pruned and trimmed to become better. Ultimately, this world is like a school. But it's a vocational school, not a playground. You put in the effort, then you take a test to see what you've learned. If you pass, you move up.

"When you're born, you have gems in you, and the job in life is to bring them out and polish them and make them beautiful. Many people don't know this and miss the whole thing. There is choice and free will, and every person has a different capacity. Some have been given a cup. Some have been given a thimble. The goal is to fill whatever you've been given."

A soul is but the last bubble of a long fermentation in the world.
George Santayana, *The Life of Reason*

༚

CHAPTER SEVEN

Righteous Lives in the Material World

Michael Lerner argues that liberals have "framed their intellectual commitments around a belief that the only things that really move people are economic entitlements and political rights"; they miss the fact that "human beings have a deep need to have their lives make sense, to transcend the dynamics of individualism and selfishness that predominate in a competitive market society and to find a way to place their lives in a context of meaning and purpose."

Stephen L. Carter, *The Culture of Disbelief: How American Law and Politics Trivialize Religious Devotion*

We are hungry to recover the sense of the sacred that is currently painfully missing from our love affairs, families, jobs and politics. No week passes when some

friend or stranger does not speak to me about the
yearning.

Sam Keen, *Hymns To An Unknown God*

If one hankers to start a fiery debate, a good topic
might be whether the office is any place to bring "deeper meaning": issues relating to philosophy, morality and spirituality. One
view is that intangible "spirit care" centers should do for the soul
what child care centers do for the child: keep them safely out of the
way until they're picked up at the end of the day. Most would
probably say that's the right way, and certainly the safest. Some
disagree. Their number may be increasing.

The concept of "righteousness" in American business culture—
how personal and social values coexist with economic realities—
has been a ponderous sine wave, moving with changing times back
and forth between tight definition and laissez faire. There have
always been conflicts between individual and business needs, between societal and corporate values. Silicon Valley's maverick culture and plethora of individualists seem to have developed their
own version of these dynamics. And, as one would expect, they're
changing at a brisk pace.

Do those who have spiritual lives necessarily derive different
moral or ethical belief systems from those who don't? It's important not to let a subtle bias creep in here: ethical and moral codes
are possessed by all. It is by no means a given that spirituality auto-
matically leads to higher standards of behavior. In fact, many who
have strong spiritual convictions are convinced they do *not necessarily* lead to better ethics or morals.

The belief-based conflicts and dilemmas which confront
people in the Valley don't generally stem from the ambient sea of

affluence. Nothing during the interviews indicated any widespread sense of guilt, or even burgeoning diffidence, regarding material success. For one thing, people work very hard. They naturally assume that anything they have they earned, and earned well. For another, most of those who have made their careers here are conscious of having been part, directly or indirectly, of a technological revolution which changed the world.

No one questions that the change is for the better. It's a given. A well-known, associated fact of life is that high-impact players reap high-impact rewards.

CASE IN POINT

A few years ago I went through a shopping experience that seemed to faithfully reflect a certain part of the Valley scene. I had decided to give myself a gift (which I felt I had earned, and earned well): a large screen television. No more 19-inch stuff. It was November. The season's big football games were coming up. I proposed to watch them on a screen appropriate to their importance. I narrowed my choices down to two: a 40-inch rear projection model, and a 35-inch direct view model. Both were newly introduced sets; both sold for over $3,000.

It was a bit of an eye-opener to find out that all the stores which carried these sets were having a hard time keeping them in stock. They came in; they *flew* out—so I was told. The first time I heard this, I attributed it to retail hyperbole and cheap sales psychology. I was wrong. They were, in fact, flying out. Most stores I went to had even sold their floor models, and could not confirm any specific date when they might have more in stock.

When I finally bought one, the store's sales manager checked his computerized inventory system and told me two units were in stock and he'd deliver one the next day. Well, he didn't. Instead he called and said that both the units had been sold the prior evening from one of their other stores. Since both those sales tickets were time-stamped earlier than mine, those customers got TVs and I got an empty promise about getting a unit from the next shipment.

I ended up buying a set from another store, which I happened to catch at the right time with exactly one unit left. Due to demand level, the first store had been unable to get another set to sell me.

The striking point was that these were $3,000 *television sets* which were selling faster than they could be trucked in. Three thousand dollars is not a small sum. A large-screen television is not a life necessity. This minor marketing phenomenon seemed to capture both the Valley's affluence level and its love of trendy technological toys.

Debra is the minister at a medium-sized church in the heart of the Valley, and she sees a full laundry list of issues which bring conflict to residents. "People in Silicon Valley know we have enough food to distribute to everyone, but we don't do it," she says. Certainly, the juxtaposition of inadequate food supplies with insatiable demand for multimegabuck TVs contains the ingredients for a

---

In Silicon Valley we hit the ground running in our 20s and spend the next 15 years trying to get what it looks like everyone else has: the house, the Beemer, the toys. We never climb up the mountain and take a careful look around at the terrain.

I'm recovering from a serious case of business ennui, and I'm trying to redefine myself with a purpose that doesn't include "stuff."

Alden, a Valley insurance broker

possible moral struggle. But I don't believe Debra's statement realistically captures the primary nature of this particular tension.

It's a fact of life that often-brutal time and energy demands conspire with high levels of expectation and uncertainty to siphon off large quantities of inner resources. In a more benign setting, those resources might be available to, and targeted for, traditional social and community concerns. As it is, moral and ethical considerations tend to swirl around a much more prosaic locus: what's right for *here*? There is widespread recognition of the uniqueness of Silicon Valley culture. No one worries how things would play in Peoria. There's a Valley way, and it doesn't have to pass muster elsewhere.

This does *not* mean that individuals in this area are less generous, less concerned, or less principled than denizens of other regions. Quite the contrary. As discussed in Chapter Ten, there is reason to believe the Valley may ultimately play a leading-edge role in social redefinition and betterment on a global scale. Issues are being pondered. Directions are being found. And the Valley is never shy about sharing its discoveries.

STACY

The evening was clear, lots of stars visible considering the right-in-the-middle-of-the-lights-of-civilization setting. A pre-Christmas cold snap was in the air: a great night for sipping Irish coffee; Hennessey cognac; or syrupy, unctuous Northern California merlot or zinfandel. I had the zinfandel, and Stacy had the merlot.

We sat in the attractive bar area of a Silicon Valley restaurant well known for power lunches and business dinners. Having beaten the crowd by a few minutes, we were able to homestead a table adjacent to the fireplace and the Christmas tree. Despite the substantial noise level from the jolly and well-lubricated holiday crowd, it was a fine setting for our conversation.

Stacy has been in Silicon Valley an action-packed four years. She came here from New Jersey to join a medium-sized network equipment company as marketing communications director. As sometimes happens, the shifting sands of corporate politics ended up depositing her in an untenable situation. She left after less than two years, and joined a startup company which had developed some leading-edge wireless networking technology.

At her new company, the monsoons of corporate temperament eventually blew her into conflict with an influential member of the senior management group. She left. She now works as field marketing director for a software utilities powerhouse. So far, so good in her new job, but she has learned to be wary of the speed and power with which things move and change in her new locale.

Stacy's mother belonged to the Church of England. Her father was Jewish. They told her she could take her pick. She feels the influence of having been exposed to Jewish culture, but ended up becoming a Presbyterian.

Stacy is acutely conscious of the tendency of work to fill all life's nooks and crannies. She's a motivated professional, but she doesn't want that to happen to her. The breakup of her 10-year marriage a few years ago threw her life into a state of imbalance. She wants to rebalance, and she wants the balancing act to include some form—the right form—of spiritual connection.

She recalls seeing one of her company's group vice presidents three times in a two-week period. Each time, the woman was wearing the same suit; the last time was on a "casual Friday."

"That's not casual," Stacy pointed out good-naturedly.

"You forget—I have no life," the VP responded. "I don't have jeans. I have pajamas, and I have suits."

Stacy does not want to live a jeans-free life.

As a matter of fact, one of her most memorable spiritual experiences involved not church and Sunday-go-to-meeting outfits, but jeans and hard labor. Some friends invited her to join them doing missionary work in Alaska. They were going to renovate a dilapidated Eskimo school building. She went, and spent days doing things like sanding overhead door frames. "My arms ached for a week," she says, "but I was proud of what we did. It was incredibly wonderful. We laughed, because we were doing things, like scraping mildew off walls, that back home we pay others to do."

During her marriage, Stacy and her husband drifted away from any spiritual involvement. On a Sunday shortly after their emotionally devastating divorce, she was driving past a church and noticed a sign that said the sermon for the day was, "God heals a broken heart." She hit the brakes and went in.

She now attends services frequently, although she's not sure what role church will play in her eventual spiritual path. She has explored New Age spirituality, but it hasn't done much for her. "You can't solve your problems by holding up a rock or a crystal," she says.

Stacy finds that her communication level with God goes up mostly when she's in trouble, although she does say "Thank you" when things turn out well. "I've had a couple of medical things that have made me get down on my knees and say, 'Please, God, let the biopsy come back negative, and I'll be a good person from now on.'"

The bumper sticker that says, "He who dies with the most toys wins" is a sad commentary.

David, a Silicon Valley minister

❧ Balancing Act ❧

Stacy's relationship with her brother has caused her to do some serious thinking about the tension between spirituality and life in the material world. His fundamentalist brand of faith is one to which Stacy most assuredly does not subscribe. He believes that buying insurance reflects lack of faith, so he doesn't buy any. Debt is counter to his beliefs (a principle of faith which, spread widely enough, could bring the modern world economy crashing down). His faith that God will provide makes him comfortable with his family's perilously marginal financial status. Stacy does not share his comfort level, and has taken him to task on this point.

"The problem is that when they're in a real bind and looking for 'God to provide,' it usually comes in the form of a check from our mother or from me. Then they feel their prayers have been answered. They're thankful to God, but not to me. I guess I'm just the vehicle. My brother knew the money would come somehow. In some respects it must be a nice way to go through life, but I couldn't abandon myself to that."

The president of the first company Stacy worked for when she finished graduate school was a mentor. Perhaps, just as parents imprint their children during formative personal growth periods, early bosses imprint subordinates during formative professional growth periods. Stacy observed this person making tough decisions that she felt were highly ethical and "right." That's how she

---

I was told it was not a good idea to discuss my Christianity at the office. Part of the reason the relationship didn't work was they weren't sure that as a practicing Christian, I could be aggressive enough for a Silicon Valley startup.

Colin, marketing manager,
recalling his brief tenure with an employer

wants to do it herself, and that's how she'd like to see businesses run.

"It's a dilemma when you see someone succeeding at work who's downright bad, downright not a good person," she says. "If the world was right, this wouldn't happen. I don't have the kind of faith that gives me an answer to this, but I don't push myself too hard on it anymore. You just have to figure that what goes around will come around.

"I believe in God, but I try not to investigate or question it too closely. I want to accept it on faith, and not have the conversation with myself about where He is, how the universe was created, or other things that might hook my scientific side.

"But I believe in right and wrong and punishment, and that it's important how you live your life. A phrase I picked up here in the Valley is the 'karma bank.' You make deposits and your balance goes up. You make withdrawals and your balance goes down. And Someone is keeping score.

"I work with a vice president who's responsible for $4 billion in annual business. He's been married to the same woman for 27 years, and I asked him how he's managed to be so successful while maintaining a balanced life and a good marriage. He said, 'You don't *get* these things, you just *keep working* on them.' In the same way, I don't think one day you can say you've *gotten* your spiritual life. You keep working on it, and that's what I'll do."

RAY

Ray describes himself as *very* competitive.

It's probably a prerequisite for his job as CEO of a small educational software company, and it contributes to his frequent success on the tennis court. But he focuses on keeping it in check when it's not needed.

It is not unusual for Ray to find his competitive side teaming up with business pragmatism to pull him one way, while his ethical beliefs are tugging back in the other direction. "You always have opportunities to treat people in an unfair fashion," he says. "It's a struggle—and it's revealing.

"Occasionally our salesmen find themselves in a position where they could charge the customer more than they should. When I don't approve it, they sometimes think that my ethics, which are closely tied to my spiritual beliefs, are a detriment to the company."

Ray's father was Roman Catholic; his mother was Protestant. He was raised Catholic, but by the time he hit college he was growing away from it. For over 10 years he had no spiritual practice. When he and his girlfriend decided to get married, they chose a Protestant church because they liked the minister and his acceptance of the fact that they were already living together.

Despite his long absence from any religious practice, Ray had always thought that life in the material world, by and for itself, was rather empty. He and his wife became actively involved in an alternative group which practiced and taught a unique blend of homegrown philosophy and spirituality. Eventually, they turned off to the group and left.

The arrival of their first child had great spiritual impact on Ray and his wife. During this receptive period, a neighbor introduced them to a church they grew to like. They have stayed there and become active members.

❧ Man Talk ❧

Ray was instrumental in starting a small men's group which meets regularly to share events and feelings relating to their spiritual lives. All the members are in the technology business. Ray's group provides a forum for members to discuss the challenges they face living out their spiritual beliefs in the material world. It also serves an important function as what Ray calls an "accountability group": they feel responsible for, and accountable to, each other for the ethical and moral content of their decisions and actions.

His description of this group struck an interesting chord, largely because of a theme that repeatedly popped up during the research for this book: men often have a much harder time than women talking about their spiritual lives. Many men are acutely uncomfortable doing it at all. Some will go to great lengths to tune out any such conversation which might unexpectedly spring up around them. If it's the only distraction available, I have observed guys in such circumstances desperately and intently focusing on television commercials for household cleaning products as a means of opting *way* out of the ambush of a discussion about some personally sensitive topic.

Five years ago, a local church published an announcement of the formation of a new support group. Twelve women showed up and started a group which still continues and has bonded many friendships. The same church subsequently announced the formation of two new groups for men: one for spiritual and general life sharing; the other to provide (euphemistically) "job transition support" for those who had been fired, laid off, or experienced other

> *"You are what you buy," is the message we get, and it's hard to remember that's not the truth.*
>
> Victor, a Silicon Valley teacher

potholes in their career path. The church had, unfortunately, a substantial number of men in this situation.

There were no signups whatever for either men's group.

❧ Court Case ❧

A challenge to Ray's ethical standards which has stayed with him long and vividly—perhaps because he believes he failed the challenge—came on the tennis court. He frequently plays in tournaments. Recognizing the strength with which his competitive juices flow, he prays before starting a match that he will compete fairly.

In a tournament playoff, at a critical point, his opponent hit a short ball that landed just over the net on Ray's side of the court. He streaked in, got there in time, and hit a winner to put the point away. However, his racket hit the net during the swing, which means his shot should have been disqualified.

Ray looked up, and realized his opponent did not know Ray's racket had hit the net. No one but Ray did. He could take the critical point and keep on playing. Or he could blow the whistle on himself and tell his opponent the point was his.

Ray kept the point. "I still feel bad that I didn't insist on the other guy taking the point," he says. "When I came to a critical spot, my competitiveness beat out my ethics. It was a real lesson for me.

> " ... people ... are working in banks, in corporations, or at the university where they find it is very difficult to live out the Christian life and they're very lonely and they mustn't be."
>
> Father Morrison, Episcopalian Rector, quoted in *Habits of the Heart—Individualism and Commitment in American Life* by Robert N. Bellah et al.

"Someone who is spiritual has a sense of something bigger than themselves. Most people would probably think of that as a relationship with some kind with God. But in sports, there's the concept of 'team spirit,' and that's also a way of connecting with something bigger than oneself. I've felt it when I was involved with athletic teams, and I've felt it sometimes by being part of a company."

Ray believes that religious or spiritual beliefs provide a basis for setting moral and ethical standards. "I'm concerned that some of those standards are going away," he says. "In American culture, tolerance is almost a religion. But tolerance taken too far is a problem, because some things should not be tolerated."

ANITA

As Anita opened her front door, my peripheral vision registered something exploding past me at ankle height, heading for the street. It appeared to be furry, and approximately the color of a Granny Goose cheese puff. It braked, executed a screeching Immelmann turn, and gazed expectantly at the front door, eyes glowing in the light from the large entryway windows, radiating self-satisfaction at its accomplishments.

"Comet, get back in here," Anita said.

Comet failed to respond with adequate dispatch. Anita strode forcefully down the path and scooped up the wayward cat. In the semi-darkness, it looked big enough to eat schnauzers.

Once back inside, Anita introduced me to her other two cats. Titus, panther-black and panther-sleek, was about Comet's size. Artemis, the only female of the group, was introduced in absentia, and did not join us. Anita explained that Titus had turned Artemis into a "Lady Macbeth of neurosis" by constantly stalking her and trying to play with her. To give her a break, Anita brought Comet into the household to be Titus' pet. As the evening progressed, Titus tried repeatedly to nibble my pen. Finding it lacking in both flavor and texture, he eventually settled for giving it a periodic nuzzle to keep it on its toes.

Anita has been in the right place at the right time twice. During the early '80s, she was with one of the Valley's legendary garage-to-multibillion-dollar technology companies. Later in the decade, she was a member of the management team at a company that correctly read the emerging market for networked desktop computing, and also joined the multibillion dollar sales club in record time. "The first company bought my home," she says. "The second one bought my theological education."

In between, she and two colleagues resigned their jobs to form a startup company. Anita's Valley experience has included two Goliaths and one David.

Anita executed a midlife career change, took the fruits of her labors at the second company, and put herself through seminary. She's now a minister. In fact, the evening we met followed her first day of work in a new pastoral job. Her life differs greatly from her days of duking it out in corporate conference rooms.

She reflected on her early work experience.

"When I came to Silicon Valley it seemed like they just started throwing money at me. I ended up with a six-figure compensation package. It was intoxicating.

Baha'is use a consensus-building style of conflict resolution, and sometimes I actually welcome conflict. It gives my spirituality a workout, and increases my spiritual muscle tone.

Terita, a Silicon Valley homemaker

"I was 29. I was visible and I was credible. We were on the cutting edge. We had great toys. We were royalty. At that time, do you think I would have considered giving that up to 'wash people's feet'? Come *ON*!

"In the late '70s the Valley culture was young, crazy and intense. People were looking for community and affirmation—that they were OK, connected. The '80s were like the T-shirt one of the company founders made up for us: '80 hours a week and loving it.' The expectation was that everyone would give their life over to the corporation."

Although most things change quickly in the Valley, this expectation has demonstrated great staying power. While enjoying her status, her money, and her new car, Anita began to sense tendrils of discontent, of something missing, snaking themselves around her inner being.

❧ Calling ❧

Her family had attended a church through most of her childhood, but after getting married she lost interest in the church and spiritual pursuits. Then she and her husband divorced. "He got our social crowd," she recalls. She felt she had been left without a community, and that church might be a quick way to find one. The World Wide Web hadn't been invented yet, so she used a tried and true, low-tech search method: the *Yellow Pages*.

The church she went to clicked. She found more than community; she found people who seemed to her to be truly committed to their spiritual path. That influence teamed up with her growing sense of needing more from life than a continuous string of technological triumphs. She felt things stirring and waking. About a year and a half later, the stirring and waking evolved into an imperative inner call to change direction, to devote herself to a life of the spirit.

She was not pleased. "I went to my minister," she says, "and asked him to talk me out of this."

He didn't. Anita embarked on the simultaneous challenges of corporate management and seminary study. This was too big a load to sustain indefinitely. Eventually, a watershed moment arose.

"We had a *major* project starting. It was part of the company's initiative to migrate to a completely new product architecture. I was given the opportunity to manage one of the groups for this project. It required a three-year commitment. It would be totally consuming for that period: everything else would have to be subordinated. It demanded *passion*.

"So I had to go home and ask myself what I was passionate about. And the answer came back that it was definitely not Reduced Instruction Set Computing. I couldn't sign up for three years of life dedicated to that. So I quit.

"I was 36 when I left, and I was already starting to feel middle-aged in that environment. I know some very young 'techies' who are still there, and I kind of enjoy their attitude about my being a minister. They're interested. They accept it. Some of them actually think it's cool. They're not impressed, but they're not unimpressed, either. Beats hostility!

"I think people here are still looking for some kind of affirmation. They want someone with some kind of authority to say, 'It's

> *God's priorities are God-community-spouse-children-vocation. In Silicon Valley we turn it exactly around: our priorities are vocation-children-spouse-community-God. Every day I try to reverse people's priorities. Can you imagine how hard that is?*
>
> Roland, a Silicon valley pastor

OK being who you are,' and there's so little of that in the Valley. Even engineers can figure out that what they get rewarded for are not the cardinal virtues.

"Part of my reason for leaving the corporate environment was the degree of spiritual bankruptcy I saw in upper management. It wasn't so much that they didn't care about the right thing; *they genuinely didn't know what the right thing was.* They're cultural role models, maybe, but not spiritual ones. They just don't show an ethic.

"At my second company, I had to lay my job on the line every 10 days. I had to go in and say, 'Look, it's ethically and morally wrong to treat people like this,' or 'We can't ship our customers bad product.' There was always the element of cluelessness."

❧ "Goofy Insanities" ❧

"I think it's very revealing that a favorite slogan in the Valley is, 'Be careful what you pray for—you just might get it.' People think God is out to get them, like a Cosmic Trickster. It's God as adversary, God as lawyer, God waiting to trip you up in the wording of your wish.

"People here don't rest in God, don't feel safe with God, don't think God wants them to be joyful. People see Jesus as a great guy, a good teacher, a snappy dresser, a moral exemplar, but not an incarnation of the Creator of the universe.

"Even in the churches, I sometimes think they're all neo-Gnostics in the pews. All that 'Flesh bad, spirit good' stuff, as if the part of us that's going to live after death will be like Casper. I'm not a Casperite. Whatever causes me to breathe in and out is what God has given us, and He's given it to us all. It's too wonderful!

"I was talking with the Bishop a few years ago, and he asked, 'What's the coin of the realm down there in the Valley?' I told him that up to a point it's money, but after that it's competition: 'What makes me better than you?' The Gospel stands completely at odds to that world, and calls us to do impossible things. I just adore that!

"Christianity invites us to necessary but goofy insanities. 'Love your neighbor' is ludicrous. 'Love your enemy' is even worse. These are nutty and counter-intuitive, and only the grace of spiritual life can get us there.

"The Valley has an almost Sesame Street mentality in terms of needing constant stimulus to keep us engaged. But the rhythm of spirituality is the rhythm of the sea: slow and eternal. It's hard to be patient and wait for the rhythm of the spirit. We want everything fast and action-packed. No sermon can run over 12 minutes—people tune out.

"Everyone wants instant communication from God, but no matter how much we want it, God doesn't e-mail us. A prayer He may hear often from this area probably says something like, 'It's almost the 21st century, Lord—please get an Internet domain!'

"We've had so much economic success in this area that we have the disease of believing everything we think is important; that we don't have to listen to anyone else; that we know best. But this makes us isolate ourselves, and spiritual life needs community.

"A type of comment I hear a lot that comes from that isolation is, 'I don't need a church, I can worship God just fine in the redwoods, alone.' I don't think it's enough. The redwoods may be the lecture, but the church is the lab, and most people need both.

"A lot of the engineers I worked with were scornful of religion, particularly Christianity. One was a friend I used to really enjoy philosophical jousting with. He was a secular humanist. He had very spiritual principles for living his life, but aggressively disavowed any God. I once asked him why he thought golden-rule concepts were valid, since in his mind they didn't come from any real voice of authority. That stumped him at first. Then he got back to me later, and said he had an answer: 'It's important to be kind, because what goes around, comes around.'

"On the other hand, many members of my current congregation have a scientific background. They want meaning. They want to make a difference. They're not satisfied with easy answers.

"In seminary they always ask, 'Why do you want to be a minister?' I used to tell them, 'I don't. God wants me to be one.' Then I wanted to say to God, 'Don't make me do this.' But I've made the change, and now I'm at the opposite end of the spectrum: spiritually rewarding work, and practically no money.

"I worked with some engineers on a book over the past year, and dipping back into the Silicon Valley culture reminded me how invigorating it can be. At first it was a problem mentally keeping up with them: my bandwidth had gone back to 'normal.' But now it's back up, and I feel like I'm running at 9600 baud while the church operates at 2400 baud. In church I feel *serene* and *content*, but not *sharp*. The spiritual life is not as stimulating in some ways as the technical life, and maybe that's what derails some people from the spiritual life.

"In the last 25 years, I think the Valley has moved from hostility to laissez faire to intellectual curiosity regarding spirituality.

I have observed that middle-aged adults who have done the demanding work of figuring out their own spiritual beliefs are more able than others to make moral decisions and stand by them, even if the decision causes them some pain. In short, these people make the best leaders.

Kathryn D. Cramer, *Roads Home—*
Seven Pathways to Midlife Wisdom

Religion in this area has been a sort of forbidden fruit: 'Don't tell me about your underwear, and don't tell me about your religion.' The new people coming into the Valley seem less rejecting. Very diverse spiritual paths are available, and it's easier to try different approaches now than it used to be. I think that's a good trend, and I'm optimistic about the prospects for spiritual growth here."

RHONDA

After the latest in a string of reorganizations, Rhonda is part of a corporate subculture she knows will take some getting used to. She works for a company that makes computer communications equipment. Her entire career has been in sales organizations, most recently as director of sales operations. She is about to say hello to a new job in an engineering group. She hopes she survives the experience.

If time devoted to the job is the key variable, she will have no problem. She's a battle-proven veteran of nonstop, 60- to 70-hour work weeks. During the rare periods when this level of commitment has not been required, she has almost felt guilty about wimping out at 50 hours.

No. Willingness and ability to work long and hard on a sustained basis are not the issues. But as Rhonda contemplates her new responsibilities, she is also giving thought to the structure of her life. The way we spend our time defines our priorities. Are hers in order? Is she making room for the right things? Is she, by any chance, using a jam-packed work schedule as a way of avoiding the contemplation of other priorities?

"It *plagues* me that I don't have a regular meditation schedule," she laments. "I just don't get my lazy butt out of bed early enough to do it. I feel guilty about it, along with many other things, probably thanks to the great guilt training I got from my parents' church. I know what I would like my daily routine to be. I just haven't disciplined myself or my workplace to accommodate it yet. But I know I could."

Rhonda was born in Wisconsin, and grew up in the Midwest. She reflected on her initial impressions of spiritual life.

"My mother belonged to the altar guild at our church, and I went with her while she did altar guild stuff. My memory is of a cold building, a cold and bleak church, illuminated by weak, wan winter light. Even now, when I go home to visit my folks and we go to church, it seems cold. There's no abundance. Everyone's pale. No one wears makeup. The organ music is thin and screechy. It doesn't feel life-giving or life-supportive."

She gave it a shot. In her teens, she read psalms and prayed for guidance before going to bed. "I never got any answers," she recalls. "I finally came to feel, 'this does not serve me; I'm not getting anything out of this.' It was pretty much like I was out there alone, and being told to go figure it out. I was kind of a rebellious kid anyway. The lack of response from God made me think that instead of staying in the Girl Scouts and becoming a fine young woman, maybe I should run off to the coffee shop and hang with the 'other' crowd and smoke cigarettes."

Her rejection of the religion of her youthful years was complete enough to let her start over, as an adult, with a blank piece of paper. Now, figuring out what to fill it with is her challenge and her opportunity.

Too many ministers fail to talk about the practical applications of spirituality. Some people turn to spiritual lives to find solace for the unethical decisions they've had to make in their professional lives.

Rochelle, CEO of a Valley counseling group

Several years ago, Rhonda took yoga and meditation classes. She realized meditation and prayer were closely related, and meditation has become her "preferred form of communion." Through calming and quieting the mind, she feels more open to receiving answers from the "All-Knowing." However, she's had to struggle with the time commitment a regular meditation practice requires.

She went through a period where she was meditating twice daily, with one 20- to 25-minute session after work. But the relaxation it brought, coupled with the energy drain of her action-packed work days, usually caused her to fall asleep for a couple of hours. When she woke up, realizing that a large chunk of time had passed while she snoozed, she became cranky and irritable. This was, of course, in self-defeating conflict with the objective of meditating.

That meditation schedule was consigned to the trash bin. She now tries for at least once every other day, with no trailing naps permitted.

❧ Loner ❧

Rhonda has tried a couple of retreats, but she characterizes her present spiritual pursuits as *very solitary*. That's not her first choice. She wishes she could find a church or group with which to participate. Although she admits she hasn't done a heavy search, she has never found it. "Whenever I go to groups or churches, everything seems so contrived," she says. "I find both overreticence and overemphasis unattractive when people talk about their spirituality. My spiritual life is more experiential than intellectual.

"Eventually—and this would be quite daring—I would like to go public, come out of the closet, and join a group or church. I don't know why. But somehow I think it would add oomph or power to my spiritual life to share it with a group. When you're fumbling around in the dark, someone might know where a light switch is.

"It could force quite a change in my marriage, though, so there's some risk. I don't know if my husband would join in that sharing. He has a rich spiritual life through meditation, but he's very much a loner. He grew up in a Unitarian Fellowship church. His mother's an atheist. UF takes 'em all."

Rhonda hopes to reap several benefits from her spiritual life. Peace of mind. Increased tolerance of her fellow humans, of situations she can't control, and of herself. Confidence that her actions, thoughts and decisions are appropriately in harmony with a Higher Power. Assurance that outcomes will be fine. Connectedness. A sense that she has a role in the grand scheme of things.

She likes to read inspiring, spirit-affirming literature, and finds that associating with successful people can be uplifting. "You can learn from them how to work through life, and be balanced and moderate," she believes. "I enjoy moderation. I don't enjoy extreme rigidity or extreme indulgence."

Rhonda attributes her moral and ethical codes chiefly to her upbringing. She doesn't see much connection between moral code strength and spiritual commitment. "Some people are very religious, but believe in the death penalty," she observes. "But some who are atheists don't believe in killing. Some people who deny a God still have an extremely ethical code of personal conduct which distinguishes them as folks of the highest caliber. Yet they may not care a whit for spiritual practices.

> *Because they live in a fast-moving, high-tech world, many people in Silicon Valley want to see the same thing in their worship. Others want just the opposite: to balance the fast pace and constant change in other parts of their lives with worship that is slow and unchanging. The two views don't meet.*
>
> Audrey, a Valley minister

"Material prosperity and abundance may be a deterrent to people feeling a call to a spiritual path. But sometimes it can work the other way: once material needs are met, people may begin to wonder if there isn't more to life than all their *stuff.* Sooner or later everyone has to face some of those personal negatives and challenges. Prosperity and abundance can't buffer us from that.

"I have a soul I'm renting from the Higher Power, and it's through my soul that I'm connected to and influenced by that Power. Part of what was going on in my childhood was I didn't know how to work this body and this soul. I've learned how to run myself now, and I hope I get good at it before I leave."

AARON

Aaron loves Silicon Valley. There's nowhere he'd rather be. And he's got plenty to compare it to.

That's not to imply he doesn't see the area's problems. As rabbi of a small, marginally funded synagogue, he gets great insight into the challenges faced by his flock, and faces a few himself. "But this is exactly the kind of place I want to be," he exults. "I enjoy the challenges, I enjoy the technology. Finding ways to use the technology to serve God is perfect for me. I love the pace. In Silicon Valley you can't tell anyone what to do. But I never wanted to direct, I always wanted to guide. This is perfect!"

After being ushered into Aaron's modest office by his assistant, I waited a few minutes while he briskly stroked the keys on his computer. "I'm putting together a newsletter, and a friend just sent me some clip art over the Internet. Let me finish my download, then we'll talk," he said.

Download successfully completed, he described his background. Born in London. Progressed through school at what might be termed an accelerated pace, starting junior high at age 9. From England, went to Israel for rabbinical studies. Lived for a while in France, then moved to New York, where he met his wife. In the Valley for 16 years.

A key word, a central, unifying concept of Aaron's view of what spiritual leadership in the Valley must embrace, is "outreach." This term is often used to describe charitable contributions made by religious organizations, but Aaron has a much broader definition. He believes spiritual leaders must be proactive, innovative, and entrepreneurial in reaching out to the community. Not just to get money in or out, but to craft a delivery system that distributes the important messages of life everywhere they need to be.

"Religious practice here is more freeform than structured," he says. "Translating the traditional into practice doesn't happen much. People don't necessarily equate traditional views of God with spirituality. They have all kinds of visions. The motto I've developed for our congregation is, 'Communicating tradition in a modern world.'

"I want to see emphasis on spiritual outreach, on getting people involved. Ninety-five percent of the people I deal with are not religious. And we're so insular. Lack of community is a real problem. I've been trying to create an environment which gets away from that.

The organization controlling the material equipment of our everyday life is such that what in itself would enable us to construct it, richly plunges us instead into a poverty of abundance, making alienation all the more intolerable as each convenience promises liberation and turns out to be only one more burden. We are condemned to slavery to the means of liberation.

Raoul Vaneigem, *Basic Banalities II*

"The need to excel in the career here often overshadows religion. That might also be true on Wall Street, but it's so consuming here. We have a competitive, dog-eat-dog mentality, and heavy emphasis on materialism. Everything's so expensive, and people have to work so long and hard just to survive. It makes introspection difficult.

"It's not so much that people here reject religion. Actually, I sense a collective backlash against the negativity toward religion. It's more that they're caught up in the excitement and demands of the technology, and they're just too busy. Sometimes we need to stop. In Silicon Valley, no one stops. But some people find their toys starting to feel a little empty, and that sometimes leads to the start of a spiritual path.

"Because everything is new here, spiritual life tends to be shallow and sparse. You don't see grandfather's plaques on many walls. It can take generations to form a solid religious organization. But the flip side is that there's an excitement to religious life here that's not available anywhere else. That's because it's based on *choice*. No one *has to* do it.

"And we have such a wonderful physical environment around us. Sometimes I look at the beauty of nature in our area and wonder if this is what the Creator's eyes saw.

"If you are religious and believe that God created you and put you here for a purpose, when faced with a dilemma you will consider it in the context of why you're here. Without religion, you might just ask, 'Will I get caught?' or 'Aren't I here to do well

---

Pure spirit, one hundred proof—that's a drink that only the most hardened contemplation-guzzlers indulge in. Bodhisattvas dilute their Nirvana with equal parts of love and work.

Aldous Huxley, *Island*

materially?' Religion gives a deep sense of responsibility and the tools to withstand temptation.

"I got a call recently from someone who had been offered big money to pirate out some software his company owned. He was very tempted, and he asked me what he should do. I told him not to do it. He didn't. The following Monday, he received a bonus check from his company, one he wasn't expecting. The check was exactly equal to what the pirate offer would have given him—*net*, after taxes."

I will conclude this chapter with the stories of two Silicon Valley couples. Both were high-achieving, two-career households. Both made the decision to trade their professional and financial success for a different model of success.

DANA AND NEIL

Dana was born into a Christian family in Illinois, but the religion wasn't a take. She regards herself as having been an agnostic until she discovered the Baha'i faith. "When I began my spiritual search," she recalls, "my plan was to start with the latest religion, Baha'i, and work my way backward. Since Baha'u'llah (the Baha'i prophet) discusses the major previous religions and explains the progression and purpose of each, it seemed the work was done for me. In their essence, without man-made rituals and dogma, they all come from God and they are all one."

> *Gossip at work is contrary to Buddhist teachings. When I notice I'm in a gossip session, I don't like it.*
>
> Marta, a Silicon Valley tech writer

For many years, Dana worked for a Valley telecommunications company renowned for its growth, its progressive policies, and the length of its employees' work weeks. She started in sales, and over time made her way into management. Although she was rigorous and active in practicing her faith, she wanted more from that part of her life.

Reflecting on the challenge of balance, Dana says, "I find myself engaged in a daily struggle to maintain a proper perspective on life and its spiritual meaning. While working in Silicon Valley, this struggle was even harder because my tendency was to awaken and start thinking about work, or whether I should cut short the prayers to squeeze in a little exercise, or whether I had time to do a few house chores before work. I always seemed to be rushing. I'm convinced it's because I hadn't given my spiritual needs the right priority.

"It took a long time to realize that when I prayed and meditated first, when I tended to my spiritual needs first, it determined the quality of my contribution during the rest of the day. I still have to stop and remind myself of this important reality."

Dana's view of her spiritual mission includes work for social transformation and human unity. Her husband, Neil, is of a like mind. This goal was destined to lead them to a bold decision.

Neil was also the product of a Midwest Christian family, and also did some early exploration of alternatives. "I attended various churches while I was growing up," he recalls. "In college, a group

All businesses have temptations. Silicon Valley is not a 40- or 50-hour per week kind of place. The danger is that the fast-moving, exciting, engrossing technology can shut one down from all other pursuits. It's a big price to pay.

Ted, a Silicon Valley rabbi

of friends would get together every week or so to party. This usually included philosophical discussion. I started reading Western philosophy, even though I hated it as a university course. In retrospect, I wish I had also investigated Eastern philosophy, but Iowa didn't have many eclectic bookstores."

Neil's spiritual path eventually led him to Baha'i. His romantic path led him to Dana, whom he met at a Baha'i meeting. His professional path led him to become a systems programmer for one of the Valley's legendary computer manufacturers. Their combined success led them to a comfortable life in a beautiful house in a very upscale Valley neighborhood. Financially and professionally, they had it made.

Then they decided to give it up.

It wasn't that they hadn't been living faithful or contributory lives. It was that they had come to a point where felt they could, and should, do more. It was time to *devote* themselves. "I remember coming to a realization that I was at a life crossroad," Dana says. "I could continue living as I had for the past 20 years—or I could move on."

They resigned their high-paying technology industry jobs. They sold the house. And they accepted an assignment to live, work, teach, help and offer spiritual resources in a South American country which is one of the poorest in the world. For three years, their existence was an exercise in the most extreme contrast imaginable to their Valley lives. While there, Dana wrote, "Upon reflection, I was quite poor in a rich country, but am becoming rich in a poor country."

Their spiritual commitment, their conviction that they were doing something important and right, didn't eliminate the impact of the traumatic change in their daily lives. They missed friends and family. They missed telephones and personal computers. They missed electrical power that worked more than two hours a day. They missed a moderate climate; convenient, comprehensive health care; not having to check the house for insects the size of fax machines; and lots more. But they stuck, prevailed, stayed faithful to the mission for which they had signed up.

"It is common for Baha'is to think of themselves as world citizens," Dana says. "Sometimes that means you leave your own country to serve others."

❧ Richer and Poorer ❧

"Living in a third-world country should be universally required," Neil believes. "Life without running water, reliable electricity, or garbage pickup, but with rampant disease, sounds unendurable. But I discovered generous, spiritual and openly friendly people throughout this environment. Also, there was a peacefulness and beauty there that I rarely find here.

"I remember one individual there who invariably described people in terms of how their soul appeared.

"Spiritual life in Silicon Valley is virtually nonexistent compared to what we found on the coast of South America. There, nearly everyone discussed spiritual concepts as part of their daily life. I think this was at least partly due to the fact that people there have almost no physical possessions.

"Unfortunately, television sets are becoming more available, and the most watched show is *The Young and the Restless*. To me, this is not instilling positive values in the minds of the watchers. Professional wrestling was also very popular, and 99 percent of those watching could not distinguish between acting and reality."

Dana observes that "... spiritual life seems easier in a less complex society where there aren't a lot of material distractions. Complexity and materialism make us struggle to stay focused on spiritual matters. I believe one can have a meaningful spiritual life wherever one lives. Some places just make it easier than others.

"Recently a television program showed Madonna singing her hit song containing the lines, 'We are living in a material world, And I am a material girl.' Here's what I'd like to have said: 'We live in a material world and many beautiful things have been put here for our enjoyment. But we are *spiritual* beings, and we must not allow material things to become obstacles to our spiritual growth.'

"The moral and ethical codes flowing from the first statement would probably be quite different from those coming from the latter.

"It may appear we gave up a lot to go to South America, but in reality it was nothing compared to the worlds and opportunities for growth which opened up to us. There was more emphasis on relationships. People spoke freely about spiritual things like breathing the air. I felt more in tune with the natural rhythm of life, waking up at dawn and going to bed about two hours after sunset. I served others more and gave more of myself.

More and more, I feel comfortable letting people know when I think what they're asking for is unethical. I try to find out what the objectives are, and then see if there's a way to meet them in an aboveboard way. For example, we've had some harassment cases. Simple acknowledgment that one person hurt another can go such a long way toward healing that breach. The healing makes sense for the company, and it's a spiritual value for me.

People might say, 'You're a lawyer, Stuart. We're not asking you for spiritual advice.' Well, they can always get rid of me if my act is wearing thin.

Stuart, general counsel for an
electronic instrumentation company

"I'm not sure what they learned from me, but I know I learned much from them. We are all related, and all connected."

I asked Dana and Neil if their Silicon Valley work experiences had caused them any spiritual conflicts. The answer was, not really.

"In the office it was generally known that I would not use or listen to obscene language, gossip or backbiting," Dana remembered. "I think I've been lucky to work for and with people of tremendous integrity, people I've respected."

"I haven't had inner spiritual conflicts," Neil says, "but there have been times when my beliefs have clashed with my manager's. We had one incident where he was yelling at and belittling a computer operator in front of several people in the computer center. I felt this was wrong, and completely unjust, and told him so later in his office. I also told him he should apologize. He did, in the presence of others. I think we both felt better.

"Our management approaches differed markedly. I tended to use a participatory, consensus-building style. He was motivated by power, and had an autocratic style. When we met several years later, he asked, 'Have you learned how to manage yet?' I just laughed and said, 'I guess not, from your point of view.' "

Commenting about future spiritual directions, both for himself and Silicon Valley, Neil says, "I see myself continuing to learn about all sorts of things, a pursuit I associate with spiritual life. Perhaps I'll leave the U.S. again, to try to assist others in learning and applying technology, while simultaneously trying to convince them that acquiring 'stuff' is not the ultimate goal of life.

Where there is the necessary technical skill to move mountains, there is no need for the faith that moves mountains.

Eric Hoffer, *The Passionate State of Mind*

"I am not very sanguine about the future of spiritual life in the Valley. Too many people, by the very nature of their jobs, do not allow themselves time to reflect on the reality of life. There are too many workaholics and too many people trying to buy the latest technological toys. There's nothing wrong with enjoying material things, but they do seem to get in the way and impair spiritual progress."

Dana is a little more upbeat. "Some observers of the sociological scene are already suggesting that as baby boomers age, they are becoming more interested in spiritual matters. We may see this trend in the Valley.

"As for me, each day presents new challenges. The quest for greater spiritual depth is never-ending. There is a beautiful quote from 'Abdu'l -Baha [Baha'u'llah's son] which sums up what I would like my future direction to be:

> *It is possible to so adjust one's self to the practice of nobility that the atmosphere surrounds and colors all our acts. ... At such a degree of evolution one scarcely needs to be good any longer—all our deeds are the distinctive expression of nobility.*"

BRETT AND ROBERTA

"I went into physics because I wanted to find out what the universe was about," Brett recalled. "Also, some nut of a physics professor said physicists made more money than anyone else."

Even in universities—bastions of the search for truth—bad information is available.

Brett is from Missouri, and was an early-life adopter of the "show me" perspective: an atheist from the get-go. He was soon to discover the art of compromise.

With many of his peers, he did a tour of duty in Vietnam. He had started dating Roberta before he left. They corresponded. When he got back home, he was ready: he proposed to her two weeks later.

"She said, 'I can't marry you because you don't go to church,'" he remembered. "My hormones kicked in. I said I'd go, but I wouldn't necessarily believe. I guess that was good enough. She said she'd marry me if we could move to California."

Move to California they did, arriving in a Silicon Valley economy ready to explode. Brett's technical degree landed him a job with a major defense electronics manufacturer. "They were hiring 19 people a day," he recalls.

He kept his commitment to give church a try. Some issues harking back to his upbringing had to be dealt with. "My parents left the Roman Catholic Church because they felt that churches were just interested in the money. My grandmother went to Rome and *bought* an indulgence so my mother could go to heaven. My parents wanted to raise moral children. But they saw God as a crutch."

Brett was baptized at age 27. He remembers the minister telling him, "You know, Brett, these things don't usually work out, coming to Christianity this late." This aroused his Missouri stubbornness. His scientific training sent him on a reconnaissance

---

Sometimes I leave a meeting where we've discussed some "political correctness"-type issues and I ask myself, "Did I just sell out?" But I can't impose my Biblical values on the corporation.

Trent, president of a Valley telecommunications company

mission for facts. He asked lots of questions. He tried to understand why people came to church. He struggled with a feeling that the Bible didn't ring true, that it could have been written by anyone. He agreed to teach Sunday school.

"But I was just teaching facts, not imparting faith," he says. "I couldn't—I still didn't have it myself. I needed help. I needed a sign."

Much of the defense work his employer did was classified, which meant there was a formal, rigorous document control system in place. A document under Brett's control disappeared. The document was classified "secret." Its absence had the potential to be a serious problem for Brett, and he was worried about it.

Shortly after the document vanished, Brett's phone rang. He picked it up. A voice he didn't recognize said, "Something lost has been found."

Mystery solved. The document had fallen behind a safe. But the unexpected words, from the unexpected voice, rang and reverberated. *Something lost has been found.* Driving home that night, he pulled his car over to the side of the road and thought about the words.

❧ Real Estate ❧

Roberta's professional route was real estate: she was a hard-charging broker working seven days a week—and seven nights. She was president of her local real estate board. She made big bucks. "I had time to do all that," she recalls, "but I didn't have time to think. My life wasn't producing fruit. Then I started to ask myself, when my life is over, what's going to be the final analysis? That I made a lot of money? That I helped people buy a house? That's all? That would be so sad."

The faith of her upbringing did not serve her well during this churning introspection. It had become a rote, intermittent practice, with neither intellectual nor emotional impact. The more she thought about the meaning of her life, the more depressed she got. She read a book which contained a chapter she felt captured her situation perfectly: *Dark Night of the Soul*.

"I got to a point where I couldn't think of anything I wanted," she says. "That's when you know you're depressed." One day she came home and threw herself on the floor, crying. "Help me, God," she sobbed.

The thought formed in her mind: "Don't worry—something good is going to happen to you."

"I knew it was God's voice," she remembers. "I was too depressed to have generated that thought myself. In a few weeks the depression was gone, and I have never doubted it was His spirit that brought me out of it.

"But I was still concerned about Brett's path. One day we were taking a walk and I told him, 'I can't stand to think of you getting to be 65 and retiring as an engineer, doing the same thing all those years.' We prayed that the strong hold that money, houses, and jobs had on us would somehow be broken. When we got back from the walk, we laughed that it was a scary kind of prayer, and the scariest part was that it might be answered.

"Not long after, Brett got a temporary transfer to the East Coast. I had to make 33 phone calls to disengage from everything I was doing. When we came back, he was told his job would be going away in a few months. I said, 'This is what we prayed for and it happened. We're free!' "

❧ Fruitfulness ❧

The new course for Brett and Roberta's lives was launched when they decided to have children—and couldn't. They tried for two years, and gave up when medical analysis found a problem. "Since we couldn't have children, we figured we'd just keep buying bigger houses and moving every six months," Brett recalls.

Then, after it was clear that it couldn't happen, Roberta got pregnant.

"It's a recurring theme," Brett says. "You try and try, and you can't get there on your own. There is no road there from here—unless it's what He wants. When you have wealth, or ability, or good looks, you rely on it, and it steers you in the wrong direction." Their child arrived. She was their "princess of the world."

"We should adopt another child," Roberta said one day, "so Melissa won't get spoiled."

"I'm not spoiling her," Brett replied. "I'm just being a good dad." But he admitted it wasn't a bad idea.

They found out that adopting a child when parents are over 40 can be tough. Someone suggested they volunteer for foster care, and they did. "Mandy, a cute little 14-month-old girl, walked into our lives and hearts," Brett recalls.

Mandy's mother had given birth at 16. She herself had been born to a 15-year-old alcoholic. ("Mandy's grandmother is younger than Roberta," Brett pointed out.) After seven months of foster care, Mandy's mother told Brett and Roberta, "You have the kind of family I always wanted. Will you raise my daughter?" They had found their second child.

Brett and Roberta had opened themselves up for new life priorities and directions. Independently and jointly, they were ready to devote themselves to work that *mattered*: a mission that would bring meaning and satisfy faith. Their introduction to the foster care system opened their eyes to its critically important role, its great potential, its many problems. Children were out there, needing help. They had found their mission.

Brett didn't look for another engineering job. Roberta no longer spends Sundays at open houses with "for sale" signs on the lawn. They refinanced their property, juggled the household budget, and started up a local affiliate of a nonprofit organization dedicated to the support of foster children and the foster care system. It's now their full-time pursuit. "This is what we were put here to do," Roberta says.

Brett is grateful for the opportunity to devote himself to community and spirit. He sees the possibility of tremendous social benefit from the formative-stage intervention foster care provides for at-risk children. He and Roberta will focus on getting foster parents trained and certified, developing support services (such as babysitting networks, to prolong foster parents' sanity by giving them an occasional night on the town), and getting charitable and spiritual organizations to do more.

"Ultimately," Roberta says, "fixing the problems that lead children into foster care doesn't depend on whether we spend more tax dollars or fewer tax dollars. The underlying issues are spiritual issues. Some people are rocket scientists, and some are babies of drug-addicted mothers. God has to find and be real to all of them."

One of the interview questions for this book was, "Do you think those who have spiritual beliefs are likely to hold different moral and ethical codes from those who don't?" Here are some of the responses from nonclergy.

We cannot judge that, cannot judge people. We don't know other people's places and situations.

Yes, but it's always important to guard against self-righteousness.

No, because the range of people's religion-based behavior is so wide. It probably parallels the scope of behavior of those who have no spirituality.

I go back and forth. There are good people in and out of churches, and there are hypocrites in and out of churches. Religion seems to promote both the best values and the worst. You can be very moral, very ethical, without religion. Secular humanism is spat on by religious conservatives, but it's a philosophy that can lead to as good values as any.

Yes. I don't see how you can have a moral code without spiritual beliefs. The existence of a moral code implies some spiritual sense.

Those who are founded in spirituality tend to be stronger and better able to stand the buffeting of the business arena.

Part of religion almost spells out spiritual and ethical codes. Some just make sense. If I don't have to worry about killing you or you killing me, I can keep both hands on the plow. "Don't have children with your sister" is just good biological sensibility.

Everyone has a spiritual paradigm, whether they articulate it or not. We are not humans struggling to be spiritual, we are spirits struggling to be human. There was a "stages-of-morality" study which seems to indicate no connection between active spiritual life and morality.

I know some religious people who are as crooked as the day is long.

Going to church doesn't make you better, and it doesn't make you worse.

Morals and ethics usually precede *religion.*

Might have the same code, but the underpinning will be different. Without spirituality, the motivation might be, "how can I look good?" or "what's in it for me?" God doesn't look at just the actions, He looks at the motivation, at the heart.

If you're just religious, *there's probably no difference. If you're truly* spiritual, *there probably is.*

You can arrive at almost any code via almost any path. Belief in God can still lead to Machiavellian morals, and atheism can still lead to good ethics.

It's not black and white, but knowing there's more to life than the material world drives a difference.

People who don't read the Bible might be less inclined to leave their money to the poor.

As people get closer to God, they get closer to good.

Not necessarily any difference, much as I would like to say there is.

Here are answers to the same question from some of the clergy:

I certainly hope so, although I'm not sure I can make such a statement. You might almost have to recap a list of what good people do. But religions have centuries of those definitions and applications behind them, and a community to support them. When people have a value system that is rooted in their beliefs, it's probably stronger.

Those with spiritual lives expect to hold themselves to higher moral and ethical codes.

It might almost be too easy for someone who does Sunday morning church, and tithes 10 percent of their income, to say "I can do whatever I want the rest of the time." So some spiritual people might have worse codes. If we feel we're only answerable to God for 10 percent of life, that sets us up as our own God for the other 90 percent.

Some nonspiritual people live wonderful lives and have exemplary moral codes. If people are brought up with good values, those values will stick around even if they never go to church.

Too many variables to say for sure.

The divorce rate in this state is 50 percent. I heard a statistic that if both husband and wife go to church, and know at least six people there by their first name, the rate is 2 percent.

Some people compartmentalize their faith journey from their work. I've seen nonspiritual people with good ethics, and spiritual people with no-good ethics.

People with spiritual lives have better views and understanding of the defects in society.

Those with spiritual beliefs tend to have a stronger sense of morality, but there's no guarantee they will live their morality.

Many people who feel unconnected with God may have moral and ethical codes which sprang from ancient spirituality, whether they know it or not.

The issue is conviction versus opinion. Those whose spiritual lives give them conviction of what's right won't deviate. Those who only have opinions might change their minds.

People on the spiritual journey seek integrity, honesty and wholeness, and are able to resist shortsighted, selfish behavior.

With a spiritual life you're likely to tune in to others more. The connection oozes out beyond you, into the world. You have less alienation, more humility, and the we/they mentality is not so acceptable. You realize you're not the center of the universe.

Without a spiritual life there's no external guarantor of ethical standards. That absence might justify anything.

CHAPTER EIGHT

Techno-Souls in Cyberspace

Cyberspace. Room for the human spirit to soar free. Earth surrounded by a digitized halo of information—a throbbing, ethereal matrix coagulating into ever shifting patterns of revelation, and giving birth to a rich stream of social, political, and environmental initiatives. The individual freedom once sought only within the cloister or in the trenches is now to flow from keyboard, mouse and glove, electrifying the initiated with raw and unbounded potential for new being. An electronic New Jerusalem, its streets paved with silicon and bridging all cultural rifts, promises the healing of nations. Even the hope of personal immortality flickers fitfully for the first time through materialist brains contemplating prospects for DNA downloading and brain decoding.

And you, self-professed infonaut—from whose
jargon I have fashioned this vision—you say you're not
religious?

Stephen L. Talbott, *The Future Does Not Compute:*
Transcending the Machines in Our Midst

"Speed is God and time is the devil."

Hitachi executive David Hancock, quoted in a *New*
York Times CyberTimes article headlined "Quicker Pace
Means No Peace In Silicon Valley"

How versatile the Internet! Shop for a car, research a paper, chat with others at a virtual cocktail party, get tax forms, read new product specs, check the latest sports statistics, ogle pictures of seminude starlets, exchange e-mail, troll for love, and—starting late but gaining momentum—pursue your spiritual path. Some may view this as technology in the highest possible service. Others may see the hand of the devil in these electrons. It's a happening thing.

Internet use is not unique to Silicon Valley. By definition, the Net is a fusion of people the world over. However, the soul, the heart and the guts of the thing were largely crafted here, and without question it throbs to the Valley beat. No discussion of the effect of technology on the spiritual and philosophical experience can ignore the impact of the Internet.

WWW.JUST.ABOUT.EVERYTHING

Many approaches extend their virtual hands to those seeking spiritual enlightenment online. Let's start with the collection of electronic documents and locations known as the World Wide Web.

The power of the Web's underlying technology has been thought out and harnessed well enough to make it relatively easy to use, even for those with limited computer expertise. This ease of use has fostered an exponential increase in the number of people logging on, creating irresistible market potential. An incredible array of organizations and individuals have created Web presences for themselves. Spiritual groups have dealt themselves in.

Websites usually consist of combinations of text, graphics, and links to other sites or pages. Organization is hierarchical, allowing browsers to "drill down" through subject areas, or peruse increasing levels of detail. The user interface is almost completely at the "point-and-click-with-your-computer-mouse" level, so Web surfers can easily navigate through storehouses of information. The biggest challenges are not technical. They are: a) figuring out what you want to see next, based on the limited descriptions, and b) patience.

The patience factor is required because use of the Web has outpaced its resources. The Internet frequently gets as choked on modem traffic as commute routes on auto traffic at 5:30 PM. Response time can be slow enough to make you want to check your modem's pulse rate to make sure it's still alive—then your own, to make sure *you're* still alive.

Everything's a package, though. Waiting for a busy website to finish downloading a document to your screen might be a fine time to catch up with your meditation.

A few months ago, a major Web indexing service listed over 5,000 links to websites in the "Religion" category. At this writing, the number of sites is around 9,000 and going up *daily*. The universe is both large and expanding. To give you an idea of the diversity of what's available, following is a partial list of what might be termed "mainstream" sites:

Category	Number of Sites Listed
Christianity	5,682
Judaism	724
Islam	257
Buddhism	175
New Age	137
Hinduism	109
Baha'i	60
Atheism	45
Taoism	12

Then, there is a multitude of what might be called "less widely practiced" offerings. Selected examples include:

Category	Number of Sites Listed
Paganism	113
Wicca and Witchcraft	82
Mysticism	71
Satanism	31
Cults	23
Shamanism	19
Druidism	17
Gnosis	11
Rastafarianism	7
Pantheism	4
Voodoo	3

And finally, some offerings in the range between "less well known" and "downright obscure":

Category	Number of Sites Listed
Asatru	17
Yaohushua	8
Santeria	4
Mithraism	4
Quan Yin	3
Cao Daiism	2
Ifa	2
International Raelian	2
Osho	1
Tenrikyo	1

A typical website access will yield words and pictures designed to give an overview of the subject, with options to select for further information or interaction. Some sites let you order books or materials, and provide event schedules. The more graphics content a website has to show you, the longer you can expect to wait and meditate while your screen fills up.

Most—not all, obviously—of the foregoing represent religious and spiritual doctrines which have existed for some time. The Net and the Web introduce a new way for them to meet up with followers, actual and potential. Perhaps a more thought-provoking dynamic is reflected by the introduction of spiritual pursuits explicitly designed for the Net. Please welcome Cyberculture Religions.

Some Cyberculture Religions are pure humor. Some are ill-disguised electronic ego trips ("**The Church of Overhead Projector**. The true religion. Currently has one member. Slowly expanding.") Some don't seem to be able to keep their Web server up long enough to matter. Some have used the new technology to attempt new blends of science and philosophy ("**Church of Virus**—A rational, atheistic religion mimetically engineered to fill an ecological niche in the idea-space of humanity created by recent advances in knowledge.") Maybe, just maybe, some will become impact players. Even if they don't, let's not underestimate the value of a good chuckle in a serious world.

Chuckle generators which somehow seem unlikely to make their mark include "**Dai-Uchu Jinja**—basecamp for the Space-Commanders. Approaching the secret of existence"; and "**Messiahs, Inc.**—How Jeremiah L. Hermastone starts a Church-In-Reverse, beats the IRS, patents God, and has more sex than Rush Limbaugh, but less than JFK."

Born-on-the-Net organizations more inviting of a closer look include such innovations as the "**First Internet Church of All**—A modern religion for modern times. A religion for environmentalists and those concerned with the state of mankind"; and "**Religion of the Humanities (ROTH)** is the first true CyberChurch. A new religion without a physical location. ROTH is completely 'of the net.' " There are others.

A quick review of the "Sermon of the Week" from the "**First Internet Church of All**" yielded a rather sensible if not groundbreaking treatise on water conservation and stewardship.

... if the excitement [about finding information on the Net] is not about actual encounters with expressions of the human spirit, what is it about? One gets the feeling that a lot of it has to do with a futuristic, almost religious vision of what the Net is becoming— and all these interim discoveries are more valued for the progress they indicate than for themselves. Signs for the faithful. Epiphanies.

Stephen L. Talbott, *The Future Does Not Compute: Transcending the Machines in Our Midst*

OK. A probe into the pastoral counseling facility of the White Oak Chapel Cyberchurch opened an e-mail window to the church. Might work for some.

A representative example of a cyberspace new spirituality shopping mall might be "**Spirit-WWW**: A Non-profit and independent Web-site," originating in Switzerland. It offers a wide array of books and links, billing itself as "A dedicated spiritual worldwide-website which comprehends spirituality in a modern context in review of ancient teachings and religious belief-systems. The site is independent of any kind of specific religious belief-system or movement, but tries to give an overview of manifold forms of spirituality."

David E. Gordon has written a graduate thesis discussing online spirituality, entitled "Religion and the Internet." Appropriately enough, he has posted it on the Internet. He makes several cogent points:

❖ The ease of access and the free flow of ideas on the Net will "… favor religions focusing on an independent relationship with the divine …" If true, this would represent a dramatic departure from traditional religious perspectives.

❖ Physical location will become less and less important in defining one's spiritual community.

❖ Exposure to a wide variety of spiritual viewpoints will encourage the continuous, fluid formation of new philosophies and organizations. Seekers will find it easy to "cut and paste" ideas from diverse sources to compose their own approaches. Then they'll find it easy to propagate their ideas and encourage others to follow. If you post it, they will come. Those who sign up will find that their followers' supply kit needs little more than keyboard and modem.

But even the most intrepid, dedicated Web spiritualist could never explore all the options. New ones get added too fast.

NEWSGROUPS

Another category of online communication which has emerged as a robust application for spiritual pursuits is the phenomenon known as newsgroups, or the "Usenet." These are series of messages sent to "folders" which are organized by topic, and available for worldwide access via the Internet. Messages may be new thoughts or responses to previously posted messages. The chain of original message, responses and counterresponses ("thread") to a particularly incendiary, thought-provoking, or common-chord-striking message can go on for months.

Some newsgroups have assigned monitors to review items before they are posted to public folders, and verify that they're appropriate for the group. Most groups are not monitored.

Historically, there were seven newsgroup topic names and hierarchies:

news	news about newsgroups
rec	recreational topics
soc	messages about social issues
talk	for general opinion-swapping
comp	messages relating to computers and networks
sci	topics regarding the "hard" sciences
misc	everything else

Now there are scads more, sometimes referred to as the "alternative hierarchy." Some of these carry the designation **alt,** and the newsgroup **alt.religion** is where a significant amount of online spiritual newsgroup dialogue occurs. Within that category, as of this writing, there were 51 subgroups, most with either self-explanatory names such as **alt.religion.zoroastrianism**; or we-can-guess-at-the-intent names like **alt.religion.course-miracle**; or in-all-probability-no-one can-figure-out-what-the-topic-is-until-they-read-some-of-the-messages-in-the-folder names like **alt.religion.spangles**.

One finds the serious, the playful, and the difficult-to-categorize. A common acronym in the online world is FAQ, which stands for Frequently Asked Questions. Many Internet services and functions maintain a list of recurring questions and the answers to them for the convenience of cybervisitors. The newsgroup **alt.religion.monica** sported 20 pages of these questions and answers. I decided to find out a little bit about the religion called "Monica."

The first question in their FAQ list was precisely what I would have hoped for: "Who is Monica and what is the purpose of this newsgroup?" The answer:

> *Monica Mi-Yeon Chung is the Venus of*
> *soc.culture.korean. In less than a month, Monica has*
> *become more famous and has more followers than Jesus,*
> *Buddha, Marx and other net-gods combined. Even*
> *after her departure to convent, her thread and*
> *popularity has exponentially grown to the point where*
> *so-called "serious debates" have become virtually*
> *impossible … alt.religion.monica is a radically retro-*
> *postmodernistic newsgroup devoted to discussing*
> *morality and subliminal messages of Monica Chung …*

Newsgroups contain energetic discourse on the full panoply of topics relevant to most modern churches, spiritual groups, leaders and individuals. The postings number in the thousands. Missives assume any and all positions on salvation, creation, women's clerical roles, gay and lesbian issues, Mammon vs. Truth, first marriages, Second Comings, third mortgages, charitable donation percentages, spiritually dead churches, prayer requests, ministerial misconduct, sudden revelation and scriptural quotation—to thinly scratch the surface. Emotions run high. Manners run low. Imaginations run wild.

The following nugget is from the **alt.religion.all-worlds** newsgroup, authored by a person identified as "SwiftRain." SwiftRain was responding to a posting from a person using the online name "Collectively Unconscious":

Collectively Unconscious wrote, "Depending on your flavor of Zen Buddhist (mine is chocolate), meditation is just an expedient method for cutting back the noise in your head. There is nothing that needs to be transcended and no one needs to be transcending it."

Actually, regardless of how off-topic we are, Zen Buddhism doesn't talk about "meditation" at all. "Meditation" is a (rather bad) translation of "zazen." Zazen just means sitting and being at peace.

(And I prefer vanilla.)

A writer using the name "SkyDotCom" offered the following thoughts in the same newsgroup:

I'd like to share an idea with those of you who may—as I do—reject the common notions of godstuff.

Though the terms "atheist/atheism/atheistic" have served well enough to lump together groups of people who "don't believe in God," I find it ironic that we *choose* to be labeled by them.

*Theism is "the belief in the existence of a god or gods."
Since I think (and you'd probably agree) that gods are
the creations of species man, it follows that the
natural state of humankind does not include any
god. A person who has no god isn't lacking anything.
Rather, the person with a belief in a god has chosen to
take on some "extra baggage."*

*Example: if a man has a tattoo on his forehead, then
he has a feature which is not part of the *natural
state* of humankind. You may choose to refer to him
as "the guy with the tattoo." But would you instead
choose to call everyone else "tattoo-less people"?*

*Then why choose to call yourself an "atheist"—a term
almost certainly coined by a "believer" (possibly to aid
in the persecution of early freethinkers)?*

*The dictionary calls an atheist "one who denies the
existence of God." I don't deny the existence of God!
There is no "God" whose existence I can deny!!!
Rather, I reject the very notion of a god. I am not an
atheist!*

Two writers identified as "Dartwin" and "Maith" engaged in
the following brief dialogue:

Maith: *"Atheists have almost as much (in some cases more) contempt for agnostics as they do for theists." Have we all got this straight?
The atheists hate the Christians, hold contempt for the agnostics, sidle
up with caution to anyone who is sexually, ah, ambiguous but *RE-
ALLY* love themselves.*

My! What hath their ever-flaunted absolute freedom wrought??

Dartwin's reply: *You're right. We're not worthy of your attention. You can leave now. Say a prayer before you cross over to the Christian bulletin boards.*

Also present are quasi-commercial messages (considered very bad "netiquette"), irrelevance, irrationality, obscenity, and incorrectly posted items. There is wheat, but there is also a lot of chaff. Usenet is a great place to check in on a very interesting subset of the world.

Despite the geographical and philosophical diversity of newsgroup contributors, the views can't be assumed to represent the population at large. Participation on Usenet is not difficult, but does require a computer and some rudimentary knowledge of how to navigate around a network. The opinions expressed are, therefore, those of a silicon-oriented community which is certainly growing, but is still a long way from including everyone.

FORUMS

With the advent of full-featured, commercial online services, the concept of the "Forum" has been deemed ready for prime time. Forums are a combination of communication channels dedicated to particular topics. Let's take a look at the "Religion and Beliefs" forums available on one of the major services.

When you select **Religion and Beliefs** from the **Life, Style and Interests** menu, you can choose from **Christianity, Judaism, World Beliefs, Spiritual Mosaic,** or **Ethics and Values.** If you click on **Christianity**, for example, the following options will appear:

❖   **Christianity Online**

❖   **Christianity on the Web** (A website Index)

❖ **The Catholic Community** (Message boards, features, websites of interest to Roman Catholics)

❖ **Focus On the Family** (Articles, functions and features sponsored by this well-known organization)

❖ **The Christian Forum**

Entering the **Christianity Online** area leads to a grouping which includes:

❖ **Message boards.** Similar to Newsgroups, with a suggested daily discussion topic. (The topic on this particular day was, "How should Christians respond to health issues facing today's society?")

❖ **Religion news update**. Click here to get late-breaking news stories regarding religion and spirituality.

❖ **Current News and Magazines**. This section provides access to electronic versions of current issues of selected newspapers and magazines.

❖ **Christianity on the Internet**. Offers an index to Internet and websites of interest. There is also a "church locator," to help people find churches in their locale and to their liking.

❖ Perhaps the most interesting resource is the gateway to **Chat and Live Events**. (Chat rooms will be discussed later in this chapter.) This is interactive communication. In chat rooms, people talk with one another, or with the "room." Live events usually involve a guest or host (often a celebrity or well-known name), who responds to questions or comments.

MERE CHRISTIANITY—AND MORE

The Christian Forum offers access to online libraries, websites, chat rooms, message boards, and a daily devotional. Approximately 500 message board topics in this forum include interfaith relationships, Christian teens, suicide, gay men marrying gay women, abortion, e-mail Bible courses, conservative churches, and "Gotta do more, gotta be more."

Curiosity piqued, I peeked into this last folder. It mostly contained exhortations to strive harder for righteousness in its various forms. Two postings, however, provided additional interest in different ways.

The first was a message which started out, "My mission in life is raising my identical twin grandsons. Custody wars, court systems and battles including welfare, military and gay issues were unknown in our past and were just as suddenly paramount. Our 32-year-old daughter ... was too busy living with her female lover to provide for God's Blessings. What a shock to us as we discovered she was Pregnant! Gay! And had no possible way to care for the newborns." This woman has written a book on these experiences, and hopes to "... reach the millions who are in our same boat."

The New Age, it appears, will be won with surprising ease. The wondrously adept principle of "emergence" accounts for everything. It will materialize delightful new organs of higher awareness, not cancerous tumors. As one Net contributor enthuses: "The nature of the organism resulting is the only question. ... Strangely, I think this organizing into a spiritual whole will occur without much effort. When human spirits gather in a common purpose, something happens."

Stephen L. Talbott, *The Future Does Not Compute: Transcending the Machines in Our Midst*

The second posting of interest contains a theme older than time itself. Its subject line is, "Cast your nets!! Are you ready?" The message reads, "Are you ready to make enough money so that money makes no decision for you? You can have all you want!!! I can show you how, it's easy! We are Christian and conduct our business in a Christian manner. We will work along side you to help ensure your success. For Free Info on how you can make BIG money, Email me ..."

Selecting the **World Beliefs** option yields invitations to forums on Baha'i, Buddhism, Hinduism, Islamic/Muslim, and Interfaith. Each of these offers a banquet of boards and sites, resources and chat rooms, similar to **The Christian Forum** menu.

If you are getting the impression that there are *many* ways to explore, communicate and share spiritual journeys from your keyboard, you are right. Many are duplicative, but that allows seekers to find the forum most precisely tuned to their individual tastes. Several stores at the mall may sell jeans, but only one may have the pair you want—in stock, in your size—on a given day.

CHAT ROOMS

Many who pursue an online spiritual path are looking for real-time interaction, not electronic document treasure hunting. Rather than browse the Web or surf the Net, they'll log on to chat rooms. Where there's demand there's soon supply, and they can find rooms dedicated to spiritual discussion—at least nominally; there's no serious enforcement. While it's true that rooms with titles like **Christian Fellowship** are not as compelling to some as rooms like **Romance Connection** or **Flirt's Nook**, they get their piece of the chat action. People share spiritual experiences, ask questions about the meaning of life and the existence of God, inquire about good Zen temples in Wisconsin, call each other spawn of Satan, and put a lot of energy into the whole thing.

The concept of chat room participation is simple, but the logistics, format and tempo take some getting used to. A loose-fitting analogy might be attending a casual, open-house style, happy-hour party where you don't know anyone. The party is in a hotel, and there are many other such parties going on at the same time. I'll use the chat room structure of one of the major online service providers as an example.

When you log on to the service and select what they call **People Connection**, you are transported to a "reception lobby." You can actually converse with other people in the lobby, if you wish, while figuring out which "party" you want to attend.

To "talk," you simply type what you want to say on your keyboard. Everyone else who is currently logged into the lobby or chat room you're in will see your name at the left side of their screen, followed by your comment. When someone else "says" something, the screen scrolls upward and that person's "screen

> ... *perhaps the most poignant symptom of the projection of a lost interiority lies in the new electronic mysticism. Images of a global, electronically mediated collective consciousness, of Teilhard de Chardin's [O]mega [P]oint, and of machines crossing over into a new and superior form of personhood are rife on the Net. Channelers channel onto the Net. Pagans conduct rituals in cyberspace. Most of this is unbearably silly, but as a widespread phenomenon it is difficult to dismiss.*
>
> Stephen L. Talbott, *The Future Does Not Compute: Transcending the Machines in Our Midst*

name," followed by their comment, appears at the bottom of the screen.

The software which controls and enables some chat rooms can accept only about 15 words at a time, so ability to communicate in one-sentence bites is helpful. The average sentence is probably five words. In an active room, the comments can fly at a very fast pace. Other rooms may have periods of "silence" when no comments are being sent. As with parties, each room has a character: shy, aggressive, anywhere between. You can participate, or just sit on the sofa and listen to the dialogue swirling around you.

Conversations take two forms: comments put out for the room in general, and comments directed to specific individuals. The live-party analogy might be the way you circulate around the room: sometimes you join a group, sometimes you're one-on-one.

One-on-one conversations usually require sharp eyes and good reflexes. If there are 20-odd people in the room and you're "conversing" with one, you need to pick the comments of that person out of the pack. Being able to think of replies quickly is helpful; so is having frisky fingers to type them.

As with real social gatherings, pests can horn in. You may be having a fine dialogue *à deux* with someone, but if it looks interesting to others in the room, they can try to get involved. If you and your cohort ignore them, there's not a lot they can do besides switch to all capital letters to protest, and say mean things about you. (Using all caps is the electronic equivalent of SHOUTING, and is considered bad netiquette.) However, if unsolicited outside comments make the two of you feel the neighborhood is going downhill, and you wish to repair to a more genteel, private locale, two options exist. You can set up a private room; or you can send "Instant Messages," which only the two of you can read, to each other.

Using the live-party analogy again, the "Instant Message" approach might be like the two of you stepping outside into the garden. The "private room" option might equate to the selected group hopping into a hot tub.

Most people don't hang around the lobby long. They head for a room with the chat topic of their choice. Major categories include:

❖   **Arts and entertainment**

❖   **Life**

❖   **News, Sports and Finance**

❖   **Places**

❖   **Romance**

❖   **Special Interests**

❖   "Country" rooms (**Germany, France, Canada**)

Chat rooms with potential interest for spiritual searchers are found in both the **Life** and the **Special Interests** categories, along with a host of other rooms. **Special Interests** rooms include astrology, ebony, art, gardens, born-again onliners, metaphysics, music, cars, computers and pets.

Life rooms offer a smorgasbord of conversation canapés for people in different stages and states:

❖   Age affinity rooms: **Teens, Twentysomething, Thirtysomething, Over 40, Senior Scene**

❖   Family role affinity rooms: **Parents, Careers and Family, Divorced**

❖   Gender affinity rooms: **Male Point of View, Women's Point of View, Gay and Lesbian**

❖ "Looking for love" affinity rooms: **Single Again, Single Parents, Widows and Widowers, In Limbo**

❖ "Searching for truth" affinity rooms: **Christian Fellowship, Philosophy**

People in chat rooms usually use "screen names," which are online aliases. Sometimes it's evident what a screen name refers to. Sometimes the choice is totally opaque, meaningful only to its owner. There's no way to find out the real names behind screen names like "Zephyr," "Silver Wraith," "Magik10," "Where'sMom1," "Angelbirdy," "Moonbats," "Bluuenikki," "HooknLaddr," "Lord Gizmo," and my personal fave, "PNutChelle," unless their owners choose to share the information. This they can do during conversation or by completing an optional member profile which is available for all to peruse. Some chat room participants do post profiles, but many choose to chat in mysterious anonymity. Such is their prerogative.

Entering the online chat world during midday in midweek revealed an interesting fact: many of the participants were midteens whom one would expect to be in school. Among their many other sociological roles, chat rooms may be emerging as a recreation of choice for the flu-ridden and/or the truant.

The words and thoughts in a chat room come and go, surge and merge, part, wane and die so that new words and thoughts may rise from their ashes. Statements range from petulantly profane to passably pithy to possibly profound, with occasional nodes of nihilistic nonsense. For some participants, the fingers on the keyboard are faster than the mind, and for some, just the reverse is true. Both mismatches represent chat challenges.

To give a touch of the flavor to those who have not been in an online chat room, spiritual or otherwise, here's an excerpt from a **New Age Spirituality** room conversation I entered in progress (speakers' "screen names" are on the left, in bold type. References to other speakers' names, which are often shortened during chats, are also in bold):

BdyMndSprt: Ah, but I do have a foundation. Faith, my own God-given religion, but it seems you are here …

STANSONELL: Silly, private room "feng shui."

Orion Zen: I don't think SSOOOOOOOOO …

BdyMndSprt: … to proselytize, so I will not get into an argument with you.

HolyGhost: No, the mind is the liaison, the soul is the operator!

STANSONELL: Orion, about what?

Orion Zen: Bible.

Sprtljrney: oh … okay, **Holy** … my ignorance of souls, maybe. Don't know much about souls.

Meemoe: Religion was god given.

WildHealer: I like that, **Ghost**.

SoulWind2: It is all one, **Holy**, no separations.

Light22: Let's do "LOVE IS"!

SoulWind2: The consciousness is …

UhOh007: Metaphysics can be argued forever … but lying can be seen easily.

Faithmom: Wide is the road that leads to destruction.

STANSONELL: Oh, must've missed something.

Silly47787: Thanks ... I need a spiritual interior decorator here ...

Sgusakov: Light ...

Orion Zen: Love is ... all of us.

Light22: Love is ... accepting others.

HolyGhost:Sprtl ... how can that be? Soul is YOU!

UhOh007: Love is ... not Manson.

RBCF Soul: Holy—Yes, SOUL runs the whole show!

Orion Zen: Love is ... you, **Light22**.

HolyGhost: Not something out there!

STANSONELL: Silly, you're telling me!!! My house is a wreck.

Faithmom: Narrow is the path that leads to eternal life.

Sprtljrney: Ghost, then maybe I don't know so much about me.

WildHealer: Love is ... healing.

SoulWind2: This world is made up of the same stuff as the "inner."

CaseCorp11: I have a question for everyone and was wondering if you guys could help me out?

Sprtljrney: Faith ... how many different paths are there?

WildHealer: Love is ... letting go of fear

Light22: Love is ... smiling at the person in the car next to you—and letting them pass.

Orion Zen: Wise words, **Wild**

UhOh007: Love is ... a four letter word.

Brando895: **Case**, go ahead.

RCBF Soul: **Wild**—yes, divine love can even heal the physical body.

HolyGhost: Perhaps! But I know how to introduce yourself!

WildHealer: Yep!

Light22: Love is ... knowing that all people long for the same thing—feeling love.

CaseCorp11: Why aren't words like Love or Compassion capitalized? To me those are more powerful than ...

Sgusakov: Love is something you have never seen until you experience it.

Faithmom: One path to heaven, many to hell ...

STANSONELL: Love is ... doing random acts of kindness.

Silly47787: Ha Ha Ha. Give ... love ... and blow the dust as I walk by to sit at the computer.

Orion Zen: **Madonna**—come on in.

The foregoing represented about two minutes of chat time. Keeping up, following the threads, getting your comments in before the topic changes, and keeping an eye peeled for someone "calling" your name end up being a fairly good workout for the intellect and an even better one for the reflexes.

Not long ago I engaged in a brief chat room conversation with a woman in North Carolina. She had recently gone through a powerful spiritual experience and mentioned that she had written about it. I asked her if she'd send me her writing. She did, via electronic file transfer. After 10 minutes of faceless screen interaction, I was reading an 8,000-word document of ultimate intimacy describing this woman's marital and physical problems, hospitalization, surgery, fear of death, and middle-of-the-night revelation. If we had met in person she probably would have shared none of this.

FACE TO FACE

When all is said and done, what does it mean to substitute screen and keyboard for live humans; to replace bricks-and-mortar meeting places with wire-and-cable connections; to have newsgroup monitors in the spiritual communication loop instead of ordained clergy? Are we seeing the search—and the means—for a new paradigm, one that seeks to distill a pure, solitary spirituality and filter out particles of traditional, organized religion?

Irving Kristol is a fellow of the American Enterprise Institute. In a February 3, 1997 *Wall Street Journal* article on what he believes is a form of spiritual crisis in our nation, he says:

> *… it is not astonishing that the search for spirituality has become so fashionable. It is what individuals, liberated from religion, desperately seek as a substitute.*

>*Spirituality is indeed an integral part of all religions—but a minor part, and it cannot be a substitute for the whole. Religion is not some kind of psychic exercise that occasionally offers a transcendental experience. It either shapes one's life— all of one's life—or it vanishes, leaving behind anxious, empty souls that no psychotherapy can reach. And for religion to shape one's life, it needs to be public and communal; it needs to be connected to the dead and the unborn.*

Public. Communal. Connected. We understand the traditional meaning of these words. But maybe they've acquired extended meanings. Perhaps those meanings force us into uncomfortable semantic conflicts. Can we be public without leaving the house? Communal without being in physical proximity to other humans? Connected without ever looking into our discussion partners' eyes?

For a good number of techno-souls in cyberspace, I think the answers are "yes." Further, the pieces are in place to support the argument that this will continue to be a high-growth phenomenon. Based on the number of churches and institutions establishing websites, or trying to figure out how to establish them, it appears many are coming to the same conclusion.

For those who want to see others, be seen, and still not leave the house, current technology provides an alternative to looking into real eyes. It's like a telephone call with video as well as voice. The necessary software runs on many personal computers, and the hardware includes a mini-camera at each end. The camera sends a continuous picture of each participant to the other's screen. Resolution isn't great, and motion is a little jerky. But it will improve, and it does allow credible visual contact without requiring people to get out from behind their keyboards. And behind their keyboards, many will choose to stay.

I don't think most people would say we're at New Jerusalem just yet—perhaps we're closer to the virtual Tower of Babel stage—but that's where some may feel their online pilgrimage is heading. As a matter of fact, at least in one vision, technology-based spirituality may be destined for a startling, infinitely more profound role. Chapter Ten will include a look at the concept of computers being the ultimate tool for achieving immortality and the promise of eternal life.

CHAPTER NINE

❦

Saying No

Irreligion: The principal one of the great faiths of the world.

Ambrose Bierce, *The Devil's Dictionary*

I ... became an actively practicing intellectual agnostic; one who took pride in explaining to others that because of recently acquired knowledge he now knew too much to be able to know any longer whether there was a God.

Dan Wakefield, *Returning—A Spiritual Journey*

What causes people to reject or leave a spiritual path?

The reasons for saying no to starting or continuing spiritual life appear as varied as 20 years of Chevy models. The purpose of this chapter is to explore some of the underlying thoughts and processes. We'll look at the topic of spiritual rejection through the eyes of some who have made that personal decision, and some who haven't but who have opinions about it. We'll also hear from some clergy why they think people decline their offerings.

In approaching this area, I guessed there were two major categories into which Valley residents without spiritual lives might fit:

❖ Those who found religion or spirituality *irrelevant* to their lives. No hook. No connection. I anticipated that this perspective would spring from a near-complete absence of exposure to spirituality, particularly during early life. Subsequent years would bring neither people nor experiences which would trigger an examination of the area. Silicon Valley life and culture would be seen as de-emphasizing or even marginalizing spirituality. Eventually, spiritual pursuits would become just something that other people did, for reasons known only to them. The topic would lack both reality and interest.

❖ Those who had explored the area, maybe even had a spiritual path at one time, but whose lives included events or experiences or changes in belief that caused them to abandon the path. The end—or the decision not to start—was not passive, not a vacuum, not a default. These people had *thought it out*. And their conclusion was that they and a spiritual life were not going to be an item. The decision represented active rejection, sometimes with a great deal of energy behind it.

Those were my guesses. I was almost, but not quite, right.

First, I discovered that everyone has had enough contact with spirituality and/or religion to have gotten past being a blank slate on which nothing had ever been written. And while some people lack interest in pursuing a spiritual path, everybody I interviewed had an opinion about it.

Second, I discovered that the reasons for rejecting a spiritual path are too varied to fit neatly into just two groups:

❖ Some say no because they see hypocrisy: spiritual values extolled on Sunday, same extollers making decisions which ruin people's lives on Monday; or spending money on frippery on Tuesday, instead of using it to make a better world.

❖ Some, as protesting kids, were dragged to church by parents. They vowed that when they grew up they would never go to such boring places again. It's a vow they've kept.

❖ Some started on a spiritual path at one time and found it enticing. Then their burgeoning beliefs presented an uncomfortable demand, and the most comfortable way to deal with the conflict was to get off the path.

❖ Some fear foolishness. Cynicism and skepticism often play better in the Valley than belief.

❖ Some feel spirituality is isolated, forbidden ground.

❖ Some feel there's an incontrovertible prima facie case against at least the Higher Power version of spirituality: too many bad things happen to too many good people.

❖ Some see rigidity: One True Way. Silicon Valley may be the least likely place on the globe for the One True Way approach to have much appeal.

❖ And the most pragmatic dynamic of all: some are just too drained after the long, demanding days at the office to pursue deep philosophical concepts. The required intellectual capital has been spent elsewhere. This may be a distant kissin' cousin to rejection by default.

There is one view of spiritual life which may make the difference between acceptance and rejection moot. Edward, a priest at a
large Roman Catholic church, says, "Spiritual life is what you are
and how you live. Spiritual life can't be separated from the rest of
life. Your life is one entity. My dad read the racing form in the car
while the rest of our family was inside the church at Mass. But he
lived the highest spiritual life."

Whether spiritual life can exclude spiritual practice is a juicy
topic for high-energy debate and highly technical theology. Or, it
may hinge on definitions. Is a moral life, an ethical life, the same as
a spiritual life? Or do they simply travel a long stretch of the same
road side by side, going in the same direction, maybe toward a
common destination, but with a different mission?

Regardless of how one lives, Edward thinks the act of rejecting spirituality is painful, always nagging at the people who do it.
Jerry, a Valley rabbi, rejects the idea that those rejections really
happen. "I don't know any human who isn't searching for meaning and doesn't want to connect to something bigger," he says. "I
know some who are misguided in their search, maybe, but none
who say 'no spirituality.' They're looking, even if they don't know
it consciously."

Sam, a Protestant minister, believes basic personality characteristics affect the decision about spiritual paths. "Thirty-five percent of the population are Myers-Briggs 'Introvert' types, who don't
like crowds or socializing. It can be hard to get them to try going
to church." He also observes that fiscally conservative types may

---

Some people reject a spiritual path because of the pain in facing
themselves. How do you accept your brokenness, your failures, your
humanity, *in a society that emphasizes perfection?*

Victor, a Silicon Valley teacher

be critical of the way churches spend money, and reject spiritual paths on that count. "Some people see the new church building and say, 'Look at that church, just suckin' dough!'"

Among the people interviewed, strong commitment to one's own spiritual journey often went hand in hand with extensive insight into why that journey is rejected by others. Maybe that's because folks remember well the obstacles they faced along their own path.

Colin, the marketing manager for a computer equipment maker, captured several variables. "People looking at churches often see them as hypocritical, controlling, freedom-robbing. Or they see them as superficial social groups without real meaning. Some may confuse spirituality with religion and get turned off to spirituality because of problems with religion."

The issue of control was a recurring theme. Frank, the bank CEO, pointed out that unwillingness or inability to conclude there are things one can't solve oneself deters many from exploring spirituality. Can't go it alone? Need outside help? You're showing weakness. You're vulnerable. Next thing you know, someone's calling in a consultant. Can a reorganization be far behind?

Gerald is the chief financial officer of a laser equipment company. In his view, a frequent factor leading to rejection of a spiritual life is that taking the high road can be tough. It's easier not being spiritual. Commitment requires you to put yourself on the line, and stand up for what you believe. Keeping the faith takes guts. You have to be willing to pay the price. You might also be dealing others into the game, and there's risk that they could suffer for your beliefs. If you have two kids to support and your boss tells you to do something wrong ...

As a journalist for a widely read Valley publication, Duane has an excellent observational perch. "Lots of things turn people in

this area off to a spiritual path," he notes. "The sense that everything is OK as it is. A sense that religion is silly, that there's a lot of
flakes involved and you don't want to be one of them. The flake
thing is a big thing.

"You see people presenting themselves as spiritual, then you
find out they're bad parents, or on their fourth marriage. Or, work
drives spirituality out because there's no time and too much pressure.

"Spiritual leaders and clergy can be the problem. Some are
good, but some are jerks, screwing around with their parishioners
and embezzling money.

"Then, there's TV and the Internet."

Rita is vice president of corporate communications for a pub-
licly held environmental technology firm. She's well positioned to
observe the challenges that being a corporate officer can offer to
spiritual beliefs. (The CEO of her company, commenting on their
internal culture, has said, "If you want a friend, get a dog.") She
sees the key issue keeping some people from spiritual paths as a
primeval one: fear. Fear of not understanding what the path is.
Fear of letting go. Fear of self-awareness. Fear of surrendering.
Fear of admitting fear. She thinks these last two are much more
issues for men than for women.

Rita also believes it's easier for women to let it be known in
the business world that they have a religious affiliation. "I've known
some men who teach Sunday school who would never admit that
fact in their work lives," she says. "I think they're afraid they'd be
considered odd by their colleagues."

*Some are simply afraid to think what it might mean if there was a
God.*

Melinda, a Valley therapist

In fact, it may be deeper than just "odd." For some, the fear might be that the "surrender" involved in that area implies the possibility of surrender in other areas. Vulnerability established, the next sound could be fins cutting through the water.

One of the dynamics of spiritual life rejection I asked interviewees to reflect on was the two-opinion household: one partner in the marriage or relationship has a spiritual life, but the other does not.

LARRY AND HELENE

Larry is a residential general contractor. He sees firsthand that the extraordinary runup in property values in the area encourages people to spend copious amounts of money maintaining and improving their houses. It's usually a good investment.

Working with his customers has given Larry ample opportunity to observe Silicon Valley lives and styles. The experience has fueled his conviction that spirituality, at least in this area, is usually synonymous with hypocrisy. "Belief systems in other countries seem to have more meaning," he says. "The only thing we grab onto are our Jeep Cherokees and our gyms. It's hypocritical to say one is spiritual when one can't get on a bicycle without wearing $300 worth of the right clothes. I couldn't do that if I were spiritual.

"Going to church just on Christmas and Easter, as many people do, is also hypocrisy. So are the proclamations of certain well-known spiritual leaders. They tell people to give up affluence, but they certainly enjoy it themselves."

He doesn't rule out all possibility that his opinion could change. But for now, Larry puts himself in the category of having said no for keeps to a spiritual path, at least as normally defined.

"My parents were Protestant. In my teens, my dad was shocked that I didn't believe in God," Larry recalls. "But he never pursued it. We were alienated anyway.

"I went to a church funeral when I was 17, and it was the longest day of my life. The bells and chimes scared me. Now, robes and candles and bells strike me as hokey. Structured religion is a joke, and I think it has little appeal to most people.

"I do have some respect for fanatical believers, though. If you're willing to kill yourself for your belief, the belief system must have something going for it.

"There may be a 'greater power' in the universe, but it's not some old man in white robes. The universe is vast. If God is there, we would be an ant farm, too small for Him to notice.

"I believe something in us does last after death. We don't get white wings or sit on clouds. But I'm interested in this, and without being morbid, death might actually be a welcome experience. It's surprising to me how many people don't like to talk about death."

Larry doesn't believe people with spiritual lives have different moral or ethical codes from those who don't. He tries to treat his customers fairly, and traces the development of his ethical values to "… my parents, and the times in which I grew up. I had no heroes along the way. It's too bad things have changed so much that people now think it's OK to cheat on everything."

Larry's wife, Helene, has a very active spiritual life, so this is an area of sharply defined difference for them. They appear to have worked this difference out well. Both display great respect for and acceptance of the other's views. "I used to tease Helene that I liked to watch Jimmy Swaggart," he says. "I knew he was a big phony, but he seemed to bring something to people."

Helene believes the key to making a relationship work in this situation is to accept the difference: that what refreshes her spirit doesn't refresh his. She knows Larry's spirit is there; he's just not acting on it. It's important for her to affirm that he does have a spiritual side, but it's OK that he doesn't express it the same way she does.

There are challenges, however. Sometimes she feels lonely because he doesn't understand what she's talking about. Having friends and professional colleagues who do is helpful. She also knows that he's very proud of her. In general, she thinks that split opinions on spirituality are a warning sign in a relationship, and it's important for the couple to work it out. "You have to have unconditional acceptance of who each other is," she says.

Larry recalls having one experience he would describe as spiritual. "I was in the bathtub. I had a feeling of total relaxation, followed by total peace. I'm not sure I could convey the feeling exactly, even to Helene. She's tried to get me to meditate, but I'm just too visual a person for meditation. I've never been able to repeat that experience."

There's no such entity as soul. The traditional understanding is that it's something inside the body which continues to exist after death. Jungians postulate that it relates to feelings and emotions. But the individual self is constantly changing, and no individual self, no "essence" of the individual continues after death. Humans have such chutzpah *to think that only we, no plants, no animals, nothing else, have something that survives after death. What arrogance! Our coming and going in life is a continuation of something great.*

Ari, a Valley Buddhist leader

"My children are like me, only more so. I would rather they believed in something, or were more open, even though I believe only half of what I see and none of what I hear.

"I do believe there's something out there—maybe a 'nothingness.' It has to be experienced, though. No one can convince me with words. But too many people to ignore have had out-of-body experiences that seem to indicate something's there.

"I almost envy people who have the certainty of beliefs. I like to think I'm open to anything that might come along. But I'm not open to easy, clichéd answers."

THREE GUYS

Once there were three guys from New York City: two from Brooklyn, one from Manhattan. Now they're from Silicon Valley, and they're friends. Marvin and Jeremy are lawyers, a fact which Lonnie, a real estate agent, has been willing to overlook in the interest of friendship.

Jeremy is a corporate intellectual property attorney, charged with protecting the patents and trademarks of a major Valley biotechnology company. He is an outspoken social commentator and a sensational chef. It's well known in his circle that dinner at his house will be a gastronomic delight guaranteed to add a pound or two to one's presence.

Marvin has a private legal practice specializing in tax law and estate planning. He has three children successfully launched into adult life, and is a scrappy sports competitor. He was probably the

---

If only God would give me some clear sign! Like making a large deposit in my name at a Swiss bank.

Woody Allen, *Selections from the Allen Notebooks,* in *The New Yorker,* 5 Nov. 1973

only 145-pound interior lineman in the last 50 years of college football.

Lonnie dukes it out in the wacko Valley residential housing market, which has recently hit new levels of insanity. Driven by an exceptionally low number of homes listed for sale in the more desirable communities, houses are selling for substantial amounts over asking price, usually with multiple offers. Prices are up 15 percent or more (over their already sky-high levels) over the past year.

It's not unheard of for Lonnie's clients to make over-list-price bids on several houses, and still end up not having bought anything because someone else offered more. Telling a client they've lost another one can be—taxing. Maybe the streets of New York helped Lonnie develop the toughness and resilience to deal with this environment, and keep his sense of humor.

In addition to their New York heritage, these three men have other things in common. They are serious about sports, both as spectators and participants (tennis, racquetball, season ticket packages to Warriors basketball and Sharks hockey). They've all gone through more than one divorce and were obliged to become midlife dating drama veterans. (Marvin and Jeremy are happily remarried. Lonnie thinks he'll recognize Ms. Right if he ever meets her.) They were all born into Jewish families. And they've all made the personal decision that pursuit of a spiritual path or practice is not going to be a part of their lives.

JEREMY

Jeremy's parents didn't attend synagogue or have a regular spiritual practice. "My mother lit a candle here and there," he says. His grandfather was "reasonably Orthodox," but he and Jeremy's father became alienated. That led to alienation between his father and most of the family, and ultimately between his father and the religion.

Although religion didn't play much of a role in his early years, Jeremy recalls an experience which might have been a crossroad. When he was 18, his maternal grandfather died, shortly before the Jewish holiday of Yom Kippur. Jeremy felt a rare spiritual urge. He wanted to connect with his grandfather, honor his passing, engage in a traditional ritual of comfort. He decided to go to temple.

Yom Kippur services often fill synagogues, and many synagogues provide tickets to their regular congregation members to make sure they can get in. Jeremy had no ticket. He was not allowed in.

He decided he didn't need to go back.

When it came time to select a place to call his home, he recalls, "I wanted to be as far away from my family as possible while staying in United States territory." California provided a reasonable fit to this uncomplicated specification.

After unpacking and settling in, he did a California thing and attended consciousness-expanding seminars such as est. They didn't expand his spiritual consciousness, but he found them useful for "opening up and looking at new things."

His skeptical views of organized religion ended up being reinforced by his first wife's path. "She became interested in 'psychic churches,'" he remembered. "She started believing what the charlatans were telling her, and was taken advantage of, financially and mentally, by some Elmer Gantry types. It had tragic consequences for her, for me, for our relationship, and for the kids. The ironic part is that she couldn't put her religious beliefs into practice in her own life. She was cruel to the children."

In what might have been a symbolic act of defiance, many years ago Jeremy sent $10 and a completed form to the post office box of the Universal Life Church. In return, he received a certificate ordaining him as a minister.

The Universal Life Church may itself be an act of defiance. Its founder despised all religion, but "wanted to get away with what the other churches got away with." The Church's theology is straightforward: everyone is free to believe whatever they want to. After substantial legal wrangling, despite its in-your-face contrariness toward what might be viewed as the usual religious perspective, the California courts ratified its right to exist.

Jeremy did not state that he joined the Universal Life Church in a mood of defiance. The attraction for him initially was the ability to obtain discounts on airline tickets, and other such benefits. However, as a Universal Life Church minister, he can legally perform marriages. He has officiated at many, and enjoys it. As a matter of fact, on the day we met for our interview, he had joined a couple in matrimony at 10 o'clock that morning.

(He mentioned that he has an idea for a revenue-generating sideline, combining his ministerial and legal training: divorce representation. He had even given some thought to a slogan: "What Jeremy has joined together, Jeremy can put asunder—for $250 up front plus costs." I *think* he was being facetious.)

Absent inputs from any religious doctrine, Jeremy ascribes his moral and ethical codes mostly to upbringing. "I was brought up in a simpler time," he says. "There were things you knew were right, and those you knew were wrong. I didn't always do right.

> *Question with boldness even the existence of a God; because, if there be one, he must more approve of the homage of reason, than that of blind-folded fear.*
>
> Thomas Jefferson, Letter, 10 Aug. 1787

But I expected to pay the consequences if I got caught, and people took personal responsibility for their actions.

"When people reject a spiritual path, it might not always be the result of a decision. It might just be evolution. But many people probably revisit the issue as life changes occur. I'm open to finding that new experience tomorrow that may cause me to take a new path.

"Some people probably lack any real need for a sense of spirituality. I don't believe in the concept of a soul or an afterlife. But I'm satisfied with my relationship with the universe, and I'm not aware of any reason exploring spirituality would make it better.

"But there's a form of spirituality that doesn't focus on religious practice or a deity. Spirituality has to deal with a contemplation of forces and natures that are beyond our experience. We need to recognize we're relatively insignificant entities in a far grander scheme, and we're lucky to be here for a short period of time. The concept of spirituality is the concept of coping with the unknown."

MARVIN

Unlike Jeremy's family, Marvin's practiced what he refers to as "the trappings of Judaism." Although he didn't regard it as a religious experience, he accompanied them to temple for the holidays. "I did it for family peace, mostly," he recalls. "My father liked to have me around on High Holy days so he'd have someone to play cards with. Our family was kosher, but I suspect it was more cultural than religious.

"I was forced to go to Hebrew school, and felt forced to go to temple when there were other things I wanted to do. It took me two years to get through one year of Hebrew school. I was also forced into piano lessons, and that turned me off to music.

"Our school taught language and customs, but not really religion. And I never felt religious there. Even if one had it, belief would not be reinforced by *that* experience. The temples were orthodox, and it was mostly old men chanting in Hebrew and the scene put me off—then and now.

"There's probably less spiritual life in Silicon Valley than elsewhere, because so many people are physically separated from their family and traditions. But it wouldn't be any different for me even if I were still back in New York."

Marvin's view of spirituality is that, by definition, it has a religious context. "Although that might not be true for Buddhism," he adds, "which is more a way of life than a religion."

Asked about his concept of the soul, Marvin replied, "It's not separate from the body. If soul has meaning, it's the character, the personality, the emotional content of the person."

A substantial part of Marvin's law practice involves representation of people who have tax disputes with the IRS. "I see a certain amount of lying, cheating and stealing," he says. "I don't like it, and I try to be careful around people who do it. It's sometimes an ethical conflict when I have to represent clients who really did what the government says they did.

"You get moral and ethical codes from family, from upbringing, from life experience. Lying is a weakness. You can't contend with a situation, so you have to resort to subterfuge to get by. I don't think people with spiritual beliefs are any more honest or ethical than people who don't have them. The worst are the ones

---

I recalled the remark of William F. Buckley, Jr. in a television interview that if you mention God more than once at New York dinner parties you aren't invited back.

Dan Wakefield, *Returning—A Spiritual Journey*

who wear their religion on their sleeve. You know you can't trust those folks.

"What causes people to reject embarking on a spiritual path? *Common sense*. Healthy skepticism. I think it can work out fine if one partner wants to pursue a religion and one doesn't. There's enough problems with relationships without looking for trouble. It doesn't seem to have the same impact as money, sex, children and in-laws.

"My wife doesn't go to church. How much belief she has, I couldn't begin to tell you. It's not a topic of discussion for us.

"I don't believe in any deity, and if there is one, there's no effect on me. The only circumstance I can think of that might launch me on a spiritual path would be if I saw an angel. Absent that, it's very unlikely. By nature, I'm a skeptical person."

LONNIE

Lonnie recalls listening to Old Testament stories at a Jewish summer camp in Pennsylvania, and finding them interesting and enjoyable. Hebrew school was different. "In those days," he recalls, "the biggest problem was that they taught rote memorization, not spiritual concepts. I was happy I was on the streets playing ball while other guys were spending seven years in Hebrew school."

Lonnie's father was religious, "... but he never pushed it on anyone. You wouldn't know." His mother did not practice the religion much.

Early in life he encountered a philosophically baffling circumstance: "Where I grew up, the Jews were noticeably less religious than people of other faiths. But the people of other faiths committed crimes, and their daughters got pregnant, and the Jews did neither. I was perplexed how the crimes and pregnancies played with those people's religion."

Lonnie observes that religion is not as important in Silicon Valley as it seemed in New York. "Is it the area or the age?" he wonders. "Can't answer. But people here would rather be skiing, or on the tennis court, or surfing the Net than sitting in a house of worship.

"I had a neighbor who was searching for the right religion all his life. He ended up joining the Divine Light Mission. But after spending a lot of money on it, he quit the Mission, went into therapy, and decided to have a sex-change operation. He never got it, but I saw him in drag once, looking like a tall Hedda Hopper.

"Many times I've asked myself, 'What's for real?' I have a hard time understanding faith. Faith alone is difficult. I'm analytical. I need to see things. I've met people of so many different faiths in the Valley, and if what they all believe is false, it's confusing. I've read a lot. I've gone full circle. And now I'm back at the starting gate.

"I don't have a clear picture of spiritual things—there's a fog out there. It would be great if there's a life after death. I'm waiting for the spirit to tell me. In the meantime, I try to live my life as best I can, and just let the cards fall. If I get a royal flush, I'll win.

"I feel sorry when I do things I shouldn't have, and that's a change from my younger life. I've always seemed to have friends who were attorneys, or found myself hanging out with attorneys, and maybe that's not so good."

If I could make one change in this area's culture to improve spiritual lives and values, it would be to wipe out bad childhood memories so adults could come to religion with a blank, open mind.

Debra, a Valley minister

(Jeremy and Marvin: is the defense ready?)

"Atrocities like the Holocaust make me wonder, 'Can the world ever be peaceful?' Most people should be forgiven for what they've done if it was a spur-of-the-moment thing, like a bar fight. As long as it wasn't an intentional atrocity.

"A woman I was dating wanted to get into Judaism, and we started going to a temple to take classes. But she wanted to get seriously into the practice, and go through the Friday night candle-lighting ritual, and I just wasn't into that. When I told her that, she made a good point. She said, 'I can't be an ethnic Jew, I can only be a practicing Jew.'

"If something is going to happen to us when we leave this world, it has to be through the soul. It's the essence, the spirit. The soul might go into another physical body, but I have a hard time understanding that. If God exists, no matter what religion you are, there has to be a soul. We're measured by good and bad.

"When striving for success, one usually steps on others and blots someone out. Maybe some haven't. But when it comes to making money, the average businessman will do whatever it takes. My beliefs have probably changed for the better since I was a kid growing up in Brooklyn. Now I'm always up front, always disclose everything. I enjoy getting people into homes they'll like. I point out the negatives because it's the ethical and moral thing to do.

"My father was a bookie, but he was well trusted and well liked anyway. My mother came across as more ethical, but probably had more larceny in her heart. She would probably have been more likely to keep an unearned windfall. New York City was dog-eat-dog. Everyone was scheming. But I sorted things out. Even in Brooklyn, I never enjoyed hurting people. Winning, yes. Hurting, no.

"Some people use the church as a way of saying 'Look how moral I am,' and some of those are the ones you better make sure you cut the cards with. But some are sincere in their beliefs. The bottom line, if you look at a cross-section, is that people in churches might have higher morals and ethics. But then there's the 'God-father' thing: while the women are in church, the men are out killing.

"I'm hearing more and more that religion is joining racquet-ball and tennis in declining interest. My guess is there's less spirituality than there used to be.

"Could anything get me on a spiritual path? Maybe if I got a message from 'beyond,' saying 'Lonnie, you've been a good person, and we want you to join the pack.' I believe that as you go through life, it's important to treat others as you would want to be treated, whether or not there's someone up there paying attention. You have to feel good about yourself when you go to sleep at night.

"Sometimes I find myself talking to God. I don't know what God I'm talking to—but I talk to God."

ROD

One of Rod's earliest memories regarding matters of the spirit was noticing that his parents dropped him off and picked him up at the church for Sunday school, but never went in themselves. "Hmmm," he remembers thinking. "What am *I* doing here?"

For a while he thought the answer was that he would "matriculate" from Sunday school to church. Finally he went into church. "It wasn't what I had in mind," he recalls. "I also remember being put off by the passing of the plate; the idea that to be there you had to give money."

Rod hails from Southern California, but he's been in Silicon Valley for over 30 years. His entire career has been in the technology world. He's worked for a peripherals provider, a microwave manufacturer and a mainframe computer vendor. He's fought the good fight as a member of management teams in materials, manufacturing and engineering. His bachelor's degree is in engineering. He has an MBA. Recognizing that in the world he's chosen you can't sit still for a moment, he's pursuing another master's degree—this one in computer science—through an evening program.

During his MBA program, Rod took courses which gave him an opportunity to do some serious noodling about the meaning of life. These included "Philosophy of Religion," "Philosophy and Personal Values," and study about "Man and His Gods." He enjoyed the exploration. But it did not end up leading him down a path.

When young love struck, Rod's fiancée wanted to get married in a Protestant church which required nuptial participants to be baptized. He had no problem with that, and went through the appropriate procedures. After the marriage, it turned out neither of them had any interest in continuing the relationship with the church, and the connection lapsed. Eventually, so did the marriage.

Throughout much of his life, Rod recalls being around people who practiced religions. It's made him want to explore, to ask questions. His engineering-oriented mind doesn't like blank areas: "I don't know, so I need to find out."

But exploration failed to uncover anything he felt would lead him to ultimate truth. "It always got to the point where it took a leap of faith," he says. "Maybe I'm too independent. Maybe I'm too technical. Maybe I'm just too stubborn. But I just couldn't make that leap of faith."

Death is an area Rod has thought about a lot. Not brooding, morbid thought. Philosophical thought. Perhaps an engineer's thought. "What has happened?" he wants to know. Has the person assumed a spiritual form? When his father died of cancer, he remembers looking at the body in the coffin and puzzling, "His body is here; where is his essence?"

During the final days of his father's illness, Rod was deeply touched by the way one of the nurses in the hospice helped his father. He was clearly in pain, and approaching the end. "She kept saying, 'It's OK, you can let go,' over and over, and finally he did. Maybe he made that leap of faith.

"But if I believe in these things, how do I test them? Are there answers or directions, or is it all fluff?"

Part of Rod's thinking about death, and the concept of soul, relates to his awareness of humans as energy producers and containers. He thinks there's a possibility that we contain energy that's separate from mind and body, that can be talked to and heard. Maybe that's soul.

If it is, everyone has one, Rod believes, and not just those who have had some form of spiritual awakening. "On a judgment basis, we may not like the form some people's souls have taken," he says, "but they have one.

"If I had to guess about life after death I'd say no, but maybe we get hung up on the terms. Does it mean we exist with no bodies? Is there a North Pole/South Pole electromagnetic implementation?"

Spirituality involves gratitude, and disbelief is the greatest form of ingratitude.

Kamal, a Valley software engineer

A recent movie named *Powder* told the story of a bald, albino mutant with the power to mentally control electromagnetic force. He was shy and sensitive, as most of us might be if we were bald, albino mutants. He was, of course, rejected and attacked by most of the people in his town. A line from this movie struck Rod and stayed with him: *Hopefully, some day our humanity will catch up with our technology.*

Rod traces the development of his moral and ethical codes to his parents and his study of existentialism in college. He believes *strongly* in the precept that individuals have sole responsibility for themselves and their actions. He tries hard to stay true to his codes, but understands the conflicts. "In philosophy," he says, "you wrestle with 'is mankind good or evil?' and it's both. We're born with both.

"It seems you can't treat people directly, honestly and openly and still move forward professionally. You have to make sacrifices, tradeoffs. Do I stay consistent with my beliefs, or do I do what advances my career and salary, and argue that I'm doing it to take care of my family? We all face that, and maybe the only person who always stays with their beliefs is Mother Teresa."

Having to lay off several people in his group presented a tough conflict to his ethical values. "But sometimes you can't avoid it. I was honest with them. I gave them a chance to share their feelings of rejection, and their pain, and their concerns for their future. Then I went home that night and cried."

Rod believes that those who adhere to a religious practice may have somewhat different moral and ethical codes from those who don't, because of their commitment to doctrines. He has a

---

I pray, even for the people I want to see fired, who should be fired, and who are going to be fired.

Celeste, a Silicon Valley attorney

serious beef with doctrines that teach that only *their* believers go to heaven. "What about believers in other religions?" he asks. "What about those who live good and upstanding lives? Not that I believe in heaven, but when someone says good people aren't going to heaven because they don't have the right belief, I think that's revolting.

"People may not have religious or spiritual beliefs, but that doesn't mean they might not at some time in the future. Humans are thinking beings. They don't take areas and set them aside and say, 'I never need to think about this again.' Particularly not in Silicon Valley. This is a thinking area.

"But some people might turn to religion for the wrong reason. They may get 'born again' because they've hit a crisis point, or an event where they feel inadequate or incapable, and they embrace a religion, unquestioningly, more from needing something than from true belief. But then they might hit some part of the doctrine they just can't accept, and leave again.

"Let me tell you what's really in my heart about this. I think some people embrace religion because everyone wants to experience a true love, and many don't get the chance to experience that in a relationship. I've been fortunate to have the experience, the opportunity, the ability to truly love another person for what they are. Every human wants that. But if they don't get it, they might find that tug takes the form of a religious or spiritual call.

"Technology is making people more isolated in Silicon Valley, and that might mean spiritual involvement will become greater. People might *need* to get together once a week to do some real touching and community and friends, and church might be where that happens.

"Religion on the Internet is an area of potential impact. It allows those who don't need that gathering to pursue their religious path without leaving their keyboard. But that might be the spiritual equivalent of just watching pornography: if you don't get real sex for too long, you may become very disturbed.

"I can see every opportunity for something to happen that would affect me emotionally and cause me to consider a spiritual path. I'm not so independent and strong that I feel I could never need something or someone to help me through my troubles, or deficiencies, or needs. But given that my life stays on a stable emotional base, I don't see any need to start on such a path."

WHAT WENT WRONG?

Roland, a Silicon Valley pastor, has been very affected by the experience of one of his parishioners. He believes the situation reflects the vulnerability of spiritual paths to failure and disappointment.

"Dale has always succeeded and done better than others around him," Roland recounted. "He had a 20-year track record of executive success. He became CEO of his company. He had *never* failed.

"But this is Silicon Valley, and things change. The company started to stumble. The board of directors decided Dale just didn't have the ability to move the company forward anymore. They voted to take him out. The unthinkable happened. He got a pink slip.

"His professional crisis caused a spiritual crisis. He couldn't accept the situation. He kept asking, 'God, what's this about? What's happening? I've been a God-honoring man. What do You want?'

"He managed to persuade the board to give him a six-month extension on the job: a trial period, to let him demonstrate he

> *When I was growing up, I had no idea what the men in our church did for a living. I just looked up to them as spiritual leaders. Now it bothers me if someone wants to know what I do for a living before they've figured out if what I have to say is worthwhile.*
>
> Trent, president of a Valley telecommunications company

could deliver what the company needed. At the end of six months they did the evaluation. It was unanimous: no, he hadn't done what they wanted. He should leave.

"He resigned, feeling abused and taken advantage of. Seventeen months later he's still unemployed. He doesn't necessarily blame God. But he has a feeling that God fell short of his expectations. He can't believe God allowed this to happen. So he's moved off his path, and is floundering in his faith. He has formally left the church."

Roland and I also discussed a more secular, less spiritual dynamic that can plague a high achiever in situations like these. For years, Dale greeted his fellow parishioners as a successful and powerful executive. It's possible that without that standing, his identity became subject to inner doubt. Image is big in the Valley. Perhaps he no longer knew how to present himself, or how his greetings would be received.

A fact of the human psyche: people can get caught up in excruciating concerns over issues that are nonexistent outside themselves. Those concerns may have caused Dale to leave his community just when he needed it most, and when it might have been able to show him its best colors. People there might never have known or cared that he was a successful executive.

For engineers, scientific or executive types, losing responsibility in their jobs is an existential crisis. They don't know who they are because they can no longer lead. They feel lost. And often they don't turn to their mates for solace, because they don't think their mates will understand.

Rochelle, CEO of a Valley counseling group

KEN

On an early summer evening, Ken and I relaxed on the patio. Warm-weather fragrances abounded, led by the gardenias my wife tenaciously nursed back to health from a freeze-induced, near-death experience a few years ago. The 6 o'clock sun slanted through laurels and pines to glint brightly off half the pool; the other half serenely captured the reflection of the trees on the shady side.

Ken came by after his work day as telecommunications manager for a computer networking company. He's a Northern California native, and has lived in Silicon Valley for 14 years. I had invited him over to talk about the reasons he's decided not to pursue a spiritual practice.

We started with a little history. His parents had introduced him to their religion, but left the decision whether or not to pursue it to him. He knew what he wanted to do by his early teens. "I bailed," he recalls.

Since bailing, he has not felt the urge to go back. I asked him to reflect on his accumulated impressions of spiritual matters, and his current philosophical perspective.

"I don't feel that I'm missing anything," he began. "For one thing, our local, fast-paced lifestyle seems more geared to consumerism and materialism. It doesn't make it easy to find time for spiritual exploration, even if one were so inclined.

"For another thing, so much spiritual stuff seems hokey: something else for people to blame instead of taking responsibility for themselves. For a while I saw a therapist to work on a problem I'm dealing with. When she started talking about a 'higher power,' I got really turned off. I thought it was a cop-out. I know I have the ability to deal with the problem, and the idea that I required a higher power to do so seemed like flaming BS.

"I'm actually an agnostic, not an atheist. Agnostics believe 'something' may have created the earth and the universe, but don't know what that something was. But believing that something had a hand in getting things started doesn't mean it is something I would worship.

"I could be convinced that such a thing as a soul exists while a person lives. But as something that continues in an 'afterlife,' I don't believe it for a moment. If the soul is what helps you make decisions and function as a person, then maybe it's there. I do have a hard time believing that all we are is electrical impulses and synapses firing.

"My moral and ethical codes come from my parents, from home-town values, and from having a great circle of friends while I was in school. We knew what was right and wrong. My ethics and morals are probably very similar to those who have spiritual lives. Much of it comes from common sense. I don't need spiritual beliefs to do right things.

"Many things can turn people off to religion. Bad, early experiences. No results from prayer. No time. Achieving success and getting to a good place in life without having had a relationship with a higher power.

"My wife is Catholic and has strong beliefs. This issue could become hard. It's something we'll probably have to address. We weren't married in the Catholic Church. I'd be willing to formalize the marriage in a Catholic ceremony, but I would not be willing to become a practicing Catholic.

"It can actually be interesting having one partner who has faith and one who doesn't. There are more important things in a relationship than views on faith. Communion is both fascinating and silly. Not in a million years could I truly believe that. But I'm willing to love my neighbor without a church telling me to.

"The race in Silicon Valley keeps getting more and more accelerated. I don't know if there's a practical limit to the stress people can take. But we're creating a lot of stressed-out individuals who are keeping it together because they have to, and they're cruising for a breakdown. Many may come to a point where they need to stop and ask where they're going, and why. They may be candidates for developing or rediscovering faith. I suspect that folks who live the good Silicon Valley life will someday come to a point where they say, 'What did I do all this for?' and want to give something back, and develop their insides as well as their outsides.

"I don't think anything would vault me onto a spiritual path, but maybe it's not that black and white. There are certain things I could never believe, such as Christ being the son of God, or maybe even that there is a God. But there are some things I need to change about myself, and I don't seem to be able to make those changes. I won't reject any discoveries I make, and that might take me down any road. I have some end results I want to accomplish. I don't know that I could put a hundred percent into any faith, but if some aspect of spirituality could help me get to my objectives, I'd consider it."

In *Roads Home—Seven Pathways to Midlife Wisdom*, Kathryn Cramer discusses "Midlife Readiness Signals for Spiritual Serenity." These include increased reflection time; consciousness of world problems; confronting the prospect of death; seeking a more satisfying philosophy; and yearning for more solitude and silence.

There's an intuitive sensibility here. Spirituality and serenity are different concepts. They can and do exist independently. But it does not require a boundless leap of imagination to picture them getting into an individual's psyche at about the same time, and finding they have a lot to talk about. Nor is it difficult to see the signals Cramer mentions emanating from many overly challenged Valley residents.

The "I've-said-no-but-I'm-open" group will stride in a different direction from the "I've-said-no-and-I-can't-conceive-of-that-changing" crowd. But the stage may be set for Silicon Valley to produce a plethora of ultimately iconoclastic new path-walkers, blazing intriguing trails and asking provocative questions.

Here are some comments nonclergy interviewees offered regarding relationships with yes/no splits on spirituality:

Pretty uniformly, the marriage will break down. With most couples it's not likely that both parties will be on the same path with the same intensity at the same time. But where one has strong spirituality and the other has none, or purely a social involvement, the marriage dies even if they stay together for economic reasons.

It can be resolved, but it's difficult. At one point I was dating a man who didn't share my beliefs, and it was always in the back of my mind. How do you address that when it's so much a part of you? Spirituality is not just the structure of religion, so maybe it can be dealt with in the realm of spirituality instead of religion.

If my husband doesn't share my spiritual life, that's between him and his God and not for me to judge, although it's very slippery for me not to judge what someone else does—particularly him. I wouldn't like it if he finally declared for no faith. It would make me sad. It would be crumbs when he could have a banquet.

My husband has a belief in God, and some spiritual life, but not on a daily focus basis. It's not something he wrestles with. We're very different, but he's very content with who he is. It would be precarious for me to judge him. That's God's job. If you have a strong spiritual life, you need to marry someone who also has one. Sometimes I think that maybe my husband wouldn't have been God's first choice for me, but he was brought into my life for some reason.

It's very common for women to be in church alone, with their husbands not sharing their beliefs. These women pray for their husbands and want the relationship to work. One of the reasons I like my current church is there's a lot of men there. The main word where one doesn't share the other's spiritual life is lonely.

I know two such instances and they both work OK. I think the issue is mostly one of personal dynamics.

The situation often brings tension. It's sad that their souls can't share.

There might be tension, but it can become a creative influence and a source of good.

My spiritual life is more important to me than my boyfriend's is to him. But he flies a small airplane, and I believe his spirituality happens in the plane. He feels it's magical and wonderful to be up in the sky, even though he's a scientist and knows exactly how a plane works. When he flies over the desert at night and sees just a few lights, he might not admit it, but it sounds to me like he's having a spiritual experience.

Sometimes a spiritual life helps women accept their partner even if he's a lyin', cheatin', drinkin', no-work guy. God bless 'em if it helps 'em get through the day. I myself wouldn't want to go through life plagued with misfits and miscreants.

It usually works OK. But it would be so nice not to have a "silent zone" between us.

Sometimes people are just in different phases of what will eventually be the same journey.

It's a struggle. Women are usually more spiritual, maybe because we men tend to be more competitive. Often men are more involved with work and women more involved with family and relationships, including the relationship with God.

Following are some responses to the same question from clergy and spiritual professionals:

If spirituality is not shared, for the friendship or marriage to work each must be mutually supportive. Both must be aware of the common good, and in supporting someone, you're being spiritual.

If one believes and one's an atheist, a basic disrespect is likely to creep in and hurt the marriage. It could probably work with an agnostic rather than an atheist, though.

What doesn't work is trying to drag someone kicking and screaming to something they don't want. If one partner manifests good stuff, the other partner may be attracted to it.

It's helpful if the spouse who doesn't have a spiritual life is at least respectful of the one who does, and doesn't deride their faith. The believing spouse should feel free to pursue the journey without feeling the need to convert the nonbeliever. Theology is important here. It doesn't work too well if you believe your spouse is going to roast in hell forever.

It can confuse the kids and be an area of constant disagreement, but if the relationship is strong it can work. Sometimes the believer has church mail sent to the office instead of home. Faith is close to the heart, and to deal it out is a huge challenge. This is a gender-equal phenomenon.

It can be delicate, but I've never seen it cause a divorce. It's actually rare when a couple shares precisely the same path.

In general, *religious differences are irreconcilable, but it can work if both people have great maturity.*

It's not a balanced, harmonic situation. The seeker gravitates to other seekers, and the nonseeker says "uh-oh."

The "different faith" scenario is easier than the "faith/no faith" scenario.

It drives the spiritual spouse crazy, because they're going someplace that their chosen mate is not.

The believers pray that some day the nonbelievers will believe.

If spiritual spouses believe they have a responsibility to convert nonspiritual spouses, the tension falls on the nonspiritual ones because they're the focus of an effort. If spiritual spouses keep it inside and hope conversion just happens, perhaps because they're setting a good example, the tension falls on them.

Worked fine for my folks. They agreed the children would be raised Catholic, and my father said, "Just don't bug me about going to Mass."

CHAPTER TEN

❧

The Path Forward

Legends of prediction are common throughout the whole Household of Man. Gods speak, spirits speak, computers speak. Oracular ambiguity or statistical probability provides loopholes, and discrepancies are expunged by Faith.

Ursula K. LeGuin, *The Left Hand of Darkness*

It is possible to believe that all the past is but the beginning of a beginning, and that all that is and has been is but the twilight of the dawn. It is possible to believe that all the human mind has ever accomplished is but the dream before the awakening.

H. G. Wells, *The Discovery of the Future,* lecture,
24 Jan. 1902, at the Royal Institute, London
(published in *Nature,* no. 65, 1902)

vi·sion quest (*n.*). A period of spiritual seeking among certain Native American peoples, often undertaken as a puberty rite, that typically involves isolation, fasting, and the inducement of a trance state for the purpose of attaining guidance or knowledge from supernatural forces

American Heritage Dictionary, Third Edition

A frequent event on Silicon Valley calendars is the offsite planning meeting. This function is by no means unique to the Valley. What is unusual here is the frequency with which these meetings are held, and the comprehensiveness of the list of participants.

The purpose of going offsite is to get people out of the daily operating environment, clear their input buffers, free up memory and processing cycles, and invite creative thought about the company's destiny. Strategic issues may be dealt with in depth, and new directions charted. Agendas for these events often indicate a time slot for a company "vision quest." Former president George Bush inelegantly referred to "the vision thing," but people knew roughly what he meant.

Many Valley workers might say that trance states and hope for guidance from supernatural forces sound like business as usual to them. It isn't easy to coax glimpses of what's around the next corner from a universe whose physical laws seem hostile to even the most modest time travel. The smart mind stays open to anything that might work, no matter how unorthodox, because prognostication needs all the help it can get.

The questions on the table for this concluding chapter are: Where is the Valley going, spiritually speaking? Where do people see their individual paths leading them? And if spiritual leaders could wave their magic wands and evoke changes in the area's culture to improve spiritual life and values, what changes would they bring?

"TWO ROADS DIVERGED IN A WOOD …"

As with most matters of opinion, interviewees' projections of the Valley's spiritual direction and destiny range across a wide spectrum. At one end are those who believe the Valley is headed for a spiritual renaissance. Borrowing from the Crimestoppers' 1A textbook, they perceive the basics of motive, method and opportunity:

❖ **Motive**. People are becoming aware of the missing pieces in their lives. Pursuit of affluence isn't filling their inner tanks, even when the hunt is successful and the affluence is captured. Technological mastery is an infinite loop of short-term illusion, because the technology mutates, divides, recombines, and grows into shocking new forms. The fight to conquer it must be re-booted, re-run, and re-won, without end. Time demands, stressful conditions, and drums constantly pounding out a ramming-speed pace are grinding people down, and creating space which needs to be filled with true values, true meaning.

❖ **Method**. Tried-and-true methods of spiritual pursuit are morphing into new forms. Limitations are crumbling. New methodology, new pathways, and custom-tailored approaches

---

I'd reduce the power of money, put a limit on CEO salaries, give every citizen a right to shelter and health care, reduce the impact of superficial material things, and make humans our number one value.

Helene, a Valley minister

to spiritual life are available in abundance. Even among the old established religions, energy is being allocated to understanding what is needed, what will appeal, and how to provide it. Valley culture features a high level of acceptance of individuality, and a low level of requirement for conformance to tradition.

❖ **Opportunity.** The diversity of spiritual offerings, belief, and leadership in the area is remarkable, particularly considering that the Valley is not really a big-city urban setting. A cornucopia of opportunities for exploration can be identified by a few moments' intimate contemplation of the *Yellow Pages*. Assuming you don't go during commute hours, you can be in the right spot to pursue virtually any spiritual path you ever heard of, and plenty you never heard of, in 20 minutes.

At the other end of the spectrum are those who anticipate a *decline* in the role of spirituality in Valley lives. In most cases, people with this perspective see the decline as continuing a trend which is already well launched. Factors cited by these people include:

❖ **Economic theory.** Those who stayed awake during their college microeconomics courses may recall a concept called "local nonsatiation." Basically, this says that consumers can't get enough: there is no point at which the demand function for goods and services flattens out. Many people see the Valley culture driven by that concept. They believe that materialism here, if not all-consuming, is close enough to declare it a religion in its own right. In this view, material pursuit will not only preclude growth in spirituality, it will continuously drive out some which already exists.

❖ **Generation X and Generation Y.** In reviewing the chronological pattern of their own lives, many of the people interviewed recalled a gap in their spiritual development. It often started in their teens and ran through thirtysomething. The nature of the gap ranged from lack of interest to active hostility. It may be endemic to young adulthood.

Technology is a youth magnet. Over the past few years, corporations throughout the country have been increasingly precarious places for older workers. But that's not news here. The Valley has always had a youthful corporate orientation. New graduates with degrees in computer science will be slavered over and fought for with increasing ferocity. More people in their 20s and early 30s will arrive (assuming they can find someplace to live). And ready or not, here they come: there's even a teenage CEO or two on the scene. These young hard-chargers will be interested in their careers, not spiritual matters.

It's true that many religious institutions in the area are acutely aware of the graying of their congregations and their failure to broadly appeal to younger adults, and they are working on the problem. But many people feel this issue won't be easy to address. They are concerned that youthful Valley trendsetters will not be attracted to spiritual paths.

❖ **Inherent rational secularism.** In the perennial tension between search for truth via science/technology and search for

> *There won't be any change in spirituality in the Valley unless an earthquake or two comes along. And even then, the change will be temporary.*
>
> Chuck, president of a computer printer accessories manufacturing firm

truth via spirituality/religion, this area's vote is hard-coded for the former. In addition to this regional predilection, there's an edge of derision toward faith followers that will discourage many people on the fence from climbing down on the spiritual side.

❖ **Time.** No one has any, and that will never change.

QUO VADIS?

Between these two extremes, interviewees saw possibilities containing elements of both visions. Celeste, a partner in a large law firm, doesn't think youth and technology are knockout blows to spiritual growth in the area. "This place is full of young, scientifically oriented people," she says, "and I think they'll have a growing spiritual awareness. Eventually it may awaken into a full hunger. Lots of spin-off interest in education and the arts in this area is a ripple effect from the technology business. This is an amazing, high-energy environment, and it may someday turn its attention to spirituality."

Stacy, the software company field marketing director, sees a similar possibility. "A lot of people talk about balance, although not many do anything about it," she says. "But there's tremendous breadth: all kinds of people trying all kinds of things. That won't change. It'll always be part of the Silicon Valley culture. We're explorers and seekers."

Many mentioned a possible change on the horizon: spirituality coming out of the closet and becoming more open and shared. Maturity and security play a role in this trend. Melinda, the therapist, thinks increased maturity yields spiritual benefits even if it's a drawback in the Valley's youth-happy professional world. "People are embarrassed to talk about their spiritual lives," she observes, "partly because they're out of balance. But one day they get jolted by a message: 'you're obsolete; if you're over 35, you're not young anymore; get out.' Maybe that gives them the chance to let something else in. I'm over 35, and my spiritual life is better than ever."

Melinda joined many of the women interviewed in expressing a desire to see the role of women in religion changed and enhanced. "I like Mary as an image in Catholicism," she says, "and I would like to see more femininity, more 'Mary' in spiritual approaches. Computers are masculine. I'd like to see inclusive, rather than exclusive, cooperative rather than competing. I hope the Valley triggers the beginning of a worldwide spiritual revolution."

Kamal, the software company curriculum developer, believes there will be strong growth in Islam in the Valley. "But it's not likely to be the people with the high standard of living," he says. "They're too caught up in their mansions and racing boats. Most converts will come from women, youth, African-Americans and Hispanics. The intelligent and the poor will enter Islam. And we'll need more Islamic educational structure to support them."

This observation touches on an important point. A key variable for the Valley is how the extraordinary increase in diversity plays out. No one doubts that the area's attractiveness and tolerance will cause it to continue as one of the most culturally and

---

I would like to say we'll see better understanding among people, but knowing people, we probably won't. The different cultures and different spiritual beliefs have the potential of leading to conflict. I hope understanding prevails. There's a trend toward smaller, less-organized churches, and an overall trend toward smaller spiritual groups. This is partly due to schism prevailing over reconciliation— a sad fact of human nature. I think we'll have a resurgence in secular humanism.

Eric, a Valley software company documentation manager

spiritually diverse locales in the world. This can happen in an atmosphere of separation or unity. Regarding matters of spirit, some think we're right on the cusp.

Stan, the technology consultant, doesn't think churches are responding well to the challenges of either youth or multiculturalism. "The group coming up now wants to be entertained," he observes. "They want multimedia approaches to functions and worship. On the other hand, I don't want to see established institutions chasing trends and abandoning tradition." He has put his finger squarely on the troubling paradox with which those institutions are wrestling: please some and you'll displease others. Or, perhaps the question is whether religious institutions should be *pleasing* people at all. Maybe that's not their mission.

Stella thinks it's possible that the area's extraordinary material affluence could blend into spiritual pursuits. She's senior public relations manager for a company which correctly read network architecture and Internet growth directions. From a standing start in the '80s, the company blew by the several billion dollar sales mark in the '90s, and made it look easy. No one knows for sure how many newly made "stock option millionaires" roam its corridors. But there's a bunch.

> *I'd bet that Bill Hewlett and David Packard had strong spiritual lives. I would not make that guess about many of today's CEOs. We seem to be in the age of "soulless technocrats," and I'm not sure there's a spiritual renaissance waiting around the corner. But people are unhappy with the decision to define their success by the titles they hold and the money they make. They're concerned about the fact that kids develop sex lives before spiritual lives. There's yearning, and there's a lot of individual searching going on.*
>
> Stuart, corporate general counsel for
> a Valley electronics company

"I look around the parking lot at work and I see $90,000 cars all over the place, and they don't all belong to the executives," she says. "One guy I work with sits in his cubicle and plays the options market. He lost $300K one day, then made $350K the next day. This is the kind of thing that makes me have to go to Idaho periodically and water my roots.

"But these young professionals often had some spiritual life in their youth, and now they're having children. Some of them seem to want to return to spirituality so their children will have it."

KATE

Kate counts herself among those who do not believe spiritual life in the Valley is on a roll. That hasn't stopped her from motoring briskly along on her own journey, however.

For 17 years, Kate worked for one of the Valley's largest defense electronics contractors, ending up as manager of a proposal group. The money was excellent. "But it wasn't conducive to a harmonious life," she recalls.

She focused on figuring out what else she'd like to do. Her program included a midcareer assessment workshop and an unpaid leave of absence to read, think, and cast about for meaningful work.

She found it. She's now the office administrator for a medium-sized Protestant church, making less than half her former salary. This experience has provided her with a fine study in contrast.

"My sense is that Silicon Valley is one of the strongest areas for exploring spirituality, but one of the worst areas for organized religions," she observes. "Alternatives are so abundant. Some people explore, but never find satisfaction. They talk about spirituality, but at a very naïve level. They're looking for something. They don't know what, but they know it's not organized religion.

"One of the most interesting aspects of this job has been dealing with the variety of people. The county inspector who comes out to inspect the church kitchen is a Muslim. I enjoy conversations with him where we swap ideas about our different beliefs. Lots of people call the church, and ask what we stand for and what we believe in. I've had ashes spend the day with me in the office before going to the columbarium.

"I was probably making too much money before. I could go anywhere I wanted, do everything I wanted. But it closed me off spiritually. It was too easy to write large checks to the church, but not do anything else. Now, the problem is at the other extreme. I'm barely making a living wage, and I've had to ask, 'Does God want me to lose my house? Is that where this is going?'

"But I can't forget the philosophical and spiritual tension I had when I was working in the defense business. I kept asking myself, 'Why are we putting billions into military hardware when people are dying from hunger and need our help?'

"When I left the company people told me privately they really admired what I was doing, but they would have too much fear of losing what they had attained to do it themselves.

"I hate to sound dismal, but I have bad vibes about where spiritual life is going in this area. I've been here 17 years, and most of the problems seem to have gotten worse. More and more, people

---

One of the most pronounced trends is the growth of experiential religion. People want to emphasize meaningful personal experience in their spirituality, not just doctrinal understanding.

Jesse, a Bay Area journalist

are getting sucked into the 'work is life, and there is no life outside of work' syndrome.

"I've reached a plateau. I'm not growing spiritually right now. But my spiritual life is really going to take off in the next few years. I'll have more time for meditating, for reading, for quiet. I might even sponge off my boyfriend for a while, and without all the distractions, I can see my spirituality getting deeper and richer."

GROWING SMALL

A trend which may have great impact is the movement to small groups for exploring and sharing spirituality. Many people are finding that small groups are much more open and inviting to individual needs, beliefs and search methods than larger groups tied to institutions. Small groups doing their own thing plays very well with Valley startup culture. We might see lots of them.

Marie, the former telecom marketing analyst, notices another benefit in small groups: people learn to talk about spirituality without getting "churchy," a style that can quickly turn people off.

Marty, the minister-turned-car-salesman, says, "The red meat of Valley spirituality will come from small groups, and the most successful churches will emphasize and support small group formation.

"Churches must adapt to the way we live. Sunday services are just not for everyone. We must develop an acceptance of people's absences, make sure people don't feel they have to be perfect to be there, and make sure they feel OK showing up whenever they want to. The Bible should be seen and taught as a love letter from God.

"I'd like to establish an informal, accessible urban ministry for everyone. Maybe the right way would be to just set up a table at Starbuck's. Then let everyone in the community know the minister is on duty and available whenever they want to quaff some java and talk about something."

Theresa, the human resources manager, sees the small group dynamic intersecting with the drive for increased community. "I know and meet many people who are becoming small church or community ministers in some way," she notes. "If you ask them what they do, they say, 'I'm a hair stylist during the day, but at night I work with teenage drug addicts.' When layoffs hit the Valley a couple of years ago and dollar contributions went down at United Way, time contributions went way up. People want to feel there's a reason, a purpose, a point to their being alive."

GHOST IN THE MACHINE

A wry thought: how long before we start seeing "Divinity in the Net," or "Spirituality in the Machine?"

> Eric, a Valley software company
> documentation manager

The answer to Eric's wry thought: as a theory, not long at all. At least one projection—a sweeping, staggering vision—closely ties human spiritual destiny to the distant descendants of the very technology being developed in the Valley today. It is a vision of the ultimate, intimate, eternal marriage of soul and silicon.

The vision is that of Dr. Frank Tipler, a physicist at Tulane University, in his book, *The Physics of Immortality—Modern Cosmology, God, and the Resurrection of the Dead.* Tipler's concept is that God, heaven, resurrection and eternal life are provable, demonstrable features of our physical universe. At the moment just before the end of time, everyone who ever lived will be resurrected into eternal life—*as a computer program emulation*. The emulation's operating system will include individually customized implementations of heaven.

Technical types might ask: how can life be eternal if it starts a fraction of a second before the end of time, and then, by definition, ends with the end of time? The answer is that time passage is subjective. Within the computer emulation, it will *seem* to the resurrected souls that they are living never-ending lives. (Technical *and* nontechnical types may not receive this message with joy. When I presented this concept at a recent "Science and Theology" seminar, the people there were absolutely horrified.)

Tipler's chronicle of how the computing power and related technology for this vision will be developed is far beyond the scope of this book, as is most of the associated theology. The time frame involved is a few quintillion years, so don't look for this in the next software release you buy at Fry's. But the striking point is that his eschatological monument, with its God of love and near-universal salvation, constructs a view of resurrection, eternal life, and heaven which seems similar to, and consistent with, that taught by many major religions. They have simply never gotten into the implementation details. Now someone has. The Valley's computer development work may now have to be considered in an entirely new light ...

IN THE MEANTIME

Olivia, the Southern transplant, thinks that meditation and spiritual retreat centers may find business booming, particularly for the 40-plus crowd. "With age comes wisdom, and part of wisdom is

---

It's not enough to just offer Sunday morning worship. Those days are gone. Our offerings must be as broad and diverse as the Silicon Valley community. I'd shift our service to Saturday night if it would help.

Audrey, a Silicon Valley minister

looking back over your life, and then at what's left, and trying to make sense of it. When sex, exercise, food and material things lose their appeal, what's left is the mind (and, presumably, the spirit). There will be a lot of 'what's it all about?' thinking." Who knows, perhaps the hot IPOs of 1999 will include retreat chains for spiritually revived techno-boomers.

Richard, the software company business development vice president, speculated along similar lines. "The '70s were the times of trying new things and changing everything, following the tumultuous '60s," he said. "In the '80s, everyone buckled down to careers and economic endeavors. Nineties people are trying to lead more balanced lives.

"We need more of a community feeling. This Valley has lots of ambivalence about distribution of wealth, but we're skeptical about the ability of government to solve much. We're starting to have doubts about the efficacy of large organizations or institutions.

"We believe in merit, but there's still compassion for the have-nots. We believe in enterprise, and performance-based awards. Some people never need help, no matter what; some people always need help, no matter what. And some people, if you can help them a little, it makes a huge difference. I think we're trying to find the Aristotelian 'Golden Mean.'

"We're doing what we can to manage tough tradeoffs in our lives. I hear more spiritual voices around, I see more spiritual books

Valley people seeking religious experiences want personal attention, a personal manifestation or revelation, from God. They reject "the Book." They tell me, "You're the minister, the Book is for you."

Roland, a Valley pastor

in stores. We're starting to ask what's important, and what's going to happen when we die. Spirituality will continue to emerge, but we also know we have to stay competitive. We have to provide for good family life, both economically and otherwise."

Some additional crystal-ball revelations people saw in the Valley's future:

❖ increased spirituality leading affluent Valley residents to do more for the disadvantaged as government downsizes

❖ growing acceptance of unconventional families

❖ increased recognition that spirituality involves a reconnection with nature

❖ an uptick in the influence of non-Western religions

At the personal level, the predominant theme might be summed up as a longing for the luxury of *time* to let spiritual exploration move far up life's priority list. Would enough affluence make this luxury widely available? Would it enable Silicon Valley to be the leader in the American Spiritual Revolution?

CLERGY PONDER THE FUTURE

Jerry, the rabbi of a large synagogue, thinks more people are making spirituality part of what they're looking for. "The question is: is it a fad, or is it lasting?" He also sees a good side to a trend

---

Shopping malls are the temples of our society. That's what people worship. I'd like to turn them all into real temples.

Jesse, a Bay Area journalist

toward less reverence for established religions. "One of the benefits of pop, idolatrous, pagan religious emergence is that some now feel it's easier to talk about religion."

Regarding the Valley's economic picture, Jerry says, "It's profoundly positive when people take risks and do entrepreneurial adventures. But telecommuting brings feelings of disconnection, which may spur more desire to pursue spirituality, meaning and community."

Justin, the pastor of a medium-sized Protestant church, sees population and consciousness change as the lead stories in the Valley's future. "Overwork will be seen as increasingly nonfulfilling," he projects. "There will be a renewal of what it means to be a parent.

"The biggest change will be in demographics, more than in belief sets. Older people are dying or moving to retirement communities, to be replaced by young families, and we need to find them and find ways to support them."

Michael, the Roman Catholic priest from Ireland by way of Kenya, has been struck by the impact of technology on the spiritual realm. "Everything is happening via e-mail," he says. "Multimedia will be used more and more for getting across the messages. Even our diocese has a Web page.

"I hope the technology will be used to address meaningful questions. For example, is the church fundamentally an institution, or fundamentally a community of believers?

The world would be so much more peaceful if people could integrate a spiritual practice into their workplace, or even their trips to the market. Maybe we have to go farther into the dark night first.

Victor, a Silicon Valley teacher

In discussing the spiritual future of Silicon Valley with clergy of various persuasions, I invited them to add another dimension. Leaving reality aside, if they could make one change in this area's culture to improve spiritual lives and values, what would it be?

Jerry: The change I would make would be that the cultural message the Valley puts out would send people more toward shared responsibility for each other, and less toward individual consumption.

Justin: An appreciation for quality over quantity. A definition of quality that says quality products *help people, they don't just make money. A definition of quality that says* quality people *contribute to the community, they don't just make money.*

Michael: My first thought about the one change I would make was to put up a catchy billboard. I'd like to see the leaders from all the different churches come together for a weekend and say, "We can't do this on our own, why can't we get together?" Maybe we ought to get some sales trainers in to show us how to get the message across, and get some of the big companies to fund the training. We need to show everyone, "We're working with you, not against you."

Erica: If I could make one change in Silicon Valley, everyone would truly take a Sabbath: a day of rest and reflection, a day to look back on the past week, and look forward to the coming week and how they want to shape it. We need to be more reflective on what we do.

Roland: My one change in the area's culture would be for people to be more committed, and more faithful to their commitments. If you make commitments, keep your promises. Too many people today nod commitment, then blow you off. Solid commitments and kept promises would improve spirituality, and honor the Supreme Being's design for us.

Ian: If I could make one change, it would be to create a strongly backed organization to bring all the diverse charitable and spiritual groups into meaningful dialogue and coordinated efforts. Every nonprofit nibbles at people's pockets. There's so many letters soliciting donations.

In my former parish in Taiwan, when it came to pledging, the congregation had no trouble giving everything they could to the church, and letting the church decide how to donate. Americans want to be involved in those decisions, in itemizing the expenditures and donations, and not just give the church carte blanche. Looking at how many solicitations people get, I can understand why. But there's not enough coming together of resources, of coordinating good work. Some really valuable efforts don't get funded, and I'd like to see us have a better way of channeling resources.

Rob: The one thing I would change would be our understanding of time. [Rock musician] Sting has gotten into Buddhism, and meditates two hours a day. He says when he does it, he has time. When he doesn't take the two hours a day, he has no time. We have to break the perception that there's not enough time, that we must always do more, that everything must be faster.

"I see growth in smaller communities of prayer and Scripture study, and I think the teachings will have more meaning in smaller groups. We'll see increased use of specialized retreats for affinity groups: mother-daughter retreats, substance-abuser retreats, businessperson retreats. There seems to be a thirst for God, and maybe more evangelization is in the cards. Cross-pollination and reaching across church boundaries might happen more. We Catholics can learn a lot from, say, the zeal of the Baptists."

Aaron's vision, from his position as rabbi of a small synagogue, echoes the cross-boundary theme. "I'd love to hire 10 more rabbis and disperse them through the area," he says. "But what I really care about is how many people are being served, not where they're being served. I'd like to see Valley spiritual leaders focus less on filling their individual houses of worship, and more on just reaching people. Why do we care where they go, as long as they go?"

Erica, pastor of a small Protestant congregation, sees Christian practice in the area opening up, being more comfortable with the idea that "… there are many pathways to God, and ours is one. Maybe we're starting to understand that God works *through us*, rather than coming down as lightning bolts. There's a sense that the inclusiveness of God's spirit is at work in the land. But there's also a rise in the more fundamentalist churches, because changes

We'll come to a point where people will move inward. This may manifest itself through churches, retreats, Heaven's Gate groups, Deep Space Nine groups, Hale-Bopp comet groups, more labyrinth walking, spiritual song and dance, or all of the above. You can't process the overwhelming amount of information and complexity out there. We'll need simple things.

Victor, a Silicon Valley teacher

and new ideas can make people uncomfortable, and sometimes change causes backlash."

Roland, pastor in a large Protestant congregation, has seen significant change in the 12 years he's been in his current job. "When I first started as a minister in this area," he remembered with a chuckle, "and told people what I did for a living, they often said things like, 'My goodness! What about money? What about achievement? What about success?' Even recently, I told a woman at my son's Little League game that I'm a minister and she said, 'Really! They actually pay you for that? I didn't know they did that anymore!'

"But I think spirituality in this area is becoming more accepted, as long as you don't try to force beliefs down anyone's throat. It used to be that when I started to talk about religion to someone I didn't know well, the response was along the lines of 'get out of my face.' Now I'm more likely to hear, 'You have some spiritual beliefs? That's cool.'

"I think the Valley will get more spiritual dimension over the next few years, but a conflict is coming. Some people won't be comfortable with the hang-loose, anything-goes brand of spirituality, and we might have some fundamentalist backlash. But it's easier for me to walk through the community than it used to be."

IAN

Ian was born in Singapore, and began his career as a Protestant minister in Taiwan. He's taken on a role which puts him front and center in an effort to meet the Valley's increasing need for diverse, multicultural spiritual offerings.

Ian moved to the San Francisco Bay Area five years ago, motivated largely by issues relating to his children's upcoming college careers. "In the U.S.," he points out, "higher education makes coaching available: English as a second language, all the help you need. Higher education in Singapore is harsh. They screen. If you don't do well, you're out."

Initially, he tried the "astronaut" approach. His wife and children relocated to the United States, while he continued his ministry in Taiwan, flying over for visits whenever he could: a commute that would make even the most hardened Bay Area freeway trekker blanch. He hung in for two years. His Taiwan parish had made him a "fat offer" to stay. But eventually he got to a point where he couldn't stand the separation. A Bay Area work opportunity arose, and he took it.

Through this period of decision and change, his prayer was, "… for God to tell me that my time in Taiwan was ended; that my mission there was over." I asked him if he had heard that. "More yes than no," he responded, "but there's still some pain."

Ian's new job was to function as "Chinese missioner," working for his church's regional organization. The post was created in recognition of the growing size and importance of the Chinese population in the Bay Area, and the need to have available bilingual, bicultural spiritual support. This was considered to be particularly important for recent immigrants.

In 1993, the head of the church's regional body asked Ian and a parish in the heart of Silicon Valley to partner on a new project: formation of a Mandarin-speaking congregation to be affiliated with the parish. By Silicon Valley standards, this particular church is a time-hallowed institution, over 80 years old. Institutions that

> *I don't find it wrong or offensive that there are spiritual absolutes. In fact, it's appealing.*
>
> Frank, a Valley bank executive

old can get conservative and often have doubts about change. No one was sure how this was going to work.

"I was willing to take it on as an experiment," Ian recalls, "and I don't like experiments to fail." He felt an affinity for the vision of a multicultural congregation. It offered him a chance to creatively address an important issue. "Churches lag society," he observes. "They pick up what society is doing later, and try to make sense out of it. But they don't lead. I felt the church should take a lead position in working toward racial harmony, and be an example to society, a living witness where people come together."

In addition to his Silicon Valley work, Ian is building and ministering to two other Mandarin-speaking congregation-within-congregations in the Bay Area. It has not been an easy task, even excluding the insane number of miles he drives each week. "You have to learn to temper the vision with the realities," he says. (I think that's a call for patience.) "There are many models of churches. In Silicon Valley, we're working to have the two congregations close together. In east Contra Costa County, there's complete separation from the Caucasian congregation. At our third location, I hope we can eventually bring the Mandarin-speaking congregation fully into the parish. Sometimes I feel there's no real understanding between the Caucasian and Chinese constituents, but we're slowly moving and learning together.

"In the '70s and '80s, churches may have been more important to the Chinese community. They were places to find help and identity. It was almost a 'golden age of conversion.'

> *I'd wipe out all the fundamentalists—Christian, Jewish or Islamic—who say there's only one right way to do it and everyone else is wrong.*
>
> Debra, a Valley minister

"But the Chinese community has broadened enormously, and there are many different parts of the community. Terminology which is sometimes used within the community to describe people's background is the '1.0 generation' for those born and raised elsewhere; the '1.5 generation' for those born elsewhere but raised here; and the '2.0' generation for those born and raised here. Each of these groups has its own needs."

We then talked about some of Ian's observations about his bicultural world. "There's a difference in the way Americans and Chinese see spiritual leaders," he pointed out. "If you meet an American and say you're a priest or minister, the image he has is mostly of you, of a person in a particular profession, which just happens to be religion. But to Chinese, the image of a Buddhist or Taoist or Christian priest is truly that of a holy man.

"Chinese Christians tend to not be philosophical about who and what God is. More experiential. Confucianism is a deep humanism, and many Chinese are humanists. So are many Christians, whether they realize it or not. You can be both deeply humanist and deeply spiritual.

"Many Chinese believe in God but not in a religion. In this area, I see the Chinese community turning more toward a religion of the heart than a religion of institution."

I asked him to comment on his community's vision of the human soul. "The Chinese tend to see a dualistic element in the soul," he offered. "It's a continuity of the ego. There's lots of stories in Chinese culture about souls, dreams and spirits. All people

---

It's not politically correct to be a conservative evangelical in this area, but some evangelicals might like that.

Jesse, a Bay Area journalist

have souls, but Buddhists, for example, believe that enlightened souls go on a different path from the unenlightened.

"The Chinese culture has always been able to be very dichotomous between secular and spiritual issues. Belief in spirits and souls is so ingrained that technology and modern developments don't affect their spiritual beliefs. But the Western mind will reorganize beliefs around new parameters such as technology."

Finally, I asked him where he thought our path was leading us. "As a Christian in Chinese culture," he said, "you always face a test of faith. In the American culture, it's more an exercise in reinterpretation. Silicon Valley will stay very pluralistic because of the diversity of the culture. I don't think the different spiritual traditions and searchers will come together."

ROB

Rob is pastor of one of the most affluent Protestant congregations in the Valley. Something one of his parishioners told him shortly after he joined this church stuck with him: "The gods of this area are excellence, creativity, and connections."

The financial solidity of his church is no illusion. In the last five years, they have raised $3 million for their building fund. (Rob says he has to continually remind himself it's for God's work.) However, a dilemma he sees in Valley culture is what he calls "the illusion of control": if you have enough money, and/or enough power, you're in control of your environment and destiny. A very Valley perspective. "It's smoke," he says. "And those very things

> If every church would adopt and find ways to support an at-risk school, we would change the future.
>
> Pat, a Valley pastor

are what can push you away from your community. But it can be seductive to be among the movers and shakers.

"One of my parishioners just sold his company, and he's gonna be rich. He's 38. He wants counseling on how to be responsible with his wealth. That's refreshing. The usual response to this situation is a new house and a new Ferrari. After an IPO, another one of our locals bought three new cars.

"But despite the distractions of money, the Silicon Valley world view of cooperation, visioning, and comfort with change could end up making us world leaders in spirituality. People here do have reverence and a sense of mystery, although it's usually the mystery of designing complex products. People here also have energy and passion!

"I'd like our church to be a spiritual resource for all of Silicon Valley. A safe place where people can be listened to, not judged. Where mystery is seen as reality. There's the potential for a new wave of spirituality throughout the country, and it just might start right here. I'd like to be a part of that."

A new wave of spirituality.

If it comes, its package might include entrepreneurial creativity; cross-cultural perspective; willingness to take risks; and new models of personal involvement. Fatima's journey seems destined to include all these elements.

FATIMA

Fatima has come full circle. She left her spiritual path—forcefully. Now she's back on it—forcefully.

Born in Egypt, her parents moved to the United States when she was 7. "My father was a pro-Western, anti-Socialist psychiatrist," she recalls, "and very critical of [then-Egyptian ruler] Nasser. We were 'escorted' out of the country."

Fatima's Turkish grandmother was a devout Muslim, but her parents practiced no religion. She attended a Catholic girls' school in Egypt. After moving to America, she became increasingly conscious of restrictions on women in her culture.

"I couldn't drink, couldn't make dates, couldn't stay out late," she says. "My mother interpreted Islam and the Koran in a very dogmatic way. I ran away from being Egyptian, being Arab, being Muslim. I married an Episcopalian who converted to Islam, and my family rejected him. I remember him saying, 'If this is the God you're worshipping, it's not the God I want to worship. Not if He separates people in love just because they're not born into the same culture.'

"I defied Islam. I ate pork and clam chowder, and drank alcohol. My parents disinherited me. My marriage didn't last."

In contrast to the tumult in her spiritual and personal life, Fatima's professional life was a fast track. She got a job as a sales clerk, worked her way up to store manager, jump-shifted to insurance industry marketing analyst, then became a manager with an equity interest in a small telecommunications firm. "I was materially successful, but I felt a vacuum," she recalls. "I woke up to the fact that there was no God in me. That feeling grew for three years. I got scared."

If I could make one change, everyone would work eight minutes from their house.

Sam, a Valley pastor

She was also troubled by what she saw at her company. "Each executive had his own territory and succeeded at the expense of someone else. For someone to win, someone had to lose. I saw corruption. I saw sexual harassment. The higher up you go the more you have to satisfy your boss, and the less personal power you really have. I was losing my spirit—becoming a robot.

"I remember going into the lunchroom one day, and everyone there looked dead. The life had been sucked out of them.

"I started reading a lot of spiritual stuff: New Age, the Bible, the Koran, the Torah. I went to synagogue. I went to Catholic church. But I felt a separation between the clergy and the people. It was as if God was the clergy's, not ours. We were an audience, just observing. I couldn't feel a connection with God."

Then she completed her circle. "As I read the Koran, I started to feel it was tying everything together. God was talking to me directly. It was reflecting my heart. It also affirmed my views about the need to fight corruption and lack of justice in society. I could relate to the trials of the prophets.

"One day I woke up and started crying. I cried for half the day. Then I prayed for the other half. Then I decided to start doing volunteer work in the Islamic community.

"All my friends at the time were practicing Jews and Christians. I was totally corporate. I never wore the traditional Muslim garb. I had some savings. I did volunteer work, and lived on my savings, and had a blast. I got to see how many subcultures we have here in America. Just in this area, there are about 35 Islamic centers, each with its own function and character. I decided to take my corporate skills and apply them to supporting this community."

Fatima was instrumental in founding an organization which has become a focal point for Valley Muslims. Her group provides organization, coordination and communication tools for the

Islamic community. She is a spokesperson and an activist. "I used to make a $100,000 a year," she says. "Now I make $7,000. I don't buy clothes anymore. But I have found God."

The God she has found is a companion: always present. Although she uses the pronoun "Him" when she thinks of God, she points out that in Islam, God is not male, but genderless.

Fatima's path forward is heavily influenced by what attracted her when she finished her circle and revisited the Koran: justice; clearly defined right and wrong; the forbidding of evil; and the need to fight against evil. She has dealt herself completely into the fray. "You have to have the community to practice Islam," she says. "There are too many temptations to be able to fight them alone.

"When I was in the corporate world my idea of success was being smarter than others, more cunning. My mother still says, 'It's great that she's an activist; how much does she make?' The corporate world trains you for 'me-me-me.' Now the competition I'm trying to beat out is evil, not other humans.

"What I'm trying to accomplish with our organization is to influence society toward Islamic ideas of social justice, which should also be appealing to Christians and Jews. There's tension between the Muslim community and other faiths, and we want to educate, be known, be respected. We're working to obtain equal treatment and coverage in the media. And we'll exemplify Islam in the best way possible. Before we can do justice to the rest of the world, we need to do justice to ourselves.

Churches must create an alternative to Sunday morning worship. All the two-career households do chores and projects on Saturday. Sunday is their only day of rest. Most of them are too tired to make love, much less go to church.

Rochelle, CEO of a Valley counseling group

"I want to get us involved in welfare issues, maybe help with implementation of the new programs, and be a service to the poor and the needy. I can see myself ending up in prison someday, standing up for what is right. I don't think you can make change without going up against major forces. But it's not the people we're up against. It's the devil.

"We've gotten involved in coalitions when events require Muslim issues to be jointly addressed. We've also participated in presenting diversity training programs. Sometimes the people taking the training don't like it, and they ask, 'Why can't you guys just fit in?' My response is, 'What is it to be an American?'

"But I never permit myself to think of us as victims. If I ever perceive myself as a victim, then I have a problem. Back in school I hated my name because kids made fun of it and teachers didn't know how to pronounce it. That's over. You can't be a practicing worshiper of God and be a victim."

DUANE

Duane is a Silicon Valley journalist whose writing focus is issues of spirit and philosophy. He's an East Coast transplant, and enjoys covering the Valley's spiritual scene. "It's not like writing about transportation," he says. "Writing about religion opens me up, makes me reflect on life."

Duane's family is Jewish, and he grew up going to a Reform synagogue. "I felt it had an antiseptic quality," he recalls, "but I loved the communal aspect, the 'lifted-up' spirits, and the emotional connectedness and richness."

As many do, Duane fell away from his religion in early adulthood. Music became the most prominent spiritual element in his life. Now he's come most of the way back: religion and music synergistically coexist as inspirations for his spirit. "I'm consciously

Jewish," he says. "I'm a respectful Jew, but not always an observant Jew."

His professional pursuits give Duane the opportunity to probe and profile the full gamut of Valley spirituality. I asked for his observations on the area's spiritual environment and future directions.

"Silicon Valley is everything from conservative Christian churches to computer company pagans," he responded. "There's a major interfaith thrust, and there's a conservative backlash against that thrust. People come here and feel empowered to pursue whatever path they want. The area seems to enable that.

"A lot of denomination-shopping happens. It's like the age of free agency in religion. There seems to be growth happening at both ends of the style spectrum. At one end, contemplative practices are becoming important to more and more people: small groups and emphasis on quiet discussion. At the other end, there's the enormous charismatic thing. Tremendous bonding occurs during charismatic Christian services and events. There's an amazing sense of community that cuts across races and classes in conservative Christian functions. The liberals would be jealous if they knew about it!

"There's a spawning of new churches and denominations. Some of them are very conscious of the need to be 'marketing-oriented.' Many of them are most assuredly not into cross-pollination with others, and have their guard up. But they can be good neighbors with each other even if the tendency is for people to stick with their own.

I'd be happy if we could just get the Y to stop scheduling swim classes on Sunday.

Audrey, a Silicon Valley minister

"Many people here return to the fold of religion because they don't want their children embracing the valueless, materialistic, 'anything goes' California culture that can suck them in. Some people are desperate to protect their kids from the garbage, and religion can be that protection. Other people turn to religion because driving over the mountain to work every day at 5 AM with their lights on and all the nuts on the road is just wearing them out. Or someone they know dies, and they start to ask, 'Why are we alive?'

"In some ways, we're without community here, in the wide open spaces.

"If I could make one change to improve the area's spiritual values, I'd have us back off from a work ethic that's gone bananas. Your kids never see you, you never see your spouse, and you're escaping into a world that doesn't include the people most important to you. There's so much data and information available that no one can remember anything. There's too much negative, jarring, frightening stuff. The complete immersion in e-culture is not good. People should turn off their TVs, get off the Internet, slow down, and get back to other people."

Everyone figures it out sooner or later, on one side of the grave or the other. I'm sometimes concerned about people with no spiritual resources, but that's more compassionate worry than existential worry. No one is going to miss the bus. Some might even come to church.

Anita, a Valley minister

THE PATH FORWARD

So, what's it to be?

Will the technology chase and the cyberculture be crippling blows to the spirit, or the source of new inspiration? Will the invasion of massively powerful computers into the nooks and crannies of life be the death knell of faith, or the door to renewal? Will the manic pursuit of technological mastery and market share mix with new-wave, leading-edge sociodynamics and extraordinary economic success to produce spiritual nihilism, or spiritual nirvana?

Call me a cockeyed optimist if you will. I find myself coming down on the side that says this area will blaze new trails to spiritual understanding and fulfillment. The partnership of soul and silicon may be uneasy, suspicious, stormy, and thoroughly counterintuitive. But I believe the group of intrepid pioneers who have chosen to call this place home will find a way to make the marriage work, and show others how it's done.

Many of the people I've encountered in writing this book find themselves in the "dark wood where the straight way [is] lost" of Dante's *Divine Comedy*. But they are bringing to the age-old questions shared by all humankind the same drive, curiosity, intellectual firepower, creativity and energy that they have used to transform the world in the past 20 years.

And who knows? Maybe Tipler is right. Maybe our road to eternal life will indeed happen via some sort of cosmic computer emulation. If it does happen, it's a good bet that the technology involved will trace its soul-preserving origins to foundations laid on a legendary, long-vanished planet, by amusingly primitive, short-lived, easily distracted biological beings, in a hallowed, ancient enclave called Silicon Valley.

Epilogue

The idea for this book popped into mind out of nowhere as I was driving down Foothill Expressway from Palo Alto to Sunnyvale at the usual 5 miles per hour over the speed limit. I was resisting the usual temptation to make it 15.

At one time, undertaking a project like this would have been about as likely as my running a three-minute mile. Most of my life was lived without spiritual content. My parents practiced no religion. Neither did their friends. Neither did my friends. I went through some exploration in my early 20s and found nothing calling, or even interesting. I placed the topic in the file-and-forget pile. Many years later, two conversations plucked it back out.

The first conversation was with my long-time girlfriend. We had been together seven years. Our many compatibilities included a comfortable, shared lack of interest in matters of the spirit—or so I thought. Therefore, I was both surprised and irritated when we sat down for dinner on a peaceful Saturday night and, after I had made play with the wine and the glasses, she asked, "Do you ever think about your spiritual life?"

We were both hard-working, hard-charging Valley technology company professionals, putting in routine 60-hour weeks. By the time Saturday night rolled around, we were drained. It was a house rule that Saturday dinner discussion topics should never be weightier than the latest *Doonesbury* episode. Her question violated the rule. I also felt that after seven years she knew, or should have known, that the answer was not just "No," but "*Hell* no." I was not pleased.

I grunted a monosyllabic negative. The Saturday mood had been soured. She proceeded to make it worse by launching into substantial detail about the sudden resurgence she felt in her own spiritual life. I did not like the sound of this at all. It seemed out of place, and a violation of my contract, that this brand of ambush was happening to me in Silicon Valley. I gloomily drank cabernet and wondered what was going on.

The second conversation took place not long after the first. On our way to a software expo in Chicago, a business colleague told me about some dreadful things going on in his personal life, and the way his faith was helping him to cope. It was a wonderfully articulate expression of the interleaving of a person's life with his spirituality. I remember having the curious feeling that our intellectual centers were being bypassed, that his heart was talking directly to my heart.

These two conversations started what we call in the computer biz a "background process." It chugged away without my giving it the slightest conscious encouragement or participation. Eventually, it surfaced and expressed itself in a form I could recognize: it asked for data.

I gathered data from reading, from people, from observation, from reflection. I attended a few worship services. I took an "inquirer's" class. The process was leisurely. I had gone over 40 years without this spiritual stuff. No need to rush now.

It took five years for the background process to chomp on the data stream, complete its processing, come to a conclusion and report back. And the conclusion was that a faith had been born.

It seemed improbable. As a matter of fact, it was a little identity-threatening. I knew myself well. And what I had always known was that I was a person who did not have spiritual beliefs. But probability and identity were irrelevant issues, glitches to be worked out. The fact of faith superseded them.

In 1989, at age 46, I was baptized, and am now a member of the Episcopal Church. My burgeoning belief was not driven by any crisis, tragedy, incipient need, internal angst, external events or sudden revelation. It was the result of a gradual process as real as my feet, but more difficult to grasp. I really can't say I understand it yet.

In 1993, I married the girlfriend who started the background process. By that time, as those who are arithmetically quick may have calculated, we had been together for 16 years. No need to rush. I have forgiven her for the stick of dynamite she added to the menu on that long-ago Saturday night dinner. And I have thanked her.

In 1995, a variety of circumstances came together to make a midlife career change inviting and feasible. I had previously written a book on computers for the nontechnical, and enjoyed it. That memory teamed up with the urge to do something different, and the recent start of my spiritual path, to give birth to this book. Why conception happened on Foothill Expressway is still a mystery.

Let me conclude by summarizing what my personal reaction was after spending almost two years writing this book, and by passing on one of the key messages I heard from the people I interviewed.

This project gave me a sense of belonging to an entirely different faith community from that represented by my church. It's not *instead of* my church; it's *in addition to*. It's the community of those who have taken widely diverse paths and perhaps selected completely different approaches to their faith. But it's a community connected by the search for truth, for righteousness, for God (however defined), and for meaningful life in a culture where the rules are new, and change before anyone can write them down.

To a great degree, clergy and spiritual leaders in Silicon Valley are aware of, and comfortable with, this "changing rules" dynamic. During interviews with them, I received a few answers which might be considered "by the book." But the vast majority of the discussions centered on the search for truth, even if the search led to places hostile to their long-established doctrines. I actually detected more than *comfort* with the free-spirited, iconoclastic, Silicon Valley mavericks among whom these people work and minister: I sensed *enjoyment* of the challenge. The doors were open, the welcome mats out.

Perhaps the single predominant theme individuals communicated about themselves in this hectic environment is captured by a term used by members of the Baha'i faith: a desire for *deepening*. In many conversations I sensed a wish, a yen, a plan, a determination that a time would arrive when spiritual pursuit, philosophical commitment, inner knowledge, and food for the soul would move far, far up the priority list. For some, it might await financial security or the fulfillment of career objectives. For others, the gating item might be the successful completion of child rearing. But for many people, the ultimate goal—in a sense the ultimate *luxury*—is to someday, some way, have the time and space to dive deep, and fully explore their hearts and souls, the meaning of their existence, and their relationship with their God. It is my profound hope that every one of them achieves this objective.

The author welcomes your comments about this book. You may e-mail him at CAGoldman@aol.com, or write to the publisher:

Rising Star Press
P.O. Box BB
Los Altos, CA 94023
Fax 650/968-2658
e-mail: HiStar@aol.com
website: http://members.aol.com/HiStar/index.htm

References and Suggested Reading

Armstrong, Karen. *A History of God: The 4,000 Year Quest of Judaism, Christianity and Islam,* New York: Alfred A. Knopf, 1994

Bellah, Robert N. et al. *Habits of the Heart—Individualism and Commitment in American Life,* Berkeley: University of California Press, 1985

Brady, Joan. *God on A Harley—A Spiritual Fable,* New York: Pocket Books Division of Simon and Schuster, Inc., 1995

Carter, Stephen L. *The Culture of Disbelief: How American Law and Politics Trivialize Religious Devotion,* New York: Anchor Books, 1994 (originally published: New York: Basic Books, 1993)

Cramer, Kathryn D. *Roads Home—Seven Pathways to Midlife Wisdom,* New York: William Morrow and Company, Inc. 1995

Cringely, Robert X. *Accidental Empires—How The Boys of Silicon Valley Make Their Millions, Battle Foreign Competition, and Still Can't Get A Date,* New York: Addison-Wesley Publishing Company, 1992

Frankl, Victor E. *Man's Search for Meaning*, New York: Washington Square Press, 1984

Friedman, Richard Elliott. *The Disappearance of God*, New York: Little Brown and Company, 1995

Hawking, Stephen W. *Black Holes and Baby Universes and Other Essays,* New York: Bantam Books, 1993

Kaplan, Jerry. *Startup—A Silicon Valley Adventure*, New York: Houghton Mifflin Company, 1995

Keen, Sam. *Hymns To An Unknown God*, New York: Bantam Books, 1994

LeGuin, Ursula K. *The Left Hand of Darkness*, New York: Walker and Company, 1969

Norris, Kathleen. *The Cloister Walk*, New York: Riverhead Books, 1996

Peck, Scott M., M.D. *The Road Less Traveled and Beyond—Spiritual Growth in an Age of Anxiety,* New York: Simon & Schuster, 1997

Saltzman, Amy. *Downshifting—Reinventing Success on a Slower Track*, New York: HarperCollins Publishers, 1991

Schwartz, Tony. *What Really Matters—Searching for Wisdom in America*, New York: Bantam Books, 1995

Sheehy, Gail. *New Passages*, New York: Random House, Inc., 1995

Talbott, Stephen L. *The Future Does Not Compute: Transcending the Machines in Our Midst*, Sebastopol, CA: O'Reilly & Associates, Inc., 1995

Tipler, Frank J., Ph.D. *The Physics of Immortality—Modern Cosmology, God, and the Resurrection of the Dead*, New York: Doubleday, 1994

Wakefield, Dan. *Returning—A Spiritual Journey*, New York: Doubleday, 1988

Whyte, David. *The Heart Aroused—Poetry and the Preservation of the Soul in Corporate America*, New York: Doubleday, 1994

Winslow, Ward, Editor: *The Making of Silicon Valley—A One Hundred Year Renaissance,* Palo Alto: Santa Clara Valley Historical Association, 1995

Wolf, Fred Alan, Ph.D. *The Spiritual Universe—How Quantum Physics Proves the Existence of the Soul*, New York: Simon & Schuster, 1996

Unpublished lecture notes for *Putting It All Together: Seven Patterns for Relating Science and Christian Faith,* a 1996 seminar series led by Richard H. Bube, Professor Emeritus of Materials Science and Electrical Engineering, Stanford University

Praise for *I, Saul*

"Jerry Jenkins is a masterful storyteller. Only Jerry can transport readers from modern-day Texas to the early days of Christianity, breathing new life into familiar biblical characters. In *I, Saul* Jerry has crafted an epic thriller that left me on the edge of my seat hollering, 'Sweet mercy!'"

—Todd Starnes

Fox News

"A terrific read with great pacing and characters that kept me turning the pages. The ending choked me up. Just think, someday we get to meet Paul, along with the other saints, gathering before the Lord to celebrate."

—Francine Rivers

Best-selling novelist

"What a great read! I took *I, Saul* to the beach planning to enjoy it over our two-week vacation. But the book only lasted a few days! I couldn't put it down! An inspirational, insightful, page-turning thriller! I have read many of Jerry Jenkins' books, but this one is his best!"

—Anne Graham Lotz

Author of *Wounded by God's People*

"A master storyteller, Jerry Jenkins has taken up the greatest conversion story of all time— the Apostle Paul's. In *I, Saul*, we see the biblical outline faithfully followed with detail that grips the heart afresh about what a life totally dedicated to Jesus Christ looks like."

—Jack Graham

Pastor, Prestonwood Baptist Church, Dallas

"A stirring fiction founded upon the facts of scripture. Jerry Jenkins brings to life one of history's greatest men: the Apostle Paul, whose life inspires us to stand and suffer for our Savior, Jesus Christ."

—Mark Driscoll

Founder and Preaching Pastor, Mars Hill Church, Seattle

"Everything I like about a great novel is here: danger, political intrigue, and cultural detail. If you enjoy mystery and history, *I, Saul* is a must read!"

—Joni Eareckson Tada

Joni and Friends International Disability Center

"*I, Saul* has everything a great thriller needs: page-turning action, intrigue, and mounting suspense, plot twists that really work and, above all, characters worth caring about. A brilliant concept and a great read."

—Liz Curtis Higgs

New York Times best-selling author of *Mine Is the Night*

"When master word-weaver Jerry Jenkins joins forces with Bible expositor extraordinaire James MacDonald, you'd better make way for something powerful!"

—Greg Laurie

Pastor, Harvest Ministries

"*I, Saul* combines the historical with the contemporary, and the outcome is compulsive reading. Vintage Jerry Jenkins!"

—Chris Fabry

Novelist and host of *Chris Fabry Live!*

"*I, Saul* is a must read book! These two parallel stories are brilliant and will leave you wanting more! I can't wait for the next one."

—Ray Bentley

Senior Pastor, Maranatha Chapel, San Diego

"Rare is the work that treats you to an equal dose of biblical insight and modern drama. But Jenkins is a rare author. Dive in, but be forewarned: you won't be able to set it aside."

—J. Paul Nyquist, Ph.D.

President, Moody Bible Institute

"*I, Saul* is plausible fiction, astute reflection, and a flat-out good read."

—Wallace Alcorn, Ph.D.

Biblical scholar and author

"Jerry Jenkins has compressed his vast talents as a biblical researcher, biographer, mystery writer, and thrill master in *I, Saul*. Hang on, friends—it's all in one breathless package!"

—Dr. Dennis E. Hensley

Director of the Professional Writing Program, Taylor University

"*I, Saul* is one of the finest books I have ever read. I laughed. I cried. And, yes, I found myself wanting to learn even more of the life of the Apostle Paul."

—Jim Pryor

westofthemind.blogspot.com

"*I, Saul* is one of those best of stories that invites you to see and live into your own future, no matter your past. I could not put this one down!"

—Wes Roberts

Leadership Mentor/Organizational Designer, Leadership Design Group

"A masterpiece. If you liked the Left Behind series, then you'll love *I, Saul*. I think it's Jerry's best."

—Sammy Tippit

International evangelist and author

"Jenkins blends reality with fantasy without compromising the biblical story. *I, Saul* captures the spirit of a man who has impacted great segments of humanity for nearly 2,000 years!"

—Dr. Gene A. Getz

Professor, pastor, author

"One of the best novels I have ever read! Jerry is a mastermind of intrigue, mystery, and historical facts. If you only read one book this year, I strongly recommend *I, Saul*."

—Paul R. Condry

President, Regional Radio Sports Network

"I enjoyed *I, Saul* more than anything I've read in a long time. Full of mystery, action, and romance, it's an utterly gripping novel and a vivid reminder of how God chooses unlikely men and women to accomplish His noble purposes. A great book!"

—Bill Armstrong

Colorado Christian University president and former U.S. Senator

"A novel that goes from mystery to history!"

—Joyce Oglesby

Host, *Just Ask Joyce*

"Jerry Jenkins has done a great job surmising the kind of life experiences that may have shaped this man who affirmed brutal murder in the name of a loving God. *I, Saul* unfolds Saul's complex life and personality against the backdrop of a modern suspense story with its own twists and complexities."

—Dr. Brent Saathoff

Pastor, Bandera Road City Church, San Antonio

"Jerry Jenkins' new novel, *I, Saul*, is truly the best of both worlds—an exciting contemporary spy thriller combined with a rich exploration of the Apostle Paul."

—Sanne McCarthy

Theatre director, Colorado Christian University

JERRY B. JENKINS

I, Saul

A NOVEL

with

JAMES S. MacDONALD

WORTHY
PUBLISHING

Copyright © 2013 by Jerry B. Jenkins and James S. MacDonald

Published by Worthy Publishing, a division of Worthy Media, Inc., 134 Franklin Road, Suite 200, Brentwood, Tennessee 37027.

HELPING PEOPLE EXPERIENCE THE HEART OF GOD

eBook available wherever digital books are sold.

Audio distributed through Brilliance Audio; visit brillianceaudio.com

Library of Congress Cataloging-in-Publication Data

Jenkins, Jerry B.
  I, Saul : a novel / Jerry B. Jenkins ; with James S. MacDonald.
        pages cm
  ISBN 978-1-61795-006-3 (hard cover)
  1. Paul, the Apostle, Saint--Fiction. 2. Bible—History of Biblical events—Fiction. 3. Apostles--Fiction. 4. Christian fiction. 5. Biographical fiction. I. MacDonald, James S. II. Title.
  PS3560.E485I4 2013
  813'.54--dc23
                              2013011238

For foreign and subsidiary rights, contact Riggins International Rights Services, Inc.; rigginsrights.com

ISBN: 978-1-61795-006-3 (hardcover w/ jacket)
ISBN: 978-1-61795-194-7 (international edition)
ISBN: 978-1-61795-339-2 (trade paper)

Cover design: Kirk DouPonce, DogEared Design
Interior typesetting: Susan Browne Design

Printed in the United States of America

14 15 16 17 18 VPI 8 7 6 5 4 3 2 1

To my brothers

Jim, Jeoff, and Jay

Torn

TEXAS

WEDNESDAY, MAY 7

"call now. desper8."

The text appeared on Dr. Augie Knox's phone at 8:55 a.m., seconds before he was to turn it off—protocol for profs entering a classroom at Arlington Theological Seminary.

Augie could have fired off a "give me a minute," but the message was not signed and the sending number matched nothing in his contacts. The prefix 011-39-06 meant Rome. He'd traveled extensively in his thirty-eight years and enjoyed many visits to the Eternal City, but such a text could easily portend one of those I've-been-mugged-and-need-money scams. Whatever this was could wait until he got the Systematic Theology final exam started and could step into the hall with his phone.

Augie had long been fascinated by his students' nervous chatter before final exams. One announced, "I looked you up in *Who's Who*, Doc, and I know your full name."

"Congratulations for discovering something you could have found in your student handbook four years ago."

"No! That just says Dr. Augustine A. Knox! I found out what the *A* stands for."

"Good for you. Now, a few instructions . . ."

"*Aquinas!* Augustine Aquinas Knox! Man, what other career choice did you have?"

"Thank you for revealing the thorn in my flesh. If you must know, that moniker was my father's idea." Augie mimicked his dad's monotone basso. "'Names are important. They can determine a life's course.'"

Many students chuckled, having sat under the elder Dr. Knox before he fell ill the year before.

"It also says you were adopted. Sorry, but it's published."

"No secret," Augie said.

Another hand shot up. "Was that a hint about the exam? Will we be speculating on Paul's thorn in the flesh?"

"He's only mentioned that mystery every class," another said.

Augie held up a hand. "I trust you're all prepared for any eventuality."

"So, what's your dad's name?"

"Ed!" someone called out. "Everybody knows that."

"Look it up," Augie said. "You may find it revealing."

With blue books distributed, Augie slipped out and turned on his phone. The plea from Rome had already dropped to third on his message list. At the top was a voice mail from Dr. Moore, who had been filling in as acting department chair since Augie's father had been hospitalized with a stroke.

Augie would have checked that one first, but next was a voice mail from Sofia Trikoupis, his heart. It was eight hours later in Athens, after five in the afternoon. "Call me at the end of your day," her message said. "I'll wait up." It would be midnight her time by then, but she apparently needed his undivided attention. That would bug him all day. How he longed for them to be together.

His phone vibrated. Rome again. "urgent. call now, pls!"

Augie pressed his lips together, thumbing in, "who's this?"

"trust me. begging."

"not w/out knowing who u r."

Augie waited more than a minute for a response, then snorted. *As I figured.* But as he headed back into the classroom, his phone buzzed again.

"zionist."

Augie stopped, heat rising in his neck. He quickly tapped in, "90 minutes OK?"

"now! critical."

Few people had been more important in Augie's life than Roger Michaels, the diminutive fifty-year-old South African with a James Earl Jones voice and a gray beard that seemed to double the size of his pale, gnomish face. Augie would never lead a tour of an ancient city without Roger as the guide.

"2 mins," Augie texted.

He rushed to his father's old office, which still bore the senior Dr. Knox's nameplate on the door. Augie knocked and pushed it open. "Les, I need a favor."

Dr. Moore took his time looking up from his work. "Number one, Dr. Knox, I did not invite you in."

"Sorry, but—"

"Number two, I have asked that you refer to me as Dr. Moore."

"My bad again, but listen—"

"And number three," the acting chair said, making a show of studying his watch, "we both know that at this very moment you are to be conducting—"

"Dr. Moore, I have an emergency call to make and I need you to stand in for me for a few minutes."

Moore sighed and rose, reaching for his suit coat. "I know what that's about. Take all the time you need."

Augie followed him down the hall. "You do?"

"You didn't get my message?"

"Oh, no, sorry. I saw one was there, but I—"

"But you assumed other messages were more important. I said we needed to chat after your first exam."

"Well, sure, I'll be here."

"Part of what we need to discuss is your father. Is that what your call is about?"

"What about my father?"

"We'll talk at ten."

"But is he—"

"There have been developments, Dr. Knox. But he is still with us."

As Dr. Moore headed for the classroom, Augie ducked into a stairwell, away from the windows and the relentless sun forecasters were saying would push the temperature at least twenty degrees above normal by 2:00 p.m., threatening the 107° record for the month.

Augie wasn't getting enough signal strength to complete his call, so he hurried back out to the corridor. Cell coverage was still weak, so he stepped outside. It had to be near 90° already. Scalp burning, he listened as the number rang and rang.

Augie moved back inside for a minute, braced by the air conditioning, then ventured out to try again. He waited two minutes, tried once more, and felt he had to get back to class.

On a third attempt, as he neared the entrance, it was clear someone had picked up a receiver and hung up. Augie dialed twice more as he walked back to take over for Dr. Moore. Just before he reached the classroom, his phone came alive again with a text.

"sorry. later. trash ur phone. serious."

Augie couldn't make it compute. Had his phone been traced? Tapped? If he got a new one, how would Roger know how to reach him?

Dr. Moore stood just inside the classroom door and emerged immediately when he saw Augie. "Talk to your mother?" he said.

"No, should I?"

Moore sighed and opened his palms. "You interrupt my work and don't check on your father?"

Augie reached for his cell again, but hesitated. If he used it, would he be exposing his mother's phone too?

"Call her after we've talked, Dr. Knox. Now I really must get back to my own responsibilities."

It was all Augie could do to sit still till the end of class. Before getting back to Dr. Moore, he dropped off the stack of blue books in his own office and used the landline to call his contact at Dallas Theological Seminary, just up the road. Arlington Sem sat equidistant between DTS to the east and the massive Southwestern Baptist Seminary to the west. Arlington was like the stepchild no one ever talked about, a single building for a couple of hundred students, struggling to stay alive in the shadows of those two renowned institutions. When Augie needed something fast, he was more likely to get it from the competition. Such as a new phone.

Like his father before him, Augie *was* the travel department at

Arlington. No auxiliary staff handled logistics as they did at DTS and Southwestern. The head techie at Dallas was Biff Dyer, a string bean of a man a few years older than Augie with an Adam's apple that could apply for statehood. He could always be counted on to program Augie's phone, depending on what country he was traveling to.

"Calling from your office phone, I see," Biff said. "What happened to the cell I got you?"

"It's been compromised."

Biff chuckled. "Like you'd know. What makes you think so?"

"I need a new one. Trust me."

"I'll just switch out the chip. You're not gonna find a better phone. How soon you need it?"

"Fast as possible."

"Why doesn't that surprise me? I'm not deliverin' it. Can you come by during normal hours?"

There was a knock at Augie's door and he wrenched around to see Les Moore's scowl. "Gotta go, Biff."

"Sorry, Les. On my way right now. Or do you want to just meet here?"

"Here would not be any more appropriate than your insisting on our being on a first-name basis," Dr. Moore said, scanning the tiny chamber in which the guest chair was folded in a corner and brought out only when necessary.

"C'mon, Les. You were only a couple years ahead of me. We hung out, didn't we?"

"Hardly. You spent most of your free time in the gym with the— what?—six other jocks who happened to enroll here."

It was true. And everyone knew the library had been where to find Les Moore.

Augie looked at his watch. *Another final at 11.* He followed his interim boss back to his father's old office. It wasn't that much bigger than his, but at least the guest chair didn't block the door.

"Would you start with my dad?" Augie said as he sat.

"I would have thought you'd have already checked in with your mother, but all right. She called this morning, knowing you were in class. Your father has slipped into a coma."

Augie nodded slowly. "She okay?"

"Your mother? Sure. It's not like he's passed. She just thought you might want to visit this afternoon."

"Appreciate it."

"Now then, Dr. Knox, I have some paperwork here that I'm going to need you to sign. Frankly, it's not pleasant, but we're all expected to be team players and I'm going to assume you'll accede to the administration's wishes."

"What's up?"

"You're scheduled to teach summer-school Homiletics beginning four days after commencement."

"A week from today, right."

"And we have contracted with you for this stipend, correct?"

Why Les felt it necessary to pencil the figure on the back of a business card and dramatically slide it across the desk, Augie could not fathom.

"Yep, that's the fortune that's going to let me retire by forty."

"Um-hm. Humorous. It is my sad duty to ask you to agree to undertake the class for two-thirds that amount."

"You're serious."

"Always."

That was for sure.

"Les—Dr. Moore, you know we do these classes pretty much as gifts to the sem. Now they seriously want us to do them for less?"

"This is entirely up to you."

"I can refuse?"

"We're not going to force you to teach a class when we have to renege on our agreement."

"Good, because I just don't think I can do it for that."

"I'll report your decision. We'll be forced to prevail upon a local adjunct instruct—"

"Like that youth pastor at Arlington Bible—"

"He's a graduate, Dr. Knox."

"I know! I taught him. And he's a great kid, but he didn't do all that well in Homiletics, and there's a reason they let him preach only a couple of times a year over there."

"He'll be happy to do it for this figure—probably even for less."

"And the students be hanged."

Les cocked his head. "Naturally, we would prefer you . . ."

Augie reached for his pen and signaled with his fingers for the document.

"I'm glad I can count on you, Dr. Knox. Now, while we're on the subject, I'm afraid there's more. You were due for a four percent increase beginning with the fall trimester."

"Let me guess, that's not going to happen either."

"It's worse."

"What, now it's a four percent decrease?"

"I wish."

"Oh, no."

"Dr. Knox, we have seen an alarming downturn in admissions, and the administration is predicting a fall enrollment that puts us at less than breakeven, even with massive budget cuts. We're all being asked to accept twenty percent reductions in pay."

Augie slumped. "I was hoping to get married this fall, Les. I can barely afford the payments on my little house as it is."

"This is across the board, Dr. Knox. The president, the deans, the chairs, all of us. Some departments are actually losing personnel. Maintenance will be cut in half, and we'll all be expected to help out."

Arlington had been staggering along on a shoestring for decades, but this was dire. "Tell me the truth, Dr. Moore. Is this the beginning of the end? Should I entertain the offers I've gotten from Dallas over the years?"

"Oh, no! The trustees wish us to weather this storm, redouble our efforts to market our distinctives, and then more than make up for the pay cuts as soon as we're able. Besides, the way your father bad-mouthed Dallas and Southwestern his whole career, you wouldn't dream of insulting him by going to either, would you?"

"He bad-mouthed everything and everybody, Les. You know that."

"Not a pleasant man. No offense."

Augie shrugged. "You worked for him. I lived with him."

"Do you know, I have heard not one word from your father since the day I was asked to temporarily assume his role? No counsel, no guidelines, no encouragement, nothing. I assumed he was angry that you had not been appointed—"

That made Augie laugh. "He still sees me as a high school kid! Forget all my degrees. Anyway, I wouldn't want his job, or yours. It's not me."

"How well I know. I mean, I'm just saying, you're not the typical prof, let alone department chair."

"I'm not arguing."

Augie couldn't win. Despite having been at the top of his classes in college and seminary, his having been a high school jock and continuing to shoot hoops, play touch football, and follow pro sports made him an outsider among real academics. Too many times he had been asked if he was merely a seminary prof because that was what his father wanted for him.

Dr. Moore slid the new employment agreement across the desk.

"Sorry, Les, but this one I'm going to have to think and pray about."

The interim chair seemed to freeze. "Don't take too long. If they aren't sure they can count on you for the fall, they'll want to consider the many out-of-work professors who would be thrilled, in the current economy, to accept."

"Yeah, that would help. Stock the faculty with young assistant pastors."

"May I hear from you by the end of the day?"

"Probably not, but you'll be the first to know what I decide."

Back in his own office, Augie popped the chip out of his cell phone and put it in a separate pocket. He called his mother from his desk phone to assure her he would see her at the hospital late in the afternoon, then called Biff to tell him he would try to stop by DTS on his way.

"What's the big emergency?" Biff said.

"Roger Michaels has himself in some kind of trouble."

"Tell me when you get here."

During his 11:00 a.m. final Augie was summoned to the administrative offices for an emergency call. On the way he stopped by to see if Les would stand in for him again, but his office was dark. The final would just have to be unsupervised for a few minutes.

"Do you know who's calling?" he said to the girl who had fetched him. If it was his mother . . .

"Someone from Greece."

He finally reached the phone and discovered it was Sofia. "Thought you wanted me to call later, babe. You all right?"

"Roger is frantic to reach you."

"I know. He—"

"He gave me a new number and needs you to call right now, but not from your cell." She read it to him.

"Any idea what's going on, Sof?" Augie said as he scribbled. "This is not like him."

"No idea, but, Augie, he sounded petrified."

"That doesn't sound like him either."

"You can tell me what it's about later, but you'd better call him right away."

Augie rushed to his office and dialed the number in Rome. It rang six times before Roger picked up. "Augie?"

"Yes! What's—"

"Listen carefully. I've got just seconds. I need you in Rome as soon as you can get here."

"Rog, what's happening? This is the absolute worst time for me to—"

"Give Sofia your new cell number and text me your ETA. I'll give you a new number where you can call me from Fiumicino as soon as you get in."

"I don't know when I could get there, Rog. I've got—"

"Augie! You know I wouldn't ask if it weren't life or death."

"Above all . . ."

FIRST-CENTURY ROME

"You must not let me die before my execution."

Memories of that ghastly exhortation from his most beloved friend robbed the elderly physician of sleep. He rolled delicately to his side to keep the wooden pallet from squeaking and waking the family who had risked everything to take him in. Hidden in a tiny chamber on the second floor of their humble, crowded house, he found his breathing rhythmic and deep.

Exhausted from the voyage and the nearly four-day race to the besieged capital, not to mention the most horrific evening of his years as a doctor, he knew there would be no rest this stifling night.

Eyes wide open in the darkness, Luke pulled aside the thin, scratchy blanket and sat up, swinging his feet onto the floor. Elbows on his knees, head in his hands, he heard the skimpy curtain billow behind him. The humid wind carried acrid smoke smelling of charred wood. He could still hear screams and shouts from blocks away in the wee hours.

Luke's desperate chase across the Mediterranean in search of his life-long friend—arrested in Troas and hauled off to Rome for sentencing (yet again)—had brought him to the strangely putrid city of Puteoli early in the morning three days previous. Frantic to find land passage to Rome 170 miles to the northwest, Luke had barely begun inquiring of traveling merchants and caravans when he heard the awful news.

Rome was ablaze.

The port was alive with rumor and gossip, but authorities made it clear that only urgently needed supplies and emergency personnel would be allowed on the long stone road to the capital. Word was that the city-wide conflagration had erupted just a few days before, during the hottest night of the year. Already called Nero's Fire, the inferno had raged through the great seat of the Roman Empire, obliterating three of the fourteen districts and decimating seven more.

Refugees from the city poured into Puteoli, lugging what little they could carry and telling blank-eyed stories of the devastation and of streets lined with stacks of countless blackened bodies pulled from the rubble. So far, all efforts to fight the fire had failed, and it continued to ravage the city.

As a slave long ago freed from Syrian Antioch and now a Roman citizen, Luke had eluded the Empire's seizure of Christians, the cult on which the emperor blamed the arson. Many refugees—and not just Christians—claimed Nero was deflecting suspicion from himself. Theories abounded as to why the narcissistic young ruler would torch his own realm, the most popular being that he merely wanted to start over and rebuild Rome to his liking. How else to explain bands of rampaging arsonists torching strategic neighborhoods all over the city at the same time?

What of the prisons? As it was, Luke's friend had been condemned to beheading, but could he already be gone in an even more excruciating manner? No one seemed to know, and Luke wasn't sure which bleak dungeon held the man anyway.

Luke laboriously swung his heavy sack onto a bony shoulder and hurried to the centurions blocking the road, allowing through only a fraction of those clamoring to get to Rome. "I am a Roman citizen and a physician!" he called out. "I have surgical tools and medicines!"

"Prove it!" a guard said, and Luke set the sack down and began to open it. "No! Your citizenship! Prove that!"

Luke dug deep into a specially sewn pocket and presented his *professio*, two small, hinged wooden diptychs bearing his inscribed Roman name (Lucanus) and identification. The guard studied it and pointed him to a two-wheeled contrivance pulled by two horses, with a place for a driver, four passengers, and a small cargo hold. "They're leaving right now, old man! Go!"

Luke rushed to the carriage, where the others helped him situate his bag and pulled him aboard. The driver whipped the horses and they hurtled over the stone pavement, bouncing and jostling for hours. They stopped only at government outposts to change horses, eat, relieve themselves, and have the driver slather the axles with animal fat.

Late each night they stayed in a shabby inn and were off again before dawn, pulling into Rome around noon three days later. Spent and aching, Luke could barely take his eyes off the orange-and-black whirlwinds of flame and smoke roiling over the whole of the capital. A citizen breathlessly told the driver, "We thought it had ended! Six days of this, and then it quit. But the monster reignited last night and now it's worse than ever."

When Luke tried to pay, the driver said, "You're here on behalf of the Empire, Doctor. May the gods be with you."

As soon as Luke identified himself to local authorities, he was pressed into service. The *vigiles*, who served Rome as both firefighters and watchmen of the night—many of whom had lost coworkers in the catastrophe—directed him to a makeshift ward in an alley just four blocks from the inferno and assigned him the worst cases. Everywhere needy victims lay or staggered about.

The tragedy had the military scrambling to maintain *pax Romana*, but the peace of Rome was turning to rubble by the moment. As day turned to night and Luke plodded on, he asked every man in uniform where he might find a friend sentenced to prison. At long last, about an hour before midnight, a massive man in uniform overheard him. "Who are you asking after, Doctor?"

When Luke told him, "Paul of Tarsus," the Roman narrowed his eyes and stepped closer. "Follow me to the alley."

In the darkness with only the shadows of flames dancing on the walls, the man asked to see his *professio*, then shook Luke's hand and introduced himself as Primus Paternius Panthera, gate guard at the dungeon. "What do you want with our most notorious prisoner? Are you one of them, as he is?"

Luke hesitated. This could mean the end of his freedom. "I have never denied my loyalties, and I won't begin now. Yes, he is my friend."

"You would be wise not to make that known."

"I just did, and to someone able to make me suffer for it."

"I admire your forthrightness, Lucanus. But you must know your friend is no longer allowed visitors. One was allowed in for several days some weeks ago, but . . ."

"I know nothing of Paul since his midnight arrest in Troas. He was hauled to a ship with only the clothes on his back. The last time he was imprisoned in Rome, he was treated with respect, and—"

"Do not mistake that sentence for this one, Doctor. Then he was bound but allowed much freedom, including many visitors. This time he sits chained in the main dungeon, in utter darkness day and night. And the ones who visited him last time appear to have abandoned him."

"So it is hopeless to think I would be allowed—"

"Nothing is hopeless, sir. Some things can be accommodated with careful thinking."

"What are you saying?"

"Only that I may have a proposition for you."

"I have no means—"

"I'm not talking about that, Doctor. Where are you staying?"

"Nowhere yet. I have been busy since I arrived."

"You look like you could use a good meal and a bed."

"I could indeed."

"And you wish to see your friend . . ."

Luke nodded. *What was the man trying to say?*

"Lucanus, my mother was severely burned in the fire. Two other doctors say she is beyond hope and that the best I can do for her is to take her to my home and let her die there. My wife and children are with her now, but of course all employees of the Empire remain on duty. Is there anything you can do for her?"

"I would have to see her."

"I would reward any consideration."

"I will do what I can."

The guard went with Luke to fetch his belongings, then they trudged through the streets, often changing course to avoid the worst of the fire. Luke prayed silently that God would somehow spare the man's mother. Whatever it took for Luke to gain favor with Primus Paternius Panthera had to be to Paul's benefit.

In the tiny home Luke found the delirious elderly woman burned over more than half her body, including her face and neck. He immediately slathered her with ointments and creams, knowing these would bring only minor relief.

"Do you mind if I pray for her?" he said.

"I have quit praying," Panthera said. "I don't know that I even believe in the gods anymore."

"I would pray to the God of Abraham, Isaac, and Jacob," Luke said.

"I don't suppose it could hurt."

Luke knelt beside the woman's bed and lifted his face. "God, the Father of my Lord and Savior Jesus Christ, I pray Your hand of healing on this woman. Bless her with Your presence and Your touch. I ask this in the name of Your Son. Amen."

The woman immediately quieted and fell asleep. Her face lost its grimace, and she lay so still and quiet that Luke leaned in and listened to be sure she was still alive.

"Is she all right, Lucanus?" the guard said as his wife tiptoed in behind him.

"This is the first time she's been quiet for hours," his wife said. "The children have been weeping and covering their ears."

"She will live?" Panthera said.

"I cannot promise. But we have hope. Rest is the best thing for her now. And I will do everything I can."

The guard whispered to his wife, she nodded, and he led Luke upstairs to the minute chamber where he would sleep. "I am grateful," Luke said. "But does this not endanger you?"

"To have taken in a physician for my ailing mother? I don't see how, unless someone finds out who you are. Now, my wife is cooking you a meal. Then I can take you to see your friend this very night."

Luke nearly wept with gratitude. He ate ravenously, asked if he could pocket some leftovers for Paul, then ventured out again with Panthera. They ascended the northeastern slope of Capitoline Hill—eerily lit by the fire in the distance—toward the *carcer*. "That is one bleak-looking building, sir."

Panthera nodded. "The largest and most desolate prison in the city."

Luke said silently, *Lord, grant me strength and peace so that I may encourage Paul.* The overnight gate guard looked puzzled but nodded to Panthera as he hurried past with Luke in tow and whispered, "A physician." Inside, the guard grabbed a torch from the wall and took Luke past the cells of commoners, where he was assaulted with smells not even the convicted should have to endure. Most prisoners lay moaning in their own filth, and Luke squinted through the flicker of the torch at their cavernous eyes and sunken cheeks.

"Have these men eaten?"

Panthera shrugged. "Twice a day a bowl of thin gruel, about half what is fed to slaves. They're not allowed visitors, let alone care."

Luke's heart ached for these wretched men, but when he hesitated at a pitiful cry, Panthera gently elbowed him along. In the front corner of the last crowded cell, three bodies lay atop one another, awaiting removal. Panthera whispered that they had been there four days.

By the time Luke reached a landing that bore a man-sized hole in the floor, his heart had quickened and his breath came short. He had to fight to keep the stink from nauseating him.

Guards encircling the hole reminded Panthera that the prisoner below was not allowed visitors. "He's allowed a visit from a doctor once a day," Primus said. "You know the emperor wants this one healthy enough to execute as a prime example."

Panthera demonstrated to Luke how to lower himself into the dungeon. "When the prisoner was put in here, he was unable to grab the lip in time to break his fall. He twisted an ankle when he hit the stone floor."

"How far down is it?"

"Just six feet, but in the darkness he had no idea." Panthera turned to one of the other guards. "Once I'm down, hand me this torch."

"He's not allowed light either. You know that."

"Is the physician to examine him in darkness? Just do what I say!"

Panthera bent at the waist and laid both palms on the rim of the far edge of the hole. He supported himself on his hands as he hopped into the opening and dangled until his feet reached the floor. Luke did the same, but not as nimbly, and his cloak tangled as he descended.

He found Paul sleeping on a small rock bench, tethered to the wall by his ankle. The floor was cold and damp, and the torch illuminated the horrid chamber, consisting of two-foot-square tufa limestone block walls, oozing an oily slime. The ceiling hung less than a foot above Luke's head.

His beloved friend lay on his side facing the wall, and Luke nodded to the guard to hold the torch so he could examine the ankle where the ridiculously heavy manacle was attached to a chain made of massive links, each wider than Paul's foot. Luke hefted the four-foot iron leash and guessed the contraption weighed at least fifteen pounds. The ankle remained swollen, likely from lack of exercise and the weight of the apparatus. Perspiration had caused the manacle to rust, which had worn Paul's skin raw. Luke fished out an ointment he spread on the affected spot, which roused the prisoner.

"My friend," Paul rasped. "You have come. Bless you."

Luke clasped Paul's hand, pressing their palms together and inter-locking their thumbs so he could help Paul sit up. Panthera settled the torch into a holder on the wall that had apparently rarely been used. "I'll give you some time," the big man said, reaching to grasp the lip of the hole and deftly pulling himself up.

Paul had always been a small man, but when Luke met him decades before, he was wiry, muscular, athletic. Until this last imprisonment, he had still shamed men half his age with his firm grip, his ability to walk prodigious distances, even his capacity to run when necessary. And that had been all too frequently.

But now the man was wasting away. Barely two years older than Luke, Paul finally looked every one of his sixty-five-plus years. Bones protruded, his grip was weak, and he sat with shoulders slumped. Luke used his foot to slide the waste bucket to the corner, which did nothing to lessen the odor. "Don't forget to return that to within reach before you leave," Paul said. "Things are bad enough as it is." He had not been bathed, and he told Luke that what was left of his garments served also as bedding.

Luke pulled food from his pockets, and Paul grabbed the bread, tearing at it with his teeth and gasping as he chewed and swallowed and offered thanks for it, seemingly all at the same time: ". . . give us this day our daily bread and forgive us our trespasses . . ."

"Slow down, friend. Don't make yourself ill."

"Too late," Paul said with a wan smile, now munching figs. "I'm starving on prison rations."

"How are you sleeping?"

Paul shrugged. "You woke me."

"But after how long?"

"It's hard to tell here, Luke. Around midday, a sliver of sunlight squeezes through the cleft in the ceiling there from street level. It casts a dim beam low on the wall behind me and in twenty minutes or so travels across the floor before it disappears. My ration of cold broth is lowered to me just after that. I sit in darkness again then, praying and singing. I feel worthless, yearning to preach. I ask about the other prisoners and wish they could hear me. I would tell them of Christ. But I hear them only when they scream, and I no longer have the power to shout loud enough for them to hear me. The guards no longer listen to me, and when they did they refused to repeat my messages to the others. They tell me to save my breath, that the others are dying long before their executions can be carried out. You must not let that happen to me, Luke. You must not."

Luke paced in the suffocating space. "But it was you who so eloquently wrote and preached about death. 'To live is Christ,' you said, 'and to die is gain.'"

"I'm not fighting death, friend. You above all know that. But I want my end to bring glory to God, to my Savior. Fortunately, they cannot decapitate a Roman citizen inside the city. They must take me out—oh, how I long for the light! But far more, I long for ears to hear me. I am desperate for any audience, Luke. But now that you are here, before long I will preach to you! Poor, dear friend, you have heard it all before."

"I never tire of it, especially from you."

"But don't let me die without one more opportunity to proclaim the good news." Luke felt Paul's weak eyes on him. "You feel I'm asking too much."

"Of course you are! How can I not feel the weight of it! People died today despite my efforts. I prayed for them, ministered to them, tried everything I knew. That's all I have to offer you as well."

"I must insist, Luke . . ."

"You're like a dog with its teeth on the hem of a garment."

"But my motive is pure. I don't want to just keep the attention of my master. I want once more to bring glory—"

"I know what you want to do, Paul! I know! And I came to do everything in my power to grant your wish. But you know what that means?"

"That Christ will be preached, God will be glorified, hard hearts will hear."

Luke faced his friend. "It means I will have to be there."

Paul cocked his head. "Why, yes, certainly. Why would you have come if I couldn't count on you? Now that you have found me, surely you wouldn't dream of abandoning me to such a fate alone."

Luke sat and shook his head.

"My friend," Paul said, "get word to Timothy and Mark to do whatever they have to do to get to me. It will take weeks for Timothy to get here from Ephesus, and I'm not even sure where Mark is. Perhaps they too can be with me at my last."

"None of us could ever abandon you, Paul. But must we watch as—"

"Rome cannot sever my soul. You can rest in the blessed hope that being absent from my body means I am present with my Lord. What glory that will be!"

"For you."

"For you, too! Your time will come, Luke, and we will rejoice in paradise forever."

Luke wanted with all his being to agree, but he could not push from his mind the image of his closest friend in the world facing a monstrous sword in the hands of an executioner, riving his head from his body.

"Tell Timothy and Mark to bring my cloak, and the books, and above all the parchments."

Luke squinted at Paul. "'Above all'?"

"Yes, the parchments."

Luke was fascinated that the fearless apostle seemed unable to hold his gaze. "What are you not telling me?"

Paul reached for Luke's garment and desperately drew him close, whispering hoarsely, "Those parchments contain my memoir, Luke. And I name names. Much of the church would be exposed if they fell into the wrong hands. I must have them, and you must help me finish them. But we have to guard them with our very lives."

Truth

―――――――――

TEXAS

―――――――――

THROUGH TWO MORE FINAL exams Augie sat as close as he could to the ancient window air conditioning units that rattled and hummed, trying to keep pace with the naked sun. Students proved creative, refilling their water bottles from the drinking fountain, then filling their palms and dousing their faces, some even running wet hands through their hair.

Augie had cured his students of whining early in the term, and they knew better than to start. "No life is messier than one in ministry," he told them. "Whiners won't last." Fortunately, everyone seemed eager now to just get through their finals and either graduate or get home to prepare for next year.

By the middle of the afternoon Augie had been agonizing for hours over Roger Michaels. *What could be so urgent?* Finally back in his office, Augie wanted to start grading the exams in case he had to leave the country in a hurry, but first he got online to find flights from DFW to DaVinci-Fiumicino. The next with an open seat was scheduled to leave two days later, Friday the 9th, at 10:30 a.m. with a stopover in Chicago, before arriving in Rome just before 8:00 a.m. Saturday.

Unfortunately, only first class was available, at almost $4,000. And with no idea what he was getting himself into in Rome, Augie would have to leave his return flight open—which could be even more exorbitant.

Even if he found the money, what if he couldn't make it back in time to start his summer-school class? What would he tell Les Moore?

Grading couldn't wait. He owed that to the students. As he gazed at the stack of blue books, Augie wondered if he could set aside his anxiety over Roger and the prospect of a trip that would totally complicate his life.

Augie would eventually give each blue book its due, but now he just leafed through to sample the essays on the question of Paul's thorn in the flesh. Many suggested various physical ailments, as well as depression, divorce, a lost love, doubt, even a secret battle with homosexuality. Augie stopped at that one, curious whether the student presented a convincing case. Primarily Augie looked for evidence that a student recognized that Paul's thorn was—as the evangelist himself had written—not of God but of Satan ("a messenger to buffet me"). For if it had been given to him by God, why would Paul have prayed three times that it might depart?

When a bead of sweat rolled from Augie's forehead onto the paper, he rose to lower the blinds and caught a glimpse of one of his Greek students in the parking lot.

Rajiv Patel, a brilliant twenty-five-year-old from Ahmadabad, India, seemed laden with more than his backpack as he trudged to his dilapidated Toyota in the blistering heat. He unlocked it, then stood staring at the ground.

Augie had long been taken with the sweet spirit of the soft-spoken student. Rajiv had shared pictures of the ministry he had left in India to seek more formal training. He had labored in squalor, sharing the gospel with the lowest castes. And unlike many foreign students whose eyes had been opened to the advantages of staying in America upon graduation, Rajiv had no such intentions. Even here he busied himself ministering to the poor during his off hours and was committed to returning home after one more year of study.

Rajiv finally opened his car door, yanking his hand from the handle, which must have burned him. Shimmering heat waves poured from the car. Rajiv slung his backpack into the backseat and removed the reflective shade from the windshield. He leaned in and started the engine, then shut the door to let the car cool, leaving the driver's side window open about an inch. Augie guessed the old car's AC would lower the temperature a mere ten degrees.

Rajiv stood shading his eyes, looking defeated by more than the heat. Finally the young man slid into the car, but rather than drive away, he rested his forehead on the steering wheel. Soon he appeared to be pounding the wheel, before finally burying his head in his hands.

Augie hurried outside, hair soaked and shirt clinging. When he reached Rajiv's car and tapped on the window, the Indian was clearly startled.

"You all right?" Augie said.

Rajiv nodded, tears rolling.

"May I sit with you?"

Rajiv unlocked the passenger door and was wiping his face when Augie slid in. He aimed an AC vent toward his face but still felt as if he were in an oven. "Would you rather talk in my office?"

"No, thank you, Doctor," Rajiv said in his native lilt. "I must be going soon."

"What's wrong, Rajiv?"

"I'm trying to have faith. But I have exhausted my funds. One year to go and my country so needy. But I cannot even enroll for the fall."

Augie quizzed him about all the avenues for financial aid, grants, and scholarships. Sure enough, Rajiv was atop all of them, and he had accumulated every cent available.

"How short are you?"

"Almost four thousand dollars."

Augie flinched. His first thought was to tell Rajiv that he would pray for him. But knowing the young man, there would have been no lack of prayer. In an instant it came to Augie that he might be the answer. "Have you got a piece of paper, Rajiv?"

The student wrenched around to reach into his backpack, handing his professor a spiral notebook.

Augie wrote, "To whom it may concern: Please charge the balance of Rajiv Patel's school bill to me for up to four thousand dollars. Dr. Augustine A. Knox."

Rajiv stared at the sheet and burst into tears anew. "I cannot accept this, Dr. Knox! You can't afford it!"

"If God wants me to do something, don't you think He'll make it happen?"

"Well, yes, but—"

"You think I just happened to look out my window when you needed me?"

"I certainly did not intend to make you feel—"

"Rajiv! Tell me you're not going to deprive me of this blessing."

"I'm sorry?"

"You heard me," Augie said, opening the door. "Remember, that's *up to* four thousand dollars. I'm pledging only to make up the difference between what you need and what you can earn or raise. I expect you to keep doing your part. Now let me out of this hotbox."

"I will never be able to thank you enough!"

"Not another word about it. We're here to train kingdom laborers, not send them home before they're ready."

Augie settled back behind his desk wondering what in the world he had done. The timing couldn't have been worse. Where was he going to come up with the money? *Lord,* he said silently, *give me the faith You gave Rajiv to believe this was of You. I'll trust You to provide.*

Augie had never seen such a fast change in the weather, especially in Arlington. Huge, roiling black clouds blew in so quickly from the west that temperatures plummeted into the 90s and flashes of light appeared on the horizon. By the time he reached US 30 heading east, the sky was black and lightning struck within a few hundred feet of the highway. The ferocious thunder was so loud it hurt Augie's ears and wind rocked the car. When the heavens opened and the rain came in sheets, Augie's wipers couldn't keep up, and visibility plunged to zero. Like everyone else, he was forced to pull over and wait it out.

With no idea how long he would be delayed, Augie was tempted to call Sofia right then, but the storm would probably keep him from getting through. He and Sofia loved to discuss their future, marriage, kids, even where they might live. Her parents had only recently realized that their friendship had blossomed into something serious.

"Daddy's cautious," she had told him, admitting that her father insisted it was way too soon for either of them to be "getting ideas." Augie deduced that Malfees Trikoupis was not yet ready for anyone to ask for his daughter's hand. Amusing, because Augie and Sofia had known each other for years as long-distance friends before moving to the next level during a tour that ended in the red-rock city of Petra.

When he was thirty, Augie had met Mr. and Mrs. Trikoupis even before he met Sofia, when the tour group gathered in the lobby of the King David Hotel in Jerusalem at the beginning of a Holy Land tour. The understated but elegantly dressed couple exuded wealth and sophistication, and Mrs. Trikoupis mentioned that their daughter was with them but that she had begged off from socializing that first night, knowing she would be the youngest member of the tour group that had congregated from around the world.

Mr. Trikoupis, dark and stocky with a shock of wavy white hair, seemed immediately taken with Augie when Roger Michaels introduced him as the host of the trip. "Young Dr. Knox knows the Book," Roger had boomed, lips hidden by his prodigious beard.

Mr. Trikoupis had excused himself and led Augie to a corner. "Perhaps this week you can infuse my daughter with a bit of an interest in antiquities, my field," he said, carefully enunciating in what was clearly a second language for him. "Sofia is a senior at the University of Athens majoring in modern art, but I would love for her to work in my business one day."

"Your business?"

"I am an importer-exporter dealing in antiquities. I have many shops in Greece, the largest near our home in Thessaloniki."

"Oh!" Augie had said. "You're *that* Trikoupis! I've been in a Tri-K shop or two of yours. So nice to meet you."

Augie had caught his first glimpse of the radiant Sofia at breakfast the next morning, and her energy alone made him feel old. Her jet-black hair and huge blue eyes captivated him, and he was struck by her firm handshake and eagerness to get on with the day. He had been miserable on his first such tour.

Her father had immediately monopolized Augie's time, and it was only near the end of that week that he'd had a chance to chat with Sofia—she had been impressed by his facility with both ancient and modern Greek—and trade e-mail addresses.

For the next few years they communicated sporadically between continents, getting to know each other via the Internet and seeking each other's advice about family and even relationships. She would send photos and resumes of her suitors and Augie would do the same with his miscellaneous dates.

Sofia had upset her father by remaining in Athens after graduating and becoming active in her church and career. "Augie," she had transmitted one night, "who wants to work for their father? Oh, sorry, you work for yours, don't you?"

"In a manner of speaking," he had written back. And somewhere along the line Augie became comfortable enough with the Greek beauty that he opened up about the most difficult relationship in his life. Sofia was far enough away that he felt free to express things he had never told anyone.

"I teach in his department, yes, but we don't talk. I'd love to think he was proud of me for following in his footsteps, but we are so unlike each other. May it ever be so."

"I must know what you're talking about, Augie. I really do care, you know. I won't pester you, but please know you can confide in me. But only if you trust me, and only if you wish."

One late night (the following morning her time) she suddenly confessed that she was considering going home to work for her father. She had been working in a fine-arts store and teaching evening classes, but, she said, despite many friends and a good church family, she felt lonely. "I don't date guys who don't share my faith," she wrote. "But even the Christian guys seem to have only sex on their minds. I miss my family."

"Funny," he wrote, "I miss the father I never had."

"You don't see him every day?"

"Of course. But he doesn't see me."

The rain finally began to abate, so Augie carefully followed the other motorists back out onto the highway. When he reached Dallas Theological an hour later, Biff Dyer's ramshackle van was pulling out. Augie honked and Biff stopped next to him. "I told you I wasn't gonna deliver, Augie, and my day is over."

"I'll owe you, Biff, but you've got to give me a few minutes."

Biff parked and slammed his door, striding back toward his office looking none too happy. Augie caught up and explained that he had been delayed by the storm. "This phone thing is critical, Biff. You know I'd never take advantage of you."

"You never have before. But it's my wife's birthday and I—"

"I won't take a minute longer than necessary."

Augie loved Biff's space. Behind a plain, efficient office sat a windowless chamber lined with shelves jammed with every electronic gadget imaginable. Biff outfitted the DTS faculty—and much of Arlington's—whenever they went overseas. Biff himself had gone only twice himself, but he'd met Roger Michaels. "Everybody's favorite," he said. "So what's up with him?"

Augie shook his head. "Petrified about something, and I've never seen him other than totally in control."

"Roger scared? Can't picture it. Don't think I've ever met anyone as worldly-wise and confident."

"I know, Biff. But now he needs me for some reason, and I can't let him down."

Biff quickly traded out the data chip from Augie's phone, inserted the old one into a drive to be scanned, got online to arrange for a new number, and loaded the new chip with several hundred minutes for international transmissions. "As secure a cell as you'll find, so guard that number. Remember, this doesn't protect anyone's phone you're connecting with. It blocks your identity, but anything that shows up on their phone is fair game."

"Got it."

"This thing sucks power like a vacuum, man. Carry a charger everywhere you go. I know you've got a converter for every country on the globe."

"I don't know how to thank you."

"I'll bill you. Listen, I gotta run, but let me show you one more thing."

Biff led Augie into the deepest corner of his electronic shack where the decades-old fluorescent lights barely reached. He pulled a tiny flashlight from his nerd belt and held it in his teeth, talking around it as he moved junk to reveal a new and very compact machine. "You won't bewieve what thith can do, Augie," he said, mouth full of flashlight. He lifted the boxy apparatus so he could reach a tiny compartment in the back. "Spring loaded." He pushed in and out sprang a chip no bigger than his finger tip. "Sound activated and can record a hundred hours."

"No way! Record what?"

"Your phone, if you want."

Biff explained that top-of-the-line phones can serve as bugging devices, even when turned off. "They can transmit to other phones, or to a recorder like this one."

"How can that be?"

"It would take me too long to explain. But if you want a record of a conversation, you just hold down this button on the side and hit your pound key, and *voila*."

"Even with my phone off."

"Miraculous, eh?"

"From how far away?"

"Where'd you say you were going? Rome?"

"Get out."

"Want me to program it for your phone, just in case?"

"Of course!"

Biff deftly slipped the chip out from Augie's phone, inserted it into the recorder, hit a button, and replaced it. "Done. And you wouldn't believe the capacity."

"You're the best."

"Just be sure to tell me the whole story someday."

"Promise. And give your wife my best wishes."

"Carol."

"Carol, right. I haven't met her, have I?"

Biff shot him a look. "The Cities of Paul tour? With Roger?"

"Sure, that's right. Sorry, Biff. My mind's already in Italy."

When Augie got back on the road toward Arlington Memorial Hospital the sky had turned that pale green that follows a ferocious storm. He realized that within an hour of connecting with his mother he needed to call Sofia before it got too late. As it was, it would be well after midnight in Greece. Difficult as it had been to tell her of his troubled relationship with his father, he had found it freeing. Revealing a part of his history he had shared with few others created a special bond with Sofia.

One of his earliest memories, he had written her online, was of his mother telling him that he was not born to them the way most babies were, but rather they chose him: "Daddy and I accepted you as a gift from God. Your father so longed for a son."

Yet only his mother seemed to have time for him. His father proved a mysterious presence in the house, quiet, sullen, unengaged. Once, Augie wrote Sofia, he had asked his parents if he could have a brother or a sister. "My mother looked pained, and my father said, 'Your mother is a little fragile, son. And one child was all we wanted.'

"But later," Augie wrote, "my father told me that when he realized how difficult raising me was on my mother, he would have been fine having had no children."

"Oh, Augie. How old were you?"

"Nine or ten. It was weird, though, because my mother frequently reminded me that my dad had so wanted a son that I was a true gift. He was an academic through and through. All I wanted to do was play sports. I badgered him all the time to play catch with me or come to my games. Once my mother insisted that he play catch with me, but he never took off his suit coat or tie. And he threw like someone who had never held a ball before. I remember hoping no one was watching. Then I accidentally tossed the ball over his head, and he scowled before he went to get it. When he bent to pick it up, his pants ripped and he stormed inside, saying, 'This is why I didn't want to do that!'

"I became a pretty good athlete, all-conference in baseball and basketball in high school. My dad never saw me play. My mother came when she could, but when she would talk at dinner about how proud she was of me and that Dad should have seen me, he'd mutter about hoping I would 'outgrow these obsessions. There's more to life than fun and games, you know.' The only recreation he allowed himself was crossword puzzles and other word games. Otherwise his nose was always buried in some scholarly book. I learned not to put posters of my ball-players on my bedroom walls. He'd just tear them down and say, 'We're not to idolize men.'"

"I'm sorry," Sofia wrote, and Augie sensed her sympathy was genuine.

"If it hadn't been for my mother's faith, I'd have never become a believer. We were all in church, every service every week. I had good Sunday school teachers and friends, and I liked the pastor. Dad was an elder. He preached sometimes, and though I always found him dead boring, everybody else revered him because he was a professor. Head of a seminary department. They say you base your view of God on your father. Imagine my view."

"How did you turn out so opposite, Augie? Or is it lucky we live so far from each other?"

"Good question. But no, people like me. They don't like him. And he doesn't seem to care."

"Your mother was strong enough to keep you from turning out like him?"

"She's a saint. Not perfect, because I wish she'd have stood up to him more often, but that's easy for me to say. He's a powerful force of nature. I don't know what she could have done to change him. But I was also taught that Christians should be known by the joy in their salvation. She had plenty, under the circumstances."

"And he had none?"

"I saw his teeth only in pictures when he was expected to smile."

"Sad."

"How did you keep from rebelling?"

"I didn't. I had no joy either. To me the Christian life was one big chore—rules, limits, dos and don'ts. By the time I was a junior in high school I was this great athlete and a straight-A student, but none of that seemed to please my dad. I thought at least my report card would impress him, but he just gave it a glance and asked if I was sure I was taking all the subjects I needed to get into college. I told him I was working closely with my academic adviser. He said, 'If your academic adviser had a clue, wouldn't he be more than an academic adviser?'

"Something in me snapped. I suddenly knew how to get his attention. Not only did I quit studying and turning in homework, I even skipped school now and then. When some buddies and I got busted for shoplifting, Dad wanted to ground me for life, not allow me to play sports, the whole bit. What pierced me though were my mother's tears. I hadn't thought that through. I wanted only to hurt him; to have hurt her crushed me. I told her I would accept any punishment if she would forgive me, and I would never do anything like that again."

"I'm guessing she forgave you."

"In an instant. But there were still scars, and that destroyed me. She didn't deserve that. He did."

"So what *was* your punishment?"

"It couldn't have been more perfect."

"Do tell."

4

The Letter

IT HAD NOT BEEN a request. No, Luke had been issued a macabre order from a man one could not deny. You might counter Paul, argue with him, challenge him, even show disdain for his opinions. But in the end the sheer power of his will prevailed.

And so the physician, drained as he was, had returned to the home of Primus Paternius Panthera. Now he sat in the dark, massaging his own temples and trying in vain to will himself to sleep.

Finally Luke stood and moved to the chunky wooden stool before a table little larger than a sheet of writing parchment. He quietly lit an earthenware lamp the size of his palm. As the flame flickered to life, he bent to review one of the last paragraphs of a letter he and his condemned friend had fashioned that night.

"Luke," Paul had said, "tell Timothy the others have deserted me and that only you remain."

"It isn't as if they have deserted you—"

"Of course they have! Don't make me try to pen this myself."

Luke had shrugged and called for Panthera, who lay over the hole in the ceiling. Luke whispered that he needed parchment and a quill and ink. "Will that arouse suspicion?"

"I'll tell the others you need it to record what you've found in your visit to the patient."

Luke spent the next hour scribbling fast as Paul dictated a letter to Timothy. The paragraph in question came just before Paul closed:

Do your best to come to me soon. For Demas, in love with this present world, has deserted me and gone to Thessalonica. Crescens has gone to Galatia, Titus to Dalmatia. Luke alone is with me. Get Mark and bring him with you, for he is very useful to me for ministry. Tychicus I have sent to Ephesus. When you come, bring the cloak that I left with Carpus at Troas, also the books, and above all the parchments.

There it was again. *Above all the parchments.* Luke and Paul had been in many desperate situations, but Luke had never seen a look like the one in Paul's eyes when he spoke of his memoir. It was one thing for him to face his own execution, and, knowing him, Luke assumed Paul would wish that other church leaders would also risk martyrdom for Christ. But that would have to be their choice. He made clear to Luke that their fates must not be determined by something found in his parchments by the wrong eyes.

But even if Timothy or Mark were able to come to Rome, and

even if they bore the treasured parchments, would they be allowed to see Paul? Perhaps Panthera could make it happen. But who knew how long it would take them to get to Rome? And what was Paul to do for a cloak in the meantime? During the day the dungeon was hot as a kiln, but at night, Luke knew Paul shivered as he tried to sleep.

At dawn the next day the doctor checked on his landlord's mother. The old woman had seemed to rest and was grateful for a fresh application of ointments, but Luke was a long way from predicting a positive outcome.

He sat briefly with his hosts and their children and enjoyed a breakfast of bread, cheese, and nuts. His sleepless night assaulted Luke all morning as he carried his leather satchel to centers for the suffering, assisting military *medicusi, clinicusi,* and *capsariori,* attempting to alleviate pain and make comfortable those beyond repair.

At noon, when much of the rest of the city partook of a light meal before taking long naps, Luke headed straight back to his pallet and slept so soundly that when he awoke he feared he had let too much of the day get away from him. Hurrying back to his work—with the small lamp deep in a pocket—Luke bought a handful of carrots and onions from an open-air market and ate quickly on the street.

As the afternoon faded, he found himself actually looking forward to seeing his friend, even though he would have to again steel himself against the repulsive surroundings. Along the way he found bargains on bread, cucumbers, apples, and figs that had sat in the sun all day.

He and Panthera conspired to avoid each other at the prison. The guard would merely wave him through the gate, and soon enough the others would think nothing of his daily comings and goings.

That early evening Paul was eager for the food Luke brought and quickly began to gorge. The prisoner groaned and slowly slid to one end of the stone bench. "Come, sit."

Luke joined his friend, the lamp in his lap. "You stink, you know."

Paul tossed his head back and laughed, putting a hand over his mouth to keep the food in. Then he grinned at Luke. "Do I?" he said, plainly exaggerating. "Every few days they strip me and douse me with two buckets of water, leaving me to dry myself with my own clothes. And yet still I offend? How can this be? Tell me, is it worse up close?"

It warmed Luke to see his friend's smile, which seemed to melt years from the weathered face. He draped an arm around Paul's narrow shoulders and fought tears as the man laid his bald head on Luke's chest. How often he'd seen Paul's glee over the years, after a day of arduous travel, contentious meetings, threats, abuse. Paul had a fierce look too, a resolve that shone in his eyes. And yet somehow, as they shared a room lent by some local believer—not infrequently a stall in someone's barn—Luke would catch Paul's beatific smile in the moonlight as he prayed before drifting off.

Luke wished he himself could find such contentment in his work, or at least in his hope for the future. God knew Paul had little to be smiling about. But the same compassion Luke had always felt for the afflicted also sobered him. Oh, he shared Paul's ultimate hope. But he feared his own sense of satisfaction would manifest itself only in paradise. There he could smile.

Here Paul sat in humiliation and despair, facing circumstances that would break a lesser man. Yet he longed to preach. And he could be amused. Luke found it beyond comprehension.

"Do you have more fruit?"

"An apple, but you must pace yourself, friend."

"When have I ever done that? This is my only real meal of the day. Let me enjoy it."

Luke stood and moved away, fetching the apple from his pocket and tossing it to Paul. He caught it deftly in one hand and took a tentative bite, Luke noticing that he was favoring fragile teeth. Paul sniffed the fruit. "It already bears the aroma of this place."

"Nonsense," Luke said. "I can smell its sweetness from here."

Paul sighed. "I don't know what I'd do without you. Until you arrived, I feared I would die of hunger. If it weren't for you and Onesiphorus . . ."

"I'm looking for a cloak for you."

"Hmm? Oh, even if Timothy and Mark come—or if they only send my things—I'll not wear my cloak. I'll use it only for sleeping and protect its hem from the floor, keep it dry. The mere thought of it cheers me."

"And yet you want those dangerous parchments above all. What will you do with those? Use them as a pillow?"

Paul devoured the apple—core, seeds, stem, and all. He pretended to pat his belly, but even in the low light Luke could see that there was scant to pat. "That feast will allow me to sleep tonight."

"The parchments, Paul. Aren't they better off in Troas, away from the eyes of the Empire? What do you want with them?"

"I am never hungrier than just before you arrive. It's as if my belly knows you're com—"

"Paul! You offend by ignoring me! You can't have me write Timothy, requesting your belongings and putting such stress on the parchments, without expecting me to ask why."

"You make me grateful I never married."

"Grateful? I know better than that. You told me so yourself."

"Mm. But would a wife nag as much as you do?"

"Not for long if you treated her with as much disdain as you do your friend."

"I have anything but disdain for you, Luke."

"Prove it."

Another sigh. "You will not leave it alone, though I clearly don't wish to discuss it."

"In the letter I'm to send to Timothy, you were clear the parchments were most important to you."

Paul sighed. "When the parchments arrive, you will need to assist me with them."

"I am to read to you?"

"You are to help me write."

"You say they contain your memoir and that you name names?"

Paul nodded. "It's my story. For years, as I have had occasion, I have chronicled my experiences. I find it most encouraging to peruse these, to remind myself from whence I came and also of the Lord's faithfulness."

"How is it that I have been unaware of this?"

"Keeping it from you was no small task. I stole private moments, when my eyes were stronger, my pen steadier. I plan to share them with you now only because I am unable to complete them myself. They are for only me, my family, and the brethren. But I will not rest until they are back under my control."

"Surely you can't risk having them here in the prison, so close to the authorities."

"True. I must entrust them to you when we are not working on them."

"And where am I to store them?"

"I cannot worry about that. I trust you. You know the danger of their falling into the wrong hands. But I do want them completed. And the account of my end can be written only by you."

Fatigue attacked Luke again. He stood in the horrific enclosure, the dim, flickering lamp illuminating the pathetic figure on the stone bench. "You know I will do anything you ask, Paul. But can you put yourself in my place? Can you imagine the pain of describing your demise?"

"Luke! We will work on it together in advance! It will be an account of the first step of my journey to where I have always longed to go. You need not emphasize the details. Everyone knows how we Romans execute our evildoers. Are you praying I will be spared? Would you have me exist like this, or to be present with my Lord?"

"I have learned not to argue with you."

"And yet you continue!" Paul said, smiling. "Ah, I enjoy the sport. Arguing with you is far better than a pleasant conversation with anyone else."

Luke jumped at a loud voice from above. "Time to go, Doctor!"

"Have I at least made you curious about my parchments?" Paul said.

"As much as you, I now long to see them above all."

Paul laughed. "Enough to cause you to get my letter to Timothy on its way with dispatch?"

"I am not dawdling, friend. You always want your letters just so."

"Indeed. But the sooner it gets to Timothy, the sooner we will see him. Of all the things I want here, the parchments and my friends are paramount. But need I say it again? You must—"

"No, you need not. It is my burden and I feel the weight of it. Keeping you alive so you may die is an awful obligation."

"So that I may die in a manner befitting Christ, Luke. You should long for that as much as I do."

Luke doused the light as Paul stood and whispered urgently, "Come to me and let me pray."

The physician approached him gingerly in the pitch dark and felt Paul gather him in. Despite the stench, what a privilege to pray with this man! "Father," Paul began, "I pray in the matchless name of Your Son and my Savior, Jesus the Christ. I praise You that I have been appointed for the defense of the gospel, and I rejoice in the preaching of Christ and Him crucified. You know it is my earnest expectation and my hope that in nothing I shall be ashamed, but with all boldness, as always, so now also Christ will be magnified in my body, whether by life or by death. And now I thank You for my dear brother and pray You will grant him health and strength and courage and power. And may the grace of the Lord Jesus Christ, and the love of God, and the communion of the Holy Spirit be with him until we meet again."

Luke thanked him and readied to leave, but Paul drew him close again, urgently telling him of a gift that had been left him by Onesiphorus of the church in Ephesus. The story gushed from the old man as he handed Luke a small bag heavy with coins. He put it and his lamp deep into Luke's pocket.

Faint light invaded from the hole in the ceiling. Luke gathered his cloak around him, then reached for the lip of the opening. He hurried out past the cells of the commoners, pressing a hand against the bulge in his pocket to keep it from rattling. He tried to hold his breath, but the stack of bodies startled him afresh and he was forced to gulp air as he reached the end of the dank, narrow corridor. At least Paul didn't have to endure this stifling torture, men crowded so close they could barely move in the putrid, muggy air.

An orange glow lingered over the rooftops as Luke rushed from the place, catching Panthera's eye on his way past. He felt as if he could taste the fresh air, such a salve it was to his lungs. His visit to the prison had both uplifted and saddened him. Paul was ever an encouragement, regardless of his circumstance. But the very place wore on every fiber of Luke's being. If only he were allowed to minister to the other prisoners in even the smallest way . . .

Luke would sleep soundly this night, he knew. And early in the morning he would make certain Paul's letter to Timothy was as perfect as he knew how to make it. He would carefully seal it, address it to his friend in Ephesus, and take it to one of the ships outbound from Ostia. He was eager to see Timothy and Mark too, but now—as was true with Paul—he wanted, above all, to see the parchments.

Revelations

DURING THEIR LATE-NIGHT EXCHANGE of online messages years before, Sofia had sounded as if she really wanted the whole story of the consequences of Augie's rebellion. And so he had told her.

"That summer I was to play in a big American Legion baseball tournament in Missouri. I'd been looking forward to it for a year. Mom and Dad sat me down and told me that was off the table. I started to rant until my mother reminded me I had agreed to accept any punishment.

"I slouched and crossed my arms, having no idea how I would break this to my coach and teammates. I was the star, and they were counting on me, but I would not even be in the country. Every summer for years I'd stayed with relatives while my parents led Holy Land tours. The way I understood it, Dad was the Bible teacher, Mom was the hostess, and they hired licensed guides. They could never afford to take me along, and it was the last thing I wanted to do anyway."

"But that year you were going."

"My mother, the eternal optimist, actually thought it would be a great opportunity for my dad and me to bond. My dad would have less time for me than he ever had at home, and I would be there against my will, angry, sullen."

"I'm trying to imagine such a trip with you not loving it," Sofia wrote. "You live for those now."

"So I stored my resentment, prepared to not even pretend to enjoy a minute of the trip. I had been raised in this very Christian, very church-oriented home with a mother who seemed to have a joy in her salvation and a father—a visible, respected seminary prof and scholar—who never experienced joy.

"Beyond getting 'saved' when I was young and being a good student, until my rebellion I was just a churchgoer. So we flew to Tel Aviv, and Mother insisted on me sitting next to my father the whole way. If he said three words to me they were probably, 'Don't embarrass me.'"

"That had to be awful."

"Pure torture. But shortly after we arrived, other members of the tour showed up at the airport, and I saw my mother in action. Dad stayed off to the side and stiffly shook hands with returning tourists and newbies, but Mom . . . Goodness, Mom was like the housemother. Most everyone knew Marie and embraced her and showed her pictures and talked and laughed and cried. Newcomers immediately recognized her from the brochures and took to her loving, enthusiastic manner. That was how it would be for the entire week and a half—Mom making the rounds every day, greeting every person anew and making sure they were looked after. People seemed to endure my father because she made up for him. All he did was read the Scripture and explain it at each site. If it hadn't been for Roger, I wouldn't have known what a cool older guy could be like."

"That's when you first met him?"

"My mother introduced us and I couldn't believe that big, resonant voice came from this elf. He was only thirty then, but his mop of curly hair and his bushy beard were already gray. Easily a foot shorter than I, he bellowed, 'I'd have known you anywhere! Your mother shows me the latest picture of you every year! Look at you!'

"He pumped my hand and said, 'I envy you.'

"'You envy *me*? Why?'

"'Why? Why, because this is your first visit to Israel, am I right?' I nodded. 'Oh, to see these lands again for the first time! You're in for the experience of a lifetime. Right now you're imagining heat and dust and boring history, am I right?' He couldn't have been more right. I was determined to hate this trip. He said, 'Talk to me again at the end of the week and tell me then what you think.'"

It had been hard for the young Augie to play the rebel, with his mother coming to life for everyone else's sake and the extroverted Roger Michaels turning every historic site into an adventure. He seemed to make it a point to sit next to Augie at meals and pull him aside for walks. "You know, I'm not a believer," he said.

Augie raised a brow. "I didn't know."

"I respect all religions. Basically I'm just a Zionist from South Africa who lives in Rome and loves history, especially the so-called sacred sites. Everybody who tours with me gains something for his own experience. But of course you evangelicals are always trying to get me saved. It doesn't offend me, but I'll bet I know more about your faith and the

Bible than you do. Except your dad, of course. Nobody knows the New Testament like he does. Why are you giving me that look?"

Augie shrugged.

"No teenagers like their parents. You'll get over it."

"I love my mom."

"Who doesn't? How could you not?"

"You can't say that about my father."

It was Roger's turn to shrug. "So he's not Mr. Personality. He sure knows his stuff. He's even respected by the antiquities authorities in my adopted city."

"Seriously?"

Roger nodded. "Don't let whatever is between you and him keep you from learning."

That wasn't easy. Augie hadn't planned to be receptive to anything. He studied the ground when his father read Scripture about the places they visited, and sometimes he pretended to nap as his father droned on.

But when Roger took over, by sheer force of his personality and that extraordinary voice he made the sites come alive. Once Marie sidled next to Augie and said, "Imagine, Jesus may have walked right where we're standing."

Augie let that invade his mind. He'd been raised on the accounts of Jesus' miracles and messages, but now the Bible came alive. The totality of the experience finally overwhelmed him in a several-hundred-years-old stone chapel in Tiberius that had been erected as a memorial. Ironically, the unbelieving guide set the tone. Roger drew everyone close before they entered and whispered, "We have this shrine to ourselves. I recommend remaining silent while we're inside."

The group shuffled in, Augie last. In the eerie stillness the tourists gazed at the chancellery, the architecture, and the stained glass. Many bowed their heads. After several minutes, Augie suddenly experienced a desire to worship, to pray, to really connect with God, something he had never really done. His mother prayed way more than he did. He couldn't count the number of times he had passed her bedroom and seen her on her knees.

Augie was a believer. He knew he was a sinner and that Jesus had died for him. He had even prayed to receive Christ. The truth was, however, that he had never really embraced it with his whole being. If it were true, if the God of the universe had really sent His only Son to die for Augustine Aquinas Knox, Augie wanted it to mean something in his life.

And at that precise moment, in the stillness of the old chapel, Roger began humming in his sonorous bass. Soon everyone hummed along to "Amazing Grace." Then Roger began to sing beautifully and the others joined in with sweet harmonies.

Amazing grace! How sweet the sound . . .

Augie opened his mouth to join in but was so overcome that he could only listen. When the truth of the next line hit him, he collapsed to his knees in tears.

. . . that saved a wretch like me!
I once was lost, but now am found;
was blind, but now I see.

It was as if he were really seeing for the first time, and the truth of everything he'd ever been taught—mostly by his mother—washed over him. He covered his eyes with his hands but could not stop weeping. Somehow he knew he would never be the same. He had no idea what his life would become, but he knew he was in love with this place, with the history of it, with the Man who had walked its streets and performed miracles here.

> *'Twas grace that taught my heart to fear,*
> *and grace my fears relieved;*
> *how precious did that grace appear*
> *the hour I first believed.*

> *When we've been there ten thousand years,*
> *bright shining as the sun*
> *we've no less days to sing God's praise*
> *than when we'd first begun.*

The feeling stayed with Augie for the rest of the trip. He drank in every detail, borrowed his mother's Bible, and followed along as his father ·spoke and Roger explained. Despite his exhaustion at the end of every day, he stayed up late in his hotel room, reading ahead, eager to glean every fact about every site.

His mistake had been exulting to his father, "Dad, I got it! I finally got it!"

"Got what?" Dr. Knox said.

"What you love so much about this place."

"What I love so much about it? On the whole, I'd rather be home or in Rome. And you might want to keep your personal reactions to yourself."

"To myself? I thought we were supposed to share Christ with everyone!"

"I'm just saying that you needn't be showy. We're not from a tradition like that, and it's untoward."

But Augie couldn't help himself. The next person he told of the change inside him was Roger.

"Singing in the chapel got to you, didn't it?" Roger said. "I've seen that before."

"Mr. Michaels, listen. I know what you said about how we Christians try to convert you, but how can you know so much about Jesus and the New Testament and everything and not become a believer?"

Roger clapped a hand on Augie's shoulder. "I told you. I admire your earnestness, but you must know there are many questions about the authenticity of your Scriptures. The last thing I want is to douse whatever fire has been ignited in you for your own faith. Good for you, I say."

Somehow this had made Augie frantic. He so wanted this wonderful man to experience what he had. His voice cracked and he tearfully pleaded with Roger to examine the claims of Christ in the Gospels and in the Apostle Paul's famous four-verse summary of the good news. "First Corinthians 15:1–4," Roger interrupted. "You see, it's not that I'm unfamiliar. I am simply not an adherent."

"Yet," Augie said, wiping his eyes.

Roger had sighed deeply. "I will say this for you, Augie. I don't believe I have ever had anyone weep over me before. They plead with me, pray for me, send me things to read, yes. But the tears are new."

"It's not a gimmick, sir. I really—"

"Oh, believe me, I have not one scintilla of doubt about your sincerity, and it touches me."

They became friends that day, keeping in touch and reuniting on every tour Augie could get to. His parents couldn't afford to bring him every time, so he worked part time and paid his own way. He became a student of the Bible, determined to be a guide one day himself.

Roger had been there when Augie first met Sofia, and also years later when they had fallen in love. Roger had always carried himself as a studied expert, confident without being cocky, passionate about his life's work.

Now he was in trouble, terrified and desperate for Augie's help.

The Roman Road

REFRESHED BY A NIGHT of sound sleep, Luke rose early, checked on his patient, then confided in Panthera that he would be gone all day to the port at Ostia, delivering a letter on Paul's behalf.

"Why not just send it by carriage?"

"I've heard delivery is spotty with the fire and the restrictions on the route. I won't rest until I know it's at the port."

"How is my mother?" the guard said.

"She is stable, and I will leave instructions on how to best tend to her burns. I hope to visit Paul this evening if I don't have trouble getting back."

Panthera squinted. "Let me send you with a document that will clear the way."

Luke settled in at the desk in his room to check every word of Paul's letter to Timothy. How thrilling was the testimony to his young protégé in the faith about his present circumstance. Even though the church in Rome had disappeared completely underground under persecution from Nero and many had indeed deserted Paul, still he averred, "I am not ashamed, for I know whom I have believed and am persuaded that He is able to keep what I have committed to Him until that Day."

How Paul loved to talk about the great and terrible day of the Lord when he would face Christ Himself at the judgment seat.

Luke agonized over the old evangelist's tone at the end, pleading with Timothy to come before winter and to bring Mark, because Paul felt all but Luke had abandoned him.

It was true, sadly. The Christians in Rome, both Jew and Gentile, had been terrorized by the emperor, and now Nero had further stirred the pot with mass arrests and proclamations against what he called the Christian cult. He bragged of having snared Paul, the biggest prize of all. Then came horrific eyewitness accounts that the emperor was using the bodies of Christian martyrs as torches to light garden parties at his palace. Little wonder that when Paul had been arrested at Troas and hauled off to the Roman dungeon, none of his formerly loyal friends admitted even knowing him. His letter mentioned Onesiphorus but not the gift that had come to Luke through Paul. Early in his greeting to Timothy and the others at Ephesus, he'd had Luke write:

This you know, that all those in Asia have turned away from me . . . The Lord grant mercy to the household of Onesiph-orus, for he often refreshed me, and was not ashamed of my chain; but when he arrived in Rome, he sought me out very zealously and found me. The Lord grant to him that he may find mercy from the Lord in that Day—and you know very well how many ways he ministered to me at Ephesus.

How Onesiphorus had encouraged Paul! Somehow this man had found Paul and talked his way into seeing him several days in a row. Naturally it helped that Onesiphorus was a timber, iron, and marble merchant, often accompanying huge shipments from Ephesus to Roman ports. Onesiphorus had a history of extending affection and tangible support to Paul. He not only served as one of the elders of the Ephesian church, but he also personally attended to the evangelist whenever he visited. And Timothy had confided in Paul that much of the monetary support the church had been able to offer was due to Onesiphorus' largesse.

Luke patted the bag deep in his pocket, filled with enough aureus coins to feed Paul for longer than he was expected to live. Rarely had he seen anyone so devoted to Paul as Onesiphorus. His selfless service to the evangelist, not just here, but whenever Paul visited Ephesus, so encouraged Paul. Luke prayed the Lord would bless Onesiphorus for that.

Finally satisfied that the letter would meet Paul's exacting standards, Luke sealed, addressed, and carefully packaged it. Getting to the small port sixteen miles away took the better part of the morning. He found his way to the land route—a narrow but solid road originally built for the Roman military—crowded with caravans weighed down with goods. For a coin he was allowed to let his old legs dangle from the edge of a wagon driven by a slave and his pregnant wife.

When they finally arrived just before noon, Luke said, "I pray the love of the risen Christ be with you on the rest of your journey."

The woman quickly looked away, but her husband bristled and turned back. "What did you say?"

"You didn't hear my blessing?"

"I heard it. I'm just astonished you would say that aloud when the emperor is putting your kind to death every day."

"Let me tell you something, friend. I will not deny Christ. I am not ashamed."

"Then you are a fool. Don't be talking like that in Rome. And don't call me friend. Life is hard enough as it is."

"My blessing stands."

"Please!" And with that the man hurried back to his perch on the wagon.

Luke prayed silently for the couple as the wagon slowly made its way down to the docks. He headed past the great warehouses and down a side street to a long, narrow, one-story stone building. The front was occupied by a small office, while light horse-drawn carriages and two-wheeled carts hauled by oxen accessed the back. The *cursus publicus* served Rome by loading the light carriages with government documents and the slower carts with the mass of mail for the general populace.

Luke presented the letter to Timothy with the proper fare and asked whether there was any correspondence for him. "I live in Rome."

"You know better than that, sir. All the mail for the capital is sorted there. Give us a few days."

"I don't suppose I could ride back with one of your carriages?"

"Not if I want to keep my station. Old man like you bounces out onto the roadway, and how do I explain it?"

"One of the slow wagons then?"

"We're not a transportation enterprise, sir. Anyway, you could walk back faster. We load those conveyances to their limit. Just stand at the side of the road looking forlorn. You'll find travelers sympathetic."

As it happened, Luke waited less than an hour in the blistering sun before he was picked up by a slow-moving camel caravan bearing spices and dried fruits. The aroma alone made the trek pleasant, the tangy and bitter spices mixing with the sweetness of the fruit. Luke had never been comfortable swaying atop a camel, especially as the second rider, but the driver shared his sun shield and eventually suggested that Luke climb down and ride in the wagon next to a plump old woman.

She did not appear to appreciate the company, nor did she seem open to conversation. She dozed for most of the trip, but when she roused, Luke asked if the pleasant aroma was fig cakes. That made her smile. Supporting herself with a thick hand on the side of the jostling cart, she rummaged deep into the inventory and produced a fistful of dried, sticky fruit. She spent several minutes pressing and forming it with her palms. Finally, clearly pleased with her handiwork, she presented it to Luke and then found the ingredients for another. When he reached for a coin, she waved him off and pointed to her mouth, as if suggesting he try it.

Luke silently thanked God for the provision and prayed for protection against whatever might have been on the woman's weathered hands. The fruit seemed to burst into liquid in his mouth. Luke closed his eyes, hoping she could see his rapturous expression. When he opened his eyes, she was beaming.

The caravan left Luke miles from Panthera's house and farther from the prison, and he had missed his midday nap. Wanting to reach Paul no later than sundown, he set off walking toward the *carcer*. Much of the route was uphill, and Luke felt every step.

He arrived at the prison later than he wished, and torches had already been lit at the entrance. The air had cooled, and as Luke stood drawing his cloak tighter, Primus quickly approached, bare arms apparently insulated with enough muscle to protect him.

"Something for you tonight, friend," Luke said, slipping the man a chunk of cheese.

Primus sniffed it. "One of my favorites, and the perfect addition to my dinner. I feel unwarranted honor."

"I'm so pleased."

Primus leaned close and whispered. "You are, aren't you?"

"Pleased? Yes! I want you to enjoy it. I'm grateful . . ."

"Indeed, it seems so. Anything else I can do for you, Doctor?"

"There might be something in a few weeks. Inconspicuous passage inside for two other friends. I don't know whether either or both will be able to get here, but if they do . . ."

"I shall do my best for you, sir. Just give me fair notice."

7

No Visitors

TEXAS

WEDNESDAY, MAY 7, 6:00 P.M.

AUGIE WISHED HE WAS already aboard the flight to Rome. There was nothing he wouldn't do for Roger.

As he hurried into the hospital that had housed his father for more than a year, he wondered what the difference would be with Dad in a coma, as opposed to the way he'd been for months—virtually unable to speak and certainly not interested in seeing his son. How many evenings had Augie sat with his mother, trying to draw out the old man?

Dr. Knox had been moved to the intensive care unit, so perhaps this was more serious than Augie had thought. What would his mother think of his leaving the country, even for only a few days?

The room in ICU bore the sign: "Edsel Knox, ThD. NO VISITORS."

That was nothing new. Difficult as it had been for Dr. Knox to make himself understood following his stroke, he made clear he wanted to see no one but his wife. After a year of pleading with him to make exceptions, Marie finally gave up. But neither did she obey his demand to keep Augie away. His heart ached for her now as she emerged, eyes red.

"I've been praying all day," she said as he gathered her in his arms. "Come see him."

Machines hummed and hissed, and Augie breathed in the ubiquitous odors of disinfectant and alcohol. There was barely room for a second chair, but Augie pulled one over and sat. Edsel Knox looked much the way he had when he was conscious—perhaps a little more gaunt and drawn. At least now there was a reason he couldn't meet Augie's gaze. If this did portend the end, would Augie be able to grieve a man who had never seemed to do more than tolerate him?

"Son," his mother said, "I know he wasn't easy to live with, but—"

"You knew that better than anyone, Mom. What was it? What made him so . . .?"

"He wasn't always that way," Marie whispered, leaning forward to lay a hand atop her husband's. "Do you think I would have fallen in love with a man like that?"

"I never remember his being any different."

"I'm sorry, August. I hope I never made you feel like that."

"Are you kidding? If it hadn't been for you . . ."

"I fell in love with his mind," she said. "Once he got a verse or a passage or a doctrine in his head, he could recite it, explain it, defend it, whatever anyone wanted. In class I sat in the front row so I could get a good look at him and hear every word."

"You're the only student I've ever heard say they could stand to listen to him at all."

She smiled knowingly. "His presentation was dry, but there was a treasure trove of information there."

"You didn't sit in front so he'd notice you?"

"Maybe. And he did. But he didn't speak to me until graduation when he couldn't get in trouble for fraternizing." She chuckled. "The first thing he ever said to me was that I had wasted my time getting a seminary degree."

"Because you're a woman."

"Exactly. I told him I had no intention of becoming a pastor, that I just wanted to be trained for whatever God called me to. But he just said I now had way too good an education for a Sunday school teacher. I could have slapped him."

"Yeah, that sounds like you."

"I just laughed and told him maybe I'd marry a seminary grad and be able to hold my own. I had no idea my calling would be to be his wife."

Augie suddenly felt claustrophobic and stood, moving toward the door.

"I'd rather not leave him, August."

"He's fine. Look at the readouts. We'll be gone just long enough to get a bite."

He walked her down to the cafeteria and they talked as they ate.

"I've never met anyone like Dad," Augie said. "Other kids' fathers had fun with their children. I mean, I'm grateful he wasn't an alcoholic or an abuser. But I swear, I never saw him smile. Did you?"

Mrs. Knox looked away as if trying to remember. "When we were dating he had plans, dreams. He would smile when he talked about teaching at Dallas or Southwestern someday."

"What? My whole life I never heard him say word one about either of those places without a smirk or a scowl. He *wanted* to teach there?"

Marie fell silent. Finally, when she had finished eating, she said softly, "I can't tell you the number of times he applied to each. He couldn't figure out why he never even got an interview, and it embittered him. But I knew."

"You did?"

She nodded. "I shouldn't say, August. I don't want to be disloyal."

"You can tell me."

"He doesn't know that I know."

"How many times did Dad apply to Dallas or Southwest, really?" he said, following her to the elevator.

"Almost every year for many years, as recently as last year. He thought it would lend him some credibility, *gravitas* he called it."

"He had all the gravitas he needed."

"Your father wanted to be legitimatized, August."

Augie shook his head. "I never got the impression he cared what anyone thought."

His mother shot him a glance as they exited the elevator. She put a finger to her lips as she opened his father's door. "We're back, sweetie," she said, laying a hand on the man's shoulder. "Augustine and I will be right outside."

In the hall she said, "August, the longer he went without respect, the darker his moods became. It was him against the world."

"So why did he never get a nibble from the other schools?"

Marie looked up and down the corridor and whispered, "He had me check the mail every day for a letter from Dallas. I called him as soon as it arrived, and he insisted I read it to him over the phone. When I got to 'I regret to inform you . . .' he told me to just throw it away.

"I was disappointed for him, August, but I was also relieved he asked me to stop reading, because the letter went on to say that since he had applied so many times, the dean at Dallas felt it only fair to tell him the whole truth. They had planted a student in one of his classes for three weeks, and he had evaluated your father's teaching."

"Oh, no. I'd love to see that."

"I kept it hidden among my things. Your father must never see it."

"Your things? What else is there?"

"Soon you'll know," she said. "I need to be back in there with him."

Augie slipped into an empty waiting room and called Sofia.

8

Timothy

FIRST-CENTURY ROME

FOR THREE WEEKS AFTER the citywide fire had finally been extinguished, Luke invested himself heavily in helping the injured and dying. Primus Paternius Panthera's mother had rallied to where he believed she would enjoy several more healthy years. A grateful Panthera assured Luke he could use the guest room for as long as he needed.

"Will you remain in Rome after, ah, your friend's demise?"

Luke didn't want to tell the guard that he had grown disillusioned by the Roman church and those who had abandoned Paul in fear of the emperor. Nero's evils acts against Christians were known throughout the city. Yet hadn't God called the followers of Christ to contend for the gospel, even to the point of death if necessary?

Luke told Panthera only that he did not know yet what he would do. "More than likely I will return to serve in Ephesus or some other city where the church remains strong. For now I feel God has called me to Rome. I want to pour myself out as an offering, the way Paul refers to his own death. Oh, for a faith like Paul's!"

The guard looked embarrassed, and Luke wondered if he had said too much. But Primus said, "I am impressed with Paul. Such courage in the face of his sentence."

"What of his message?" Luke said. "Surely by now you know it by heart."

Primus looked away, which told Luke that he—like all the guards in Paul's proximity—had heard Paul urgently preach from the end of a chain in the black pit. "I was raised to revere the gods," he said.

"You know Paul worships the one true God."

Primus nodded. "He makes that clear, and there is no question he believes it. That alone makes him admirable."

"But not believable?"

Primus studied the ceiling.

"Panthera," Luke whispered urgently, "these gods, do they love you? Forgive you? Would they die for you?"

Primus shifted his weight. "They're supposed to have created the world and now superintend the affairs of men."

"Tell me, friend, do these gods actually exist? Are they real beings?"

"How can we know? I believe they are real if one believes in them."

Luke cocked his head, brows raised. "By that reasoning, if one does not believe in them, do they then not exist?"

Primus sighed and shrugged. "You are too clever for me, Doctor. Leave me to my beliefs."

"Ah, I care too much for you for that," Luke said, but Primus' look told him the conversation was over.

After his visit to the prison that night, Luke stopped at an inn for a cup of wine on his way back to Panthera's. The proprietor, who knew him from his work with the fire victims, said, "A man came asking after you today. I told him I didn't know where you were lodging."

"Dark-eyed, trim, about fifty?"

"That was the man. Carrying a large satchel. Looked weary from travel. I suggested Flavia's."

"Oh, sir!"

The innkeeper shrugged. "There are not many other places."

Flavia Sabina was the widow of a senator who had left her a rather large home she had turned into little more than a brothel. The formerly handsome estate was now a rundown box full of small rooms rented by the hour, the night, or the week. The proprietress cared nothing about who stayed or for how long, let alone what their business might be—provided they paid in advance.

Luke found her lazing about the dingy foyer of the place. "Only a couple of closets left," she said. "Cheap."

Luke asked if she had rented a room to a Timothy of Ephesus.

"How would I know?" she said. "Names and hometowns are nothing to me."

Luke described him.

"Upstairs, last room on the left," she said. "If you're staying with him, that's extra."

Luke assured her he was not and hurried up the stairs. He knocked at a thick, creaky wood door.

"Who goes there?" came a whisper.

"Timothy, it's your friend!"

The door swung open to a tiny room lit by a dim lamp, illuminating Timothy's disheveled hair. He wrapped Luke in a huge bear hug and lifted the old man off the floor. "How soon can I see Paul?"

"Tomorrow evening, but where's Mark?"

"He's on the way from Troas with Paul's scrolls and books and parchments. Should be here within the week."

"You didn't bring the parchments?"

Timothy pointed to the bed, where Luke sat, and the younger man squatted on the floor. "Only the cloak made it to me. We got conflicting reports on the whereabouts of Paul's documents, so Mark is searching personally. I can't stay until he gets here. I am obligated to the brethren at Corinth on the way home."

"That's not exactly on the way."

"Nonetheless, I must go."

"Paul will be so pleased to see you!"

"I can hardly wait."

"Neither can Paul."

"Will I have any trouble getting in?"

Luke told him of his relationship with Panthera. "We will have breakfast at his home in the morning."

Timothy rose and dug Paul's cloak from his cargo. Luke fingered it, remembering it well. Thick and smooth and warm, it had been a gift from the believers in Troas. Roman soldiers had wrenched Paul away from there so quickly that he had not been able to take it with him. He told Luke he had longed for it on the prison ship, and now even more. Stifling as the dungeon was during the day, it proved frigid at night.

The next morning after breakfast, Luke tried to slip Primus a coin on their way out "for the extra meal," but his wife rushed to refuse it. "Your friends are our friends, Doctor."

Timothy helped Luke on his rounds that day, fetching water, helping carry patients, and running any errand Luke needed. When the sun finally began to wane, Luke and Timothy set out for the prison, stopping to eat and to buy foodstuffs for Paul and for Primus.

Primus was conferring with fellow guards who stepped away as Luke and Timothy approached. Primus called out, "So you have brought an assistant!"

"I have," Luke said.

The three passed through the front gate and up to the entrance, where Primus led them past more guards and down the long corridor with the crowded, awful cells on either side. Luke had forgotten to pre-pare Timothy for this and heard the younger man gasp as they hurried toward the hole leading to the dungeon.

The guards there seemed to come to life and puff their chests as Primus and the visitors entered. "These two are authorized to visit the condemned," he announced.

"By whom?"

"By the front gate guard," Primus said evenly, his tone grave. The others backed off.

"Would you aid my assistant after I'm in?" Luke whispered as he approached the hole.

"I'll help you both," Primus said, offering a meaty forearm. Luke grasped it with both hands and dropped into the black cell.

"Luke!" he heard as Paul sat up, chain rattling.

Luke lit his lamp. "I've brought a surprise. Your cloak."

"Don't sport with me, Luke."

The doctor joined Paul on the stone bench and pointed up at the hole. The old man squinted, then started as—*Plop!*—down came a large bag, then dangling feet.

"My friends have come?" Paul rasped.

"One has," Luke said, as Timothy dropped into sight.

Paul stood and tried to approach the younger man, but the chain quickly reached its limit, and Luke leapt to keep Paul from falling.

"Timothy, my son! Come to me!"

They embraced and Paul pressed his face, tears streaming, into the taller man's chest. "I knew you would come! I knew it! And Mark?"

"Maybe in another week," Timothy said, his voice thick.

"Wonderful! And you brought my things?"

"Only your cloak, Paul. Mark is hoping to bring everything else."

Paul pulled back and looked both Timothy and Luke in the eyes. "The parchments—"

"We know," Timothy said, digging out the cloak and wrapping it around the old man. Paul hummed with pleasure as he found his way back to the bench. Luke was stunned anew at how much weight Paul had lost.

"Timothy, son," Paul said, "come sit with me. Tell me everything of the brethren."

Sofia

AUGIE FOUND HIMSELF NERVOUS calling his beloved. Though they were engaged, the diamond was on layaway. He hoped to give it to her in Athens late in the summer at the most romantic place he could find. Neither wanted a long engagement. He hoped they could be married during his fall break, then he would bring her to live with him in Texas.

She answered immediately, her fluent English beautifully laden with the consonant-rich Greek accent.

"Oh, Augie," she said, "I wish you were here. I'm so worried."

"I'd ask you to meet me in Rome, but I don't know what I'm getting into."

"Don't tempt me."

"I won't leave Europe without seeing you."

"You'd better not."

He loved the longing in her voice. But he had to bring her up to date on his father. She asked about how he and his mother were doing.

"Fine, just worried about leaving now, but there's nothing I can do here."

"I need to get your new number to Roger, and your ETA."

He recited it and told her he should arrive in Rome by eight Saturday morning.

"I don't like living apart, Sof."

"I don't either. And I'd love to talk with you all night. But let me get back to Roger and let's talk tomorrow. Give Marie my love."

Augie felt light-headed as he made his way back down the hall. He'd never known anyone like Sofia, never loved anyone this way. After so many years of texting each other, the day had finally come when she joined another of his tours. She had tried to make that a surprise. But after replacing his father as the tour leader, Augie made it a practice to know the name of everyone in the group.

He was taking just over sixty tourists into Egypt and Jordan, ending at the famed red-rock city of Petra. He had seen her name and those of her parents on the manifest and found himself strangely excited about seeing her again after six years. He was thirty-six and she twenty-eight.

The tour group met in Cairo, and after a few days in Egypt flew to Amman. Her parents had greeted him with appropriate enthusiasm, her mother adding, "And you remember our daughter."

Augie reached to shake her hand. "Yes, your name again?"

Sofia had punched him. "Helen of Troy," she said. "How are you, cyber pen pal?"

"You failed your assignment, Dr. Knox," Mr. Trikoupis said, smiling.

"You were to get Sofia to see the light and join my business. But she's happy, and that's all I care about."

Augie and Sofia had sat with each other at a meal here and there, and he noticed her rapt attention when Roger answered a question from one of the tourists.

"Impressive, isn't he?" Augie said.

"Fascinating," Sofia said. And when she smiled Augie melted inside. What a wonderful person she seemed to be, and so magnetic.

"These trips are all about emotion," Roger told Augie for the ump-teenth time. "Move the people, inspire them, give them memories, and always save the best till last."

On this trip, that meant Petra.

On the final day, Augie found a heavy-eyed Sofia in the seat behind her parents near the back of the bus. Mr. and Mrs. Trikoupis appeared to be napping, so he slid in next to Sofia.

"Wait till you see Petra," he said. "Roger knows this place like the back of his hand."

"He knows every place like that," Sofia said, and Augie noticed their bare arms touching, yet neither pulled away.

"I probably won't see you till dinner tonight," he said, "but I hope you come to love Petra as much as I do."

"I'll save you a seat and let you know."

Petra had the desired effect on the entire group, which Roger insisted was due to its beauty alone. "This is one place where the guide is mostly in the way," he told them as they gathered at the eastern entrance to the long, narrow gorge that eventually spills into the city carved in stone. He quickly outlined the history of the place a famous poet once called "a rose-red city half as old as time." Inside, Roger told them, they would see the treasury, the monastery, a Byzantine church, a temple, rock-cut tombs, a street of facades, and dozens of other breathtaking works of architecture, all cut directly out of the rock.

"You can climb all the way up to what they called the high place," he said, "but I recommend that for only the most fit. Don't say I didn't warn you."

Before they all split up to explore, Augie chose to tell the story of his own spiritual journey, recounting how he had gone from an angry teenager to a man who had come to love the Land of the Book, the Book, and the Author of the Book.

Roger went over his heat- and sun-avoiding tips, pulling a gadget from his pocket that told him the temperature was already well over 110 degrees. "Dangerous," he said. "Hydrate. Take frequent breaks. And enjoy."

Augie caught sight of Sofia here and there throughout the day. Once, when she was shopping at a trinket stall, she said, "I want to climb to the high place and see the altar."

"Oh, I don't know," Augie said. "You're in shape, but this is as hot as I've ever seen it here."

"I won't forgive myself if I don't do that. When would I ever come back here?"

"Tell you what," Augie said. "Promise you won't do it this afternoon and I'll personally climb it with you later."

"Seriously? When? After this it's the pool, dinner, and bed."

"Not for you and me," Augie said.

She seemed to study him. "All right," she said slowly. "Let's see if you're a man of your word."

Back at the hotel Augie wanted just one dip in the pool before dinner. As he climbed out he was surprised to see Sofia stretched out on a chaise lounge. He knew she was trim and in shape, but he had not expected the spectacular body he found shaded by a huge umbrella. It was all he could do to keep his eyes on her face.

"Remember your promise," she said.

10

The Message

LUKE WAS IMPRESSED THAT Paul was so warmed by Timothy's visit that he ignored the bread and cheese Luke put into his lap. While the old friends reminisced about their experiences on Paul's missionary journeys, Luke busied himself pawing through the bag Timothy had brought, sorting trinkets and gifts and a scarf. It pleased him to hear Paul and Timothy laugh, recounting their years of adventures. Luke found himself cheered by Paul's enthusiasm. "You act as if you haven't seen each other for ages! It's been only a few months."

"It seems like years," Timothy said.

"It does," Paul said. "Now, the work at Ephesus . . ."

Timothy brought him up to date, asked advice on conflicts, thanked him for his letter—"which, with your permission, I would like to copy for several of the other pastors"—and said it was a gift he would always treasure.

Paul seemed to puzzle over the suggestion. "I suppose it's all right. But it was intended for only you. I'll trust your judgment."

Eventually Timothy got to the question Luke knew was coming. "What is so crucial to you in your parchments?"

"I do pray Mark finds them and can bring them," Paul said. "When might we expect him?"

"A week or so. Unfortunately, I must be in Corinth when he's here."

"But he knows where to look."

"If they're there, he'll bring them. You know he still feels bad about the falling out between you two."

"Oh, please, no! We have been over that and over that! It was so long ago. And he has since proved himself so many times."

"But he feels he was wrong."

"He *was* wrong! But that is not the point. No one has been wrong as many times as I, yet the Lord is patient and forgiving. How can I be otherwise?"

Timothy chuckled. "You weren't patient at the time."

"That was not the time for patience. He had to face his error. But we must not revisit painful pasts. I have never held it to his account."

"So, the parchments . . ."

"Merely personal things, Timothy. Forgive me."

Timothy leaned close. "You know that makes me only more curious."

Paul threw an arm around him. "I know, beloved. But listen, my fate is sealed. The brothers I have mentioned in my parchments must be allowed to choose for themselves whether they are willing to die for the cause of Christ. I dare not expose them to the Empire through my writings."

Later, at the entrance to Flavia Sabina's excuse for an inn, Timothy whispered, "You will be with him at the end, Luke?"

"How could I not?"

Timothy nodded. "His biggest fear is dying before—"

"Oh, believe me, I know. As you might imagine, he has made that quite clear."

Timothy grinned through his tears. "Perhaps looking forward to Mark's visit will help."

"No question. And your having been with him has likely been the best medicine."

"I assured him all the churches are praying for him, but of course that prompted him to ask where the other brothers have been. He wanted to know, could not anyone else have found their way to him? 'Only Luke, Onesiphorus, you, and soon Mark.'"

Luke saw Timothy off a few days before Mark was expected and found himself so eager to finally see Paul's writings that he could barely sleep. The next time he visited his friend, he said, "Your writings won't embarrass Mark, will they?"

"There's nothing for him to be embarrassed about," Paul said. "He had to see, to learn, to grow."

"To repent."

"Well, yes. And Timothy's report that Mark still regrets it shows he fully learned his lesson. If you were so worried about his embarrassment, why did you mention our differences in your own account of the first days of the church?"

Luke's writings, including his account of the Christ, based on extensive interviews—mostly with Peter—were being copied and starting to make the rounds of the churches. His recounting of the earliest acts of the apostles included a summary of Paul's falling out with Barnabas—Mark's cousin—over having Mark rejoin them in their efforts. Paul refused, and he and Barnabas parted company over it. Though they never ministered together again, Paul often spoke kindly of Barnabas. Luke's account included Paul clarifying his objection to Mark, so no reader was unaware. If Paul's own memoir shed more light on the subject, including how they reconciled, so much the better.

At long last a message arrived from Mark that he had reached Puteoli. "Greet Paul with my sincerest affection and all blessings in Christ, and assure him I will get his belongings to him. I pray you are both well and eagerly look forward to seeing you."

Paul seemed barely able to contain himself. "My parchments! But you know what I most look forward to beyond those? Having Mark read to me his own record of Jesus. Like Matthew, he was there."

"You *have* read it! We have delivered copies all over the world."

"Yes, but to hear it from his own lips, and to be able to ask questions . . . How is Mark able to afford to get here?"

Luke told him of the gift from Onesiphorus, which made Paul immediately tear up. "Is there no end to the tenderness of that man's heart? God bless him and his household!"

"I don't know that he intended the money for such a purpose, but if you—"

"Knowing him," Paul said, "he would want me to use it in any way I see fit."

"Mark will be eager to get out of that smelly port city. What is it about that place?"

Paul shook his head. "It makes even this place smell like a garden. Whether it's all the wells or the mineral springs, I don't know. Many have no choice, but how anyone would choose to live with all that sulfur . . ."

Four days later Mark sent word to Luke that he had arrived at military stables a few miles outside Rome. Luke hired a carriage and, after embracing his old friend, explained why he had gone to the expense. "It's too far to walk, and I'll not be carrying you."

"There's a denarius in it if you do," Mark said, his bag over his shoulder and a long walking stick in his other hand.

"I charge five denarii per mile for such service."

"You're a mean-spirited doctor."

At Panthera's home, Luke and Mark sat at the table as the guard's wife busied herself at the oven. "I'm sorry there's no room for a guest in your quarters," she called out.

"There is if I sleep on the floor," Luke said.

"Then he is most welcome, as is any guest you bring. I just want you both to be comfortable."

Mark said, "I'm happy to pay for the inconvenience."

"No!" she said, setting a hot pan of food between them. "We don't charge." She laughed. "If you want to stumble over each other, what is that to me?"

When it was time to leave for the prison, Mark immediately rose and began stuffing his bag.

"Take your time, friend," Luke said. "And I can help carry some things."

"You have enough with all the food," Mark said.

When they finally reached Primus outside the prison gate, Luke made the introductions. Primus lit a small torch and led them into the building, Mark following with his walking stick.

"How has the prisoner been?" Luke said.

"Quieter than I ever recall. Lonely, I'm sure. I slipped him a lamp at the start of my watch the other evening, but someone confiscated it."

"So he's been in the dark the rest of the time."

"I'm afraid so."

Luke noticed Mark holding his nose as they passed the commoners' cells. More bodies had been stacked, awaiting disposal. As they neared the end of the cell block, Luke was startled by Mark's cry as he dropped heavily to the filthy floor.

Luke and Primus whirled, and as Luke bent to help Mark up, Primus handed him the torch and reached through the bars to retrieve Mark's stick. A prisoner had thrust his hand out and snatched it. Now he was trying to keep it from Primus.

Luke had never seen the guard so furious. His face turned a deep red and his veins bulged in the flickering light as he reached deep into the cell. The other prisoners tripped over each other to avoid his massive arm. He spoke quietly but with such ferocity that Luke feared he would hurt someone.

"Make me unlock this cage and come in there," he said, "and you'll not see midnight."

The prisoner with the stick appeared gleeful, as if any attention was better than none. The others watched with what appeared fascination and fear, as if unable to believe their cohort had done something so rash.

The prisoner edged one end of the stick toward Primus' hand, touched his fingers with it, and pulled it back again. Primus stood to his full height and began pawing at the keys on his belt.

"Here! Here!" the prisoner said, poking the stick out through the bars.

Primus wrenched it away so fast that it flew from his grip and clattered to the floor. He grabbed it and now wielded it like a club. Luke ducked and covered Mark as the guard swung it full force at the bars.

With a loud clang and crack, the whole cage seemed to move. The prisoners fell back as the wood splintered. "What did you want with a stick anyway, slave?" The prisoners filling the cell scrambled to the wall and squatted on their haunches, terror in their eyes.

"I'll execute your sentence right now!" Primus hollered, keys in hand again.

"No!" Mark cried out. "Forgive him! He was just curious!"

Luke rose and whispered to Primus, "He's not long for this world anyway, friend. Look at his eyes. It's all right."

The man's eyes nearly glowed yellow. Whatever was killing him would not be remedied in here. "It's your lucky day, scum!" Primus hissed.

The prisoner was on his knees now, hands clasped before him. "Thank you! Thank you!"

The guards surrounding the hole had emerged to see what was going on. Now they backed away from Primus, who still looked as if he wanted to take off someone's head. "Now I've gone and damaged your stick, Mark. I'll find you another."

"Don't worry about it," Mark said, peering into the hole. "I won't need it down there anyway."

"Mark!" came the weak scratchy voice from below. "Is that you?"

"Paul! I'm on my way down!"

"Praise God!"

Primus helped Luke down first and dropped him the satchel. Luke lit his lamp and embraced Paul, and they stood together watching Primus slowly lower Mark through the opening. He rushed to Paul and fell into his arms.

Paul wept and prayed and exulted over his friend. "And you were able to find all my things?"

"Everything. I brought it all."

"Even your own account? You can read it to me?"

"I'll be pleased to, Paul, but I know what you want most of all."

"Just knowing my parchments are here is enough for now."

"Since when have your writings been private? We copy your letters and take them all over the world. Timothy is even having your last letter copied."

"With my permission, though that wasn't my intent."

"Everyone benefits, Paul. The brethren in all the churches are encouraged by your letters only slightly less than if you joined them in person."

Paul sighed and sat, whispering to Mark of the danger to the brethren contained in his memoir. "I will leave them in Luke's custody and trust his judgment about who should see them."

Mark nodded with a knowing look. "You don't want me to see what you have written about me."

"Not until I'm gone. But you have seen my latest letter to Timothy, so you know I speak well of you to all. Now I want you to read to me from your account of the Master."

While Mark was finding it among his things, Luke whispered, "Paul, have you been able to talk with Primus?"

"Some. He always looks about, worried his comrades are listening. I believe he has a soft heart, Luke. You must keep in touch with him after I'm gone. He greatly admires you."

"We have become friends."

Luke held the lamp as Mark sat next to Paul on the stone bench and spread out his gospel. He began:

The beginning of the gospel of Jesus Christ, the Son of God.

As it is written in the Prophets:

"Behold, I send My messenger before Your face,

Who will prepare Your way before You."

"The voice of one crying in the wilderness:

'Prepare the way of the Lord; make His paths straight.'"

John came baptizing in the wilderness and preaching a baptism of repentance for the remission of sins. Then all the land of Judea, and those from Jerusalem, went out to him and were all baptized by him in the Jordan River, confessing their sins.

Now John was clothed with camel's hair and with a leather belt around his waist, and he ate locusts and wild honey. And he preached, saying, "There comes One after me who is mightier than I, whose sandal strap I am not worthy to stoop down and loose.

"I indeed baptized you with water, but He will baptize you with the Holy Spirit."

It came to pass in those days that Jesus came from Nazareth of Galilee, and was baptized by John in the Jordan . . .

Luke could not remember Paul ever looking so content, so fulfilled, so rapturous.

1 1

Love Story

—————————

JORDAN

ONE YEAR PRIOR

—————————

SOFIA HAD SAVED A place for Augie at dinner that night at the hotel near Petra. Though he had to fight to suppress a smile, he kept things polite and formal with her—which seemed to amuse her too.

"By the way, you're off the hook for the climb to the high place," she said. "I couldn't walk another step. Sorry. I appreciate it. And I really wanted to see Petra from up there, but—"

He held up a hand. "I know you're beat. But it would mean a lot to me if you'd come. I promise you won't regret it."

She lowered her chin and narrowed her eyes. "You're serious. Well, if it's that important to you . . ."

"It is."

"And if you want to give me a piggyback ride there and back . . ."

He laughed. "I'll at least find us a ride to the base of the climb."

"And what's my guarantee? You promised I wouldn't regret it. What if I do?"

"Then I'll never do it again."

Her smile and laugh made Augie feel her look had been created for his pleasure.

When dinner was over, Augie and Roger stood at the door as people filed out, thanking them for the week. When the Trikoupises reached them and were talking with Roger, Augie whispered to Sofia, "We'll have to hurry to beat the crowds. I just have to run to my room for my flashlight and a jacket. You'll want a sweater or something."

"It's still in the 90s out there."

"Suit yourself." *Got to admire a woman with her own mind.*

"Now that's what I call a flashlight," Sofia said a few minutes later when Augie showed up with a boxy contraption that emitted about ten times the light of a standard one. He also had two bottles of water and had tied a hooded sweatshirt around his waist.

They hurried across the road, past the souvenir shops—most still open—and finally reached the long expanse that led to the Siq, the mile-long, narrow gorge into ancient Petra. There Augie hired a horse-drawn carriage to take them directly to the base of the high place. As soon as they crowded into the back, they were off, bouncing and jostling, Augie fighting to keep from landing in Sofia's lap. He loved her giggle.

Finally they reached the Siq, where crowds had gathered, and soon the shambling carriage was the only conveyance in sight.

"Oh, Augie!" Sofia said, "it's beautiful!"

The entire length of the narrow passageway, lit by the sky during the day but pitch black at night, had been lined with candles stuck inside paper bags. The eerie pink glow reflecting off the red-rock walls guided them all the way to the end, where they found hundreds more of the lights scattered before the treasury building and throughout the city.

"It's called Petra at Night," Augie said. "And you can see why so many people line up to experience it."

"I sure can, but I wouldn't want to do this on foot. Those people must think we're royalty."

"Aren't we? I thought you were Helen of Troy. That makes me Brad Pitt. Or something."

At the base of the high place Augie told her, "You can go first and I'll shine the light on the path from behind you. It's steep and can be treacherous, but just keep moving. When you need a break to catch your breath, let me know." He pointed the flashlight at their destination high in the distance. "It'll take a while, but we can do it. Just stay close."

When she started up, Augie was impressed by the muscles in her long legs. "I think I'd rather shine the light on you," he said.

"Dr. Knox! We don't know each other that well."

"I'll behave."

Sofia stopped occasionally, bending at the waist and resting her palms on her bare thighs, breathing deeply.

"You okay?" Augie said, offering her a bottle of water.

"Just need to refuel." She drank deeply and started up again.

"Hey," Augie said, "before you get too far, look down."

Sofia turned and gasped, scanning the ancient city lit by all the candles. "That may be the most beautiful thing I've ever seen."

"And you come from one gorgeous country. I promised you wouldn't regret this."

"No matter what, I won't. Bet you wish you weren't weighed down by that sweatshirt. I'm sweating."

"We're not at the top yet, girl."

Sofia gave him a funny look. "Well, then let's get going, boy."

Augie took the lead. He had always found the last part of the climb the toughest, and he was relieved to finally get to flat ground and reach back to help her up. He led her to an outcropping where she sat on a rock to catch her breath. "When you're ready, I'll show you the altars," he said. "You'll see where the blood of the animals drained, where they put the coals, everything."

Sofia lowered her head and breathed deeply. Finally she stood, hands on her hips. "I'm so glad you talked me into this. You can say, 'I told you so.'"

"Just happy you're enjoying it," he said, shining the light in her face, making her cover her eyes. "You have the best smile."

"You make me smile," she said.

After he showed her the altars he shone the light down into the valleys.

"I could stay here all night," she said.

"You'd be lonely."

"You'd leave me here?"

"It's been a long week," he said. "I need my sleep."

She laughed, then crossed her arms and rubbed her biceps. "Oh, no! I didn't want you to be right."

"About?"

"Now that I'm up here, I'm cooling off."

Augie set the light down and pulled the sweatshirt off his waist. "No, that's yours," she said. "You planned ahead. I didn't."

"Don't be silly," he said, slipping behind her and draping it around her shoulders. "I brought it for you anyway."

"You did not."

"I did," he said, turning her to face him. "My thermostat runs high."

She relaxed as he helped get her arms into the sleeves. The sweatshirt enveloped her and the long sleeves hid her hands. He zipped it to her neck and put his hands on her shoulders. "Better?"

"Yes," she whispered. "Thank you."

And in that instant Augie pictured Sofia with him forever. The vision raced through his mind, their waking together, eating together, going to church together, raising a family. The scenes were as clear as day and stunned him speechless. In the shadowy light he gently cupped her face. "You know, there's nowhere else I'd rather be than right here right now."

He drew her face toward his, and as their lips met she wrapped her arms around him. When he pulled back they stood gazing at each other, inches apart. "August Knox," she said, "I was not expecting that."

"Need I apologize?"

"You'd better not. All the way up here I was planning what I was going to say when we reached the top. Like what a great guide you are. How smart. How wonderful with people. How passionate about these places and about your faith."

"Okay, I'm listening."

"That's not what I want to say anymore. I want to say what you said, about not wanting to be anywhere else."

He drew her close again and they held each other tight. "Have we started something?" he said.

"I sure hope so," she said, her voice thick with emotion.

He pulled back. "Tears?"

"I'm already missing you, Augie. We fly home tomorrow. When will I see you again?"

"As soon as I can arrange a trip to Athens."

Precious Gems

―――――――

FIRST-CENTURY ROME

―――――――

LUKE WAS SORRY TO see Mark go, especially after the lift he had given Paul. But with Paul's memoir waiting, Luke didn't mind having the old missionary all to himself again. The writings had the potential to be priceless. Paul had never penned a simple letter to a friend or a church without loading it with truth so poignant and beautifully written that the whole of the body of believers benefitted from it. Better than that, Paul's thoughts and reasoning seemed to be born of his rich relationship with Christ. He wrote with an urgency and authority that amazed and thrilled his readers. Would his memoir prove any less?

That evening in the dungeon Paul riffled through the parchments, asking Luke to move the light higher. Finally he pulled a huge sheaf of sheets from the rest and handed them to Luke. "We must not wait any longer. Take these and start reading them. Guard them with your life, and bring them back to me. I need your counsel. We need to talk these through, make certain they are accurate, complete, and most of all meaningful."

Luke tucked the documents away and rushed to Primus' home as if bearing precious gems. His body ached from the fatigue of the day, but his mind was alive. In his room he disrobed, then wrapped himself in his cloak and sat at his table, lamp lit, parchments stacked before him. He lifted the first and tipped it toward the light.

13

The Offer

AUGIE KNOX STOOD OUTSIDE his dying father's room in the ICU, pre-occupied with getting out of town. Growing up, had it not been for the oasis of his mother's gentle spirit, he would have died of thirst in the desert of his father's indifference.

Edsel Knox was widely respected, a precise, articulate, brilliant theologian. But nothing of the truth of what he knew so thoroughly seemed to reach his heart. He could explain anything. He seemed able to personally experience nothing. Despite all this, Marie Knox spoke lovingly to him and about him, caressed him, held his hand.

At home he was a roiling cauldron of silence. Jokes were anathema. Never a smile. Never a kind word. Not even a thank you for dinner. He was not a TV watcher but rather a reader. When not studying theology, he read history. Before bed it was word games.

Edsel rose at the same time every morning, six days a week, shaved, showered, dressed, ate, left, and returned late every afternoon like clockwork. Even on Saturday he spent the day at his office. Sunday he went to services morning and night, napping in the afternoon.

Augie hated to think what he might have become had his mother not been, in essence, both parents to him. Yet he could never elicit one disparaging comment from her about his father. She defended her husband, spoke lovingly of him, and said she felt privileged to help him to be the man of the Word that he was. *Man of the Word maybe,* Augie thought, *but no man of God.*

Had his parents ever—even in the distant past—enjoyed a magical experience like Augie and Sofia enjoyed at the high place in Petra? His father's reaction to the news of Augie's engagement was simply, "You think they're going to let their daughter marry so far out of her class?"

His mother said, "August is good enough for anybody."

"Tell a Greek millionaire that."

Augie shoved his chair back. "I wouldn't be the first man in this family to marry outside his class."

"August!" his mother said.

His father gave him a look that would have made Mona Lisa frown.

Now Augie wondered if the man ever fathomed how fortunate he had been to find such a wife. Who else would have put up with him for so long?

The elder Dr. Knox had proved maddeningly prescient. Nearly two months from their first kiss Augie arranged a short trip to Athens, leaving just enough time to get back for his fall teaching load. During the flight he couldn't sleep, couldn't read, couldn't concentrate, paced whenever he was allowed, and jabbered so long to a flight attendant about Sofia that she said, "Tell me any more about her and I'm gonna have to be in the wedding."

When the eternal flight finally touched down at Athens International Airport Eleftherios Venizelos, Augie was haggard and unshaven, but he found her smile above the crowd, and it was all he could do to keep from running over people to get to her. Had any couple ever been more in love, more destined for each other?

That night, after he had napped and freshened up, Sofia introduced him to her friends over dinner. They were pleasant and talkative, but Nomiki, one of the guys from her work, seemed to be studying Augie. Finally the man said, "You guys are in love, right?"

"Of course," Sofia said. "Now don't start . . ."

He shook his head. "I don't get why you've exiled him to a hotel. Who does that?"

"Do you really want to know?" Augie said.

"No, he doesn't," Sofia said. "We've already been through this. He didn't think there was anyone left in the world like us."

"There's not!" Nomiki said. "You're adults. You're in love. You're planning a future together. Get on with it!"

"Don't think we wouldn't love to," Augie said.

Nomiki smiled. "So you agree with her that you're somehow honoring God this way?"

"She's worth it."

"Sorry I asked."

Sofia held up a hand. "Enjoy your dinner, Nomiki."

At the end of the evening, when the group was saying its farewells, Nomiki shook Augie's hand. "You're a lucky man," he said. "More power to you."

Two days later the flight to Thessaloniki took less than an hour, and Augie was surprised when Sofia headed for the rental car counter.

"Dad and Mom are both busy at the main store."

"Too busy to—"

"They need a little time to get used to this, Augie. I am their one and only, remember."

Tri-K Imports' anchor store occupied half a block in downtown Thessaloniki. Malfees Trikoupis emerged from the back to warmly embrace his daughter. The man seemed to always dress the same way— gray slacks, tailored white shirt, navy blazer with gold buttons.

He shook hands with Augie while keeping a protective arm around Sofia. "You've been here before, no?"

"Many times, but always with responsibility for a busload of tourists. Never time to really enjoy all you have to offer."

"Allow me to show you around."

"Daddy, let us say hi to Mom first. I'll bring him right back."

They found Eris Trikoupis in the office looking anything but busy. She seemed to force a smile, remaining seated as she tepidly greeted Augie. "Sofia, are we going to be able to get some shopping in today?" she said. "Just you and me?"

The tour of the store, no surprise, proved a ruse to cover Mr. Trikoupis's agenda. "You're not here to ask for my daughter's hand, are you, Dr. Knox?"

"What if I was?"

"Have you slept with her?"

"I assure you I have not. You know I share both your faith and your values."

"I can only hope. Are you prepared to support a family?"

"No, sir, I'm not. I'm prepared to support her. The rest of you will have to fend for yourselves."

Malfees looked up sharply, and Augie grinned.

"I did not find that amusing."

"Forgive me, sir. I'm well aware you have all the resources you need."

"And I fear that you do not, Dr. Knox. How much do you make?"

"Sir?"

"Don't make me repeat myself. It's a fair question. You come to tell me you're in love with the most precious possession I have in the world. Surely it cannot surprise you to find me curious as to how she will be cared for."

Augie told him how much he made at the seminary—which was embarrassingly paltry.

Malfees Trikoupis cleared his throat. "Would it surprise you to know I make fifty times what you do?"

"Seriously?"

"Easily. My daughter is used to a certain lifestyle."

"I know better than that, sir. You have done well to require her to live within her own means."

"That's just good parenting," the man said. "But naturally she has a safety net few enjoy."

So Augie's own father had been right. A Greek millionaire would be hard pressed to let his daughter marry a pauper.

"Would you deprive Sofia the love of her life, the desire of her heart?"

"Of course not. But I could find a way to immediately quadruple his income while making full use of his intellect, his education, and his unique skills—particularly his knowledge of our language. Too many of our so-called experts are only guessing at what they see inscribed on ancient artifacts. Would you not find it interesting and challenging to use your skills that way?"

"I'm all ears."

Augie followed Malfees Trikoupis through an Employees Only door and down a narrow hallway that opened into an office wholly unlike the rest of the cluttered back rooms. Despite that it was windowless, the room was large and pristine and as exquisitely appointed as the office of any head of state.

A glistening hardwood floor bore a marble-top desk and a teak boardroom table surrounded by expensive guest chairs. Side tables and shelves showcased pieces that made the best artifacts in the store look like bric-a-brac. "Take a moment," Malfees said. "Drink it in."

Augie wandered among the artifacts, agape.

"Literally priceless," Sofia's father said. "I would not sell one of them for any amount."

"I thought everything in this world had a price."

"Not everything. Not these. Not my daughter."

"Mr. Trikoupis, please. I would never refer to Sofia as anything other than the treasure she is to both of us."

"Sit," Malfees said, pointing to a chair.

Malfees moved behind his massive desk and settled into his leather judge's armchair. "I insist on total honesty on the part of every employee. No misleading. No fudging on prices. My policy is one you Americans would call zero tolerance. I consider it the only way to do business. I have been told by the government that I keep the most meticulous records of any merchant in Greece. With all the fraud and black-market sales, all the illegal trading in antiquities, I may be the only one left who is known by all to be totally aboveboard. I'm often consulted by the authorities when something goes wrong."

"Sofia is quite proud of you for that."

"In this trade, a reputation is all a man has. Greek law establishes that the state owns all antiquities found on land or in the sea. Anyone who finds something, even by accident, must report it to the authorities. And there is no exporting of such items without permission of the Antiquities Council. I have former colleagues who tested that law and wound up in prison for five years, plus having to pay a fine."

"But I assume you have loftier reasons for being ethical."

"I've never even been sniffed at by the Police Antiquities Squad."

"I'm impressed."

"Enough to come to work for me?"

Malfees outlined a dream job that included being his right-hand man, leading tours, consulting with antiquities experts, and an obscene salary. In the middle of it, Malfee's intercom buzzed. He shook his head as he pressed the button. "Busy."

"It's Dimos Fokinos on the line, sir."

Malfees sighed. "Just tell him I'm not here but that you'll get me the message."

He turned back to Augie. "That's your competition. He is currently a grossly underpaid archaeologist, a civil servant in the Hellenic Ministry of Culture. Anywhere else, in any other economy, such a gifted specialist in artifact dating would be a wealthy man."

"So you'd be fortunate to land him."

Malfees shrugged. "That would be your misfortune. It's only fair to tell you he's as tall as you are, darker, Greek. And if I may say so, he looks a lot like my daughter."

"So he's gorgeous."

Mr. Trikoupis raised a brow. "That's what people say."

"So you haven't invented this position just for me?"

"I will hire the most qualified and the most interested. Think it over. Talk it over."

"Sofia and I will pray about it."

"Well, that too. But don't delay."

Attractive as the offer was, Augie knew before he got out the door that there was no way he would subject himself to it. Besides his love for his students, being beholden to her father would be toxic to their marriage.

He did not look forward to disappointing the man.

I, Saul

FIRST-CENTURY ROME

LUKE WAS STRUCK BY the neat, compact handwriting of the opening sheet of parchment and wondered how long ago Paul must have begun this project. He reached to the bottom of the stack to examine more recent entries. Sure enough, the script was larger, the characters shakier, the pages more blotched. Besides Paul's failing eyesight, his hand was less steady and his poorly lit environments had made writing nearly impossible. Now, in total darkness, there was no way he could finish this himself.

Fortunately, the writing at the beginning was precise enough to overcome writing so small that Luke had to hold his lamp directly over the pages. He was instantly drawn into the narrative, forgetting where he was, the time of night, his exhaustion, or his responsibilities the next day.

I, Saul, begin the recitation of my most vivid memories by acknowledging an incident that has affected my entire life, even with all that came after it. And as you shall see, all that followed even I would deem the creation of a fanciful mind had I not myself lived it. I will describe this horrific occurrence, which took place in Jerusalem many years ago, as it falls chronologically in my narrative, but I mention it now to clarify that rather than shape me, it instead revealed the essence of the man I was. Though the memory of it is seared so deeply in my mind that I recall it as if it happened today, it was merely the first in a long line of momentous events that led to this writing.

My account of that day—in due course—will detail my part in the death of a man, a murder which at the time I considered a legal execution, and thus just. But first I must establish who I was, what shaped the man I had become by the time that violence occurred.

I should also clarify that I call myself Saul here as I begin my writings, not because I was once Saul and became Paul. I was also called Paul—my Greek name—even as a child. But it's true I was more commonly called Saul then. Even after the great change in my life, when in an instant old things passed away and all things became new, I was still as frequently called Saul as Paul. Only many years later in my ministry did my Greek name become most common.

I have established clearly in my preaching and my letters to the churches that I am the chiefest of sinners. This is anything but false humility. It would be folly for me to even pretend to justify the depth of my depravity.

Ironically, my older sister Shoshanna bat Y'honatan—the victim of my boorishness when we were growing up in Tarsus and then Jerusalem, and who now does not even claim me as kin—would be the first to corroborate that, for whatever other faults I bore as a child (and there were many), I was dispassionately honest. To this day she might call me many unsavory things, but never a liar.

Was I born truthful? I think not. But I had been taught to fear God. Relatives and neighbors came to refer to me as Judge Saul or Honest Saul. Aunts and uncles would tell my mother, "Rivka, that boy has the bearing of a leader."

She would smile and whisper, "A rabbi."

My fear of God began with a reverence for my father's quiet depth of character. He was a respected businessman, a leatherworker, a tentmaker. But beyond that, he was both a Roman citizen and a Jew of the highest order, a Pharisee of the tribe of Benjamin. Before I knew what that even meant, the privilege and responsibility of both my citizenship and my race had been ingrained in me. I had been named after the first king of Israel, who had also come from the tribe of Benjamin. To be a Jew, I was taught, meant much more than just nationality. To my father, and thus to my family, our Jewishness was more religion than race. We weren't just Jews; we practiced Judaism.

I rather enjoyed having a smaller than usual family and being the only male child. I could tell Shoshanna was proud of me. I knew why. I was smart.

Again, I say this not to boast, and again I credit my father. I cannot remember a time when I did not clearly know my place in the world, in the Empire, in the city, in my family, and in the synagogue. How did Y'honatan the tentmaker accomplish this? All I can tell you is that he educated me daily, and not just in the Scriptures. My father did not merely assign me chores, but he also performed my tasks with me. From a very young age, when I was barely old enough to understand and much too young and nowhere near strong enough to actually do the work, he taught me every step in the tent-making process. He showed me how to make short work of what appeared big jobs. But, beyond that, we took walks. And on these walks he said the same things over and over and over.

Such repetition might have tested the patience of other boys. That was not true with me. Even when I got to where I knew what he was going to say and could have recited it with him, I felt honored to be entrusted with such truth and wisdom.

My father impressed upon me that our very lives, our daily living, comprised a ritual meant to honor the God of Abraham, Isaac, and Jacob. He was the one true God, to whom we owed obedience and allegiance. Father told me the story from before I was born when he and my mother had been forced as Jews to flee to the magnificent city of Tarsus, and yet they retained their Roman citizenship. I was fascinated by Tarsus' great history, architecture, shops, and the marketplace.

Sabbath soon became my favorite day, because it meant assembling at the central meeting place, the synagogue. There I heard confirmed what my father taught me every day—that the husband and father was both the legal and the spiritual head of the house, responsible for the family. It fell to him to be certain his wife and children were protected, sheltered, and fed. I never even considered a future that did not include exercising those roles within my own house.

I loved that we were Pharisees, set apart, devoted to God and the Scriptures. Even before I began my formal education in Judaism, my father ingrained in me that there was one and only one way to do whatever task was set before you: the right way. We were to honor God in everything. This conviction would lead to that great watershed day and my approving of the condemnation of a man known to be an enemy of God, and to my involvement in his execution. As you will see, I hesitated not in the least, believing with my whole heart that I was fulfilling one of my life's purposes. It was not the first and would hardly be the last of many times I would feel that way. No contemplation, no questioning, my whole being engaged in doing the right thing for the right reason—harking back to my father's counsel.

I had been born into an unusual family, a unique circumstance. We were Jews, yet we were Roman citizens, and our culture was influenced heavily by the Hellenists—the Greeks. Greco-Roman *was the term for the Empire as it was known then. I spoke Hebrew at home and in the synagogue, and I picked up Latin from the Romans. But the Empire was so influenced by Greece that I learned Greek as well. My father said that being civilized meant being Hellenistic, but he was also careful to warn me not to let Greek philosophy invade the purity of our orthodox religion. "We are Hellenists," he said. "But we are not Hellenizers." To me that* meant that we were religious Jews in a Greco-Roman world.

Only when I matured did I realize the advantages of being fluent in three languages. As a child this came naturally. I knew one had to be multilingual, religious, and patriotic. Being citizens brought with it privileges that few others enjoyed. Most of the people living in the Roman Empire were not citizens, and yet my father cautioned me that our first allegiance was to God, and our law was found in the Scriptures. So where most Roman citizens were philosophical in their beliefs—either Stoics or Cynics—and the Hellenists concentrated on linguistics, the arts, the sciences, and the fitness of the body, we Jews elevated the spiritual life.

The Romans revered citizenship. I was, by birth, a citizen. The Greeks held intelligence and thinking paramount. I was taught the best their culture had to offer. And among Jews, the tribe of Benjamin—my tribe—was elite.

Having all this in my favor could have led to arrogance and conceit, and I can't deny I bore much of that. But believe me, I stored all this away and determined at a very young age to be the absolute best Benjaminite-Pharisee-Roman-Hellenist I could be. I could barely pronounce those words as my fifth birthday approached, but I knew what turning five meant. I would learn to read and write, and this would be based on the Scriptures.

Though this all began as a colossal mystery to me, I somehow grasped that what my father tried to tell me every day came from the holy book. When first I began haltingly reading it, I was reminded that the Torah (the five books of Moses) was the true source of all knowledge. My religious training, my study of history, my learning of ethics would all be based on the Scripture.

Just as I couldn't wait for it to begin, I was unique among others my age because soon I couldn't get enough of it. I caught on to reading quickly, memorized lengthy passages, and enjoyed the attention that brought me when I was called upon to recite them in the synagogue. Most fascinating to me were the stories of great men and women who walked and talked with God Himself. I knew no one who did that. My father was good and devout, but I did not sense he conversed with God the way the patriarchs did. When I raised the question, I was told that I should worry about doing what God wanted and expected of me, more than trying to become personal friends with Him.

I was struck that God knew the men in the Scriptures. Perhaps if I learned all there was to know, followed every rule, honored God in everything I did, He would notice me. Know me. How I longed to walk with God as my ancestors had!

As I neared my tenth birthday, when I would begin schooling in Jewish law, my father also taught me more about the city of my birth. He did this in the most casual way, merely talking about what an impressive place we lived in. He told me it was one of the largest cities on the Mediterranean, half a million people living in about ten square miles. It was also a port city, exporting minerals and timber from nearby mountains, and producing cilicium, a fabric woven from the hair of the black goats found in the Tarsus mountain range. Cilicium was named after our province, Cilicia, and it was the raw material my father used for the *black tents he crafted. The Roman army was one of his biggest buyers.*

Tarsus was the capital of Cilicia, and while it was under Roman control, the senate gave it the standing of libera civitas, *or "free city," which meant we could govern ourselves. I was also fascinated that ours was a university town, a metropolitan center of Hellenism, though my father warned me that they taught a pagan education. He reminded me to stay on a path that taught me only the best of their culture.*

I was proud to be from the city that was the first stop on a trade route that connected the Mediterranean to the Black Sea. I wanted to stay there, grow up there, become a religious leader there. But it was not to be. Both my rabbi, Daniel, and my father saw in me something more. By the time I was thirteen years old, I was well along in the study of the law. I was so far ahead of other students my age that Rabbi Daniel told my father it seemed a waste for me to stay in Tarsus. A real, advanced education could be afforded me only in Jerusalem.

Jerusalem! That was 375 miles southwest of Tarsus. I loved my hometown, my friends, my relatives, and in no way did I want to leave my family—even if it meant formal training under one of the great, noted rabbis in Jerusalem.

"We would not send you," my father told me. "We would go with you."

"With me? The whole family?"

"Of course! I am responsible for my children. I would not abandon you to someone else's care."

Naturally all this leads to the fateful day I have been

foreshadowing, but allow me to take you there as I was—step by step. My father had a huge order of tents scheduled to go to Damascus in Syria, and I overheard him talking with my mother about accompanying the load.

"You haven't traveled with your goods for years," she said. "And you always hated those long voyages."

"That's the beauty of this," he said. "We are taking advantage of cargo room available in a caravan carrying dry goods that will take the land route to the Syrian gates and through Antioch. It's a long journey to Damascus, but I could then go on to Jerusalem, perhaps a hundred and sixty more miles south, and look into the two rabbinic schools for Saul."

Mother sat silent. "I don't know," she said finally. "You'll be gone such a long time."

"Several weeks, but there is much to learn about Jerusalem before we relocate there."

"Didn't the rabbi say only one of the schools would be suitable for Saul?"

Father hesitated. "Both are Pharisaic, but they take decidedly different approaches. Rabbi Daniel leans toward the school founded by Rabban Shammai over the one founded by his contemporary, Rabban Hillel. Both are long dead, but their schools reflect their views of the faith."

"Why does the rabbi prefer the Shammai school?"

"Because it's more orthodox, emphasizing strict obedience to the law. The other, now run by Hillel's grandson, Gamaliel, is more open and tolerant."

"That does not sound good."

"No," Father said. "It doesn't. So it doesn't surprise me

that our rabbi prefers Shammai. But Gamaliel is considered a great and wise teacher. I cannot imagine he is actually apostate. He too is a Pharisee, after all. I just want to visit both schools."

"Perhaps you should. This is a critical decision."

The next Sabbath, my father revealed his plans to Rabbi Daniel as our family was leaving the synagogue. The tall, thin man seemed not at all disgruntled that my father had not immediately adopted his suggestion, but rather amused. "I encourage the trip!" he said. "Be sure in your own mind before you turn over Saul's training to any man. Better yet, take the lad with you! See where he would be most comfortable."

"Oh, Rabbi!" Mother said. "Please don't put such notions into the boy's mind. How would he ever keep up with his studies? And what would I do without either man in the house for all that time?"

"Forgive me," the rabbi said. "I should have been more discreet. But you know Saul is so far ahead in his studies that he need take only a copy of the Torah with him to keep reading as he travels. As for your needs, rest assured that our congregation will look after you. Anyway, knowing Saul as I do, I'm convinced that in the end he will agree with me about which school to choose."

My mother chuckled at the real reason the rabbi wanted me to go, but she didn't seem to take seriously even the possibility of it.

I had never been outside Tarsus and only knew what my father had told me about the outside world. The very idea of such a long journey to a foreign province, then *actually visiting Jerusalem, the temple, the schools . . . It was nearly more than I could take in, but I began pestering my mother about it the moment we arrived home. To my great surprise, she did not reject the idea out of hand. And of course I enlisted my father as an advocate. Even more astounding, Father had me begin riding one of his business's packhorses for practice, telling me it was likely he and I would make the last leg of the trip—from Damascus to Jerusalem—on horseback.*

When Mother began warning me that the trip would be more arduous than I could ever anticipate, I knew she had opened her mind to the possibility. I assured her I was prepared to endure any hardship for such a blessed opportunity.

That trek would become my greatest early memory.

Luke sat back and rubbed his eyes, imagining what was to come in the manuscripts. He had so many questions for Paul, but he was also exhausted and knew he had to rest before a busy morrow. As he lay on his pallet he imagined the young boy and his father on the adventure of a lifetime, and while at first the visions kept him awake, soon he was drifting, his mind carrying him across the rugged terrain that led from Tarsus all the way to Jerusalem.

15

Marie's Klediments

———

TEXAS

WEDNESDAY, MAY 7, 9:00 P.M.

———

As Augie drove his mother home from Arlington Memorial, all he could think of was Roger, desperate for his help. He had to force himself to concentrate on his mother's question.

"Have you ever regretted not taking Sofia's father up on his offer?"

He shook his head. "I started imagining what I could do with all that money, living in a beautiful city, giving Sofia the kind of life she grew up with, still leading tours, plus evaluating antiquities, using all my training. But nothing could compare with multiplying myself every year by dozens of students serving churches all over the world. I tried to explain it. Malfees claims to be a fellow believer. I thought he would get it, but he was not happy."

Augie's cell chirped. A text from Roger. "I need to check this out, Mom. Sorry." He pulled off at the next exit and parked on the shoulder.

"hope Sat soon enuf. have 9mm S&W 4 u. Time 2 get familiar w/1 b4 dep?"

Augie texted back: "Smith & Wesson? Haven't shot in 20 years. Why do I need a gun? And why're you up? 3 a.m. there. Call me."

"no more calls. b sure 9 is a parabellum. text when u get here."

Augie pulled back onto the expressway. "What is it?" his mother said.

"Roger's in trouble. I've got to get to Rome by Saturday and I have no idea how I'm going to do it."

"If it's that dire, you'll get there, that's all."

"It's going to take a lot of money I don't have."

As he walked his mother into her house, he suggested they talk about it in the morning when he came to pick her up.

"Nothing doing, August. You're going to tell me what's going on with Roger or I won't sleep."

"You look asleep on your feet now."

She waved him off and disappeared, emerging a few minutes later in robe and slippers and carrying a large wooden box. Augie leaped off the couch to help her, amazed at how heavy it was as he set it on the coffee table. "What's this?"

"All in good time," she said, sitting next to him. "Now out with it."

Augie told her he didn't know much beyond the cryptic texts and one urgent phone conversation. He did not tell her about Roger's mention of the gun.

"Whatever could be wrong?" she said.

"No idea, but if he needs me, I have to get there. I've got to sneak in a trip to the bank tomorrow, I guess."

"I have money."

"You do not."

"I do, August. For such a time as this. Your dad put me in charge of the checkbook, and I have saved a little from every bit of income he's had for more than forty years."

"Does he know this?"

"He never asked. Thank the Lord, we've never needed to touch it. It's in one of those interest-bearing accounts connected to a credit card I have never used." She leaned over and rapped on the box. "It's right in here."

"How much are we talking about, Mom?"

"Just a tick under forty thousand dollars."

Augie sat speechless as she beamed.

"And you'd lend me—"

"Nonsense! You will take the credit card and use what you need."

"Mom, I couldn't—"

"Don't you dare deny me the freedom to do what I want with my money."

Augie was reminded of his own conversation with Rajiv that afternoon. What's fair was fair.

"You're a lifesaver, Mom."

"You're my life, August. Now I'm going to entrust this box to you. Guard it with your life. It's full of my klediments."

"Your what?"

"June Carter Cash said klediments were anything you hold near and dear to your heart. Your father has never seen most of these, August. I need to warn you, though. Things in there will shock you, some will break your heart. But do me a favor, get to this before you leave."

"Mom, there's so much I have to do before I go, but if it's that important to you . . ."

"It is."

Curious as Augie was, he was also exhausted, pulling into his tiny bunga-
low just before 10:00 p.m. He opened his mother's box of treasures and,
after digging through a three-inch layer of keepsakes and bank statements that would have discouraged his father from pawing any deeper,
found the credit card, still gum-stuck to the letter it had come with.
Online, he booked the Friday flight that would get him into Rome the
following morning, still unable to find a seat other than in first class.

He Googled pistol ranges and found the Wildfire Gun Shop about
ten miles south of the seminary. He added "firearm training" to the end
of his to-do list for the next day, then opened his mother's klediments.
Deep in the bottom of the box lay a thick, oversized manila envelope
secured with twine and also heavily taped shut.

He sliced it open on his kitchen table and tipped out a couple of
inches worth of smaller envelopes and documents. Augie was surprised
to see more than a dozen business-sized envelopes from both Southwestern Baptist Theological Seminary and Dallas Theological Seminary.
He finally found the one his mother had mentioned. It contained an
evaluation of his father's teaching by an anonymous auditing student
who had been surreptitiously sponsored by Dallas.

The form called for the evaluator to rate the professor 1 through 10
in the following areas:

Knowledge of subject

Ability to explain information

Delivery

Engaging of students

Finally came an assessment of the suitability for the candidate to
teach at Dallas.

The evaluator had awarded Augie's father 10s in each of the first two
categories, notes stating that "It's clear Dr. Knox possesses as exhaustive

a mastery of his subject as a lifetime student of the Bible could. And he articulates this precisely and completely so that any student listening and taking notes could learn it thoroughly."

For the second two categories, however, notes next to the zeros included, "Dr. Knox's recitation of facts is so monotonous that it's amazing even *he* can stay awake through it. No inflection, no passion, nary an indication that the material even interests him."

No surprise, the essay on the candidate's suitability to teach at Dallas was brief: "I'd rather be tortured than be forced to sit one more minute in a class taught by Dr. Edsel Knox."

Augie was stunned that someone at Dallas thought it necessary to include such a biting review. This must have come after years of having turned down his father's applications.

Augie sat with his head in his hands, hurting for his father, despite the rigid lack of emotion the man had shown his whole life. What made him so grim and yet so deluded that he apparently did not see himself that way?

As he began to put things back into the box, Augie noticed an envelope from a urologist's office postmarked forty years before.

Dear Dr. and Mrs. Knox:

The attached printout confirms the disappointing news I shared with you last week. The figure of fewer than five million sperm per milliliter of analyzed volume is conclusive, as any figure under twenty million is too low to predict viability. I wish you all the best as you consider other family planning options.

Augie was suddenly overwhelmed with anger. How dare his father insinuate to him—and to many others over the years—that adoption proved their only option because his mother was too fragile to bear children?

It was one thing for a man to be negative and nasty, but what could make him so small and insecure that he would blame his own infertility on his wife?

Augie dug to the bottom of the stack he had slid from the envelope, only to find a manila folder on which his mother had written "Private and Confidential."

Augie tore it open and out fell a pile of yellowing newspaper articles more than sixty years old. A handwritten note had been penned in shaky script and signed by his late Great-Aunt Gladys: "Marie, Ed must never know I sent these. Please."

The headlines, the pictures, the captions assaulted Augie, making him hold his breath, his heart jackhammering. He quickly stepped back from the table, as if to separate himself from the poison of this history. Here was something he wished he had not opened, not seen, not been exposed to.

This was a game changer that would affect everything he thought he knew about his father.

All Augie Knox knew about his extended family was that his mother had a brother and a sister, both married, both with families, and so he had the normal complement of aunts, uncles, and cousins on her side.

Dr. Edsel Knox had spoken only occasionally about the fact that his father had been an itinerant evangelist and then a pastor in Florida before dying when Edsel was not yet two years old. "Needless to say," he had told Augie once, "I remember nothing of him and know only what my mother told me. My mother's sister Gladys said he was quiet and humble."

Augie could not forget his father's faraway look and the slight shake of his head when as a youngster he had said, "So Grandma never got married again? You didn't get another dad?"

Augie was puzzled by his father's silence and his mother's quick change of the subject. Augie's grandmother died before he was ten, and his memories of her two visits and their one visit to her home in Florida were fading. One thing was clear, however. Whenever they were in her presence, the only person who smiled was Augie's own mother— who seemed to scurry about trying to keep everything civil. His father and his grandmother barely spoke and rarely looked at each other, and strangely, she seemed to take little interest in Augie either. At her funeral, his father neither wept nor spoke.

The few times Great-Aunt Gladys had visited, she doted on Augie, seemed to get along famously with his mother, and was cordial with his dad. Augie had a vague recollection of a tense conversation in which Aunt Gladys suggested that his father could be more attentive to her sister, Dr. Knox's own mother. "She lives with regret every day of her life," his great-aunt had said.

Over the years, Augie began to see his dad as almost an orphan. Aunt Gladys passed when Augie was a young teenager, and it seemed his father now had no connection to any family but his own wife and adopted son.

Now Augie knew why. Though his father was not named in any of the newspaper articles, it was clear he was the child in question—protected by a quaint journalistic convention that would not be practiced today. "The lad, 9," one article intoned, "has been awarded to the custody of his aunt, the court determining his mother failed to protect her own son, despite obvious wounds and scars." Edsel's mother had been sentenced to a year in prison, five years' probation, permanent loss of custody, and limited visitation rights.

Augie's body seemed to pulsate and he was unable to sit. He bent at the waist, palms flat on the table, squinting at the truths that screamed from the pages. "Oh God," he prayed. "Oh God, oh God, oh God . . ."

It turned out that his father's mother had remarried when his father had just turned eight. That man, according to the torrid articles, was convicted of aggravated child abuse and sentenced to fifteen years in prison. While in a county holding cell awaiting transfer to the Florida State Prison, he took his own life.

Augie finally sat, overwhelmed with pity for the child his father had been. To lose your father as a toddler, then endure the intrusion of a replacement and then the abuse . . .

What other kind of a man could have grown from such a wounded child? And how in the name of heaven had he become a theologian and seminary prof?

Augie awoke eight and a half hours later, locked his mother's storage box in the trunk of his car, then took off for a brisk run. He assumed he felt out of sorts because of the revelations that had assaulted him, but after about a mile it came to him. For the first time in as long as he could remember, he had forgotten to start his day with prayer. But he had awakened with such dread, so many emotions, he was eager to get on with his day and get to his mother.

As he ran, he called her, telling her to skip breakfast so they could go together when he picked her up. Forty minutes later Augie drove her to her favorite restaurant on the way to the hospital.

"August, don't punish me for fulfilling my vow. Your father was livid that his aunt had told me anything, and he still doesn't know I've seen the newspapers. But she felt I needed to know."

"Why?"

Marie put down her fork, avoiding Augie's gaze. "Your father and I actually separated for a few weeks during the first year of our marriage."

"Are you serious?"

"I couldn't make him happy. We'd actually had fun when we were engaged, but as soon as we were married, he withdrew emotionally. I know you grew up with that, August, and I'm sorry. I didn't know what to do to snap him out of it. I suggested counseling, talking with our pastor, getting out and doing things, changing our routine. He wouldn't hear any of it, so I left him a note that I would be at my parents'. Would you believe that for the first week I didn't hear a word from him?"

"Somehow I do, yes."

"I was humiliated. I couldn't imagine living with him the way he was, yet I would never break my wedding vows. So what was I to do? I called his mother, whom I had met at the wedding, where it was obvious something was really wrong between them. She said, 'Welcome to my world,' and hung up on me. The only other person I could think to call was his Aunt Gladys. That woman traveled hundreds of miles to see me. I'll always be grateful for that."

"And she told you the story."

"She also told me she felt inadequate to help Edsel, so she just raised him as a Christian, kept him going to church, and discovered he was very bright and inquisitive."

"But always sad."

"And angry. I made up my mind I would not stay away from him any longer. He was surprised to see me. Said he was glad he didn't have to tell his superiors at the seminary that his wife had left him. I held him and told him he could trust me, that I would always love him and be there for him." She sighed. "He said, 'I hope so. We'll see.'

"He also said he would never speak to his aunt again. I scolded him, told him she loved him and had rescued him and made him the man I'd fallen in love with. That was the first and last time I ever saw him break down. I thought I had reached him, August, and that he suddenly realized what an angel Gladys had been. But no. He could only sob and rage that every time his stepdad took him to the basement or the attic, he prayed God would rescue him. He said he prayed for hours every night, crying himself to sleep, but God never listened to him."

"He must hate God to this day," Augie said. "How did the guy finally get caught?"

"Gladys saw welts on Edsel's back and demanded to know what was going on. It was torture for him to finally spill the full story, because his stepdad had threatened to kill him and his mother if he ever told. Your father made me swear I wouldn't tell you. But it seemed time."

"I wish I could talk to him," Augie said.

"I pray he regains consciousness," she said. "I'd like to tell him one more time I love him. And I'd like to say good-bye."

Marie couldn't go on, and when Augie covered her hand with his, she wept. When she was able to speak, she said, "I tried now and then to suggest that God *had* answered his prayers by sending Aunt Gladys. But he said it was too late. Too much had happened. In my naïveté I actually expected him to be a good father, the opposite of what he experienced. But he was simply incapable."

Augie shook his head. "He should have gotten help and been a better dad. But I can forgive him. I want to. Yet none of this explains why he always blamed you for not being able to have children."

"Imagine his shame, his horrible self-image."

"But blaming you, that was wrong, plain and simple."

"August, your father may be a senior citizen, but to me he's a stunted, wounded nine-year-old boy. I wish I could have gotten through to him, seen him grow up, mature, reclaim some joy in his faith. But if people seeing me as too fragile to bear a child somehow deflected further humiliation from him, I was willing."

"Some would call that misplaced loyalty, Mom, even enabling."

"I call it love. He chose me to be his wife, and God called me to it too. It's been an honor to serve them both for all these years."

"You're a giant, Mom."

"I wish."

Augie had planned to walk his mother to the elevator and be on his way, but now he felt a need to see his father—especially before leaving the country. A different Edsel Knox lay tethered to the machines and pumps and IVs. His hair looked thinner, wispier, his face gray and gaunt, his body bonier. But for the whirring and clicking, and a readout showing his pulse, BP, and respiration, the man could have been dead.

Marie held one of Edsel's hands in both of hers and whispered, "Good morning, sweetheart. August and I are here."

Augie placed a hand atop his dad's head and tried to look him full in the face, despite that Edsel's eyes were closed and an oxygen mask covered his mouth. Augie leaned in and laid his ear on his father's chest, strangely comforted by the strong, regular rhythm of his heart.

"Stay with us a while, Dad," he said.

16

The Journey

OVER THE NEXT SEVERAL weeks, Luke spent his days caring for victims of the fire. As the rubble was hauled off and the healing centers released more and more patients back to their homes, the great city slowly came back to life. In some quarters, the emperor began to rebuild.

Luke hoped that as reconstruction began and the masses of the dead were finally buried, his volunteer work would abate. But no. After his initial excitement ebbed, he felt every one of his years.

By the time he visited Paul each evening, his legs felt heavy and his breathing shallow. It encouraged him to know that when he couldn't be there, Panthera often visited his prisoner. Still, Paul sat alone in the darkness most of the time when Luke was not there. And except for the infrequent occasions when other guards might briefly light a lamp in the dungeon while they doused him with two buckets of water, or came to retrieve and empty the waste bucket, all Paul could do was sit or stand or pace as far as his bulky chain would allow.

According to Paul, his bowls of cold gruel—one delivered early in the morning and the other in the middle of the afternoon—tasted as bad as they smelled. "Primus has begun slipping me an apple now and then, which tides me over until your visit. He seems needy, Luke, and yet he is a proud man and will not be pushed. All I can do is to explain the gospel and tell him what Christ has done for me. He worries about his family and their future, but he admits that he can no longer bring himself to pray to the Roman gods. But neither is he convinced that the one true God exists and that Jesus is His Son. It might take something dramatic to persuade him. You know what I am referring to."

Luke harrumphed and sat heavily on the stone bench as Paul stood shifting from foot to foot. "You think he'll attend your execution?"

"I intend to invite him."

"I can't imagine even a prison guard would want to see your head severed by some gigantic executioner."

"Fetch him for me, would you?"

"You want to talk to Primus right now, tonight, with me here?"

"Especially with you here. You should hear how he talks about you, Luke. He admires how kind you were to his mother and now to his wife and children. And in your faithfulness to me, he's seeing what true friendship, real loyalty, is all about."

Luke sighed and moved beneath the hole in the ceiling, then laboriously hoisted himself through the opening and hurried through the smelly corridor, ignoring the cries and moans and outstretched hands.

When Luke told him Paul wanted to see him, Primus whispered, "I was with him earlier. The others are suspicious."

"If you don't think it's a good idea—"

"No, if he needs me . . ."

He summoned a young guard. "Man my post until I return."

Once in the dungeon, Primus said, "I mustn't stay long. What is it?"

"I request the honor of your presence at my execution."

"I've watched heads strike the ground. Such gruesome sights have lost their fascination."

"I need to know that some in the audience will give me a fair hearing. You and Doctor Luke may be the only ones. Knowing you will be there would give me peace of mind, Primus. Please. As a friend."

"I am your friend, Paul. That's one reason I would rather not witness your end."

Luke nodded. "That is how I feel too."

"The only two friends I have in Rome would both abandon me in the hour of my greatest need and not extend that small kindness?"

Luke tended the lamp. "To you it seems small. To me it is a great sacrifice. I could never abandon you. I just wish you could see what a horrible obligation it is."

Paul moved slowly, carrying his chain, and sat next to Luke. "I'm not entirely insensitive," he said, draping an arm around the physician's shoulder.

"Not entirely. But you must admit that your truth telling often gets in the way of your peacekeeping."

"Do you still have need of me?" Primus said. "Entertaining as it is to see old friends squabble . . ."

"Forgive us!" Paul said. "I just need the same commitment from you that I have from my colaborer here."

Primus cleared his throat, clearly overcome. "I prefer not to see you die, but if you wish me there, I will be there."

That night in his chamber, Luke returned to the parchments, the reading giving him an entirely new view of his old friend, revealing the history and perspectives of the man he thought he knew so well. Somehow they had never discussed much of this in all their years together, despite the miles they had walked, ridden, and sailed. A chunk of bread tucked in his cheek, Luke settled in to read again.

Traveling by land with dozens of camels, their drivers, and slaves, Father and I took the long route, north and west of the Mediterranean, that led to Issus near the southern border of our province. From there we would laboriously make our way through the Syrian Gates mountain pass and eventually into Antioch.

We had said our tearful good-byes to Mother and to Shoshanna—who told me she was actually going to miss me. I felt the same but couldn't bring myself to say it. I could see from the look in her eyes that she knew how I felt.

I was the only member of the vast traveling party under the age of twenty. Not only was I not assigned any tasks, but I was also told to stay out of the way of the slaves and their masters. Father explained that the transport company had goals they had to reach every day to make the trip profitable, and they intended to succeed.

Besides the camels that each transported almost a thousand pounds of food and water and wine, horses carried the masters who made sure the colossal flatbed wagons, pulled by oxen, remained steady on the stony roads built for the military.

Father told me the animals could cover about thirty miles a day but that the wagons would slow the entire caravan to the pace of our walking. With the ruts in the roads jostling the loads, the slaves had to re-secure the cargo whenever the carts stopped so the drivers could grease the wheels with animal fat. It was a slow journey.

The wagons bore high piles of tents, which could be easily assembled by the buyers as long as the pieces stayed together and didn't pitch off onto the ground when the wagons tipped.

Ingeniously, Father had the slaves store on top of two of the wagons tents that could be easily used every night and disassembled every morning, allowing the whole party to sleep in privacy and comfort—as comfortable as one could be in that barren, dusty terrain.

I was so full of enthusiasm and energy that as soon as we started out I dashed in and out of the way of the camels and horses. Footpaths ran along either side of the eight-foot-wide road, and while Father kept to these, I ran ahead and wondered why we couldn't go faster. At this rate it would take forever to get to Syria, let alone to Damascus. And Jerusalem was several days beyond that!

Every thousand or so paces we found great, heavy, stone markers that Father said were a little less than a mile apart. Every twenty or thirty miles we saw inns, often very nice ones. Because of the size of our party, we used Father's tents rather than pay for lodging.

The worst part of the trip was the sheer boredom. There was little for me to do but walk along with the slow caravan or sit on one of the bouncy wagons, trying to hang on.

When I complained, Father reminded me of the scrolls and my responsibility to keep up with my schoolwork, memorizing the Scriptures and the law. It was not easy to read on a bouncing wagon, but Father created a sun shade for me, so all I had to worry about was keeping myself aboard and not dropping the scroll.

Much of my adult life would consist of traveling thousands of miles, so I am grateful that I learned to use the time for lively conversation, prayer, even reading and studying.

The rest of the people on our journey, none of them Jewish, seemed fascinated or even amused by our pausing to pray three times a day, beginning at dawn. Father and I would attach our tefillin (small boxes filled with Scripture) to our foreheads, bind upper left arms with leather straps, and wear the tallit (shawl).

By the end of the second week I was bored to the point of madness and had to remind myself that Jerusalem was the reason for this ordeal. It seemed to me a mirage by now, but I just aimed at the great day when we would arrive and I would see all the things I had heard about the Holy City.

17

Nine Millimeter

TEXAS

THURSDAY, MAY 8, 8:50 A.M.

AUGIE PULLED INTO THE Arlington Seminary parking lot a few minutes before his Greek final. How he'd love to have been taking this exam rather than monitoring it. Greek had come easy to him and was one subject in which he'd scored perfectly.

As he headed inside, going over everything he had to accomplish before his Friday morning flight, Sofia called from Athens.

"Augie, I'm worried. My last message from Roger said he had something he would leave for you—everything you needed to know in case anything happened to him. What could he have gotten himself into?"

"Wish I could be there now," Augie said, and he told her about Roger saying he'd also have a gun for him.

"There's a pleasant thought I can chew on the rest of the day."

"So where do I find this stuff if I can't find him?"

"He doesn't want me to tell you by phone or text," Sofia said.

"So you're coming to Rome? I know you're a daredevil, but I don't want to be responsible for—"

"Roger is my friend too, Augie. If I go, I know the risks."

"I've got to get to class."

"Just one more thing. The guy my father hired to take the job you turned down, Dimos Fokinos—"

"Your dad told me about him. Everything I'm not. Gorgeous, ambitious . . ."

"Anyway, my father's trying to set us up."

"You and Dimos? That's just great."

"He's brilliant, I'll give him that. He guesses the age of an artifact on first sight, then examines it to see how close he came. Pretty impressive."

"Uh-huh."

"Augie, you have nothing to worry about. You know I've already made my choice."

The final was uneventful and Augie was preoccupied with the conversation he had to have with Les Moore. Augie dropped the blue books in his office, and as soon as he arrived at Les's office, the man rose and pulled on his suit jacket.

"That's certainly not necessary," Augie said. "This is just me as a friend with a couple of—"

"Dr. Knox, seriously, we're not friends."

"—difficult requests."

"If you're asking that I reconsider the salary cut—"

"No, I'm accepting the offer."

"Good thinking. You have the cushiest job in the place."

"Let's not get ahead of ourselves," Augie said. "You may want to withdraw the offer when you hear what I need. Dr. Moore, tomorrow morning I'm boarding a flight to Rome and—"

"Surely you don't mean tomorrow morning," Les said, running a finger along the top page of his calendar. "You have two finals tomorrow, not to mention your summer-school class that starts next Wednesday."

"About that . . ."

"No. Whatever it is you're asking, no. This budget thing is decimating us, Dr. Knox. We'll be short staffed like never before, and we can't have you gallivanting all over—"

"Les, sorry, but I need you to cover my finals tomorrow and to take the first few days of my summer-school class next week if I'm delayed getting back."

"You can't be serious! I can't do that."

"Then you'll have to find someone who can. It doesn't even have to be a faculty member, just someone to sit in there and then gather the blue books."

"What's so pressing in Rome?"

"I'm not at liberty to—"

"You think I'm going to drop everything, inconvenience myself, not to mention anyone else, to let you run off on yet another trip? What's so all-fired important about it?"

Augie sat back and sighed. "A dear, trusted friend needs me. A guide I've worked with for years. That's all I can say."

"Have I met him? Was he on that tour I took a few years ago to—"

"Israel, yes! Roger Michaels."

"What's his problem?"

"All I know is that he needs me and I'm going. I'll be back as soon as I can."

"This Michaels is not a believer, is he?"

"What in the world does that have to do with—"

"I'm just saying."

"We're only to help needy friends if they happen to share our faith, is that it?" Augie stood. "You can keep that contract."

"Calm down, Augie. I was just making an observation."

Augie dropped back into the chair. "See how easy that was, Les, to call me by my first name? Can't we just talk this through? Let me be clear. If going costs me everything I love here, so be it. Now I'm asking you, as my superior, to help make this happen."

Les Moore folded his arms and stared into his lap. "You'll owe me, Dr. Knox. No more shenanigans, no more asking to have your classes covered. And, you know, the wife and I wouldn't mind being invited on one of your trips this summer."

"I've been asking you for years. We cover everything for those willing to serve as hosts."

"We'd be happy to do that."

"Then are we good for tomorrow and next week?"

"But not beyond next week."

"I wish I could promise that," Augie said.

11:00 A.M.

In the parking lot of the Wildfire Gun Shop, Augie locked his briefcase, bulging with blue books, in his trunk next to his mother's box of klediments. The shop was a low, concrete-block building painted industrial green. He heard *pop, pop, pop* from the range in back and was surprised to hear the same inside. A handsome woman with gray hair to her waist introduced herself as Katrina, the wife of the owner, and explained that they had "an indoor range too. By noon won't be nobody wantin' to shoot in that sun. 'Cept maybe me. I don't mind the heat."

Augie told her he needed to be brought up to speed on a Smith & Wesson nine millimeter that would be waiting for him in Rome.

"Good thing," she said, "'cause you'd have to jump through so many hoops to take one with you, it wouldn't hardly be worth it. This nine, is it a parabellum?"

"Yes! What does that mean?"

"Just tells me the kind of ammo it uses. And it'll take me twenty minutes to run you through the safety procedures, how to load it, the safety, grip, aim, all that. Then you can shoot a few rounds. Have to charge you for that. Nothin' for the training, just for the bullets, cheap target ammo. If you need it for protection over there, you're gonna want high-velocity hollow points."

Augie was taking notes. "How can you do this for nothing?"

Katrina laughed a throaty chortle. "You're gonna get hooked, young man. Then you'll be in here looking for your own gun, bullets, ear protection, holster. I'll make some coin off ya."

She stepped behind a glass counter, pulled out the nine, and showed him everything from where to seat the handle in his hand to how to determine his dominant eye, and how to dry fire. When she was satisfied he knew how to load the pistol and handle it safely, she handed him a pair of ear muffs he worried had been used by dozens before him. She put on her own and signaled for him to follow. "You mind shootin' outside?"

Augie found the weapon loud and explosive. Within half an hour he had emptied four ten-round magazines. *God, deliver me from ever having to use a thing like this.*

"You know enough to protect yourself," Katrina said, beaming. "Just remember, average response time by the cops—here or in Rome, I bet—is about twenty minutes. Response time of a nine parabellum is about eleven hundred feet a second. Make sure if an attacker gets to you, he's comin' through a hail of bullets. If he kills you, it better be with your gun empty."

1:00 P.M.

At the hospital Augie's mind was already in Rome, but over lunch his mother wanted to talk. "I should have told you about your father," she said. "It would have made your life a little easier, at least."

"I just don't get why he didn't want help," Augie said. "Smart man, well-read, he had to know a professional could help walk him through this. He couldn't have enjoyed living the way he did. Is he still mad at God?"

"I'm afraid so. There's no question of his faith. He believes what he studies and teaches, but I know the little boy in him still resents feeling like his prayers were ignored. Truthfully, August, I don't understand that myself. To allow a defenseless child to be abused . . ."

"I can't make it compute either. I know God is mysterious, but I believe He's omniscient and omnipotent. I can't pretend I accept what God allowed."

"Trusting is the hardest part of my faith," his mother said. "All I could do was be someone to love your father and care for him in spite of it all."

As Augie walked her back up to ICU he said, "You know I'm leaving tomorrow morning. No idea when I'll be back."

She nodded. "I'll be all right. Just take care of Roger."

Bewilderment

FIRST-CENTURY SYRIA

The rugged mountain pass called the Syrian Gates may not have been the longest part of our journey, but it proved the most arduous. Father said the Romans should have built the road in a serpentine fashion so it wouldn't be so steep, but apparently they saved materials and money by making it as straight as possible. The men and the animals leaned into the inclines and huffed, pushing themselves onward. It was as if someone warned them that trying to stop, even for a breath, might send them tumbling back down.

"They seem so eager to get there," I said. "And yet they still have so much farther to go after that, from Antioch to Damascus."

"And we have to go almost that far again to reach Jerusalem," Father said. He pointed far into the distance to explain how the more than five thousand acres were fed by fresh water from the south by what was called the Plateau of Daphne.

"I heard some of the masters talking about going there," I said.

"You and I will stay away from that plateau," Father said. "They hold ceremonies there to worship Apollo."

"But we worship the one true God."

"That's right, Saul. Apollo is a myth, and I daresay most of the Greeks know that. Yet they worship him anyway. You know the commandments. It is a dangerous thing to worship any god but the God."

I could hardly keep my eyes open when we finally arrived outside Antioch in what seemed to me the middle of the night. I felt safe as long as I knew Father was awake, but when it was clear he had fallen asleep, I lay staring at the dark walls of the tent, shuddering at every strange sound in the night.

We had recited our prayers that evening, but still I longed to converse with the God of the heavens and the earth, the one true God of Abraham, Isaac, and Jacob. The great men of Scripture walked and talked with Him. Why couldn't I?

It seemed strange to address Him without the formality of our daily recitations, but somehow I believed He would forgive a child. I dared not even whisper for fear of waking Father, but from my heart I prayed, Great Creator God, I am afraid. Give me courage like Jacob and strength like David. And please answer me. Show me You hear me and are with me.

God did not speak to me, but I took my drowsiness as His answer. That I could slumber in spite of my fear meant that perhaps God had granted me courage. I didn't feel bolder, but I did drift off.

When the morning sun forced its way through the tiny slits and openings of the tent, Father remained still, snoring quietly. I crept out and relieved myself in the privacy of a thicket, then wandered back to where the watchmen sat around a small fire, toasting bread and roasting small strips of a meat I did not recognize.

One gestured toward the pot and said, "Enjoy!"

I hesitated, so he tore a chunk off his loaf and sopped some juices from the pan, handing me the bread with a bit of the meat atop it. I must have been hungrier than I knew, for I found it mouthwatering. The man ignored my thanks and turned back to chatting with his mates, so I strolled off to a bluff overlooking Antioch.

As the great city came into view and the sun fought the chill of the morning, I stepped up on a rock and was suddenly overcome. I had no idea what was affecting me so, but as I stared over the walls into the shimmering town, I felt something I could not describe then and still find difficult to put into words. It was not the sheer size of the city, though I knew only Rome and Alexandria were larger. No, it was something else, something personal.

From my vantage point I could see the common wall

that encompassed the entire metropolis, and beyond that
Antioch's four quarters, each with its own wall. Father had
promised that we would visit and get a look at its aqueducts
and baths, race courses, and temples.

I couldn't wait, and yet neither could I move. Something about this place seemed to invade my soul. It was as if
God Himself was impressing upon me that this would not be
the last time I saw Antioch, that regardless of how much of
it I toured with Father today, that would be only an introduction. I cannot explain it. I simply knew deep within that
Syrian Antioch would become an important place to me.

I started at a voice behind me, Father whispering,
"Antioch the Beautiful." We made our way down the hillside and into the city, quickly finding ourselves on the main
street, lined on both sides with covered colonnades. I was so
tempted to tell him of the strange feeling the place gave me,
which only increased with every step. What was it about this
city that so drew me? I couldn't imagine why it would play
a role in my future, especially when I would be studying in
a rabbinical school in Jerusalem. Was God trying to tell me
that this was where I would one day be assigned?

Father pointed out various carvings and statues to the
city's deity, the goddess Tyche. "It means luck in Greek," he
said, "Fortuna in Latin. It seems all anyone here cares about
is prosperity. The God of our fathers has no place here."

Was it possible I was meant to one day bring the truth
of the Torah to Antioch? Its sights and sounds and smells
stayed with me for days as our caravan slowly made its way
south toward Damascus. My attraction continued to grow

as the city faded from view. My young life had centered on the Scriptures, ancient texts and teachings and laws. Now something visceral called to me. What it was I had no idea.

Strangely, many days later as we slowly came upon Damascus, the same deep feelings rolled over me. What was happening? Was God calling me to something? I couldn't bring myself to mention it to Father. He was one of those who, along with our own rabbi, had told me to concentrate on my studies and not worry about becoming personal friends with the Creator. "That was for those great men, the patriarchs, at that time. Our job is to learn and to know the truth of the law and to practice it daily."

For weeks I had felt alone with my deeply emotional thoughts about Antioch. I was curious about Damascus and enjoyed learning all Father knew about the city, but in no way did I expect it to have the same effect on me that Antioch had.

I could not have been more wrong. We had been peering at Damascus for hours that hot morning, but when we were nearly upon the great city, I was overwhelmed. It lay some fifty miles inland from the Mediterranean on the south bank of the Barada River.

Father said it stretched about a mile by a half mile, surrounded by a wall that from a distance appeared dotted with ramparts on its northern and eastern sides. As we drew nearer we could see how massive these ramparts were.

When the caravan settled just outside the city, Father and I quickly set off. I stayed close to him and stared at the looming ramparts. "How does bread and fruit sound for our meal?" he said. I just smiled and nodded and followed him to a street called Straight.

The same deep stirrings that had overcome me above Antioch came rushing back. In a strange way, while I felt separated from the God I knew about from the Scriptures, it didn't seem this was my fault. I didn't know what else to do to get close to Him. I loved the stories of His speaking to my heroes. All I could do was believe my elders that God did not work that way anymore and take some solace in the fact that neither my father nor my rabbi, nor anyone else I knew of, had enjoyed the experiences described in the sacred texts. But not until years later did I attribute to God Himself my feelings about the city.

Father must have noticed. "Something on your mind?"

I shook my head, immediately riddled with guilt for my lie of omission. "I'm a little homesick, I think. I miss Mother and Shoshanna."

"So do I. But we are to be guests of my buyer, Samuel, this evening. Maybe we'll feel better in his home."

Father's customer proved to be only slightly younger than my father and, I could tell from his fringed tzitzit, he was also Jewish. In a Jewish home the rituals and practices would be familiar, and I wouldn't feel conspicuous. Samuel's eyes lit up and he asked if I was of age and had been recognized as an adult.

"Yes, sir," I said.

"My David—the eldest of our five—will come of age two months from now, and I fear he is hopelessly behind in his studies. Maybe you can encourage him."

Father laid a hand gently on my shoulder and said, "Saul will very much look forward to that."

When all the business was done, we walked with Samuel, guiding our horses, to his home less than a mile away. David, taller and thicker than I despite being a little younger, introduced himself and his siblings. His handsome mother told us dinner would be ready in an hour.

David asked if I wanted to go exploring in the city.

"I'd better ask my father."

"You have to ask?" David said.

"I have to at least tell him," I said, and again I was stabbed with guilt. I never told my father anything. I sought his permission. But I didn't want to admit that, even though I hated myself for this. Father's quick approval made me feel even worse. I determined to not let this boy influence me in such a way again. I was so shaken, by the time I walked back to David I had told myself that this was about me, my character, my resolve. Maybe I was thinking too deeply for a boy my age, but whatever had pushed me past my peers intellectually was now working on my behavior. Every decision I made from that time on would be my own, influenced by no other. Was I growing up too quickly, taking things too seriously? Perhaps. But this was an important moment in my life.

I followed David into the street and toward the heart of the city. Soon he stooped to pick up a rock and gave it a mighty heave over the top of an apartment building.

I stopped. "Won't that land in the street beyond?"

"That's the plan. But it didn't. When it does you hear

screams or shouts or—the best—curses. That's when you know you've hit a donkey and a cart is out of control."

"And you think that's funny."

"It's hilarious. Try it."

"I would never risk hurting someone."

"No one would know who did it."

"But someone could even be killed."

"I've been doing this for years, and nobody's ever died that I know of."

When David bent for another rock, I charged him. "Drop it!" I said.

He shoved me, and I stumbled and almost fell. When he raised the stone as if to throw it again, I lunged at him again, knocking him to the ground. "Do that again," I said, "and I'll drag you home and tell your father."

David struggled to his feet. "Relax, Saul! I was just playing! You've got to remember, I was named after a guy famous for throwing rocks."

"That's not funny. You were named for a hero, a man God chose because of his heart for Him."

David shook his head. "You want to climb the city walls, or do you want to go back and ask your father?"

I had been eyeing those walls all day, fascinated by the ramparts and wishing I could get a closer look. Sure enough, as we drew near, several people were walking along the top of the city wall, and children were climbing the sides, carefully positioning their sandals or boots in the cracks between the bricks.

I studied the wall, and the places for my feet and hands

seemed to form a pattern. I leapt into action and scampered up the side as if I had done this all my life. I followed David across the broad top of the wall to the other side, where he told me to take hold of the side of one of the ramparts and look down. The outside of the wall had been sealed with something that made it smooth, impossible to climb up or down. It made sense that Damascus authorities would make it impossible for their enemies to climb the walls. I couldn't imagine a way in or out of Damascus if the gates were locked.

From this vantage point I could see for miles, the surrounding area dotted with rocky outcroppings and flowering jasmine bushes.

That night, after a tasty meal, Father and I were directed to a small room off the kitchen where we would sleep. After our prayers, we lay on mats, and I whispered, "I need to tell you what happened this afternoon, but only if you promise not to tell Samuel."

He stared at me in the low light. "I'm not sure I can make that promise, Saul. If it's something egregious, I might be forced to."

I wished I hadn't even broached the subject. But now I was stuck. I told him of David's rock throwing.

Father sat up and sighed heavily. "I can't believe you allowed that, Saul."

"I didn't! I knocked him down and threatened to tell on him if he did it again. And he didn't, so that's why I hate to go back on my word."

Father shook his head. "You please me when you do the right thing merely because it's the right thing. But if I were

Samuel, I would want to know about this. Are you confident David won't do it again when we are gone?"

I shrugged.

"That is not a good answer, Saul. If you are to become a rabbi, truth must always be your hallmark. You must be brave, courageous, devout, and unafraid to expose wrongdoing. It's not enough for you to obey and be righteous. You must ignite a lamp in the darkness, bringing sin into the light."

"Are you going to tell his father?"

"I will pray about it."

I had little doubt that Father would tell Samuel. My misgivings quickly passed. Rather than dreading David's reaction when he learned I had exposed him, I found myself looking forward to it.

Might I grow up to be one who is unafraid of hard, even harsh, truth, bold enough to call people to holy living? Surely that would be a noble pursuit, and I might gain more of God's favor if I became His instrument to keep people on the path to following His laws.

19

Napoli

PRESENT-DAY ITALY

SATURDAY, MAY 10, 7:55 A.M.

ONE THING AUGIE KNOX had learned from his taciturn father was how to travel. Much as the old man had hated it, and happy as he was to turn over the bulk of it to his son, Edsel Knox knew all the tricks of the trade. Besides keeping his passport and visas up to date, he never checked a suitcase and carried on just one leather shoulder bag. It contained just three of every piece of clothing he needed. While having one cleaned he could wear the second and have one in reserve. He'd washed enough of his own shirts, underwear, and socks to get by in a pinch. He was wearing the one pair of shoes he would need for every contingency.

All his reading had been downloaded to his phone, with its nearly unlimited capacity, and his toiletries were the smallest, most compact he could find.

The only extra bulk on this trip was the dozens of blue books, but he had discarded each as he graded it and electronically stored his evaluation. Except for a brief layover in Atlanta, Augie had devoted about three-quarters of the ten-hour flight to plowing through the finals.

He had catnapped, and now as the plane taxied to the gate, Augie felt remarkably refreshed. He would grow drowsy by early evening, but finally finding out what was going on with Roger kept his mind off his own fatigue.

As Augie hauled his bag out of the overhead bin and slipped his passport into his pocket, he transmitted grades back to the seminary, then speed-dialed Sofia. It was an hour later in Greece, and she would be on her way to work.

"Glad you called," she said. "You haven't tried Roger yet, have you?"

"Soon as we hang up."

"Don't. He still sounds petrified, Augie."

"My phone is secure."

"He's afraid his new one has already been hacked."

"Yet he called you?"

"He's talking only in code now, Augie. Told me to tell you to go to the exact spot where you and he met to discuss the cruise to Malta. Said you'd remember."

"I do, but that's—"

"Don't be specific, Augie. He's frantic we not give anything away by phone. He doesn't think anyone knows you're coming, but don't bet on it. He'll be in disguise."

"Disguise?"

"He made a big point of the *exact* spot."

"I know the place." *Problem is, it's in Naples.*

"Augie, keep in touch, will you? I'm dying to know what's up, and I'm worried about you both."

"Just wish I knew what he wanted from me."

"I know you'll do whatever you have to do, love."

Fortunately Augie knew his way through Fiumicino Aeroporto and instinctively followed the crowd through Terminal 3 to Customs, checking his phone for trains to Napoli. One was to leave a few minutes after nine for the 110-mile trip and would cost him eighty dollars.

"Business or pleasure?" the customs agent said, studying his face and his passport photo.

"Business. American tour guide meeting with—"

"I can see where you are from, sir," she said, smiling.

"My bad. Visiting a colleague."

"Where?"

"Napoli and then probably back here in the city."

"I see you're leaving your return open."

He shrugged. "I do love this place."

"Welcome to Italy, Dr. Knox."

The temperature in Rome would be thirty degrees lower than Dallas by noon. Augie hadn't imagined enjoying 72 degrees again for months, but the cloudless sunny day was idyllic.

Onboard the train Augie texted Sofia. "Tell him my ETA is 11:15."

She responded, "OK. Praying."

Augie's phone bore nearly two hundred downloaded books for just such a time as this. But try as he might, he couldn't find a thing that held his interest. Nothing could take his mind off whatever jam Roger was in.

In all the years Augie had known Roger Michaels, he had never seen the man rattled. Unflappable, Marie Knox had called him. On tours, schedules changed without warning. Bureaucratic delays were common. You never knew when to grease a palm or stare down an implied request for a bribe. Worse, the members of the tours themselves often proved difficult. Some were impossible to please. Others shadowed you, eager to ingratiate themselves.

Roger seemed to respect people of faith. Jewish by birth, he didn't practice that religion either. He didn't call himself an agnostic, let alone an atheist, "more of a deist." He was deferential to the many Christians drawn to Augie's tours. Few people detected—without probing—that Roger was irreligious. He easily quoted from both the Old and New Testaments. Only if someone directly asked would he allow that he was "still on the path, searching, but not in the market for more input, if you don't mind."

People all over the world who liked, admired, respected, yes, loved Roger Michaels were praying for his soul. Augie often teased him, "You're surrounded. You have no hope."

If Roger's life was truly in danger, would he be more receptive? Or less?

Disguise. What might that look like? Augie thought he'd recognize him regardless. Roger was short, solid, and anything but fat. At about five eight and two hundred pounds, still he was agile and quick. He almost always wore tan hiking boots with one-inch soles, laced all the way up and double tied, revealing two inches of white sock. Unless he was at a site that required long pants, he wore khaki cargo shorts. Outlined in one bulging pocket were a half dozen or so granola bars, and in the other his phone and a passel of pens.

He wore flannel lumberjack shirts that had been crudely tailored into short sleeves, topped by a thin, breathable vest laden with guidebooks, maps, and more pens. Though he was fair-skinned, Roger's massive arms were dark from the sun, sporting downy bleached hair. His watch could be mistaken for a small Buick.

He often wore a floppy fisherman's-style cap over longish hair that had gone from blond to gray in the years Augie had known him. Same with the full beard that started just below Roger's sun-reddened cheeks.

The most popular guide in Israel, largely because of his stentorian voice, Roger was good humored but never silly. His pale-blue eyes danced and he loved to weave stories. Augie could not remember even a hint of frustration clouding the man's face. He seemed to always be smiling, radiating confidence without conceit. He had been such a mentor to Augie, especially early in their relationship, which was why Augie considered Roger his best friend today.

As the train neared Napoli, Augie found himself fighting dread. He hated the idea of his mentor and best friend being worried about anything—let alone terrified.

The Malta cruise meeting had come on Augie's second solo trip. His father had finally fully ceded the work to him, and he and Roger spent an hour sketching out the six-day excursion. Roger had invited Augie to stay at his Rome apartment, but business had taken Roger to Napoli, so they met there at one of Roger's favorite haunts.

The South African had an affinity for local eateries. The Portauovo, a tiny square box decorated largely with rough-hewn wood, boasted a dozen tables and served breakfast twenty-four hours a day. It lay tucked between shops and bigger restaurants across the street from Piazza Giuseppe Garibaldi station, one floor down from Napoli Centrale, where Roger's train would pull in.

Roger had quizzed Augie about the name of the place the first time they ate there. Augie wracked his brain for the little Italian he knew. "Egg something?"

"Very good. The Egg Cup. I recommend the—"

"Eggs?"

Roger had roared. Augie could never bring the man's face to mind without imagining a toothy grin surrounded by that massive beard.

NAPLES, 11:30 A.M.

Finally disembarking, Augie had to remind himself which escalator to take. When the Portauovo came into view, Augie looked for the very table in the back corner where they had met the first time. It was the only empty table as lunchtime approached and waiting customers spilled into the street. They had to wonder why a table sat empty with so many in line. But a tiny tented card read *Riservati*.

Augie slipped to the front of the line in the face of scowls. The host frowned at him until Augie nodded toward the reserved table. "Knox," he whispered.

"*Si. Seguimi.*"

Augie followed him and as soon as he sat down his phone chirped. "1 minute," Roger had texted. "no big greeting, K?"

When Roger approached, only his body was familiar, if not quite as broad. He wore navy Crocs, no socks, dress slacks, no belt, a tuxedo shirt, cuffs rolled up. The beard was gone, revealing a pasty, babyish face that contrasted with his rosy forehead and newly bony cheekbones. A beret covered his head, but when Roger doffed it at Augie's astonished look, he revealed a shaved head.

It felt strange not to bear hug the man, but Augie had to squint even to be sure it was the same person he'd known so long. Gone was the smile, the twinkle. And in place of the usual broad-shouldered posture, Roger sat slumped, folded in on himself. His eyes darted and his fingers twitched. Besides scared, Roger Michaels looked embarrassed.

"Sorry about my look," he said simply.

"You do what you've got to do, Rog. Now what's going on?"

A waiter appeared and pointed to the menu chalked on the wall.

"Nothing for me," Roger said.

"Nonsense," Augie said. "We both want the three-egg omelet and a large orange juice."

"I can't eat," Roger said as the waiter left.

"Force yourself. You look gaunt. Now give . . ."

Michaels looked around, leaned forward, and whispered, his voice shaky. "Augie, I've been entrusted with the greatest find in history."

"What, the Dead Sea Scr—?"

"Bigger." Roger wrenched around again, staring.

"Who are you afraid of?"

"I can't trust anyone. This is so huge, Augie. Have you ever known me to exaggerate?"

"Never."

"I'm talking about the most important document since the New Testament. You'll have to see it to believe it. Sometimes I wish I'd never laid eyes on it."

20

On to Jerusalem

FIRST-CENTURY ROME

"TELL ME, LUKE," PAUL said the next night, "have you made any changes in the manuscript, any suggestions?"

"Not a jot or a tittle yet. The story has captivated me."

"When you get to the latter years, you will find that my mind was not as sharp and my pen much shakier. I will need your help making sense of all of it and putting it into a form where people can read it. Keep it among the brethren and my family."

When Luke embraced Paul for his usual farewell, he felt an urgency in the old man's grip he hadn't noticed for weeks. Was he afraid the end was near? Luke found Primus most interested in Paul's health. "I confess, Doctor, I wish he would pass in his sleep. I don't want to see his execution any more than you do."

Later, as he ascended to his guest room, Luke wondered whether

Primus and his wife treated him so kindly only because he had treated Primus' mother. They had to know the risk of harboring a Christian. If and when Nero wanted him, he would not be hard to find.

He sat wearily before the parchments, and at the haunting, lonely call of the night watchman announcing nine o'clock, Luke decided he would allow himself three more hours of escape into Paul's narrative from fifty-five years before.

The next morning at breakfast I found myself looking forward to David being found out by his father. Only now do I realize that it was then that I began to see my role as a model of one who not only knew the law, but also abided by it.

Father had taught me to look adults in the eye, shake hands firmly, and speak clearly. I bade thanks and farewell to Samuel and his wife, waved at the other children, and stuck my hand out to David. He hesitated, but I think he realized his father was watching and finally offered a limp hand.

"Samuel, if I may have a private word," Father said, "Saul, please wait down there at the crossroad."

I tugged my horse under a tree and twisted to look back at Father and Samuel engaged in serious conversation. Samuel suddenly grew rigid, and now only Father was talking.

Samuel called out for David as Father mounted up, and the boy glared at me as he slowly approached his father. I returned his gaze, unafraid. I had nothing to be ashamed of. He did. And it felt good to be God's instrument in bringing him to justice.

21

Carabinieri

"SWITCH SEATS WITH ME," Roger Michaels said. "I don't want to be surprised."

"By whom?" Augie said, rising.

"See the carabinieri station over my shoulder, across the street?"

"You're afraid of the police?"

"I told you, I can't trust anyone."

He settled with his back to the wall of the Portauovo, pulled his beret down over his eyes, and rested his chin in his hand. Augie would not have recognized him, so he couldn't imagine anyone else would.

When the waiter brought their omelets, Roger left his silverware wrapped in a paper napkin as if to follow through on his insistence that he couldn't eat. "Say a blessing if you want," he said. "You will anyway."

As Augie bowed his head, a boldness chilled him. It was as if God Himself had given him utterance. He reached to cover Roger's hand, stunned anew at his friend's shuddering. "Father," Augie whispered, "we are grateful for this food. Bless it to our bodies. And would You use whatever Roger is going through to draw him to Yourself? I pray in the name of Your Son and my Lord, Jesus Christ. Amen."

Augie unrolled Roger's napkin and slid his silver to him. "You're going to eat, Rog. I'm here to help, and I can't have you running on empty."

Roger sighed with a catch in his throat. "Oh, Augie," he said, sounding as weary as Augie had ever heard him, "you remember Klaudios?"

"Giordano? Of course. The Vatican guide with the—"

"Limp. Yes. He's dead."

"What?" Augie said, mouth full and struggling to swallow. "How?"

"Murdered. I didn't think they'd do it. They needed him to get to me. How are they supposed to get to me without him giving me up?"

It was all Augie could do to breathe. "Roger, you've got to back up. What are you talking about?"

"I owe him my life," Roger said, eyes filling. "He was even more in my face about his faith than you were. You know how Catholics can be."

"I'm lost, Rog. What are you into?"

Roger covered his eyes, appearing to doze. Finally he slid his hands away. "You know they've been working on Mamertime."

"The prison, sure. Shoring up the foundation or something?"

Roger nodded. "It's been a mess over there, tourists coming all this way, disappointed not to get a look at Paul and Peter's dungeon."

"Right."

"The plan was to leave the tufa rock walls just as they are to stay as close to authentic as possible. It took 'em weeks to brace those so they could replace the two rows of blocks below floor level."

"Makes sense."

"Well, Klaudios made friends with the workers over there, even a couple of the supervisors. You know him—wanted to be the first to know when the place would be open to his groups again."

"That's him."

"So apparently one day there's a big to-do at the site and Klaudios happens to be there jawing with the supervisor. The engineers had seen some sagging, I think, and they guessed the foundation was deteriorating somehow."

Augie wanted to leap across the table and grab Roger, demanding he get to the point. "So what caused the commotion?"

"Turns out the engineers might have been wrong about the foundation. The stones were cold but they were dry and appeared in decent shape."

Roger paused to take a bite, and suddenly he was shoveling in eggs and cheese like it was his last meal. He kept peeking over Augie's shoulder.

Finally the big man took a long swig of his orange juice and said, "Thanks. This was a good idea. I needed that."

"Roger, I'm going to kill you myself if you don't get on with the story."

"The supervisor shuts down the work late in the afternoon—"

"When was this?"

Roger shook his head. "I can hardly remember when my life ended. A little less than three weeks maybe? Anyway, down deep behind one of the stone blocks a worker finds something wrapped in a kind of primitive burlap. The cloth was in pretty rough shape, but it had pro-tected whatever it was wrapped around, and that felt intact."

"He didn't unwrap it . . ."

"No!" Roger said. "Valued his job."

"So somebody called the Art Squad . . ."

"'Course," Roger said, "even though nobody knew what might be in there. Could have been garbage, but the supervisor had to follow the rules. Whoever he called at the Carabinieri Art Squad told him to secure the site and said they would send someone in the morning to check it out."

"Routine."

Roger nodded. "But ol' Giordano was curious."

"Never knew a guy with more questions," Augie said. "Everything interested Klaudios."

"So when everybody's gone but a couple of guys from the crew who are supposed to watch the place, he—"

"They assigned laborers for security?"

"They didn't know it was anything important, Augie. Probably fig-ured it wasn't, like nine times out of ten these so-called finds turn out to be meaningless. So Klaudios tells the guys he's going to nose around inside before he goes back to the Vatican, and they probably don't think a thing about it. Why would they? He's on the Vatican payroll. They know him, he's been friendly with their supervisor, so they don't care. Pretty soon he comes climbing out of there and tells 'em he's going to go get his stuff but that he'd like to spend a little more time in there before he goes home. Asks them if they want anything and comes back half an hour later with snacks and his big old satchel over his shoulder. While they're enjoying what he brought 'em, he's back in the dungeon."

"You're not saying he stole an artifact."

"Augie, you may be the only person on God's green earth who wouldn't have, and I wouldn't put it past you."

"But that's a major crime! Doesn't he have a family?"

"He's got kids in college."

"What'd he find, Rog, and how'd you get mixed up in it?"

"Can we walk and talk? I feel like I'm sitting under a spotlight here."

"This place was your idea, Rog."

"Not all my ideas are brilliant. Like letting Klaudios rope me into this."

Augie paid the bill and followed Roger across the street and into the underground station. "We taking the train back to your place?" Augie said.

"My apartment is where they're going to kill me. I haven't been there for days. Anyway, I drove. You can ride back with me. I've booked you into a place less than half a mile away from my neighborhood."

"Who wants to kill you, Roger?"

"Guy from the Art Squad. He'd use a Tombaroli hit man."

A tomb raider? "All right," Augie said. He dragged Roger to a bench in a secluded alcove and made him sit. "So what did Klaudios haul out of there?"

"You ready?"

"Enough to beat it out of you if I have to."

"Only the memoir of St. Paul the Apostle."

2 2

City of David

Father's plan was that we travel a little more than thirty miles that first day, stopping about halfway for a light meal and to water and feed the horses. Merciless as the sun had been, we soon entered what seemed an oven so bright and hot that we could barely go on. Our animals stumbled and stutter-stepped and I turned to see Father looking as alarmed as I.

We lived in an arid country, and we knew it would grow worse in this direction, but could anyone travel in such conditions? Father said we needed to press ahead. Later I would remember those last few miles to the rest area as the longest, most labored, torturous part of the whole journey. At the watering station we met travelers coming the other way who offered no accounts of unusual heat. And people who arrived from the same direction we had come didn't appear to have suffered as we had. The torture of that leg of the trip seemed to have been put exclusively in our way. I could not understand it.

The entire rest of the way to Jerusalem we never again encountered a stretch as punishing. With our Sabbath break it took us about six days from Damascus. And it all faded into one unpleasant memory when I got my first glimpse of the City of David.

Father and I reined in our horses on a ridge as the sun was setting. I thrilled at the fading orange light as it bathed the crowded rooftops, a variety of shapes that represented palaces, temples, shops, houses, and apartments in the Holy City.

We found lodging at a small inn just inside the city walls. In the morning we would seek out the two schools between which we would choose. I would not have been surprised to be unable to sleep before such an auspicious day. But I had not taken into account how weary I would be from the travel of that last week.

I lay back and closed my eyes, and within seconds my dreams were filled with important meetings and introductions and decisions. The entire rest of my life, I knew, would be influenced by whom I met the next day, what I saw, what I experienced. Fortunately, everything connected with the trip had conspired to make me so tired that I slept soundly, knowing I was ready for whatever God had for me.

23

Klaudios's Demise

WHEN AUGIE FOUND HIS voice, he rasped, "What are you saying, Rog? Original manuscripts?"

Roger nodded, eyes darting. He looked as if he hadn't slept in days.

"Of which epistles?"

Roger waved him off, leaning close. "Listen, you're the Greek expert. I know just enough to be dangerous. But from what Giordano showed me and from what I could decipher—"

"Klaudios knew his Ancient Greek."

"He sure did. And neither of us doubted that what he stole was a personal memoir. It begins, 'I, Saul . . . ,' and from what I can make of it, it tells Paul's story from his childhood. Augie, I believe it's written in his own hand."

Augie sat back, nervous about who might be watching. "You think Klaudios stashed it before he was—"

"I know he did, Augie. I told him to. I know there are forgeries of lots of stuff claimed to be first-century documents and are eventually traced to centuries later, but who else but Paul himself would have written something like this and stored it there? It's real, man, and that makes it, well, you know . . ."

"If it's authentic, Rog, it's the single most priceless artifact ever uncovered. I mean, the Dead Sea Scrolls are dusty, crumbling fragments, and look what they've become."

"You've got to see these. I don't know what it was about the underground humidity, the tufa, or what, but the ink has hardly faded, and every word is readable. The work is pristine. Stunning. If the parchments can be dated by an expert, that'll seal it for me."

"That's out of my field, but come on, Roger. No fading after almost two thousand years?"

"Some, sure, but it's totally readable. We'll have to find an expert we can trust. I can't imagine Paul intended to store it for centuries, but he couldn't have picked a more perfect spot."

Augie shuddered at the possibilities. "Could it really be legit?"

"Would somebody kill a man over a fake?"

"Who killed Giordano?"

"I'm telling you, this guy from the Art Squad hired a goon from the Tombaroli. And I'll be next."

"Please . . ."

"It was professionally done, Augie. One twenty-two slug through the temple at point-blank range. The coroner says it was one of those cheap, lightweight, slow bullets propelled by just a primer, used for plinking at stuff like small rodents. He said the weapon would have to have been placed directly on the temple for the tiny slug to have kill power."

"Where was this done?"

"Carport outside the Giordanos' apartment. Witnesses said they saw a tall dark-haired man in a suit chatting with Klaudios through the driver's-side window just after he had parked. Then they saw the man casually walk away, so they didn't think to get a good look at his car or plate. Said Klaudios just sat in his car after that."

"Already dead."

Roger nodded. "Mrs. G. saw her husband's car in the usual spot from her window, but when Klaudios never came up and didn't answer his cell, she went down and found him. Can you imagine? Tiny hole in his temple, no exit wound. All the bleeding was internal."

"Had to kill him instantly," Augie said, "even a tiny bullet like that, through the brain."

"Professional. Hired gun for sure."

"But it doesn't make sense the Art Squad would kill him. Just arrest him and get the manuscript back. Back up and tell me how you got involved."

"Well, Klaudios had to know it wouldn't take long for the Art Squad to discover nothing was still in the dungeon the next morning, and of course the construction guys would tell them he'd been down there. So he called me that night. He said, 'You know who this is. My office. Now.' I'd just returned from a tour and was in for the night, so I had no interest in getting dressed and heading out again. I called him back and he didn't even greet me. Just said, 'Now. This is nonnegotiable.' He's an old friend and had referred a lot of people to me for trips—"

"Me too."

"—so I owed him. As soon as I get to that arched hallway that leads to his office, he grabs me and drags me in there. Shows me those first few pages. He's got cotton gloves for both of us, and he handles those parchments like glass. I don't know Ancient Greek, but it took him a couple of hours to work his way through just the first few sheets of parchment. It looked real to me, and if his translation is right, it sounded like it would corroborate everything Paul wrote in the New Testament. That tells me that when he gets to the part about his missionary journeys, all those age-old arguments about which letters he really wrote and whether his theology was changed later by scribes—all that—will be put to rest."

Augie studied this hollow, desperate shell of the man he knew. "And you'll have to reexamine everything you've thought about the Bible."

"If I can stay alive long enough. This is my fault, Augie. You know me. I'm not about money, the big score. Poor old Giordano had stars in his eyes. I told him he had to go straight to the Art Squad and tell them what he had before they came looking for him—like your father did here once years ago when one of his tour group members found a coin and wanted to keep it."

"Sounds like Dad," Augie said. "A legalist through and through."

"I told Klaudios there might be a reward in it for him. He laughed. Said, 'Roger! I stole these out of a historical site! My reward will be the rest of my life in prison.' I told him, 'Just tell 'em you were curious and as soon as you saw what it was, you knew it shouldn't sit in Mamertime a minute longer. You'll be a hero.' He didn't want to be a hero. He wanted to be rich. Said he was going to hide the parchments, deny he ever saw them in the prison, and then make a killing on them when the dust settled. He said, 'You and I are the only ones who know what this is.'

"I asked him why he didn't leave something there so the Art Squad would think that was all. You know he actually considered going back and planting something else? Wanted me to go with him. I told him he was crazy."

"Rog, I need to know what happened. How did he get himself killed?"

Roger looked up quickly and blanched. Augie turned carefully to follow his gaze and saw carabinieri huddling near the tracks, then fanning out.

Each carried a sheet of paper they seemed to compare to every middle-aged man who passed.

"We've got to get out of here," Roger said.

Augie put a hand on Roger's arm. "Don't draw attention. We're just nobodies, travelers. We're not in a hurry. We're not worried about anything."

"Easy for you to say."

"If you've ever playacted, Roger, now's the time."

Augie rose and Roger followed. Most of the carabinieri seemed to head for the platforms, but strangely they seemed interested only in the departing trains. "If they're looking for you," Augie said, "why do they think you're here and headed somewhere else?"

"No idea, but we'd better hurry."

"Slow down, Rog. Look at this shop. Aren't those toys interesting?"

"Augie, what the—?"

"We're blending in, man. Breathe. If a cop checks you out, just smile. Where's your car?"

"The big lot, out back."

"Linger a little longer, then just stroll that way. I'll stay with you."

Roger seemed to struggle to remain nonchalant, and less than a half minute later he began moseying toward the escalator that would take them to street level and the parking lot. Augie saw him hesitate at the sight of an officer at the base of the moving stairway. Roger whispered, "If necessary, call me François."

What? When he put a hand on Roger's back to urge him to keep moving, he felt knotted muscles.

Augie stepped in front of Roger, then smiled and nodded at the officer while approaching the escalator. The cop stopped him, thrust in his face a photo of the Roger Michaels he had known for years, and said, "*Avete visto quest'uomo?*"

Augie spread his hands, palms up. "No Italian. English."

"Have you seen this man?" the officer said, carefully enunciating with a thick accent.

"*Il mio amico Americano sa molto poco Italiano,*" Roger said, stunning Augie by speaking Italian with a thick French accent. Roger was multilingual, but what was this?

"You speak English?" the cop asked Roger.

"*Oui. Un peu.*"

"A little, huh," the cop said. "As your American friend speaks very little Italian, and I speak very little French, we will speak English then. Okay?" He pointed to the photo. "We're looking for this man."

"Why?" Roger said, accent still thick. "What's he done?"

"He's just wanted for questioning." He turned to Augie. "Passport, please."

How do I keep him from asking for Roger's ID?

"Me?" Augie said, laughing as he dug through his bag for it. "Do I look like that?"

The cop chuckled and shook his head. To Augie's surprise, Roger pulled out his own wallet. The officer leafed through Augie's passport. "World traveler," he said. Augie nodded. "And you've just arrived. Business or pleasure?"

"Visiting my friend, François."

"Welcome to Napoli, eh, Naples, Dr. Knox. And you, sir?"

Roger removed from his wallet a worn driver's license bearing his current likeness.

"Ah, you live in Roma, Mr. Tracanelli?"

"*Oui. Si. Yes!*"

Roger's moving from French to Italian to English clearly amused the carabiniere. "Thank you, gentlemen. If you should see this man, would you kindly inform one of us?"

"Is he dangerous?" Roger said.

"I do not believe so. We are simply looking for him on behalf of another agency."

At the top of the escalator Augie said, "I thought that was the end of you, Roger. How'd you do that? License and all?"

"Have you ever known me to be unprepared?"

"No, but I've never known you to fear for your life either."

"They go hand in hand. And don't think it was easy to find a forger. Never used one before and don't ever want to again. Scared to death the whole time."

"The whole time what?"

"When he was shaving me, photographing me, working his magic. I mean, these guys stay under the radar because their clients are hiding too."

"You didn't use your own address, did you?"

"You kidding?" Roger pulled his license out and showed it to Augie.

"I know that street. Businesses district, isn't it?"

"Mostly. Lots of second-floor apartments. If they pinpointed this address it would be above a pharmacy. A one-story pharmacy. But who's going to go to the trouble of checking it out?"

"Roger, now that the carabinieri are on this, how long before the press gets hold of it?"

"Don't think I haven't dreaded that. This find may be the best kept secret in the world, but the other agency that officer mentioned is the *Comando Carabinieri per la Tutela del Patrimonio Culturale*, the TPC."

"In English?"

"Division for the Protection of Cultural Heritage. It's the Art Squad under the National Military Police."

"Why would anyone there have Klaudios killed?"

"Same reason Klaudios risked his whole career. Guy has to be a rogue agent. I've never heard of a scandal there, but the prospect of the big score does things to people. That's on me too, Augie. Rumor had it that the original worker who found the parchments told the Art Squad guys the next day that it looked like ancient writing. I told Klaudios again that he should just tell 'em he recognized it was valuable and was holding it for them. He said no, he was off to hide everything and would be back in a day or two."

When they reached the exit leading to the parking lot, Augie stopped. "So where did he hide the parchments?"

"The Art Squad guy, would you believe the second-in-command, named Aldo Sardinia, told him they knew from airport records that he had flown to Greece and that he would do himself a favor if he just told them everything. Said he shouldn't need to remind an expert like Klaudios that taking an artifact out of Italy was a major crime."

"And . . .?

"I think the crafty old gimp sent Sardinia on, what do you Americans call it . . .?"

"A wild-goose chase?"

"He had them looking all over Greece. Next thing I know, I get a call from the Art Squad."

"Klaudios gave you up?"

"He swore he didn't. Sardinia must have gotten numbers from Giordano's phone and hacked into any he might have called around the time of the disappearance."

"So when was this?"

"Three days after he met with Klaudios. But the thing was, the guy calling claimed to be Colonel Georgio Emmanuel, head of the Art Squad. Now I know they believe the find is real. He tells me their investigation of the disappearance of a valuable antiquity had led to me and that I could help myself by coming clean. He says his right-hand man, Sardinia, will be coming to see me and that not only would he appreciate it but that I would be wise and protect myself if I would be as forthright and forthcoming with him as I can be. I assured him I would. He warned me to tell no one we were meeting and added, 'We'll know if you do.'"

"What did you make of that?"

"That I was being watched and that my phone had been compromised. But when Sardinia showed up, I recognized his voice as the man I had talked to on the phone who had said he was head of the Squad, so something didn't smell right. But he made it clear the Squad knew Giordano had confided in me and said he hoped he didn't have to bring me in. I said I hoped not either. He said if Klaudios had stashed the documents with me, or if I knew where they were, I'd tell him what I knew or wind up in a cell next to Klaudios's.

"Fact is, I believed him. Somehow I mustered the courage to tell him I'd be honest with him if he'd be honest with me. He looked surprised when I told him I knew he was the one who had called me saying he was Georgio Emmanuel. He dismissed that as standard operating procedure, something they often do to gauge how cooperative a person is going to be. He even said that sometimes Emmanuel himself does call, but that he was busy. He told me I was pretty astute to figure out it was him but that it didn't change anything and I needed to tell him what I knew. You know me, Augie. I don't lie. I figure the truth can never hurt you."

"That's biblical," Augie said. "Jesus said—"

"'You shall know the truth and the truth shall set you free.' Forgive me if I'm finding that hard to believe right now."

"He was talking about Himself," Augie said.

"Whatever. I told the truth, and I'm about as far from free as I've ever been. I told him Klaudios Giordano had told me what he'd found, that I'd seen it and urged him to turn it in. Guess I should have told him the whole truth."

"Which is?"

"That Klaudios left me with the first original page, photocopies of the rest, and a sealed envelope I wasn't supposed to open unless something happened to him."

"So something happened to him. What was in the envelope?"

Roger looked around and whispered, "I don't know yet. Before I could call the Art Squad to see if lying to someone on the phone was really one of their tactics, I saw on the news that Klaudios had been murdered. I stashed everything he gave me and haven't been able to get back to it since. It's obvious Sardinia is convinced he can get the original manuscript through me, and that's why he didn't need Klaudios anymore."

"You think he wants this for himself, not for the Art Squad."

"I do. I believe he's in cahoots with the Tombaroli, had one of their guys shoot Giordano, and they're going to make millions with this thing on the black market. Sardinia will implicate the Tombaroli or somebody else for Klaudios's murder, and nobody else at the Art Squad will be the wiser that he's in on it."

"Don't lie to me, Roger. We've got too much history and I've put my life on hold for you. Do you know where the parchments are?"

"No."

"Where'd you put what Klaudios gave you?"

"In a locker at Stazione Termini along with the gun I promised you."

Augie closed his eyes. "Tell me you're kidding."

Roger fished in his pocket and produced a key. "I'm not."

"You left a page from a priceless artifact at the Rome train station."

"I don't have a safe-deposit box, Augie."

"You don't think it might have been worth the investment? We've got to get it out of there, and fast."

As they pushed through the doors to the parking lot, Roger froze and gripped Augie's elbow. "Follow me," he whispered. "The carabinieri are digging through my car."

"Can they do that?"

"You want me to tell 'em they're breaking the rules? We've got to figure out how to get back to Rome."

"Train?"

"I don't want to risk bluffing my way past the authorities again. Other carabinieri down there may not be so easy to fool. We need to rent a car. In your name."

"Sure," Augie said. "But where will we go? Where've you been staying?"

"On the streets. I was hoping we could upgrade your room to a suite."

"I'm in this deep," Augie said. "Might as well harbor a fugitive."

SATURDAY, MAY 10, 2:00 P.M.

Wending his way out of Napoli at Roger's direction, Augie said, "You didn't leave any evidence or anything of value in your apartment, did you?"

"Only everything I own. Clothes, computer, all of it. I've been on the run since the first time I called you."

"But you left nothing that would hint at what you've done with what Giordano gave you."

"No. I put your gun, the original page, the photocopies, and Klaudios's instructions in that locker. He said he had put the rest of the memoir where only he could find it."

"But this Sardinia is convinced Klaudios told you where, right? That's why you're in trouble."

"That's why he had Klaudios killed. Giordano was in the way of Sardinia's lifetime score."

"And now so are you."

"Now you're getting the picture. But what he doesn't know is that I don't know any more than he does. What he wants is in the envelope I promised not to open unless something happened to Klaudios. Once he was murdered, I couldn't risk going back to the locker. I changed my look, got new documents, and tried to disappear. It's the only way I know to stay alive. This guy's got the resources of the biggest antiquities protection agency in the world."

"But if you're right, Rog, Sardinia is your life insurance policy. Without you, he has nothing."

"And without the envelope, I wouldn't know what to tell him if I was being waterboarded. And I'll never give it up."

"Why not just send the envelope to the head of the Art Squad? Let them find the parchments, keep Sardinia from marketing them to the Tombaroli, and give scholars all over the world a chance to translate and parse every word? It'd be a gift to the whole planet."

Roger fell silent and turned to face the passenger-side window.

"What did I say?" Augie said. "You haven't stolen anything. You'd be in the clear. You'd be following the law. The memoir would be protected and eventually get to where it belongs. What am I missing?"

"You're just underestimating Sardinia. You think my new look is for the Tombaroli?"

"You're sure this guy is really who he said he was this time?"

"Yep. Looked him up online."

"Risking his career for this, not to mention his life."

"Paul's memoir is the once-in-a-lifetime prize that could turn the best carabiniere anywhere. You realize what he and the Tombaroli could do with this, Augie? A few square inches of each page would be worth a fortune."

"Cut it up? They wouldn't."

"Because it's sacred? Don't kid yourself. It's gold."

2 4

Shammai

FIRST-CENTURY ROME

LUKE WAS FASCINATED TO read of events Paul had never mentioned but which had clearly shaped the man he knew today. And he was eager to learn what went into the decision of where to train to become a rabbi. Luke knew where Paul had studied, but how did young Saul and his father choose?

I was so excited in the morning that I was up before Father and tempted to go looking for breakfast for the two of us. But I knew he would be displeased if I did anything before Tefillah, so I strapped on my phylacteries and waited for him. Soon we were reciting the Schacharit, including one of my favorite parts, the 100th Psalm:

Make a joyful shout to the Lord, all you lands!
Serve the Lord with gladness;
Come before His presence with singing.
   Know that the Lord, He is God;
It is He who has made us, and not we ourselves;
We are His people and the sheep of His pasture.
   Enter into His gates with thanksgiving,
And into His courts with praise.
Be thankful to Him, and bless His name.
   For the Lord is good;
His mercy is everlasting,
And His truth endures to all generations.

What a thrill it was, half an hour after breakfast, to hear this same psalm recited as an incantation by a choir in the court of Herod's Temple. The holy site, which had already been under construction for years and which—Father told me—would not likely be completed for many more, proved so overwhelming to him that suddenly he could no longer speak.

I was in awe too. I told him, "When we move here, I'm going to study this place inside and out and know everything there is to know about it."

I didn't know then how significant it was that the two rabbinical schools we were to visit that day sat on opposite sides of the temple. All I knew was that both had been founded in the previous century and that one, Beit (House) Shammai, was stricter about Jewish law than the other, Beit Hillel.

For all I thought I knew back then, it's hard to imagine how little I understood. I was thirteen years old, but I felt like an adult. I believed I was equal with men my father's age. I should have known better, because Rabbi Daniel privately reminded me that "much responsibility comes with the recognition we have bestowed upon you. You realize that you are now accountable under the law for the full penalty of breaking the commandments."

Certain freedoms had attended being a child, smart and learned as I had been. But I should have known that the biblical commandment to serve God brought with it this adult accountability.

That all came rushing back to me in the shadows of the great walls of the temple in Jerusalem. Eventually Father was able to speak, and he rhapsodized in hushed tones about this fulfillment of a lifelong dream and how much it meant to him that I would one day be a rabbi, "perhaps right here in this place. You could be a leader, Saul, a doctor of the law, a member of the Sanhedrin . . ."

We trekked out of the temple and down a broad street that led to the Shammai rabbinical school, which proved to be a compound of long, one-story buildings encompassing a courtyard where mostly the young boys ran and played. We were greeted by the director of the school, a pale man of about forty with long, light-colored hair and generous lips. He introduced himself as Rabbi Enosh and took us on a brief tour of small rooms where classes of young men and boys gathered near—and "sat under" or "sat at the feet of"—

the teacher. Soon we found ourselves in Enosh's small office, where he offered us chairs and he sat beside his wood table.

"Your rabbi, Daniel of Tarsus, has informed us that you are an exceptionally outstanding student," he said, "gifted in memorization and meticulous about the Law. That is why Shammai is the place for you. Our founder, Rabban Shammai, believed only worthy students should be allowed to study the Torah. You will flourish here. Those who receive our training have gone on to become some of the most respected and accomplished rabbis and temple leaders in all of Judaism."

Eventually he got around to one of the differences between his school and the competition. "They would allow what they consider a harmless lie, like telling an ugly bride that she is beautiful. Would you do that, Saul?"

"A lie is a lie," I said. "I'd sooner say nothing than to bear false witness."

Enosh looked pleased. "And what about divorce, young man?"

"Divorce? I'm a little young for—"

"But you're old enough to think this through. We hold that the law teaches that a man may divorce his wife for only a dire transgression. Do you know that there are those—again, claiming to be Pharisees—who would allow a divorce over something as trivial as a wife preparing a bad meal?"

"That's terrible," I said.

"Of course it is. As advanced as you are and as far ahead of your contemporaries as you may be, here you will be challenged, tested, perfected in the Law of Moses. You will have not only memorized the Scriptures, you will understand them, be able to teach them and, best of all, strictly live by them. A devout Jew, especially one committed to becoming a rabbi, should want no less."

I resonated with this from the core of my being. I wanted, above all, to please God, and I knew of no other way than to be perfect in His sight. What I really wanted to know was whether the Shammai school had graduates who had reached a point where they were worthy to walk and talk with God, and to hear God speak.

"With the support of your rabbi and the elders from your synagogue, I know our council would quickly approve your admission."

"Let's not be hasty," Father said, and I saw Enosh's smile fade. "We have much to think about, and another house of learning to visit."

Enosh grew rigid. "Tell me, Y'honatan, is the other school Hillel?"

"Is there another in Jerusalem worth perusing?"

"No," Enosh said, sniffing. "But I don't consider Hillel worth looking into either."

"Perhaps we will come to the same conclusion," Father said. "But it is only fair that we base our decision on a thorough evaluation of both."

Enosh was clearly not pleased, and I have to say I was alarmed too. If Shammai was the stricter of the two schools, wasn't that all we needed to know?

"Let's leave it at this," Enosh said, "why don't you come back and visit me tomorrow only if your decision is that Saul attend here. *If you do not reappear, I will know your deci-sion and would not care to see either of you again anyway.*"

Father cocked his head. "*You feel that strongly against Beit Hillel?*"

"*Frankly, Y'honatan, it concerns me that you would even consider entrusting the religious education of your son to apostates. We have not even broached the subject of their view of Rome, sir. They do not deny that they remain open to commerce between Jew and Gentile. This in light of that fact that the pagan nations all around us side with Rome in our disputes with the Empire. A man, a nation, is either a friend of God or he is not.*"

Enosh shook hands with us. "*I hope to see you tomor-row, but if not, may God have mercy on you.*"

25

Manhunt

PRESENT-DAY ITALY

SATURDAY, MAY 10, 2:30 P.M.

DURING MOST OF THE more than 120-mile drive from Napoli to Rome, Roger sat with his head in his hands, moaning about what would happen to his car—and to him—when he never returned for it.

"This isn't like you, Rog," Augie said.

"Excuse me if I've never been an assassination target."

"C'mon, man. You're the only one with a clue as to where the parchments are. As long as you keep that to yourself . . ."

"What happened to Klaudios was a message for me."

"That's why I'm here, Rog. Your life is my only priority."

"Be real. You're dying to see the memoir yourself."

Augie's phone vibrated. He put it on speaker and punched the connection. "Hey, babe."

"I need news, Augie. Roger okay?"

He told her everything, interrupting himself only when he saw Roger's terrified look. "This is secure, Rog. Untappable, guaranteed."

"Nothing's guaranteed anymore," Roger muttered. "How about *her* phone?"

"Who would even know to tap it?"

"They discovered yours, Augie! I was calling her too, you know."

Augie winced.

"Do you need me there?" Sofia said.

Augie hesitated. He didn't want to subject her to mortal danger, but neither did he want to make her decisions for her.

"I only want to help, love," she said. "What can I do?"

"We've got a lot to do, and with Roger having to stay out of sight . . ."

"Say no more," she said. "I'll book a flight and let you know when I'm arriving."

"Keep track of your expenses and I'll—"

"Augie, stop! I've got this. Or at least my father's got this."

"You think it's wise to tell him what's going on?"

"If I can't trust him, who can I trust? Anyway, he may have an idea or two."

"Won't he try to talk you out of coming?"

"I'm coming either way, Augie."

"He'll understand how crucial it is to—"

"Please. He keeps confidences better than anyone I know. In his business, he has to. I'll rent a car as soon as I get there. Where will I find you?"

Roger chimed in, telling her where Augie's hotel was. "Just to be safe, you should stay somewhere else. I'm hiding out there too."

"You sound better, Roger."

"I don't feel better, but it's nice to not be alone in this."

"You were never alone," she said. "You knew we'd be there for you."

"I hoped."

"Don't be silly. We love you."

The men agreed that when Augie checked in he should upgrade to a suite and add François Tracanelli to the account. "Then you can head out and round up clothes and stuff for me. After that it should be dark, and you can take the key to the train station. I don't want that stuff in there a minute longer."

"What're we gonna do, put it in the hotel safe?"

"Got to be more secure than the train station. But at least there I didn't have to fold it to make it fit."

"Hadn't thought of that," Augie said. "No way we're folding it. It's protected, right?"

Roger nodded. "Klaudios sandwiched it between acid-free sheets and wrapped it with cellophane."

"Can't wait to see it. Gives me chills."

SATURDAY, MAY 10, 4:45 P.M.

Only when he was deep enough into Rome that he sensed he was nearing its northern border did Augie realize that Roger had never told him where to turn and was clearly no longer just gazing out the window.

He laid a hand on his stocky friend's shoulder and said, "I've gone too far, haven't I?"

Roger's breathing was even and deep. He must have been drastically sleep deprived if even a touch didn't rouse him. Eager as Augie was to get settled in and get his errands run, he couldn't bring himself to wake the man. He entered Roger's address into the navigation app on his phone and turned down the volume. As soon as his phone had geo-synchronized with the satellite, a woman's voice said, "*Fare una inversione a u quando possibile.*"

He knew enough Italian to know he had indeed ventured north of where he wanted to go. Augie switched the narration to English. "Make a legal U-turn when possible."

It would have been safer to do this alone and at night, but with Roger asleep and unrecognizable, Augie followed the directions to Roger's apartment. Was there a chance he could slip in and out without being detected?

But the place was crawling with men in suits and unmarked cars the same make and model as police cars. He drove past, wishing he'd paid attention when Roger had told Sofia. All he knew was that it was within half a mile of Roger's apartment.

Augie pulled onto a side street and parked, reclining his seat and selecting a novel on his phone. He was determined to let Roger sleep, imagining how long it must have been since his friend felt safe enough to soundly slumber. Augie opened his window an inch and felt the cool air. Before he turned off the engine he noticed the temperature had dropped to 57 degrees.

6:15 P.M.

The last thing Augie was aware of was that the words of the novel began to swim and he had to fight to keep his eyes open. He was startled awake by a gentle rap on his window and squinted up into the face of a female carabiniere.

"*Identificazione, per favore.*"

"Um, yeah, sorry. English, please?"

"Identification, please."

Augie handed her his passport.

"And your companion?"

"Sleeping."

"I see that. Also American?"

"Oh, no." Augie gently reached into Roger's bag and pulled out his wallet, from which he produced the phony driver's license. "Need me to wake him?"

"That may not be necessary," she said. "Excuse me one moment."

When she went around the front of the car, Augie noticed her partner through the rearview mirror, standing near the left taillight. The female officer bent and compared the license photo to Roger's face, which Augie guessed was mashed against the window. She went to her *polizia* car and returned several minutes later.

"Are you lost, Mr. Knox?"

Augie explained that his friend knew the way to his hotel but that he didn't want to wake him.

"I see you have arrived in Italy today. We cannot have you sitting idle at the curb. Please wake your friend so you can proceed to your destination. And welcome to Rome."

"Thank you." Augie stared at her, wondering if she expected anything else.

"I'll wait," she said.

"Oh." He shook Roger. "François," he said. "The carabinieri need us to move along to our hotel."

Roger sat up with a great heave, grunting. "What? Augie, what?"

Augie calmly referred to him as François again, hoping Roger would have the presence of mind to affect his French accent. "Just need you to tell me how to get to our hotel."

"*Sacrebleu!*" Roger said, and the carabiniere immediately bent to stare past Augie at him.

"*Sortez de la voiture, s'il vous plaît, Monsieur.*" ["Step out of the car, please, sir."]

"*Oui. Certainement.*" ["Yes. Certainly."]

Roger quickly emerged as the woman approached, and they spoke in French. Looking none too pleased or sure she was doing the right thing, she marched back to her car.

"What was all that?" Augie said as Roger climbed back in.

"A colossal goof. When you woke me I was using my South African accent."

"You seemed to recover quickly."

"Yeah, but then I resorted to the first French thing that popped into my head."

"*Sacrebleu*, so?"

"Nobody in France says that anymore. Only foreigners who want to sound French. She asked why I had used such a clichéd idiom if I was really French. I told her it was an old family joke—that we all said that when rudely awakened. She's running my name through the system."

When the carabiniere returned, she handed Roger his documents. "*Sacrebleu* indeed," she said with a wry smile. "No relation to the Olympic pole-vaulter of the same name? From the seventies?"

"No," Roger said. "But I get that a lot. Just a coincidence."

"Carry on."

"We have to do better at blending in," Augie said as he pulled away.

"You think? I get accosted by one more carabiniere, I'm going to just let them cuff me."

Augie told him of his drive-by of Roger's apartment.

"That was risky. What'd you expect? I can never go back. My car and my place, both history."

"Don't think like that. We're smart guys. We'll figure this out and get it fixed."

"Glad you think so."

6:50 P.M.

Augie and Roger checked into the Terrazzo Hotel and as he stretched out on the bed, Roger scribbled a list of necessities. Augie headed out, finding clothes and toiletries easy, but the language barrier made finding Roger an electronic tablet tricky. He bought the best he could find, with every bell and whistle available.

Roger roused when Augie returned after dark, thrilled with the tablet and quickly connecting it to his own private network. He began downloading all his personal stuff, telling Augie, "Sardinia or the Tombaroli would have to be pretty sophisticated to crack my encryption."

Roger gave Augie the locker key, directions to the train station, where to park, and the quickest route to the treasure. "And bring us back some food, man. There's a meatball sandwich place in the terminal."

Augie had just reached the rental car when he got a call from Roger. "Better get back up here."

"What's up?"

"Just hurry."

Back in the suite Roger had the TV on and had triggered the English captions for Augie's benefit. Every channel bristled with a nationwide manhunt.

"Michaels, a South African émigré, is an international tour guide by trade, sought for the murder of popular Vatican guide Klaudios Giordano. The carabinieri say the murder weapon and a sketch of the victim's carport were found in Michaels's Rome apartment and his car had been abandoned in Naples. While a witness identified the only suspect in the murder case as tall and dark and thin, police say the evidence points to Michaels as the one behind the slaying. The actual shooter remains at large."

Roger looked more agitated than worried. "They didn't find any weapon in my apartment. All I have is a nine-millimeter twin to the one I left for you in the locker. And it's in my backpack."

Augie felt a pang when he saw on the screen the rawboned, pointy, smiling face of the late Klaudios Giordano. The man had always been a delight. What could have caused such a rash choice? Did he really think he could get away with a monumental theft like that?

Then came the pictures of Roger. Fortunately, they were of the man the way Augie remembered him, buried under the bushy gray beard. Unfortunately, they'd already had an artist guess what Roger would look like with his beard dyed, with it short, and with it gone.

"They underestimated my chin," Roger said, showing Augie how wide his was compared to what was depicted on television. "I guess that's good."

"There's nothing good about this," Augie said.

"Sure there is! There's a reward for my capture. I'm worth more alive than dead."

"Are you serious?" Augie said. "If you're right about Sardinia, he's just multiplied the number of people looking for you. Once he has you in custody he'll get what he wants and find a way to eliminate you."

"Well, thanks for that encouragement," Roger said. "I'm just wondering how anyone could think me smart enough to mastermind a murder and stupid enough to leave the evidence in my apartment."

26

Hillel

I was giddy, certain I had found the perfect place to study under learned men who cared about every jot and tittle of the Scriptures.

Father could not hide his displeasure. I followed him to the western side of the temple where the wall blocked the harsh morning sun.

"Son, you know that I am loath to speak ill of a man, but I found Rabbi Enosh haughty and condescending, entirely without charity. He speaks of his opponents with disdain."

I had been so certain of my future, but to go against my father's wishes was unthinkable.

"*Saul, how would you feel about Rabbi Enosh if he were against you? Let's say you raised an objection to something he taught...*"

I had to smile. Our own Rabbi Daniel had become exasperated with me more than once, even when I was right and my arguments prevailed. "*He would be a worthy opponent, a challenge.*"

Father shook his head. "*I deduce he would be less than charitable. He would dismiss you like a pest.*"

"*Is there no way that you would choose Shammai for me?*"

"*I have not said that. It's possible that Beit Hillel will prove so counter to our view of the Scriptures that it will not prove acceptable.*"

"*What if you don't find either place right for me?*"

Father stood and stretched. "*We will always have the memory of this rich journey. And you will become heir to my business and the brightest Pharisaical scholar to ever make tents.*"

I must have looked stricken, for my father immediately clapped me on the shoulder. "*I am teasing you, Saul! I know you are called to serve God. Before the end of this year, you will be in rabbinical school somewhere.*"

Crowds passed from the upper gate, including many men still wearing their phylacteries.

"*I believe Hillel is just down this way,*" *Father said, pointing.*

"*You're looking for Hillel?*" *The voice was loud, friendly.*

We turned to see a large man, easily a foot taller than my father and perhaps twice his girth, accompanied by a boy who seemed a bit younger than I and a girl about my age. The man introduced himself as Nasi and his children as Simeon and Naomi. I could not take my eyes off her, the very image I had conjured of a young Cleopatra when I read that the beautiful queen of Egypt was said to have once visited Tarsus long before I was born.

Naomi was darker than her brother and her father, with skin so beautiful I wanted to touch her face. Her expressive eyes made her look at once both radiant and shy.

". . .my silent son's name is Saul, and yes, we have an appointment at Beit Hillel."

"I am going that way," Nasi said, excusing his children. As she turned to leave, Naomi looked me straight in the eyes and said softly, "It was nice to meet you, Saul." I could have died.

Simeon had already run off when we followed the man. "You are to become a student at Hillel?" he said.

"Hillel or Shammai," I said.

"Indeed?" Nasi said with a smile. "The schools are wrestling over you? They are very different, are they not? From a distance one would think Shammai is a prison and Hillel a banquet hall. Which way are you leaning, young man?"

"I am proud to be a Pharisee," I said.

"Ah, you would prefer the more strict. Admirable that you would not immediately choose the school that sounds easier." Nasi swept his hand toward a three-story building

hemmed in by shops and apartment buildings on a narrow street. "I'm grateful the decision is yours and not mine! May the Lord bless you."

The man bowed and set off down an alleyway next to the school. I started toward the entrance but noticed Father was not moving. "Do you know who that was?" he said.

"He said his name was Nasi, why?"

"Nasi is not a name, Saul. It's a title. I've heard it only in reference to high officers of the Sanhedrin. And I'm not talking about local councils. Here in Jerusalem it is the Great Sanhedrin."

"We asked directions of a member of the Sanhedrin?" I said.

Father chuckled. "Perhaps later we will go back by the temple and inquire. And we can thank him."

Inside a woman edged past, carrying a tray laden with freshly baked bread. "Looking for someone?"

"Gamaliel," Father said.

"Upstairs to your left, but I'm not sure he's here yet. He's also president of the Sanhedrin, as you may know. He has been at the temple all morning."

Father whispered, "He will know the man who showed us such kindness."

We mounted a curved, stone stairway that deposited us into a narrow corridor. A man carrying sheaves of parchments hurried past. "Gamaliel?" Father said, and the man pointed to a door down the hall.

We knocked, heard a "Come in!" and pushed open the door, only to see Nasi rise and come around his desk to welcome us. "No trouble finding the place?" he said, roaring with laughter. "Yes, I am Nasi Gamaliel. As soon as you mentioned Hillel, I knew who you were. I was hurrying here for my meeting with you. Sit, sit, please."

"Are you the high priest?" I managed, thoroughly intimidated.

"No, that role is officially held by Eleazar ben Annas, but his father, Annas, is really the high priest. I preside over the council." (Father told me later that Annas had been ousted by the Romans for acting too independently, even executing illegal capital sentences.)

The massive Nasi Gamaliel found a sheet of parchment and dipped a quill into an inkpot. "So, Saul," he said, pen poised over the paper, "it's between the zealots and the apostates, is it? I am not blind to our perceived differences. I do not care to dwell on those unless you have specific questions. For now I want to get acquainted with you. Your decision will come in its own time and will, I hope, be based on your own values. So I'll leave that to you. Tell me about yourself. Your first memory, your home, your family, that sister of yours, your synagogue, your studies, interests, what you're passionate about."

I started with my earliest recollection, my sister holding me back when a cart rolled past our house. "Tiny and young as I was, I understood that she was protecting me, and I felt loved."

Gamaliel's pen remained still. "That is a beautiful story," he said.

I told him everything I could remember about my life,

my studies, my faith, right up to this adventure, traveling by land all the way from Tarsus. The big man was scribbling, nodding, looking up, smiling.

When I finally paused, he dipped his quill again and said, "Tell me about you and God. Do you feel as if you know Him, or just about Him?"

This friendly man with the open face seemed to be looking right through me. My voice became thick and raspy, as if I had been caught. "I have told my father and my rabbi that I wish I could walk and talk with God the way Abraham, Isaac, and Jacob did."

Gamaliel nodded. "What a wonderful desire."

Father cleared his throat. "Both Rabbi Daniel and I have cautioned Saul not to expect so much. The men he cites are patriarchs, heroes of the faith. We are called to remain faithful to God's Word, to obey His Law and His commandments."

Gamaliel looked kindly at my father and spoke softly. "You are wise to protect your son from disappointment. And you are right that the mighty men of Scripture are chronicled for a reason. But has God changed? Does it not remain a noble pursuit to want to truly know Him?"

Father looked puzzled. "I believe God is unknowable. We are called to know about Him and to obey."

"I tend to agree, Y'honatan. But I choose not to forfeit the hope that we may know Him as did the patriarchs." He turned to me. "And this is where you find yourself, am I right?"

I nodded, hoping Father was not disappointed in me.

Gamaliel set down his pen and leaned forward, speak-

ing earnestly. "Saul, I cannot promise that if you come to Hillel, you will one day walk and talk with God as our ancestors did. But I can tell you that we will never discourage that pursuit, and I for one would not limit God to where He would never be available to you in that way.

"And, Y'honatan, I do not pretend to be ignorant of the differences between the two schools. Where the Shammaites believe that if one breaks one of the laws he is guilty of breaking the whole, we would say that God will take into consideration the preponderance of good over evil in one's life. We summarize the intent of the Law this way: what is hateful to yourself, do not to another."

Gamaliel led us out of his office and down the stairs. He whispered to the woman we had seen with the tray of bread, and we waited while she left for a few moments and then reappeared with three cloth bags, handing one to each of us.

We followed Gamaliel into the street and about half a mile from the city where we came to a grove of trees on a quiet hillside. There we sat, opened our bags, and found bread and fruit and cheese. Gamaliel blessed the meal, and as we ate he said, "Rabban Hillel, who founded our school, was my grandfather. My charge is to maintain what he began, a reverence for the Word of God, passing along the oral traditions, and calling young men into rabbinical ministry who are deeply committed to God and His Law. I seek peace with all men, even those with whom I may disagree."

When we had eaten he smiled and rose, gathering up our scraps and slowing heading back down the hill toward the city. When we reached the Hillel school again, Gamaliel *led us to a bench outside, where he squeezed his big body between us.*

"I do not wish to compete with Shammai for your son, Y'honatan, but let me simply leave it at this: Should Saul decide to enroll here, I will personally be his teacher. If my opinions trouble you in anyway, perhaps you would be more comfortable elsewhere. Whatever you decide, you may rest assured I remain at your service. Even if you choose to study at Shammai, you know where I am and should feel free to call upon me at any time if I can be of service to you. Questions?"

"One more," Father said, "if I may. Would you summarize the difference between the two schools then that Shammai emphasizes the letter of the Law—in the Pharisaical tradition—while Hillel is more concerned with the spirit of the Law?"

The rabbi cocked his head. "Insightful," he said. "I would add this: I would not want to speak for our friends at Shammai, but I can say that the spirit of the Law always keeps the person in mind. The Person of God and the Jewish person."

"Interesting," Father said. "One doesn't often hear God referred to as a Person."

"And isn't that tragic? The God of the Scriptures, the One your son and I have confessed to wanting to walk and talk with personally, is clearly a Person! Oh, He is the same yesterday, today, and forever, and in Him is neither change nor even shadow of turning. He is above all, Creator of all, and He sits high above the heavens. There is no God like Him. But He walked and talked with Adam in the garden.

He spoke to Moses and Abraham and Isaac and Jacob. That is the Person I want to know as revealed in His Law."

Gamaliel turned to me. "Questions?"

I shook my head. "Not about Hillel. I am curious, though. Why is it your daughter does not look like you and your son?"

"Saul!" Father shouted.

"No," Gamaliel said, laughing. "It's all right. The simple truth is that I married a beautiful woman who was somehow able to overcome my plainness to give me a handsome son and a beautiful daughter. Naomi, thankfully, has her mother's coloring and appearance."

The big round man slapped his thighs and rose, putting a hand on my shoulder. "You, sir, would be welcome to begin your studies here—if Hillel is your choice—two months hence, if you would just let me know within the week."

"Oh," Father said, "I expect we'll be able to announce our decision by tomorrow."

"I'll look forward to hearing from you then, either way."

"Either way?" I said. Was he just being polite? Wouldn't he, like Rabbi Enosh at the Shammai school, rather not see us if we decided against him?

"Of course," Nasi said. "I expect your decision will be made with much thought, and whether you choose to come here or not, it has been my pleasure to meet you both, and I wish you all God's blessings."

27

The Page

SO IT WAS OFFICIAL. Augie was harboring a fugitive. He drove through the ancient streets shaking his head at what he'd gotten himself into.

Suddenly overcome by jet lag, Augie felt a deep love for Roger. Augie had always admired the man and looked forward to their trips together.

However, what he was feeling now was a deep concern for his friend's eternal soul. He honored Roger's right to believe—or not believe—whatever he chose. But what kind of a friend would he be if he didn't press the issue—given that he truly believed that if Roger was killed he might be forever separated from God?

Sofia would understand. He phoned her but first told her of the manhunt.

"It's all over the news here too," she said. "My father is making me bring Dimos."

"You said he would tell no one!"

"Fokinos is an expert. We need all the help we can get, don't we?"

Augie sighed. "This is complicated enough, Sof."

"We'll be there tomorrow."

Augie told her of his urgent concern for Roger's soul.

"I'll be praying," Sofia said. "We just have to look for opportunities."

"First we have to keep him alive."

When Augie pulled to within sight of the train station the night sky was filled with flashing blue lights and the street was barricaded. He parked two blocks away and jogged to the barrier. "I need to get to my stuff," he told a carabiniere. "It's in a locker."

The cop signaled to a colleague who hurried over. "English," the first said.

The second turned to Augie. "Yes, sir."

Augie repeated what he needed.

"Apologies, Mister. Bomb threat. Locker contents are being moved to this gymnasium." He handed Augie a card with the address. "You can retrieve your belongings there tomorrow."

"I don't suppose the meatball sandwich place is open."

The cop laughed and pointed down the street. "Try there. Just as good. Maybe better."

On the way back, Augie called and filled Roger in.

"Oh, man," Roger said. "Did you tell 'em you need it now?"

"And make them suspicious? No."

"If they open that envelope or the paper box or get curious about what's so carefully wrapped . . ."

After they devoured the food, Roger looked more discouraged than ever. "Goin' to bed," he said.

Exhausted as he was, Augie found himself too agitated to sleep. What if he were arrested the next afternoon? What would happen to Roger? He slipped out of bed and padded to the door of Roger's room. Mustering his courage, he said, "Man, I've got to talk to you. You don't have to say anything, just hear me out."

Augie rehearsed their history and assured Roger he knew how he felt about the differences in their beliefs. "But I wouldn't forgive myself if something happened to you and I didn't try one more time."

Augie prayed silently as he spoke, asking God to give him the words to explain what it means to be a true believer in Christ. He quoted a lot of Scripture and finished, "I'm just hoping that Paul's memoir will corroborate everything you've read in the Bible and that you share Paul's heritage. You wouldn't be the first skeptic who became a believer."

When Roger didn't respond, Augie said, "We can talk later. Just tell me I haven't offended you. I sure haven't meant to."

Still nothing.

"Roger?"

But his friend was snoring.

SUNDAY, MAY 11, 11:00 A.M.

Augie received a text from Sofia that she and Dimos Fokinos had landed.

Roger said, "I gotta get out of here. But I'll be back in time to camp out in the lobby behind a newspaper, and—"

"Whoa, don't forget you're not as incognito as you were yesterday, François."

"C'mon, I told you. They got my chin wrong. Plus I'm gonna go crazy sitting here all day. I want to see if Sofia recognizes me."

"She won't. I wouldn't have, but take your tablet with you. And you know what to do if you think you've been made."

"Been *made*? Talking like a spy already."

"Just be prepared."

"I speed-dial you, and when you see my number but hear nothing, you know I'm in trouble."

"How secure are these new phones you keep trading?"

Roger shrugged. "Not very. I don't use 'em long."

Eager as Augie was to see Sofia, he texted that she should let him know where they checked in and then come by the Terrazzo at three o'clock. "directly 2 r suite, look like u belong, draw no attention."

12:55 P.M.

Augie drove to the address the police had given him and stood behind half a dozen people in a line outside. As soon as the door was unlocked, they all hurried in. Black plastic bags lay on folding tables, some bulging, some nearly flat. Locker numbers had been written on cards and taped to them.

Augie peeked at his key and headed for his bag, only to be intercepted by a uniformed carabiniere. "*Identificazione e la chiave, per favore.*"

"Sorry, *chiave*?"

"*Parli Italiano, sir?*" the cop said, nodding when Augie produced his blue passport. "Aah, English. Key. I need to see your locker key."

As soon as Augie produced it, the carabiniere said, "I have been instructed to inform you that you will not be allowed to leave here with all your contents unless you show me more documentation."

Augie froze. "And what documentation is that?"

"I think you know, sir."

He wanted to be neither belligerent nor a pushover. "If I knew, Officer, I would not ask."

The cop leafed through his passport. "You are an experienced traveler. You know you are required to have official clearance on your person for one specific item in your locker."

Augie smiled and shrugged.

"What is your work?"

"I lead tours, mostly to holy sites."

"And to which of these have you been allowed to carry a handgun?"

"Oh! The nine millimeter! That is not mine. It belongs to a friend."

"I will need the name."

"Will I be getting him in trouble?"

"He will have to come himself to retrieve it. But I must tell you, its serial number does not show up on any local police database. Our constitution does not recognize the right of citizens to bear arms."

"It doesn't? Then I wouldn't want to deliver it to him."

"His name?"

"That isn't necessary, is it? If I inform him it is unregistered, he would be wise to abandon it, wouldn't he?"

The carabiniere hesitated, a look coming over him. "It is a nice gun, sir."

Augie nodded. "How about I tell him he should just forget about it?"

"To keep himself out of trouble."

"Precisely. And would you personally dispose of it for him?"

"As his representative, you are instructing me to do that?"

"Yes, Officer, I want you to take personal responsibility for it. As you say, it is a nice gun. And that way, it doesn't have to be officially processed, does it?"

"Not if you are entrusting it to me."

"I am."

"Sign here."

A multipart form listed the contents of his locker. "Oh, I don't read much Italian either," Augie said. "Do you mind?"

The cop read, "One large sealed envelope addressed to R.M., unmarked. One five-hundred-sheet paper box, full. One wrapped and protected photograph or document."

Augie leaned in to peek at the form. "No mention of the, uh . . ."

"The . . . ?"

"The nine."

"What nine? Is something missing, Dr. Knox? Something else you want listed on this official police form?"

"No, I think that covers it."

The officer grabbed the bag and swung it into Augie's arms, clearly without an inkling that the single page of parchment alone was worth millions of euros. "Be sure everything you just signed for is there."

Augie peeked in at the three items, one drawing him like an undertow. He nodded and the officer walked away.

Augie started back to the hotel, driving as carefully as if he had been transporting cocaine. He tried to appear nonchalant as he strode through the lobby, reminding himself to slow down, maintain his composure. Only when the elevator doors slid shut did he realize he had forgotten to look for Roger lounging in the lobby.

2:20 P.M.

In his suite Augie hung a Do Not Disturb sign outside, applied the dead bolt, and attached the quaint chain. He rummaged for a clean pair of socks. They weren't ideal, but they would have to do until he could find cloth gloves. He sat at the desk and gingerly emptied the bag, setting Klaudios's envelope and the stationery box aside. He peeled the tape from the edges of the sheets protecting the parchment, making sure he kept the entire package out of the sunlight streaming through the drapes.

Finally, before him lay a parchment page about eleven inches by fourteen, sandwiched between thin, custom-cut, acid-free sheets. Augie slid the socks over trembling hands, then lowered his head to where he could softly blow on the top leaf until it began to slide away and expose the parchment.

Augie held his breath and slowly nudged it with his awkwardly covered fingers until the entire page came into view. *Oh, God,* he prayed silently. *Let this unspeakable privilege be real.*

The page was written in Ancient Greek that appeared to be from the Hellenistic period. Earlier texts, and even some during the beginning of that period, were written both right to left and left to right, alternating every line so the writer barely had to lift his hand from the page. This one had been written right to left, and, as Roger had told him, the script was remarkably readable for being as old as he hoped.

He began reading, meticulously translating for himself as he went, careful not to touch the parchment even with a sock-covered hand.

I, Saul, begin the recitation of my most vivid memories by acknowledging an incident that has affected my entire life, even with all that came after it. And as you shall see, all that followed even I would deem the creation of a fanciful mind had I not myself lived it.

Augie sat back and exhaled heavily. Was he actually reading something written in the Apostle Paul's own hand? It was almost more than he could bear. Was Paul referring to his dramatic conversion experience on the road to Damascus? Or something earlier? Augie couldn't wait to find out.

2:55 P.M.

Augie stacked everything on the side table in his bedroom, setting the heavy ream of paper over the one original page.

He heard footsteps outside the door and moved close to listen. Sofia's voice: "Δήμος, θα μου δίνετε ένα λεπτό για να σας χαιρετάει αρραβωνιαστικός μου?" ["Dimos, would you give me a minute to greet my fiancé?"]

He opened the door to her knock and she wrapped her arms around his neck, kissing him deeply.

"My love," he said.

Still entangled, Sofia said, "Let me introduce you to Dimos Fokinos, who works with my father. His English is pretty good."

Fokinos, who had remained just out of sight, appeared. The men traded pleasantries, Augie telling him his reputation had preceded him. Sofia's comment about his English proved an understatement. Though his speech was heavily accented, he clearly knew the language. He said, "Mr. Trikoupis tends to exaggerate."

But he hadn't. Dimos was everything the man had said: tall, slim, with longish, black, curly hair. He was dressed almost as stylishly as Sofia. Genteel, however, he was not. As he shook Augie's hand he slipped past him and into the suite. "Come on in," Augie said, the sarcasm plainly eluding Fokinos.

The Greek draped his jacket over the back of the couch, then sat. "We need to get down to business. Your man is all over the news and it won't be long before he is in custody."

"Not if I have anything to say about it," Augie said.

"You need to be very careful if you don't want the same fate. Where is he, anyway?"

"You didn't see him in the lobby?" Augie said.

"Had I seen him, I would know where he is, wouldn't I?"

"His disguise is working, that's all."

"I saw no one in the lobby," Sofia said. "It was empty except for staff."

"We don't have time for this," Dimos said. "Your friend needs to stay out of sight, and we need to find the parchments."

"We?" Augie said. "You're a guest here, sir. And our priority is not the parchments. It's our friend's life."

"Which is as good as over, so don't play games, Dr. Knox. You're talking about an artifact which, if I can verify its authenticity, is priceless."

"*You're* going to authenticate it?"

"That's why Mr. Trikoupis sent me."

"Do you read Ancient Greek, Mr. Fokinos?"

"I thought that was your job. Mine is to evaluate the parchment itself. When can I see it?"

"All in good time. Right now I need to find Roger."

Fokinos huffed and began pacing.

Augie texted, "where r u? they're here."

Dimos pulled on his jacket. "Are we going to sit around here all day?"

"Where do you propose we go?" Augie said. "I'm not leaving until I reconnect with Roger."

"Make it fast. If you really care so much about his eternal soul you wouldn't let him out of your sight."

Augie shot Sofia a glance. She looked ashen. Was it guilt over revealing to Dimos her private conversation with Augie? Or had her phone been compromised?

28

Trouble

FIRST-CENTURY ROME

THOUGH SUMMER WAS ALMOST over, the great capital city was as hot as it had been during the great fire. The sheer number of dehydrated government workers kept Luke from tending to the general populace, including many mothers and children. Well after the sun finally, mercifully, set, Luke had not had time to pick up his lamp and find something for Paul to eat. He prayed Panthera had been able to visit Paul and provide a little food and light.

But when Luke got to the prison, a young sandy-haired guard from inside patrolled the gate.

"Primus on break?" Luke said.

"No, Doctor. He's being disciplined, and—"

"What for?"

"—if the gods favor me, he'll be discharged and I will get his post."

"What did he do?"

"Showed favoritism to a prisoner, and you know about whom I speak."

"So he checked in on Paul. What was the harm in that?"

"Did you know he had been feeding the prisoner too?"

"A scrap now and then. What of it?"

"Worse, he was caught providing light. He may lose his position, sir. For now he has been suspended for a week without pay."

"That's horrible."

"It's policy, sir."

"Then Paul has not eaten today—beyond the gruel, I mean?"

"Probably not."

Luke hurried inside, surprised that even the guards manning the hole stood in virtual darkness. He could barely make out their forms in the dim light.

"Even *your* torches have been doused?" Luke said.

"Orders, Doctor," one said. "They were sending light through the hole, and the prisoner's sentence calls for complete darkness."

"But for months he has had that little bit of light."

"And none of us cared much, except Gaius."

"Gaius?"

"You passed him at the gate. He grew tired of Primus enjoying the privileges of position while violating protocol and reported him. Our superiors have reminded us—strongly—to enforce the sentence as written."

"Why don't you just cover the hole? Why should you have to stand here in darkness?"

"A cover will be in place by tomorrow."

"Must I visit my patient in darkness also?"

"I'm afraid so, sir."

"A travesty." Luke stepped closer. "Does this mean I cannot bring a little extra food for him either?"

"You will find us looking the other way, if you are discreet. We have become fond of him. We know nothing of his guilt or innocence, but not one of us doubts his sincerity."

"But I have no food this evening."

"I would give you some of mine," the guard said. "But we've just had our break and nothing is left."

"I worry about Paul living through the night."

"The outside guards do not break for another hour. Perhaps one would slip you something."

Luke knelt over the hole and poked his head through. "Paul!"

"Luke!" came the raspy reply. "The darkness torments me! And I'm hungry! Come quickly."

"Hold on, friend! I'll be down soon."

Luke rushed out to the new gate guard. "May I call you Gaius?"

"That's my name."

"I need a bit of food for my friend. Some bread, cheese, anything."

"I told you, he's not allowed—"

"Do you have a price?"

Gaius hesitated. "You wish to put me in the same predicament as Primus? What kind of a hypocrite would I be?"

"Who would report you?"

"None would dare!"

"Then a bit of food?"

Gaius looked around, then spoke softly. "If, as you say, the price was adequate. You must not let the other guards know where you got it."

"I am prepared to do my part for the life of my friend."

"You could not afford me."

"Try me, Gaius. Surely you could use an extra coin or two."

"It depends on what those coins were made of."

"I need food only for tonight. I can bring my own from now on."

"Selling you food is one thing. Ignoring you giving your own to the prisoner is another."

"I've never had to pay for that."

"You can't tell me Primus was never accommodated."

"Please. Your price."

Gaius whispered an exorbitant amount, "which would pay for my ignorance for a month."

Luke countered with half the price, "to cover this until his execution." Gaius surreptitiously shook Luke's hand. "I have another proposition," Luke said. "I'll pay the full amount you asked for if you will not testify against Primus."

"But I brought the charge! I will be the primary witness."

Luke shrugged. "If you don't want the money . . ."

"I do! But how will that look?"

"Just say that you feel the suspension was adequate for the offense and that you are confident that such a good superior as Primus will not repeat it."

"But then I will not be promoted to this post!"

"Would it pay that much more than I'm offering?"

"No. But it comes with privilege and honor."

Luke wanted to ask what kind of honor was due a man so easily bought. "The decision is yours."

"And you'll pay me immediately?"

"Tomorrow." *Unlike you, my word is my bond.* "But tonight, what do you have for my friend?"

"No bread, but cheese."

"I need more."

"A handful of olives."

"Any fruit?"

"A few grapes."

"And how will I get these?"

"I shall bring them to you after my break. I'll invent a reason to check on you and the prisoner."

Luke's inclination was to thank Gaius, but he couldn't muster the words.

Inside he found Paul lying on the floor, the chain on his manacled ankle stretched to its length. "I'm just trying to get close to any hint of light, Luke. I can endure much, but not constant darkness. I don't know how long I can carry on."

Luke promised to try to find a way to continue bringing his lamp. If they indeed covered the hole, perhaps he could then light it without the guards seeing. "And tonight I must wait to feed you until after the guards take their breaks."

"The one they call Gaius is not our friend, Luke."

"Have no fear. I have bought his favor."

Luke helped Paul to the stone bench. The older man said, "So, he will be guilty of the very thing he reported about Primus. Hypocrisy knows no bounds. I hate to see him prosper by my predicament."

"We both know he will not prosper in the end," Luke said.

"I will pray for him. Will you too, Luke?"

"It won't be easy."

"Was it easy for Jesus to pray for those who led Him to His death? He asked His Father to forgive them!"

"May God grant me the same grace."

An hour later Gaius slipped nimbly down into the dungeon. "Approach, Doctor," he whispered. "And speak quietly." Luke reached for him in the darkness and accepted the food.

"Do I also have to hold my tongue?" Paul said.

"You should say nothing at all."

"Fearing what consequence? Can you mete out a punishment worse than execution?"

"I could flog you, limit you to the gruel. Utter darkness will become your closest friend."

"I am able to endure all things for the sake of the gospel."

"I know, I know. Does saying that give you some sort of peace, make you feel better about yourself?"

Paul spoke between bites. "I consider myself nothing compared to the matchless perfection of my Savior."

"I've heard this all before."

"Why may I not see your face?" Paul said.

"You have seen me. I've been down here before."

"You're the sandy-haired one, the one who never had anything good to say about your superior."

"Primus was not really my superior."

"No? He only outranked you and gave you orders."

"But where is he now? Even he had superiors. And they listened to me."

"I like to see the face of a man I'm speaking with. I need to ask you something, and I can't do it in the dark."

Gaius sighed and moved back under the hole in the ceiling. "Hand me down a torch!"

"We're not allowed, Gaius! We were told—"

"Just do it! I will answer for it. I need to check conditions down here."

Luke and Paul covered their eyes until they grew accustomed to the light. Luke was stunned as the flame, so much larger than his lamp, illuminated Paul.

The man had become a faded image of himself. His dark eyes seemed more piercing than ever, staring out from his bony, emaciated face. Luke wondered how long the manacle would be secure on such a skinny ankle.

The physician was overwhelmed with memories of a young, vibrant Paul, traveling the world to visit the churches. He had never been a big man, but he had been muscled and wiry.

"All right, here I am," Gaius said. "What is it?"

"I do remember you," Paul said. "A handsome young man in the prime of life, lost in your trespasses and your sins."

"How dare you?"

"Do not fight the truth, son. We're all sinners. Isaiah said we had turned, every one, to his own way."

"Isaiah? You think I care what a Jew writes?"

"What is your own way, Gaius? Do you believe in the gods?"

"Of course!"

"Worship them? Follow their commands? Oh, wait, they have no commands, no claims upon you. Do they care for you, forgive you, live for you? Would they die for you?"

"Stop! You said you had a request of me, so get on with it."

"I want to prove to you that God loves you."

"Save your breath."

"Nothing can silence this message."

"Your execution will."

"Oh, no, there you're wrong. This message will long outlive me. It is the story of forgiveness, redemption, salvation. I am merely a mouthpiece. The movement has begun and will never die, because it is all about One who conquered death."

"No one can conquer death."

"One already has. Surely you want to hear more about Him."

"I do not! I'm leaving."

"But my request . . ."

"Last chance. What is it?"

"Promise to attend my execution."

"By the gods, I wouldn't miss it!"

"I don't put any stock in their word, but if you tell me you will be there, that is good enough for me."

"I'll be the one cheering the loudest."

"As long as you also listen."

29

A Billion Euros

"SOFIA AND I ARE going to look for Roger," Augie said.

"Suit yourself," Dimos Fokinos said. "I'll get my equipment from the car and start examining the parchments."

"I will have nothing for you until we find the manuscripts."

"But what about the one——? Listen, we——you've got to find this thing before the Art Squad does. Once they have it, you lose access. No looking at it. No studying it. No credit for uncovering it. No money."

"There's no money in this, regardless," Augie said. "Whoever finds it has to turn it over to the Art Squad."

Fokinos slowly closed and opened his eyes. "Are you seriously that naïve? We've——you've got to milk this thing for all it's worth. Parcel it out, make them pay for the privilege of seeing it a little bit at a time."

"Put a ransom on it? We'd wind up in prison for the rest of our lives."

"They're setting your friend up for that already! So use the parchments as bargaining chips. Trade information for immunity. This is the perfect antiquity to engender one huge reward. The last thing you want to do is to just give it up."

"Provided it is what we hope it is."

"I can determine that for you."

"Why would I show it to someone who encourages me to commit a crime? What would your employer think?"

Fokinos seemed to fight a smile, then sat and rested his elbows on his knees. His tone grew earnest. "Listen, Dr. Knox. I don't need to tell you the value of this find."

"That's right, so spare me."

Fokinos held up a hand. "No, hear me. We're not talking millions of euros."

"I know."

"Not even tens of millions."

"I'm aware. This is my field."

"Hundreds of millions, Augie—may I call you Augie? Maybe even a billion. I don't mean to insult your intelligence, but you don't seem to grasp the magnitude of the discovery."

"If you'd take a breath, I'll tell you what I grasp."

"Please do, I beg of you."

"You're implying that the dollar value supersedes ethics, even laws."

"I'm not implying it, Augie. I'm saying it outright. You're not going to hurt anyone or even defraud anyone. At worst you're going to break a rule—an unfair rule that says antiquities found in this country belong to the government. Well, I prefer finders keepers."

"One word of this to my father," Sofia said, "and you'll be back to your old job."

Dimos spread his arms on the back of the couch. "So shortsighted."

"I know my father."

Fokinos snorted. "Actually you don't. Do you really think he and I have not already had this conversation? Are you not aware that he and I have friends in the Art Squad and every other such agency around the world? That we protect ourselves by also knowing everyone on the black market, from the diggers to the middlemen to the financiers?"

"My dad is the most ethical purveyor of antiq—"

"How do you think he maintains that reputation, Sofia? By keeping his friends close and his enemies—"

"Closer, yes," she said, "I know the adage. But you have him all wrong."

"Would you bet Roger Michaels's life on it? I'm here on a mission. While you and Augie—"

"He may be all right with you calling him Augie," Sofia said, "but I prefer you address him correctly."

"Fair enough. While you and Dr. Knox pretend you are trying to keep your friend alive long enough to find out where he stashed the manuscripts—as if you don't have them in hand already—I will be cultivating every contact I can find so we can maximize our profits once the goods are in hand."

Augie narrowed his eyes. "You wouldn't even know where to start."

Fokinos smiled. "You have no idea. I start with the Art Squad, placing my services at their disposal on behalf of my employer, who, with his compliments and best wishes, lends me and my expertise to help evaluate and protect the single most valuable artifact ever to surface."

Augie shook his head. "And with his gratitude and blessing, you gain access to anyone you need in Italy."

"You're catching on."

Augie's phone buzzed. He peeked at the readout and stood. "Roger!" he said. He went cold when there was no response, but couldn't let on to Fokinos. "Yeah! We were worried about ya. Be right there."

"That's a relief," Sofia said. "Where is he?"

"About twenty minutes north," Augie said, inventing a location the opposite direction from Dimos's and her hotel. He was desperate to keep Fokinos from mucking everything up. "And he's hungry. Let's all go and have a meal with him."

"Not smart," Fokinos said. "Just get him back here and order room service."

"Come on. You need to meet him anyway."

"I'm staying as far away from him as I can. You want to risk it, feel free. I've got places to go."

"It's Sunday," Sofia said. "Come with us."

"The people I need to see don't keep regular hours," Fokinos said. "I'll catch up with you later."

As soon as he was gone, Augie told Sofia his side of the conversation with Roger had been a sham, that the call and the silence meant trouble. "It was reckless of him to leave the hotel, but he's a grown man. I can't tell him what to do."

"Somebody needs to," she said. "Augie, you need to know I said nothing to Dimos about our conversation about Roger's soul."

"Or the first page of the manuscript, I hope."

"Of course not."

"You know what that means," he said.

"He must have seen our texts or overheard our calls. But your phone is secure, right?"

"Guaranteed."

"Who would have even given him my number?"

"I don't want to think about it," Augie said.

"Oh, no. Dad wouldn't."

"Who else?"

"I'm calling him right now," Sofia said.

Saul's Decision

"HE'S NOT HERE," PRIMUS' wife whispered desperately when Luke arrived late that night. "He doesn't want his mother or the children to know what has happened. He said he would meet you at midnight, and it's almost that time." She told him to wait in the back room of an inn not far away. "I hope you don't mind meeting him there. They stay open late for men who enjoy their ale and mead. I know you are not one of those."

"No, but I know the place."

"Don't let him stay out too late. Or drink too much."

Luke smiled. "Try not to worry. Your husband will survive this. Bless you."

Luke hurried through the streets, reminded that for the first time in weeks he felt he was actually making progress. His daily workload was becoming more manageable. The rebuilding of the city progressed slowly, but people were being gradually relocated. While they seemed grateful to have shelter again, many grumbled that the emperor himself had been behind the disaster. "It's only fair he provide for me and my family," one woman told him. "His fire put us on the streets."

As Luke made his way toward the inn, he wondered what the magnanimous Onesiphorus would think of how he was using the treasure the man had provided for Paul's care. Luke assumed he would be in favor of whatever made Paul's life better—even bribery.

Luke slipped into the alley behind the inn and found the back door. The place was crowded with revelers, many already past their thresholds of strong drink. The proprietor handed a tray of decanters to a chubby woman and headed for Luke. "I didn't expect to see you here after hours, Doctor," he said, leading him to a small table near the bar. "I don't imagine you'd care for mead or ale?"

"No, thank you. Just meeting a friend. He might like something when he arrives."

The man leaned close. "I have some aged wine that few here can afford. I'd be honored to offer you a sample, with my compliments."

"That sounds wonderful," Luke said.

"When your friend gets here, I'll bring you each a cup."

Luke sat facing the door and waved tentatively when Primus entered. Someone broke into song, accompanied harshly by flute and lute and drums. People rose to dance with the servant girls. Primus appeared annoyed by the merriment. With his job in jeopardy and a family to support, Luke couldn't blame him. The guard weaved through the revelers to Luke's table.

"Have you eaten?" Luke said.

Primus nodded. "The children don't notice the lack of meat, as long as they get their honey and bread."

The proprietor delivered the wine and refused Luke's offer to pay. "I told you, my privilege."

Primus sipped. "It's been a long time since I've tasted something like this. And I don't expect to again soon."

Luke told him of his arrangement with Gaius.

"You know you can't trust him," Primus said.

"That is clear. However, I believe he will not testify against you. In fact, he may help you regain your post."

Primus looked dubious until Luke told him the man's price.

"You'd do that for me, Doctor?"

"A hypocrite should never prevail."

"I'm no better. Until I got to know Paul, I thought nothing of accepting your gifts for ignoring what you were doing for him. I'm too much like Gaius to hate him."

Luke held his closed hand out to Primus and dropped several coins into his palm.

"Oh, no, I can't."

"You must. You can't be expected to miss a week's pay. Consider it a favor from Paul himself. A wealthy friend provided for him."

"If it weren't for my family, I would refuse."

"I know you will use it wisely. Anyway, you deserve no less than Gaius. Paul will be pleased to know we have been able to help. When is your hearing?"

"Day after tomorrow."

"We will be praying."

An hour later Luke sat in his room at Primus' house. He was glad to have been able to help, but how it broke his heart to see both Paul and Primus in such despair. It was a relief to lose himself again in Paul's memoir.

Father seemed to walk more slowly than ever as we trudged back to our lodging. "Those two headmasters wore me out," he said. "Rabbi Enosh with his negativity, Rabban Gamaliel with his generosity."

We entered our chamber and sat on our cots.

"We are strict Pharisees," Father said. "That part of Shammai appeals to me."

"Me too. But I also long to know more than the Law. I want to know God."

"If He is knowable," Father said. "Be careful what you wish for. My fear for you studying at Shammai is that you might develop the same attitude as Rabbi Enosh."

"I didn't notice it until we met Rabban Gamaliel. He is certainly compassionate."

"A man of character," Father said. "I would never want to see you soften your view of the Law, but you could do worse than to develop a bearing like his."

"I would not come here just to have a good time," I told my father, "but somehow I think studying under Gamaliel would be more pleasant."

"That should hardly be your priority. You must promise me that you will give yourself wholly to your studies for as long as you're in Jerusalem. We are uprooting our whole

family and moving far from our home just so you may get the best religious training."

I lay back on my pallet and intertwined my fingers behind my head. "Studying here is a gift I never imagined."

"You have been diligent. You have earned it."

"I want to study under Gamaliel," I blurted, surprising even myself.

Father turned and seemed to search my face. "Really? That would be your decision?"

I nodded. "I know it's not up to me, but yes."

"I don't know what Rabbi Daniel will think, but I too lean toward Hillel. Naturally, you must tell me of any teaching contrary to orthodoxy. But I rather like the idea of your sitting at the feet of Gamaliel."

31

Closing In

Sofia put her phone on speaker.

"Dad, how much did you tell Dimos?"

"Only what you told me. What's the problem? He's trustworthy."

She shot a glance at Augie. "Maybe, maybe not, but he knows more than what I told you."

"What have you not told me, dear? How can I help if I don't know everything?"

"I'm talking about private stuff—things that happened since I talked to you."

The pause was too long to suit Augie. And when Malfees Trikoupis began again, he spoke deliberately, as if taking great care to not trap himself. "Private? And recent? Then—then how would I have been able to tell him something even I did not know?"

"That's my point, Dad. He shows up gung ho and ready to go, but he slipped up. He knows too much. Roger's life is not the only one on the line here, and we feel like we've already been compromised by someone who's supposed to be on our side."

"He is on your side! He is there on my behalf. You know I would do nothing to jeopardize your safety."

"Then how does he know all this stuff?"

"You're absolutely certain he has knowledge of your private conversations."

"Yes, at least two. He had to have access to my phone."

"No! How?"

"I just asked you that."

"On my life, darling, I would never—"

"Augie and I are going to have to get to the bottom of this before we can continue working with Dimos. If he's here to examine the parchment and determine its age, there's nothing for him to do until then. Yet he's already trying to make connections."

"I have contacts who could be helpful, Sofia."

"But what if Dimos were to say too much to the wrong person? Why don't you call him back to Greece and let us call for him when we're ready?"

"No, no. Now, he's there. I can talk to him, but let him establish the contacts and—"

"Then we'll have to confront him. We have to know how he got access to my phone."

A long pause. "Just be careful not to accuse before you give him a chance to explain. Maybe it's not as sinister as you think."

"What are you saying?"

"Nothing. It's just that at my age I have been through many misunderstandings. You don't want to jump to conclusions. Now, was Dr. Knox able to learn where the manuscript might be?"

Augie shook his head. "No," Sofia said. "I'll keep you posted."

As soon as she was off the phone, Augie said, "Let me try something else. It's what, seven hours earlier in Dallas?"

He called Biff Dyer.

"Augie! What's up?"

"You, I hope. Did I wake you?"

"Honestly? Yeah. But we've got to get the kids ready for church anyway. You find Michaels? He okay?"

"We're all fine for now, Biff. I just need a little help. We think someone's hacked Sofia's phone, and we have to know who. Any way to figure that out?"

"Won't be easy. But give me her number and the serial number on her chip and I'll try."

5:00 P.M.

Augie kept checking his phone for word from Roger. "No sense heading out unless we have a clue where to look."

"Maybe he dialed you by accident."

"One way to find out." Augie called Roger. No answer. Augie texted him, "on r way soon as u say where."

. While they waited, Augie showed Sofia the first page of the memoir. "It has to be real, doesn't it?" she said. "It just has to be. Has anyone ever discovered an older document?"

"The Dead Sea Scrolls, and even some older fragments, but this is hundreds of pages all intact."

"What's in the envelope?"

"It's addressed to Roger, who was to open it if anything happened to Klaudios. I shouldn't open it unless something happens to Rog. He believes it tells where the rest of the originals are. The box is full of reduced photocopies of the rest of the manuscript. It'll take me a long time to read through, but I have to do it when I won't be disturbed."

Augie's phone chirped. "It's him! A picture."

They studied the image. "A corner," she said. "Both street names are visible. He's in the center of Rome on a Sunday? Isn't that the Vatican across the Tiber there? Maybe he's trying to hide in the crowd."

Augie reassembled the protective covers for the parchment. "We've got to get to him."

"Better take a cab," she said. "Don't want to be driving in that mess."

"What if we need to get him out of there fast?"

"You wouldn't be able to do it in a car anyway. Unless this were a James Bond movie."

Augie's phone signaled a text.

"br ur 9."

"cops kept."

"br mine. mattress."

Augie found the nine millimeter between the mattresses in Roger's bedroom. It felt heavy enough to be loaded, but he made sure by releasing the magazine, then snapped it back in.

"Pray I don't have to use this," he said.

"I'll pray you don't get caught with it."

As he threaded his belt through the holster and positioned it in the small of his back, Augie said, "We can't leave this stuff here." He put the envelope in the safe and found a plastic laundry bag in the closet big enough to hold the parchment. He looped the bag over the top of a hanger, draped a shirt around it, and they headed for the parking lot.

Augie hung the shirt in his rental car and stashed the laundry bag and the box in the trunk.

At the main entrance the doorman waved for a white car with a *TAXI* sign on the roof. The crest on the door bore the Latin acronym *SPQR* (The Senate and People of Rome). Augie studied the picture on his phone and told the driver, "First street west of Piazza Navona."

Sofia whispered, "Think he's running?"

"I'll ask," Augie said. But before he could punch in the text, Sofia reached to turn his phone toward her.

"This says he sent that picture from his tablet, Augie. Why not his phone like the original call?"

"I don't know. Better quality?"

Augie tapped in, "on r way. u ok?"

Nothing.

"Driver," he said, "could you hurry, please?"

"*Perdono?*"

"*Potrebbe sbrighi, per favore?*" Sofia said.

Within minutes the driver had picked his way through heavy traffic, most of it heading toward the Vatican, and stopped at a curb near Piazza Navona. "We'd better split up," Augie said. "You go north, then east. I'll go south, then east. We'll meet in the middle on the other side of the piazza. Don't make it obvious we're looking for anyone. Let him find us."

Augie didn't expect to be recognized, but since someone had compromised his phone after Roger had called him in Dallas, they could have Googled him and found out what he looked like. If the number two man at the Art Squad really was behind all this, he could have tracked Augie's flight from DFW to FCO.

Augie had to consider all the possibilities. He had shown his passport to the carabiniere in the Naples train station, to the car rental clerk, to the policewoman near Roger's apartment. He had even used it to check in to the hotel and to retrieve the stuff from Roger's luggage locker. Augie could only hope the cop at the gymnasium who absconded with the Smith & Wesson had reason to not report that encounter.

Sofia's phone had been hacked too. For all Augie knew the Art Squad had been tailing them since they arrived. Could they have seen him stash the parchment in the rental? He didn't want to be paranoid, but surely someone as highly placed as Aldo Sardinia could be that technologically savvy.

When Augie turned north on the east side of the piazza, his phone vibrated. Augie fought to remain casual as he pulled it from his pocket. Roger had texted: "screwed up. ditched phone. holy cross now."

Fortunately Augie had led enough tours to know the Pontifical University of the Holy Cross was almost immediately north of him. When Sofia rounded the corner at the end of Piazza Navona, he signaled her to wait there. As if she'd been born to espionage, she stopped at a kiosk and appeared to be studying what was posted there.

When Augie passed behind her, he said under his breath, "Holy Cross." As he reached the corner where the great university stood, he slowed as if just taking in its expanse. His phone vibrated twice. Texts from both Roger and Biff Dyer in Dallas.

He checked Roger's first. "c u. where 2 find me in a min."

Biff's read, "success. can u talk?"

"No. Text pls."

"K."

Roger again: "walk in shadows."

The sun was deep in the west already, so Augie moved to the east side of the complex where the buildings blocked its rays. As he turned the corner he noticed Sofia behind him.

Another photo appeared on his cell, the sign for a tiny eatery. Roger texted, "200 ft left & down."

Roger must have believed he had eluded whoever was after him to feel safe below street level. Augie would have chosen higher ground, but then neither had he ever run for his life.

Augie squinted into the sky at the *thwock-thwock-thwock* of a helicopter. The chopper looked official, military or police. His phone read, "that's 4 me. u armed?"

Augie responded, "u got 2 b kidding."

"have the 9?"

"2 many people."

"b ready."

"Not 4 aircraft."

"hurry."

Augie thought it better not to be seen running rather than gawking like everyone else, so he just kept walking and looking up. The whirlybird drifted south toward the other end of the piazza. Several *polizia* cars headed that way, as well as a few uniforms on foot.

Augie slowed when he thought he'd gone about sixty yards, and Roger texted, "don't miss it. where'd chopper go?"

"South, past Navona."

"whew."

Augie saw the sign and trotted down a short flight of stone stairs, knowing Sofia was close enough to see him. The place was nearly empty, dingy with dark wood paneling lit only by a dim knockoff Tiffany. Roger peeked over the top of a menu from a booth near the back.

The restaurant was secluded, but Augie feared they could be sitting ducks. He slid into the booth but didn't like having his back to the door. "There's an exit behind me too," Roger said, nodding toward a rusty door under a sign with an arrow: *Bagno*.

"Got to go?" Roger said.

"Thankfully, no. Now what happened? How'd you wind up here?"

Roger hesitated and looked up as a *cameriera* approached and set a dog-eared menu before Augie. "*Caffè?*" she said.

"Please, and some bread and olive oil."

She hesitated, so Roger said with a heavy French accent, "*Per favore e solo pane.*" He turned to Augie. "The *olio d'oliva* is on the table."

When the waitress left, Augie said, "I don't know how you do that."

"Helps to know lots of languages."

Augie heard footsteps and saw Roger make eye contact as Sofia moved past and slid into the next booth with her back to them, close enough to listen.

"So I go for a walk," Roger said, "and I want to be back to the Ter-razzo by the time Sofia and the other guy get there. But I'm convinced I can't stay hidden much longer with the whole government looking for me."

"You're right," Augie said.

"So I grab a cab and head this way, thinking I'd just like to see the sights again, maybe for the last time."

"You said you screwed up."

"Did I ever."

Roger fell silent again when the *cameriera* delivered warm bread and approached Sofia, who ordered a salad.

Roger continued, "You know I've been changing phones almost every day, but like an idiot, while I'm walking around here I start wondering whether Sardinia has been trying to call me. The only number he has for me is my old voice mail. So I dial in and listen to a bunch of messages from travel agencies, then to a few calls from people horrified by what they saw about me on the news. I finally get to one from Sardinia. Says I'd better find him before he finds me or I'm gonna regret it. What else is new, right? Then it hits me. All that time I spent listening to messages left my new phone vulnerable. Of course they'd be monitoring my voice mail."

"But your distress call to me was from that phone."

"Just before I ditched it south of Navona. I was a couple of blocks from where the carabinieri had set up a checkpoint. With that phone I'd been carrying I might as well have fired off a flare. I speed-dialed you, tossed the phone, and got moving north."

"You should have grabbed a cab back to the hotel."

"I should have done a lot of things, Augie, but I've never been hunted before. That chopper went south because they tracked my phone to the trash bin."

"Creative. Why not down a sewer grate?"

"Like I said, I'm an amateur."

Augie's phone buzzed and he found a text from Biff. "See below number used 2 hack ST's." Augie didn't recognize it, but slid his phone across the table to Roger. "Slip this to Sofia."

Roger stretched and reached the phone behind him to Sofia. As soon as she looked at the screen she whirled in her seat and glared at Augie.

Anticipation

FIRST-CENTURY ROME

THE NEXT NIGHT THE guards lifted away the new wood disk that covered the hole in the floor, and as Luke descended, Paul darted toward the light as a moth to flame. When the covering slid back across the opening, Paul moaned.

"Patience, my friend," Luke whispered. "I've brought the lamp."

"I have been in utter darkness other than around midday when they delivered a bowl of the wretched cold gruel."

Luke lit his lamp and pulled food from his pockets. The condemned man sighed and bowed his head to give thanks. With a crust of bread in his shaking hand, he said, "I have lived through shipwreck, stoning, flogging, and prison, but this blackness is the worst. When my friends who walked with Jesus quoted Him about casting men into outer darkness,

I could barely comprehend it. Now I shudder at the thought. At least I feel His presence, even while enduring this."

Luke reached with the hem of his sleeve to wipe tears from Paul's cheeks.

"Luke, I look forward to heaven more every day."

"You know what I look forward to every night? Your wonderful story. I pray for you constantly while reading it."

I hardly slept that night, so eager was I to break the news to Rabban Gamaliel in the morning. During breakfast I pestered Father about things at Hillel he would have no way of knowing.

He merely smiled. "Life is easier when you simply let it unfold."

"What will I do onboard when we sail home?"

"Stay out of the way of the crew, study, pray, try to keep from becoming seasick."

"Have you ever been seasick?"

"Once on a short fishing trip when I was a little older than you, and once was enough. As I hung over the bow, adding chum to the water, someone assured me I wouldn't die from seasickness. But it was the hope of dying that was keeping me alive."

I laughed. "You need to tell Rabban Gamaliel that story!"

"No I don't, and neither do you. He's probably heard it. It's an old joke."

All the way to the Hillel school I ran and threw rocks and sticks at trees and even whistled. I couldn't help imagining coming back here with my whole family. No more sitting in a classroom with a bunch of kids just memorizing and reciting and asking a question or two. I would be conversing with a leading scholar, digging deeply into the texts.

Gamaliel welcomed us into his office.

Father said, "Can you tell our verdict by the boy's smile?"

"I'm pleased," the headmaster said. "Too often new students are fearful, knowing the work will not be easy."

"I don't want it to be easy," I said. "I want to be challenged, to learn all there is to learn."

"That's the kind of a student I was," Gamaliel said. "I still am. I work every day with members of the Sanhedrin who clearly feel that because they have attained some status, they can no longer be taught. I hope you find, as I have, that the more you know, the more you realize how much you don't."

"I can't wait to get started."

"You are going to be a joy to teach. But beware, bright and thoughtful as you are, even you will find we push students to their limits. At home you may be far ahead of others your age, but we attract the best students from all over the world. Distractions may creep in. What else are you passionate about?"

"He's very athletic," Father said, "but he is a scholar at heart."

"Females are not a distraction?"

"Not until yesterday," Father said with a smile.

My face burned. How could he say that in front of the girl's father?

Gamaliel said, "It was not lost on me that you were taken with Naomi. As you become interested in the opposite sex, you may find your studies suffering. We will strive to keep your mind on your education."

Embarrassment shut my mouth. While Gamaliel and Father chatted, I sat studying the floor, hoping my humiliation would pass.

Father must have noticed, because he changed the subject. "I'm told there is a good market for quality tents here."

But before Gamaliel could respond, someone passed his door and he called out, "Oh, Nathanael, a moment please!"

That was the first time I laid eyes on a man for whom, as an adult, I would work for many years. He was dressed in priestly robes and had an orange beard. Gamaliel introduced us and said, "Nathanael is vice chief justice of the Sanhedrin and teaches here when he has time. My own son Simeon is one of his students."

I must have looked surprised, having just met Simeon, because Nathanael said, "Rabban Gamaliel's son is a fine-looking lad but does not yet look his age. And you," he said, nodding at me, "though small, if you had a beard, look as if you could teach here."

The three men laughed, but I felt very much my age.

Four days later Father and I arrived at the great port at Caesarea. Anchored there was a magnificent ship, its hull sealed with tar so that it looked like a great black beast. I guessed it was at least a hundred feet long. The crewman assigned to guide us aboard was barefoot and unkempt. I found him hard to understand.

"How many will be on this boat?" I said.

"Not boat, ship! About three hundred."

"How heavy is this boat—ship?"

"Afraid she'll sink?"

"Just curious."

"Something like four hundred thousand pounds fully loaded. All powered by that huge foresail up top. Once it's open to the wind, that will be all we need to sail us to Tarsus."

Other passengers and cargo were being loaded, and the ship was already rocking. I rather enjoyed the motion. On the main deck I was fascinated by all the activity, and the ship itself. What fun this was going to be!

When I asked a man tending the ropes one question too many, he said, "You want to learn to tie this knot?" It proved nowhere near as easy as he made it look. My hands were too small and smooth to manipulate the thick cords.

When I finally produced a sloppy knot, he asked if I wanted to meet the captain. Did I ever! I followed him to a cramped space with a small bunk, a few instruments, and a map.

When the captain welcomed me aboard, I blurted, "How big a storm can this ship survive?"

That launched him into a litany of his most harrowing voyages, from squalls to waterspouts to hurricanes. He recalled "waves higher than three stories, which almost cap-sized us."

"Ever been shipwrecked?" I said.

"Only once, long before I was a captain, and on a much smaller vessel. Ran into a storm that broke us up off the coast of Egypt. Crew of a dozen, and only ten of us reached the shore. But don't you worry, lad. It would take a bigger storm than I've ever seen to threaten this craft."

We finally cast off late that afternoon, and I became enraptured by the whole idea of sailing. This was the life! I loved the sights, the smells, the sounds, all of it.

As the craft leaned into the waves, I could hardly wait for us to reach Tarsus and then make the return trip in time for school. I couldn't imagine much sailing as a rabbi, but neither had I expected to become so enamored of sailing from city to city. Now I couldn't get enough of it.

33

Hacked

PRESENT-DAY ROME

SUNDAY, MAY 11, 6:00 P.M.

"WHAT IS IT, BABE?" Augie said, no longer able to pretend he and Sofia were strangers in adjoining booths.

She stood, thrust the phone into his hands, and started for the entrance. "See you back at the hotel."

Roger whispered, "Sofia! Go out the back."

She spun on her heel.

"What's wrong?" Augie said.

"*Si vuole andare, signorina?*" the *cameriera* said.

"No, I don't want it to go."

Sofia was out the back door before Augie could get to his feet. He caught up with her in the alley and took her into his arms. She was trembling. "Who was it, Sof? Your dad?"

"It was my mother's number! Why would—how, how could she—?"

"I don't know, but we've got to get Roger out of here."

Sofia yanked the phone out of her purse and threw it against a brick wall so hard it shattered. Hands in front of her as if to steady herself, she said, "I'm all right. Just tell me what to do."

"Grab a cab and have it wait at the end of the alley. Tell the driver we'll pay double to avoid the checkpoint."

By the time Augie got back inside, Roger had settled up with the *cameriera* and was on his way out. When they saw Sofia standing by the cab, Augie grabbed Roger's arm to keep him from running to it. "We're just tourists. No need to rush."

The cabbie was a young woman eager to try out her limited English. "You are desperadoes, no?" she said, laughing. "Stay away from checkpoint because you robbed the bank."

She shot down side streets until she was able to get across the river and find a clear route south. When the cab pulled up to the Terrazzo, the three agreed to go to the suite separately. Roger would go first while Sofia lingered in the lobby, heading up when she saw Augie return from retrieving the parchment from the car.

Once they were all in the suite, Sofia said, "I've got to go get my stuff. I'm not staying in the same hotel as Dimos. I can't believe he's risking his career like this. When I tell my father . . ."

"You think your mother's in on it?" Augie said. "She never struck me—"

"No! It makes no sense. She has everything she's ever needed and doesn't want half what she's got. Dimos had to have turned on the charm and talked her into it, but for what purpose? Let me use your phone, Augie."

He tossed it to her and she began talking animatedly to her father in Greek. Augie made out her first line: "We found out how Dimos knew our private conversations."

Finally she plopped onto the couch. "He's going to find out what's going on. Sounded shocked."

"You sure you want to switch hotels?" Augie said.

"I'm done with Dimos, that's all I know. You want me to stay somewhere else?"

"No, I'm just wondering if it's easier for us to stay under the radar separately?"

"If they're onto us," Roger said, "they're onto us. But she's gonna need a car."

"I'll rent my own."

"No," Augie said, "I'll run you back to your hotel. In the meantime, Rog, don't answer the door."

7:30 P.M.

In the car Sofia said, "You must be dying to start reading the rest of the manuscript. Translate it for Roger. Maybe that'll start a conversation."

Augie told her of his effort the night before. "And he was sleeping the whole time."

When they got to her hotel she said, "I'll be quick. Just got to pack and check out."

"Wait, don't check out. If anyone's tracking you, let 'em think you're still here."

Augie's phone rang, making Sofia stop halfway out of the car. "Is it my father?"

"No, it's my mother."

"Say hi for me," she said, and hurried inside.

"I've been worried sick, August," his mother said. "How's Roger?"

"In a little trouble, but he's safe for now."

"Thank God! I've been praying. You all right?"

Augie said he hoped to wrap things up quickly and be home soon.

"Good," she said, "because I have news. Your father is conscious."

"No! Seriously?"

"I'm not sure he recognizes me, but his pulse and respiration are strong. His pupils react to light and he can follow the doctor's finger. They keep telling me his prognosis hasn't changed, but this has to be better than a coma, right?"

"Seems like it, Mom, but don't get your hopes up."

"Of course my hopes are up, August. I'm wringing every drop of hope out of this I can. I'm praying that by the time you get back, he'll seem like himself again."

A beep told Augie he had another call: Malfees Trikoupis. "Mom, I'm so sorry, but I've got to take this. Thanks for the good news, and I'll be praying."

"Well, all right, good-bye."

"Mr. Trikoupis!"

"Yes, Augie. Is Sofia there?"

"She'll be back in a few minutes."

"That's good actually. Listen, I got to the bottom of the phone business with her mother. I'll tell Sofia later. But you understand my priority, don't you?"

"Your daughter, of course."

"I know you're watching out for her. I'm talking about the manuscript. I don't need to tell you the value—"

"I'm well aware," Augie said. "But, if you don't mind my asking, how would you characterize your interest in it?"

"What—are you joking?"

"We may not be on the same page."

Mr. Trikoupis paused. Then, "Well, you, I—I thought you agreed, that, ah, that I don't need to tell you the magnitude . . ."

"But, sir, its value is to the Italian state."

"You didn't make me aware of it because I am one of the top purveyors of antiquities in the world?"

"I didn't make you aware of it, sir. Sofia confided in you, and I hope no one outside you and Dimos is aware of it. Even he should not have been told."

"Oh, rest assured we understand the need for confidentiality. We don't want anyone else competing for this."

"I'm not following."

"Augie, surely you know I will take care of you. Your finder's fee alone—"

"Sir, you've somehow jumped to a conclusion."

"Augie, listen to me. It's no coincidence that you made sure I was brought into this. Who else would understand the potential of such an antiquity?"

"A find of this magnitude could never be marketed."

"Don't be naïve," Mr. Trikoupis said.

"It would never be allowed outside Italy. If you somehow acquired it, you would never be able to tell anyone you had it."

Mr. Trikoupis's voice suddenly dropped. "Naturally I'm not going to display it in my front window! Don't worry. No one will know except those who trade in such things, and they will have as much reason as I to keep it quiet."

"I could never be part of something like that."

"Don't insult me by implying that I would expose you. I am just as dependent on your confidence as you are on mine."

"Mr. T., I need to be clear. If I am fortunate enough to find this manuscript, it will not be coming to you."

Trikoupis suddenly sounded avuncular. "All right, let's stop and back up. First, I know you have the manuscript or at least know where it is."

"Sir—"

"Second, you know few people alive have the ability to maximize the return on a treasure like this. *Priceless* is just a word. The parchments have a price all right. If you guessed within several hundred million euros, you could multiply that exponentially because of my involvement. Your one percent of the total proceeds will set up you and my daughter for generations."

"There will be no—"

"I would not dream of shortchanging you. The value of your silence alone is worth that."

Clearly, Sofia's father was not the man Augie had been led to believe he was—let alone who his own daughter believed him to be. He was so desperate to get his hands on the Pauline memoir that he couldn't imagine Sofia's fiancé would deny him. In that instant, Augie decided to change his approach. He would play along.

"Honestly, Mr. Trikoupis, I am at a loss for words."

"No need to thank me. You will have earned it. To tell you the truth, it takes a score like this to get my juices flowing, and believe me, I have been involved in some incredible projects. That said, I do expect you to do your part."

"I'm sure you do."

"For starters I need your full cooperation with Dimos. Frankly, he fears you're not seeing the big picture."

"If *I* may be frank, sir, you seem to have a better handle on the scope of this than he does."

"Let's not hold that against him. He's always been a salaried man. Though I pay him multiple times what he made working for the government, it's nothing compared to what he'll see from this deal."

"I understand."

"So you'll follow his lead and assume he speaks for me?"

"You can be sure I'll follow him."

"I knew I could count on you."

"Oh, here's Sofia."

"Thank you, August. I'll tell Dimos that you and I have had this chat and that we understand each other."

"Yes, sir."

Augie put the phone on speaker and handed it to Sofia after she tossed her bags in the backseat.

"Sweetheart, your mother feels terrible that she went behind your back, but she did it with the best of intentions. She was worried about you, that's all. I think it's taken longer for her than for me to accept that you're a grown woman and don't need us checking up on you everywhere you go."

"How is hacking into my ph—"

"She merely asked Dimos if there was any way she could keep an eye on you, and he suggested that connecting your phones would allow her to know where you were and that you were safe."

Augie could tell Sofia was about to erupt. "Roll with it," he mouthed. "We'll talk."

"She realizes," Sofia said, clearly fighting anger, "that this gave Dimos access to my private conversations?"

"She does now and admits she just wasn't thinking. In any case, she has turned it off, so you need not fear further invasion of your privacy."

Sofia rolled her eyes, but Augie faked a smile. "Well," she said, "that's a relief."

"May I tell her you understand and that she need not feel awkward the next time she sees you?"

Sofia hesitated and Augie knew it was a tough pill to swallow.

"Of course."

"That's my girl. Probably best if you didn't bring it up with her at all. She knows she crossed the line. No sense beating her up, is there?"

"No, I guess not."

As they headed back toward the Terrazzo, Sofia said, "Pull over."

Augie pulled onto a side street and parked at the curb.

"What the devil is going on?" she said.

"You wouldn't believe it."

"I just might after enduring that performance. I have never known my father to lie to anyone, let alone me. I'd bet my life if I called my mother right now, she wouldn't have a clue about the phone. It's not something she'd ever ask for or agree to. That's why my dad doesn't want me to bring it up."

"I heard your dad lie once, Sof."

She recoiled. "You did?"

"I passed it off as a white lie, but—"

"Augie, a lie is a lie. You let it slide?"

"It wasn't my place to lecture him. Ironically, he lied indirectly to Dimos."

"All right, I'm confused."

Augie reminded her of the time her dad tried to hire him. "Fokinos called while I was in your father's office, and he told his secretary to say he wasn't there. I know people do that all the time . . ."

"I don't."

"Well, I don't either, but it's fairly common."

She shrugged. "It still makes him a liar. And he just now lied to me. The same man who taught me from childhood how a person's word and reputation are what life is all about. I bought it. I see it in you, and it's one of the reasons I love you."

"You trust me to tell you the truth?"

"I do, Augie. If you ever gave me reason to doubt you, I'd be out of your life before you could blink."

"I would never want that, love."

"Me either. Augie, you've told me you love me, that I'm your whole life. I've given you my heart. I'm planning to leave my family, my job, my home, my country for you. I'll follow you to the end of the earth. My future is built on trusting you."

She leaned into him and he held her.

"It's a good thing," he said. "Because before we get back to the hotel I have to tell you what I've finally realized. I said you're not going to believe it because I hardly do. You're not going to want to believe it, I know that. But you know I wouldn't tell you something like this unless it was true."

3 4

Until Dawn

FIRST-CENTURY ROME

LUKE BECAME SO IMMERSED in Paul's memoir that he read through the night. Knowing he would be spent by morning and worth little to his patients, he kept telling himself he would put aside the parchments at the end of the next interesting story, only to forge ahead to discover more.

The physician pored over Paul's account of his family's voyage to Caesarea and then the land journey to Jerusalem, his father setting up his business and almost immediately becoming a supplier both to the Jews and the Romans—particularly the military. Paul also told of his mother becoming acquainted with the new area, setting up house-keeping, getting involved in the synagogue, and of Shoshanna matur-ing into womanhood.

Young Saul had immediately established himself—according to what Gamaliel told Y'honatan and Rivka in front of their son—as the most motivated student the rabban had encountered in all his years of training rabbis. Paul recounted his own eagerness to learn, to engage, to discuss, to debate. He told of his humiliation when Gamaliel privately cautioned him to "remain charitable when others disagree," and to "offer them the courtesy of time to also make their points."

Gamaliel's prediction that the young scholar might not find himself ahead of his peers at such a prestigious academy soon proved incorrect. During his first year, Saul progressed to where he held his own against older students. Soon he grew confident enough to challenge even Gamaliel, especially when the headmaster emphasized the heart of the law rather than the purity of it.

Gamaliel cautioned him, "The Word of God is a lamp, a light, a direction, a path. But we must remember that the rabbi ministers to finite beings—frail, imperfect men and women."

"I would argue," Saul said, "that our duty is to remain true to the purity of the Scripture, to learn its every nuance, so that we may hold our congregants to its standard."

Gamaliel, according to Paul's account, told Saul how much he appreciated his zeal and pleaded with him to season his orthodoxy with compassion. That, Paul admitted, made the young Saul entrench himself "only more deeply into what I considered pure Pharisaic doctrine. I was blind to how I was perceived by others. All that mattered was that God was perfect and that rabbis were called to point their people to His model."

As Saul's years of schooling continued at the feet of Gamaliel, Luke saw the young man grow into an exceptional intellect powered by a fanatical confidence in his own views. When Rabban Gamaliel informed him he was "becoming a man with whom no one can argue, indeed who intimidates any who question you," Saul accepted it as the ultimate compliment. "That my mentor saw this as a character flaw and counseled me to become more diplomatic did not dissuade me. I felt empowered, knowing I was right and that I could state my case with such force and intellect that no one could hope to prevail over me. My goal became to become the youngest leader among the elite Jews of Jerusalem."

Saul's account of young love came as a colossal surprise to Luke, as Paul had never mentioned that he had been close to marriage. His writings showed that he had found himself in ferocious competition academically and athletically with both Gamaliel's son, Simeon—also a prodigious scholar—and another young man, Ezra, whose aim was to become a priest.

That triumvirate with similar goals and intellects should have become fast friends, but it soon emerged that the other two resented Saul and could barely abide his presence. Not only did he prove overbearing in theological discussions, but he also turned every leisure activity, every sport, into a personal competition. And because of his athletic ability and robust physique, he prevailed in every physical contest.

From his adult perspective, Paul wrote, "I never neglected to lord my superiority over my two rivals. I was still taken with Simeon's sister, Gamaliel's daughter Naomi, and seized every opportunity to shine in her presence. I either invented arguments wherein I could impress her with my knowledge, or if she happened to watch us playing at any sport, I competed with all my strength."

That seemed a good place for Luke to set aside the manuscript and steal a few hours' sleep, but a glance at the next line persuaded him to keep reading.

When finally I succeeded in turning her head by outrunning

her brother and Ezra, she approached shyly, brilliant eyes and smooth dark skin rendering me speechless for once. "May I talk with you," she said, "when you have time?"

I wanted to tell her and the world that I had all the time she needed and that there was nothing I'd rather do than have an excuse to gaze at her.

But, desperate to impress, I calmly said, "How is this moment right now? I have worn out those two gentlemen, who are no challenge anyway. They'll have more fun without me."

Naomi sat on the ground. "That is what I wanted to talk about."

I dropped near her and lay on my side. "You enjoy my speed, my ability?"

She seemed shy and looked off into the distance. "You are impressive, Saul, in everything you do. Running, leaping, talking, even just walking. You have passion, as if you are on your way somewhere."

"I am," I assured her, prepared to tell her my plans. She had to know her father, as well as his vice chief justice, Nathanael, were already urging me to think about beginning my rabbinical life in some administrative role under the Sanhedrin.

"Simeon tells me you have more of the Scriptures memorized than most of the other students," Naomi said, "even ones who have been at Hillel for years. He says sometimes you can quote a passage faster than even my father."

"The truth is I have memorized more than all the other students," I said, "and it isn't that I can sometimes quote a *passage more quickly than your father. It's always. You can ask him."*

"I don't doubt you. Father is impressed with you, but you know that."

I nodded. "If I may be frank, Naomi, I care more about what you think of me."

"Do you really?" she said, looking directly into my eyes, which compelled me to sit up. "Or do you just want to know you have yet another admirer?"

In my naïveté, this strangely emboldened me! I told her, "If you admired me, I would not care what anyone else thought." I watched for the delight this was bound to bring her.

Instead, she challenged me. "So if I began a passage, you could complete it for me?"

I had to chuckle. How much time would a female spend memorizing the words of God? "Anything you know I certainly know. Try it!"

Naomi said, "'Let another man . . .'"

"'. . . praise you!'" I said. "The Proverbs of Solomon! 'Let another man praise you, and not your own mouth; a stranger, and not your own lips.' Correct?"

"Yes," she said, rising before I could even assist her. When I leapt to my feet, she stared at the ground and said quietly, "That you know the words but not the wisdom they contain is no surprise."

She had done it again—rendered me speechless. Still in my teens, I knew the history of the Jews, all the kings and kingdoms, good rulers and bad. I knew our lands, our sac-

rifices, our rituals, our laws, and not just in part but the whole. Already I was qualified to lead a congregation and instruct them in the proper ways to conduct their lives. Yet this fetching young woman dared say I knew the words but not their wisdom?

As she walked away I stood transfixed, wondering what a man has to do to impress a woman. I had outrun her brother and his friend. I was the top scholar at Hillel. I had finished the passage she cited before she reached the fourth word. Yet she insults me? I could only watch as Ezra ran to greet her. He looked nervous and immature. Yet as they chatted she smiled at him, even gently touched his shoulder!

My entire walk home I was consumed, not by what she had said—I hadn't even thought that through. No, I could not get my mind off her obvious affection for Ezra! He was a competent enough student, but he was awkward and rarely serious. Clearly he was enamored with Naomi, but who wouldn't be? And she had plainly engaged him, encouraged him.

That may have been the first time I allowed myself to be distracted from my studies. Naomi had invaded my mind. Over and over I relived our brief conversation, bewildered that I had failed to impress her.

For the sake of accuracy, I must admit I lost track of how many times I went over the encounter in my mind before finally falling asleep that night. I woke before dawn, as usual, and something about walking in the crisp air allowed the truth of the proverb to reach me.

I had been so focused on failing to impress Naomi and

then tormented by how happy she seemed with Ezra that I had entirely missed her point—the wisdom of the proverb, not just the words I had memorized.

"Let another man praise you, and not your own mouth; a stranger, and not your own lips."

To Naomi this was not just an answer to a challenge. It had been her message to me! How was it possible a student as accomplished as I could prove so ignorant?

More importantly, why was it I felt so compelled to praise myself? Because so few others did? Was the praise of Gamaliel himself not enough?

I was suddenly overwhelmed with shame. Not only did my peers not compliment my successes, but neither was the object of my longing impressed with me. Why? Because I praised myself. I knew the Word of God and claimed to obey it to the letter, yet somehow I had not applied the pithy sayings of Solomon to my own life. I had not obeyed them as Law.

During my prayers that morning I asked God if this was why I had never enjoyed the kind of friendship with Him that the great patriarchs of the Bible had. Was this why we did not converse? I believed He heard my every prayer, but why had I never heard Him?

I did not hear Him that morning either, though I asked forgiveness for violating the Law. And I determined that I must follow the proverbs with the same vigor as I did the rules for sacrifices. Only now, with the benefit of years, do I see that I did not become humble, did not become kinder, more thoughtful, or more compassionate. I became deter-

mined. I would not praise myself, not because of what that revealed about me, but because the Scripture forbade it. And because Naomi would be watching, I could scale the last barrier between me and her affections.

Luke stood and stretched. It would be futile to sleep now. Besides, he had to find out what became of his old friend and Naomi during Saul's remaining years at Hillel.

Somehow the young rabbinical student, by the sheer force of his will, succeeded in keeping quiet about himself and his achievements. He remained the first to answer any question, and he was no less aggressive on the fields of play, but he stopped taunting his opponents and bragging.

Naomi did notice. Once she even told Saul she had heard someone else praise him. Thrilled as he was, Saul did not insist she expand on what she'd heard. However, he still frequently saw Naomi and Ezra together.

Luke continued reading, fascinated.

It was not easy to compete for her affections while suppressing that part of me that wanted to argue that I was the better man. Could she not see it? Ezra was nice enough, but he was not accomplished. Did Naomi not want the attention that would come from a relationship with the man everyone knew and talked about—especially now that I was not talking about myself?

Eventually I prevailed. It was not easy, becoming more active and obvious in my pursuit of her while still stifling my ego to remain obedient to the Law. Perhaps Ezra saw he was unable to compete and stepped aside. For whatever reason, Naomi gradually found more time for me.

Within a year, as I neared graduation, we were in love and everyone knew it. Many said she was good for me, made me quieter, less arrogant. Only I knew the truth. Inside I was a cauldron of frustration, battling my true nature to remain obedient to the Law and to keep Naomi's heart. She had a calming influence on me only to the extent that I would do anything to keep us together.

Gamaliel himself allowed that the "obvious infatuation with my daughter has not seemed to negatively impact your scholarship. Do you see a future together?"

"I would be honored to become a member of your family," I told him.

"Let's not get ahead of ourselves, Saul."

But I longed to make Naomi my wife. She was not only beautiful, but she was also a woman of deep character— kind and humble and eager to serve others, not because the Law required her to, but because that was her nature. She was an obedient woman of God for motives I did not possess.

I burned to consummate our love, and the only hindrance to formally pursuing her upon my graduation from Hillel was my focus on establishing myself among the Pharisees of Jerusalem. By now the puppet high priest, Annas' son, had been replaced by Annas' son-in-law, Joseph Caiaphas. Annas himself remained the real power behind closed doors.

With Gamaliel and Nathanael cordially competing for my services, I enjoyed allowing them to try to outdo each other in securing me for their staffs. While it might have been more advantageous to my climb to a station of influence to immediately begin working for the man I assumed would become my father-in-law, eventually he and I both thought better of it. "We will have plenty of time together if you accept a position with Nathanael," Gamaliel said, "and we will avoid any suspicions of nepotism."

Naomi was too genteel to press me toward marriage, though often on our long solitary walks we discussed our future home and children, as well as my plan to become the rabbi of a large, influential synagogue. I think she liked the idea of our settling in one place eventually, because my role for Nathanael took me all over Israel on various assignments. I could not bring myself to tell her that from almost the first week of my new job I realized I would never be content staying in one synagogue.

I loved everything about the Great Sanhedrin, from the sound my sandals made as I strode through the long dark corridors, to the beautiful harmonies of the all-male choirs whose chants and songs greeted the sunrise and announced the sunset. They practiced throughout the day, so the ancient temple and the Sanhedrin's meeting place, the Hall of Hewn Stones, reverberated always with rich, deep melodies of praise to the one true God.

The haunting strains should have prodded me to a deep sense of private worship, but I had by now given up on knowing God. My father and my rabbi from Tarsus had been right. I could not hope to have the same standing with the God of

Abraham, Isaac, and Jacob that those patriarchs enjoyed. We would not converse. He was unknowable, and the best I could do was, in essence, to worship His words, His Law.

If I had been exacting on orthodoxy as an obnoxious teenage scholar, now I was entrenched. There was no middle ground with my doctrine and theology. I took every word of the Holy Scriptures literally and demanded that even the most tolerant disciples of Gamaliel try to prove me wrong. Not only were they unable, but almost daily I succeeded in exposing their arguments as soft and self-centered. Even Gamaliel wearied of my fundamentalism and warned that marrying myself to such a rigid standard might threaten any future I hoped for as a member of the Sanhedrin.

And this was no Lesser Sanhedrin of twenty-three members who sat in judgment over every other city. No, this was the Great Sanhedrin, in which sixty-nine members sat under Gamaliel and his lieutenant, Nathanael. To even dream of becoming a member of such an august body, I had to be diligent, resourceful, hardworking, and impress all the council members. Plus I would have to be married. My educational credentials were a given, known to all.

The council of seventy-one met when matters of national import arose, like war or political insurgence or an appeal from a lower court, or when the Lesser Sanhedrin could not come to a verdict. Such meetings convened in the hall that had been built into the north wall of the Temple Mount, half inside and half outside the sanctuary, giving access to both the temple and the outdoors. I had learned at Hillel that it was the only part of the temple complex not used for ritual purposes, and thus it was constructed with stones hewn by iron implements.

Both Gamaliel and Nathanael occupied offices within the complex, and I was assigned a tiny alcove near the vice chief justice. I spent little time there as I did his bidding. Nathanael sent me scurrying all over the Temple Mount and the city, as well as to other cities, researching, interviewing, fetching documents, whatever he needed.

I was busy, excited, fulfilled in my role, especially when Nathanael, and at times even Gamaliel, used me as a confidant and sought my opinions. While both continued to counsel me against rigidity, they still sought my input and often used it. When either the Lesser or the Great Sanhedrin met, I stationed myself out of sight but within earshot and smiled when I heard either of them quote me without acknowledging their source. That was all right. My day would come.

Naomi grew more distant the busier I became. When we were together, often at the end of a very long day, all I could talk about was what I was doing. I sensed sadness in her when months flew by with no change in our status. My own sister had long since married and had begun a family. But what could I do? I was special assistant to Nathanael, and his needs and wishes became my priority.

I served in this role for years, establishing myself as the person to go to when a member of the Sanhedrin wanted to influence either of the top two men. I was the most accessible, and the most knowledgeable, and I developed a reputation as one who was ever present, hardworking, and dependable. No one questioned my devotion to the Law.

But everyone, including her father, questioned my devotion to Naomi—something of which my former rival would take advantage.

35

Baiting the Hook

PRESENT-DAY ROME

SUNDAY, MAY 11, 8:30 P.M.

AUGIE MIGHT AS WELL have punched Sofia in the stomach. From the look on her face, his recitation of what her father had told him destroyed her lifelong worship of the man.

The pain in her eyes made him wish he hadn't had to tell her. She looked like a four-year-old who had just learned the truth about Santa Claus.

Trikoupis had been Sofia's rock. She often talked of how she admired him, looked up to him, considered him a model of class, sophistication, and, most of all, honesty. She adored him.

"Let me borrow your phone," she said as they headed back to the Terrazzo.

He knew she wouldn't compromise him with her dad, but she was dialing a number she didn't have to look up. She put it on speaker.

"August?" her mother said.

"No, Mom, it's me. Just borrowing his phone."

"Is he in Greece, Sofia? Surely you'd have said something if you were going to the States."

"I met him in Rome."

"Rome! How nice! Why didn't you tell us?"

"Daddy knew."

"He didn't say a word! What is it, a surprise? Do you have news?"

"What more news could there be, Mom? You know we're engaged."

"No, I just thought, I don't know, that you set a date or something. Just don't tell me you're eloping. We'll travel as far as necessary to be there for your wedding."

"No, just checking in. Wanted to tell you my phone broke, so if you need me, call me on Augie's." She read off the number.

"So what's going on in Rome?"

"Augie's here on business, and you know it's less than a six-hundred-mile flight for me, a little over two hours."

"Give him my best."

When they finished talking, Sofia leaned over and let the phone slip into Augie's shirt pocket. "So, one of the three of you is lying," she said. "My money's on Dad."

That sounded flippant considering how devastated she had to be. Augie said, "You know she's going to ask him why he didn't tell her you were in Italy."

"I hope she does! I'd like to see him answer that. Let him squirm."

"Wow."

She looked miserable. "Just like Dimos doesn't care about anything but his share of the take, my dad doesn't care what I think about it. Nothing—not even his love for me—is going to get in the way of this deal."

Back at the hotel Sofia booked her own room three floors below Augie's suite, then joined him and Roger.

"I had to lie to Dimos," Roger said. "He showed up just after you left."

"You weren't to open the door."

"Even to him? I'm not thrilled about his knowing what I look like now, but he knows I've been with you. Anyway, he tells me he knows I've got the first page of the parchments and photocopies of the rest, plus a letter from Klaudios that tells where the rest of the originals are. I tried to play dumb, telling him he doesn't know what he's talking about, but he didn't buy it. He told me he knows the truth and to quit worrying about how he found out.

"What could I say? He was right. It was all I could do to keep him from searching the suite. I told him everything had been hidden in a new location, but he said if he could just examine that first page, we'd all know what we had. Like an idiot, I told him I already had a pretty good idea, because guys don't get killed over nothing.

"To reassure me, he adds that I'm in the driver's seat, that my guy can be bought. 'My guy?' I said. 'Who's my guy?' and he said, 'Who do you think I've been talking to today?'

"I didn't want Dimos to see I'm freaking out, so I just kept listening. I had to know if he had really talked to Sardinia."

"Good thinking. And . . .?"

"He wouldn't come right out and say it, but he did tell me the guy's lined his own pockets before, and that he uses the Tombaroli to do his dirty work. He told Fokinos he'll decide how much he can afford to share with us. If Fokinos is telling me the truth, he and this guy both really believe that anybody can be bought."

"We need to encourage that," Augie said.

"Way ahead of you," Roger said. "I told Fokinos I'd be happy not getting whacked and even coming away with a little something. He laughed and said, 'A little something? You'll be set for life.' So I said, 'What about my friends?' and he said there's enough for all three of us— not to mention—" Roger hesitated and glanced at Sofia.

"Don't spare me, Rog. I'm a big girl. There's also my father."

"Right. Dimos says he told his contact to figure a couple of million euros each for you two and me—and that if the parchments were proved real, your father would buy the goods for around five times his expenses—"

"Meaning paying off the three of us," Augie said.

"Right, you and Sofia and me, plus certain services by the Tombaroli. So this Art Squad guy gets about thirty million euros and we get two each. Imagine how much that investment of thirty-six million euros will be worth for Sofia's father in the end."

"If it is Sardinia, wouldn't he know I'm already supposed to get a finder's fee?"

Roger shrugged. "I'm only guessing it's Sardinia. I asked Fokinos what's in it for him, if the three of us are getting a total of six million. He told me not to worry about him, because he's guaranteed a percentage from Trikoupis, not on the purchase but on the profits. He claims that in the long run, his piece will be bigger than what his contact at the Art Squad gets."

"The manuscript is really worth that much?" Sofia said.

"If Fokinos is right, parceled out in pieces on the black market it could gross a billion euros. Why? Thinking about taking him up on it?"

Augie was pleased to see her finally smile. "I don't mind letting him think we're interested," she said. "If that would get you out of danger."

"Then what?" Augie said. "We entrap him, pull off some kind of a sting?"

She nodded. "Something like that."

Roger seemed to study Sofia. "You realize your father is the buyer, so he also gets caught in whatever trap we set."

She shrugged.

"He could spend the rest of his life in prison, Sofia," Roger said. "Can you live with that?"

She sighed. "It would crush me. But it would be his own doing."

Augie began to pace. "If Sardinia *is* behind all this, it's been way too easy for him. Klaudios makes the heist and leads him to Roger. Dimos shows up on Sardinia's doorstep with a gift-wrapped buyer waiting in the wings. Sardinia's looking at netting thirty million euros, after our six million and whatever other expenses he's incurred. That's some lucrative civil servant job."

"So how do we reel these guys in?" Sofia said.

"We have to give them something," Roger said.

Augie nodded. "Something real."

"Such as?" Sofia said.

"We need to let Dimos examine the parchment."

"But he can't perform real tests on it," she said. "It belongs to the Italian government. It's one thing for you to protect it until you turn it over to the state, but there's no way Dimos could cut out a sample, no matter how small, for carbon dating."

"That's what it would take?" Augie said.

"It's not my field, but I know my father has invested in manuscripts several hundred years old once they were authenticated by carbon dating. But they had to slice thin strips from the parchment to do that."

"Is there a simpler way, something he could do that wouldn't affect that first real page but be a good indicator until the government can have it tested?"

"You'd have to ask Dimos," Sofia said. "If I wanted to talk to him, I wouldn't have switched hotels."

"He'd have to do it here," Augie said. "I don't want to keep moving that thing around. Tomorrow I'll put it into a safe-deposit box."

The three sat silent for a moment. "Want me to call him?" Roger said.

"Do it," Augie said. "But remember, we're playing him."

"Meaning?"

"Don't sound eager. Make him work for it. Then get him to meet me someplace."

"Thought you said it had to be here."

"He doesn't need to know that till he picks me up. That'll keep him from tipping off anyone else."

"Good idea," Roger said. "I wouldn't put it past him and Sardinia to kill us and keep the manuscript for themselves."

"You're getting a little dramatic, aren't you?" Sofia said. "Whatever the first page is worth, the whole stack of—how many?—"

"Around five hundred pages."

"—is naturally worth that many times more. As long as we don't give them Klaudios's envelope, they need us."

Roger brightened. "I say we don't open that envelope till we nail 'em. That way we couldn't reveal where Klaudios stashed the pages even if they tortured us, because we don't know."

"Better yet," Augie said, "we send them in the wrong direction. Once they start looking, we find the memoir and turn it over to the government."

"Why don't we do that now?" Sofia said. "Life would be simpler."

"Problem is," Roger said, "the Art Squad could already be watching us everywhere we go. Surveillance is their specialty. They could follow us right to the goods and catch us red-handed. Nobody's gonna believe we weren't stealing a priceless artifact."

"Klaudios's envelope is in the safe," Augie said. "We need to stash the photocopies of the pages somewhere else. They aren't worth much, but I don't want them in the wrong hands."

"We need to keep Roger on the move, right?" Sofia said. "Put the box of copies in the safe in my room for when Dimos is here tonight. Tomorrow Roger can wait for us there."

"Works for me," Augie said.

The three of them huddled around the landline phone. "Have him meet me at ten at the Keats-Shelley Memorial House," Augie told Roger.

"Nice," Roger said. "Confuse the devil out of him."

As soon as Roger identified himself, Dimos said, "You alone?"

"Dr. Knox is here."

"Put me on speaker. Augie?"

"Hi, Dimos."

"Anybody know where Sofia is? She's not answering her phone and she's not in her room."

"Couldn't tell you," Augie said, winking at her. *That*, he thought, *is how you mislead without lying.* "I'll see her tomorrow."

"So what's up, Roger?" Dimos said.

"Been thinking about what you said today. Got a few questions."

"I thought you might. Fire away."

"Remember I told you I was sure what we have is real because somebody paid the ultimate price for it."

"So you did, but neither my buyer nor my seller will commit until I've examined at least that one real page."

"That's asking a lot."

"It's mandatory, Roger. We're dead in the water until we know for sure. And face it, you're in danger."

"I don't know, Dimos. How do you test it without damaging the goods?"

"Listen, I have what I need to be able to satisfy both parties—a bright, safe light and a high-power microscope. I use no liquids and I do no cutting. The buyer and seller will have to do that at some point, but it will be out of our hands by then. But if this is what we think it is, my examination will allow me to assure my contacts with a degree of certainty that will allow them to proceed."

"And then I'm off the hook? I'm gettin' tired of living like this."

"You'll be not only safe, my friend, you'll be comfortable for life. That goes for you too, Dr. Knox. I mean, if that appeals."

"Let's just say I'm open-minded," Augie said.

"Good. And no one ever has to know your involvement. How sweet is that?"

"Very. But Roger's not entirely convinced and I can't say I blame him."

"He can ask me anything!"

"Okay," Roger said, "how do we know that as soon as you're satisfied the thing is real, you don't tell the wrong people where we are?"

"What would be the point? One page is something, but we want the whole memoir."

Roger rolled his eyes at Augie. "We're going to need a few days to think about it."

"Roger! They had an all-points bulletin out on you today, a Sunday! You think you're going to survive a Monday when the whole force is working? You've got a small window of opportunity. It has to be tonight, man."

Roger paused as if struggling with the idea. "If we tell you where to meet us, you tell no one and you come alone."

"On my honor. Just make sure that wherever we're going has electricity for the light. I'll wait till I'm back in my hotel room before I let both parties know my findings. If I determine it's real, you'll be cleared, the Tombaroli get blamed for Klaudios's murder, and you get credit for helping thwart whatever they were doing. Best of all, you get your life back. Not to mention a nice allowance."

"Dimos," Augie said, "why would anyone cut me in on this deal?"

"Consider it services rendered, and the first service is your silence. Then we need a translation, your specialty. But you understand, everything hinges on finding the whole original manuscript."

"You said it hinged on your seeing the first page," Roger said.

"Well, initially. But no one gets paid until Trikoupis takes delivery of the entire document."

"We're not sure where that is."

"Right!" Dimos said, laughing. "You haven't read Klaudios's instructions yet!"

"Correct."

"Okay, have your fun. When I've seen the page, we'll talk about the rest. Now where and when?"

"*Piazza di Spagna* 26, ten o'clock."

"You're kidding. The museum house at the steps? Tell me you didn't stash—no, you wouldn't. They're closed Sundays anyway."

"That's just where you're meeting Dr. Knox," Roger said. "Then he'll tell you where you need to go."

Confrontation in the Moonlight

FIRST-CENTURY ROME

AT BREAKFAST THE DAY of Primus Paternius Panthera's hearing, the guard was dressed in his finest uniform and freshly shaved, but he looked haggard.

Primus' wife whispered, "We both heard the crier's call of fourth watch."

"You were still awake at three?"

Primus nodded. "I worry that the man will renege, he's so ambitious. If he does, I am out of a job, you lose what you paid him, and—"

Luke held up a hand. "I may be new to this underhanded business, but I know enough to withhold payment until services have been rendered. Young Gaius had better weigh his options. He can feed you to the wolves and perhaps see his pay increase, or he can follow through on his commitment to me and immediately double his income."

Primus said, "Many was the night I enjoyed food from your hand to look the other way when you visited my prisoner. I was no better than Gaius."

"But now you break small rules," his wife said, "only for the benefit of others, not for yourself."

"I confess I remain skeptical about Paul's message, Lucanus. But you both are so passionate about it. And you know I don't believe in the gods anymore, if I ever did. But to step all the way over to the other side . . . No one could know or I could lose my citizenship, my job, even my freedom."

"Maybe your life," his wife said.

"Should you commit yourself to the one true God and Father of the sin-forgiving Christ, you must commit heart and soul."

"It is not selfishness that keeps me from it."

"Fear?"

"Maybe some. But neither am I fully persuaded."

Luke smiled. "Say that to Paul, and if it does not prompt him to tell you of another who said the same, ask him to tell you of his defense before King Agrippa."

Primus rose. "I must go. I only wish I were as confident as you of Gaius' testimony."

"I am under no illusion," Luke said. "I pray he does the right thing, even if for the wrong reason. Regardless of today's outcome, Paul and I consider you our friend."

Primus was obviously touched. His wife said, "If we lose everything, we will still be rich in friendship."

Luke wanted to run back to Primus' house in the middle of the day, knowing his wife would have news. But he could not pull away from his patients. Late in the afternoon he returned at such a pace that he knew he would feel it in his joints the next day.

Primus' children ran out when he arrived. And when Primus' wife joined them, he knew. The news was written in her eyes. "Reprimanded, on probation, but back to work. He can't wait to see you."

"Same post?"

"Reinstated."

"Praise God!"

Gaius stood watch at his usual position at one corner of the block that housed the prison. Luke stopped. "I am grateful you did the right thing."

"I didn't do it because it was right. I did it because it was profitable. You know what you owe, and I know what I was promised. My whole family thanks you."

More likely the brothels and pubs will thank me.

"Just don't forget your other promise."

"The execution? As I said, I wouldn't miss it."

Luke smiled as he reached Primus. "Greetings," the guard said formally. "Identify yourself and your business."

"Lucanus, physician to the condemned."

"Your *professio.*"

Luke dug it from his pocket and Primus studied it. "I am obligated to inform you that you are not to provide light for the prisoner beyond what is necessary for your examination. Neither are you to feed the prisoner beyond what is medically necessary."

"Understood. Thank you."

Primus snorted. "You're thanking *me*?"

Luke whispered, "I need a little extra time tonight for a longer examination."

"I shall inform the others. Carry on."

Luke was eager to tell Paul the news but found he had known since morning. "There are no secrets here, Luke."

Late that night he dived back into the memoir.

At times when we were sharing kisses alone overlooking Jerusalem, I would tell Naomi she had my whole heart. One late evening it became apparent she had heard this once too often. "Saul, we're nearly thirty. You have a nephew and nieces who will marry in a few years. My father is not happy, and I am hurt."

That pierced me. "Oh, Naomi, you know what my life is like. Someday . . ."

"I am not pressuring you, Saul. In fact, if you asked me tonight I would say no."

Was she serious? "Is there another?"

"I should be asking you that," she said.

"You know there is not!"

"Well, when have you ever had time for me?"

"I'm with you now!"

"And yet you lie to me."

"Naomi! How can you suggest such a thing? I lie to no one, especially not to you." I knew I was too opinionated for most people's taste, but a liar? No, I would not admit to that.

"You lie to yourself. I know you think you love me."

"I do!"

"You desire me, I can see that. I desire you too. I want to be in love with you."

"But you're not?" I said.

"I am going to stop talking if you do not listen."

I raised a hand in surrender.

"You just told me I had your whole heart," Naomi said. "If you don't see that as a lie, you are deluded."

I fought to hold my tongue.

"How do you feel about your place with the Sanhedrin?"

I didn't have to think before I blurted, "It is my life! It is what I was born for, trained for. I am not even a member of the Sanhedrin, and yet I am pressed into service every day to carry out the wishes of the council."

"You love it with your whole heart."

"I do! Aah, I see. You trapped me."

"I merely prodded you to tell the truth. I do not have your whole heart."

"Naomi. God has to be my first priority."

She put a hand gently on my shoulder. "Saul, hear me. I could never be jealous of God. If He truly had your heart, I would love you only more. But this is the first time you have mentioned Him in ages."

"It is His business I do every day."

"No, it is my father's business, Priest Nathanael's business, the council's business."

"All that is God's work."

"But you don't talk about Him. You talk about rules

and regulations and rituals and obedience. And you are so good at it. Everyone says so. My father praises you all the time. To some it may appear that your first love is the Law. Perhaps your first love is your position."

I brushed her hand away. "So I am a deluded liar who puts himself before God."

I had silenced her. I had not wanted to hurt her, but I had dedicated my life to becoming a Pharisee among Pharisees. It had made me the person I was.

"Tell me, Naomi. There is another suitor, isn't there?"

Her hesitation wounded me. "Not presently," she said.

"What does that mean?"

"Someone has asked my father if he knows your intentions."

"My intention is to marry you! It has always been. How did your father answer?"

"He said you had not formally asked for my hand, but that he would ask me if I knew your plan."

"Now you do."

"And you know mine."

"Who is it who wishes to pursue you if I do not rise to your expectations, or is he a coward who would rather remain anony—"

"In fact he prefers that you know."

"You are asking me to step aside?"

Again a pause that crushed me. "I am."

I struggled to find my voice. "For whom, then?"

"Ezra."

The Examination

AUGIE SAT ON THE nearly three-hundred-year-old Spanish Steps, flanked by identical three-story buildings, the one to the south a museum, its second floor dedicated to the works of John Keats and Percy Bysshe Shelley and other Romantic poets. The steps lay less than a mile northeast of Piazza Navona, where he and Sofia had been just that morning. Now the cold steel of Roger's nine-millimeter Smith & Wesson pressed into his back.

A few minutes after ten a late-model sedan pulled to the curb. Not wanting to appear overeager, Augie ignored Dimos's honk and sat as if taking in the sights. Finally the passenger window slid down. "Let's go!"

Augie felt his breast pocket as if to be sure he had his phone and sauntered down the steps, noticing a large black trunk in the backseat, presumably holding Dimos's equipment.

"Just you?" Dimos said.

"Who'd you expect? Someone has to stay with the goods."

"You find Sofia?"

"I wasn't looking for her," Augie said. "Were you?"

Fokinos shrugged. "Where to?" he said as he pulled away.

When Augie told him the Terrazzo, Dimos hit the brakes. "What? That's your hotel."

"So?"

"So why didn't I just meet you there?"

"Playing it safe."

Dimos looked at Augie as if he had just figured things out. "You still don't trust me."

"Why should I? I just met you."

Dimos shook his head. "I'm the guy who's going to make you rich."

"Wait a second, friend. You and Trikoupis wouldn't have even known about this if I hadn't been dragged into it."

"Don't be silly," Dimos said. "This is the world we run in. We'd have found out sooner or later, and whoever had the prize would be looking for buyers with deep pockets. Fact is, Dr. Knox, you need me. Until I authenticate it, your priceless find is just a rumor."

"What was the holdup back at the steps, Doc?" Dimos continued. "Making sure no one was following me? Don't worry, no one else knows."

"Yet."

"Well, of course I'll need to inform my Art Squad guy tomorrow."

That was a laugh. Augie knew Fokinos would report his findings to both Sofia's father and Sardinia within seconds of leaving the hotel.

"You were playing spy, Augie. Watching me like a hawk."

"No. Just needed to see if you would be reckless enough to holler my name."

"You think I'm an amateur, don't you?"

"C'mon. A few months ago you were working for the Greek government, weren't you?"

Dimos chuckled. "That's what it said on my business card. I've always worked for me."

"Meaning?"

Fokinos weaved through traffic as if he'd spent a lot of time driving the city's confusing streets. "You remember a few years ago when the Art Squad confiscated about fifteen million euros worth of antiquities that had found their way to Switzerland?"

"Vaguely."

"Well, Google it. A Japanese art dealer was storing the stuff in Geneva. I helped verify a lot of it, pieces between seventeen hundred and three thousand years old. Got a nice fee from the cultural heritage police, but that was nothing compared to what I got from the art dealer."

"He paid you even though you helped Italy get all the antiquities back?"

"Well, there's 'the antiquities' and '*all* the antiquities,' if you know what I mean."

"I don't."

"Let's just say we helped make our Japanese client look like an unsuspecting victim rather than the thief he really was."

"I thought you were working for the Art Squad."

"So did they. We charged them for our time, but the dealer paid us even more for our, uh, consulting."

"Who's this *we* you keep talking about?"

"Oh, no you don't. You're testing me again, Augie, seeing if I talk about my compatriots. I don't. Let's just say he's very highly placed in the Art Squad, has a sterling reputation, and plays the colonel—I mean, the top guy there—like a fiddle."

"Pretty lucrative for your contact then?"

"Of course! You think he authorized payouts to the so-called art collector and to me without getting substantial kickbacks? And don't think he didn't get a percentage of all the stuff that was never officially recovered."

"I assume you did too."

"That should go without saying."

"So, why'd you take the job at Tri-K when you can cash in on deals like that?"

"Well, it wasn't to greet tour groups. in Thessaloniki and ring up their souvenir purchases, I'll tell you that."

10:40 P.M.

"You guys are pros, all right," Dimos said as he rolled his trunk up to the suite door. A Do Not Disturb sign was in place. "Let me guess, the door is locked and bolted and chained."

"I hope so," Augie whispered. "You know what's in there."

"Why don't you just announce it to everyone in the hotel?"

"The sign is overkill?"

"Don't play scared is all I'm saying. Nothing is going on here, so it should look that way. Now tell me, you have a code, right?"

"You're good." Augie rapped three times, they heard the chain and the deadbolt, and Roger let them in.

"Okay," Dimos said, pushing the trunk in, "resecure the door, but take that fool sign down."

They followed Roger to Augie's bedroom, where the sheet of parchment lay on the table, still sandwiched between the acid-free protector sheets. Dimos rubbed his palms together and looked around. "All right, take the lamp off the table, shut the drapes. Ambient light will only distract me. Unplug the radio. Let me use the adjustable chair. And be prepared to turn off the overhead light once I'm ready."

While Augie and Roger arranged things the way Dimos wanted, he hefted his trunk onto the bed and pulled out a tripod, which he set to the right of the chair. He removed a huge conical apparatus covered with elasticized cloth, which he removed to reveal a lamp with a huge floodlight. He secured it to the tripod, then crawled under the desk with an oversized power cord.

Next he lifted out a monstrous microscope with an unusually large viewing platform. The scope itself rode on what appeared to be a miniature dolly and could thus be maneuvered over the viewing area without moving the document. He adjusted the chair and put on a pair of filtered goggles and what looked like a hunting cap with an extra-long bill.

Finally, Dimos rummaged in the trunk for a pair of cloth gloves. As he put them on, Augie said, "You wouldn't have an extra pair of those, would you?"

"Sure, take what you need. And grab me those forceps. They look like oversized tweezers with the pinchers covered in cloth."

"I could use a pair of those too," Augie said.

"No. Unfortunately they're as expensive as they look. Imported from Russia."

Dimos set the forceps to the right of the parchment. "Room light off, please." Augie hit the switch and the room went dark. "Shade your eyes, gentlemen," Dimos said. He clicked on the floodlight and the room came alive with intense whiteness.

"Heat's not a problem?" Augie said.

"No," Dimos said. "A unique filter diffuses it. The parchment is perfectly safe." He used one hand to slide the protective sheet away from the parchment, then the forceps to grasp the document and guide it to the base of the microscope. He edged the top eighth of the page onto the base.

Dimos sat for at least twenty minutes, slowly maneuvering the lenses over the viewing area, as if carefully studying every molecule. Augie strained to make out what he was mumbling.

"Um-hm, guessing split goatskin. Somebody figured it out when papyrus got scarce. For centuries you could get papyrus only from Alexandria. When prices went up or production fell off, people had to adapt. Parchment became the answer."

Still peering through the lenses and slowly scanning the exposed part of the page, he said, "I got a look at the famous Jesus-had-a-wife fragment, but that was Sahidic Coptic written on papyrus, and I concurred it could be dated to the fourth century."

Augie whispered, "This has got to be the most intact, pristine sample of the oldest readable manuscript ever, right?"

"I've seen pieces of parchment from two thousand years before Christ, but they're just barely readable bits on crumbling fragments. I'll be telling both buyer and seller that this is the oldest readable manuscript found to date. It'll have to be carbon dated eventually, but there is no doubt in my mind it will be authenticated. How this remained intact for two centuries, underground—parchment not being waterproof—I don't know. Had to be a perfect mix of temperature and lack of humidity."

"So you're looking at a miracle?"

"I'm looking at the biggest payday I'll ever see."

"Really," Augie said. "It does nothing for you that you're handling the very page on which the Apostle Paul wrote in his own hand?"

Dimos cocked his head. "When you put it that way, yeah, that's kind of special."

Roger said, "It's a lot more than that, man."

Augie suddenly felt dirty having a character like Dimos Fokinos handling the parchment. But for all Dimos knew, Augie and Roger were as eager as he to get their millions.

"I'm satisfied," Dimos said a few minutes later as he packed his gear. "I know you know where the rest of this manuscript is. You probably already have it in your own custody."

"Possibly," Augie said.

"Well, just so you know, that's where the money is. I'll talk to my people tonight and we'll be in touch tomorrow."

MIDNIGHT

When the coast was clear, Sofia rejoined Augie and tossed Roger her extra key card.

"I want to get this into a safe-deposit box as soon as the bank opens in the morning," Augie said. "And then, Rog, you can hang out in Sofia's room while she and I pay a visit to Piazza Sant'Ignazio."

"Art Squad Headquarters?" Roger said. "What if Sardinia is there?"

"What if he is? He doesn't know us."

"You'd better hope not."

"If he did, he'd have had us eliminated already. We're going as tourists. We'll ask for a tour, see what we can find out."

"You're crazy."

"I know. But carrying your nine millimeter tonight wasn't the only precaution I took."

Entrenched

FIRST-CENTURY ROME

As the sun began to set earlier, Luke found ways to smuggle more cloth into Paul's dungeon. It had become chilly by the time he left the prison each evening, and his own cloak was barely enough to protect him. It would get only worse as winter set in.

One night Primus beckoned him and whispered, "You must hide those extra coverings during the day. Certain guards are grumbling about special treatment again."

Luke set his jaw. "I'd like to see one of them live at Paul's level of luxury for one hour."

"I know. Just be careful."

"Where would I hide anything down there, Primus? There's no room behind the bench. And any guard's faintest light would reveal anything out of the ordinary."

"I'll go down tomorrow and take a look."

That night Luke read nearly a hundred more pages of Paul's memoir, learning more than he ever dreamed about his friend's deep sense of loss over Naomi. The parchments were filled with a despair that had haunted Paul his entire life, apparently even to this day.

To my shame, I longed for Naomi until I feared I might die. I missed her look, her touch, her voice. When she married, I felt a fool. No other woman has even given me pause since those days of my youth when I neglected my one true love. I look back and wonder how I could have imagined any other result after the way I treated her. Was I so enamored of myself that I couldn't imagine she would ever feel otherwise?

Even decades later, traveling thousands of miles for the sake of the gospel, I often find myself weeping at the end of the day. Sometimes I even plead with God to deliver me from this obsession with a woman who has long since made her choice. She is a mother and a grandmother by now, and yet her visage is ever before me. My conscience condemns me for my adulterous yearning, and sometimes it is all I can do to surrender my old nature to God and trust Him to help me stay my course.

My only balm has been to pour my whole self into serving Him, striving to return to my first love of Christ, His salvation, His message, His truth, His saving grace. Naomi will never know how the pride that repelled her grew into a determination to daily offer myself wholly to the Lord.

My becoming a Christ follower had to appear blasphe-

mous to her, and for years I tried to justify finding her and pleading with her to consider Him. I could not allow myself that mission, having never been able to fathom the depth of my true motives. All I could do was pray for her soul and that God Himself would, in His mercy, put the right person in her path to show her the truth.

Though this created a lifelong war within me, the bitterest season had come early when it became known that we were no longer a couple and that Ezra had soon after become her intended. I wanted to hate him, and for a long time I did. Yet it was not his character or his actions I detested. He was not vulnerable on those points. I hated him because he had taken my place.

I must have been a sight back then, short and wiry with bowed legs and already losing my hair by age thirty. My face offered little to desire—friends teased me about my hook nose, bushy eyebrows that met in the middle, and light-gray eyes contrasting with a ruddy complexion. Naomi herself once said my eyes would have been my redeeming feature, "were they not always ablaze."

Well, if I was afire before she abandoned me, I soon became a raging inferno. Enemies and colleagues said I spoke twice again as loud as I needed to in order to be heard, and that I gestured so aggressively that I often physically struck someone in my audience without realizing it.

Such assessments had no tempering effect. I wanted nothing less than to be known throughout Judea as the most exacting Pharisee alive. I represented the strictest sect of my religion, among whom I strived to be singularly devout.

No issue, no argument, no subject of conversation was any more important to me than another. Whether it was a member of the Sanhedrin who may have committed some egregious act or merely a child's sandals clacking too loudly in our sacred corridors, I reacted with equal vehemence. Whatever the infraction, it propelled me into a rage. I was known to curse the infidels, call down the wrath of heaven on them, even rent my clothes at the very thought of their impudence.

Some worried I had lost my mind, and more than once Nathanael pleaded with me to be reasonable. Often he called in Gamaliel, whose generous moderation had once served as a standard I strived to emulate. But now he seemed to me a capitulator, weak and indecisive, always open to hearing both sides of a dispute and trying to come to a mutually satisfying middle ground. Often I marched home long after the rest of the clerics had ended their workdays and paced my apartment, forgetting to eat, talking aloud to myself, convinced that I alone was correct in my assessment of every situation.

Imagine my fury when yet another mystic appeared out of nowhere to capture the imaginations of the people. What children they were! What sheep! How many charlatans had we seen in Judea, inventing their own doctrines and persuading the masses that, finally, the chosen one had arrived?

This one is different, they said. This one performs miracles. This one speaks in parables and dichotomies. Even members of the Sanhedrin were impressed. I demanded examples. One told me this man preached that those who would be great must first become servants; that to become rich, one must give his money away; and that people should love their enemies, do good to those who hate them, and pray for those who mistreat them. Such lunacy!

Many pleaded with me to come and hear Jesus of Nazareth, the one they began to refer to as Master and Rabbi and Teacher. I flatly refused. I knew that like others before him, when he moved on, the clamor would fade.

But when his fame grew and accounts of his miracles became so pervasive they could not be ignored, the Sanhedrin sent scribes and Pharisees to report back. They challenged him and he answered in riddles. He worked on the Sabbath. And while it was not illegal for a layperson to speak in the temples, it was frowned upon. Yet he did this without hesitation or shame.

Some believed he might be our long-awaited Messiah. Now they had my attention! The man had quickly moved from a curiosity to a blasphemer. When one of his admirers asked him if it was true, if he was the Messiah, he did not deny it.

I confess I became curious and privately wanted a peek at this man, who was at least a remarkable performer. But I had made a point of being one of the very few religious leaders in Jerusalem who had not joined the flocks who heard him. Now my pride kept me from going. I told anyone who would listen that he would eventually be exposed. He would somehow offend the very ones so enamored with him now. Something would portend this charlatan's end.

It came as no surprise to me when even those closest to him betrayed him and abandoned him and he indeed ran afoul of Rome. He was hauled before the high priest and the Sanhedrin. He had chosen the wrong audience for his claim to be king of the Jews.

Though I might have enjoyed witnessing it, I pointedly refused to attend that debacle, smugly reminding everyone that I had been right all along.

He was put to death on a cross like a common criminal. To my mind, the man had served but one purpose—to elevate my position as the most astute Pharisee in Jerusalem.

The death of the Nazarene meant the end of a nuisance.

Raising the Stakes

AUGIE AND SOFIA KISSED goodnight at the suite door. She buried her head in his chest. "Hasn't been a good day for me."

"I just hope your dad's smart enough to back away from this, for your sake."

She shook her head. "Too lucrative. If he really cared about me, he wouldn't be in this deep already. Honestly, offering you a finder's fee . . ."

"I think I convinced him I'll play ball, if that makes you feel any better."

"It doesn't. And neither does your plan for tomorrow. Roger's right. Dimos had to tell that number-two guy all about us or he wouldn't have agreed to pay us off. And that alone is worrisome, don't you think? Once he has what he wants, we're as expendable as your Vatican friend was."

"That's why we've got to play this to the end, Sof. Give them nothing until we're paid, then the money becomes evidence against them."

"But somebody in authority has to know that in advance. If we get caught, it'll be too late to claim we were just setting them up."

"Then I've got to get to Colonel Emmanuel, the top guy," Augie said.

"Without Sardinia finding out? How?"

"I wish I knew, Sofia. You've got to wonder how much Emmanuel knows. Probably only what Sardinia wants him to believe."

"If they *have* been tracking us by our passports, Sardinia probably already told his boss you're a friend of the guy who had Klaudios killed. How do you prove whose side we're on before this blows up?"

"First we've got to get that original page secured. Roger says the banks open at 8:35. We start there. Then go straight to the Art Squad to establish where we stand."

"How sure are you that this Emmanuel is clean, Augie?"

"Don't think I haven't wondered. But Dimos says his contact there plays the colonel like a fiddle. If he was just trying to impress me, why wouldn't he claim he had the whole squad in his pocket?"

"I just hope my mother will visit me in prison," Sofia said.

"You joke, but you're not invested in this. You can back away whenever you want, and nobody will hold it against you."

"No thank you. Right is right. If you and Roger and I are going down, it'll be together."

Sofia left with another kiss, but not five minutes later called Augie's phone. "I'm an idiot," she said. "I left a bag in the closet at the other hotel."

"Let's go get it."

"It'll wait. Good thing I didn't check out. Can we leave a little early tomorrow so I can pick it up before we go to the bank?"

"Your hotel lies between the bank and the Art Squad. Bank first, then hotel, then squad headquarters, okay? And bring the photocopies. Might as well put them in the bank too."

They agreed to meet in the lobby at eight.

Augie lay on his back in the darkness, hands behind his head. Across the way he heard Roger call out from his bed, "Still awake, Augie?"

"Yeah."

"Think Fokinos has already reported in?"

"'Course. Those guys can't see past the dollar signs. They're probably not sleeping either."

"Fokinos is convinced we're sitting on the rest of the manuscript. I'm dying to know where Giordano stashed it, but I'm glad we haven't even opened that envelope. As long as they think we know, they need us. I just hope whatever's going to happen happens soon. I'll go nuts waiting in Sofia's room all day."

"When I get to read the whole memoir, it will all be worth it. Listen, Rog, what's it going to mean to you if the rest of the memoir is as clear as that first page? What if it proves that Paul is the author of all those letters in the New Testament?"

"You're wondering if I heard you last night."

"Sorry?"

"Every word."

"You were pretending to be asleep?"

"I guess. I'm not ready to talk about it yet."

"Can't ask for more than that."

Augie had finally drifted off—he didn't know for how long—when his cell phone buzzed. He squinted at the screen. *Oh no!*

"Mom! What time is it there?"

"A little after five-thirty. I didn't mean to wake you."

"Dad okay?"

"As a matter of fact, he is."

That was a relief. Augie hoped to get one more chance to talk to his father, but it hadn't seemed likely. "That's good. Hope to be home soon. But I need to get some rest before tom—"

"Someone wants to talk to you, August. Hold on."

"Mom, I—"

"Augustine?"

"*Dad?*"

"I just wanted to hear your voice."

"You did?"

"It's been a long time, son. Longer than I knew."

"You sound pretty good, all things considered."

"Surprised you can even hear me. Your mother has to hold the phone for me."

"Dad, I'm so glad you're back with us—"

"Probably not for long, I know that."

"Well, I didn't know if I'd even get a chance to say good-bye, Dad. I'll try to get back soon so we can talk."

"I'd like that."

"You would?"

"Stop acting so surprised, Augustine. I'm not dead yet."

"I'm just happy. There are things I want to tell you, need to tell you."

"Nothing needs to be said, son. I'm glad I got to talk with you one more time anyway."

One more time? When did we ever talk before? Augie wanted to get home in time to say his good-byes without bitterness. A lifetime of pain would not be erased by one last conversation, but to have one relatively normal conversation with a father he had hardly ever known would be a bonus. "I'll look forward to telling you about my trip," Augie said.

"Um-hm," his father said, clearly ready to nod off again. "Rome, your mother said. The one place I didn't mind visiting. That's where Michaels lives, you know. You remember, the guide who—"

"I'm with Roger, Dad."

"I'm 'bout to fall sleep again here, son, but greet him for me, would you?"

Augie heard a rustle and his mother came on. "Be safe and hurry home, August."

"How about that?" he said.

"I know. I feel like it's a gift from God, just for us."

8:40 A.M.

Augie felt conspicuous striding through the cavernous bank lobby, certain the nine millimeter was obvious under his jacket.

More than one customer looked up as he and Sofia passed, but Augie quickly realized that each was a man with his eyes on Sofia.

He and Sofia sat across the desk from a middle-aged woman as she explained to them the options for a safe-deposit box. Augie found his knee bouncing and reminded himself that no one knew what was in the bag on his lap.

"*Dimensione?*" she said at last.

"Oh," he said. "Big enough for this?"

The woman produced a tiny tape and came around the desk to measure the bag. "*Quarantatre da trentotto centimetri,*" she said.

Augie looked to Sofia. "Seventeen by fifteen inches," she said.

The woman checked a laminated card. "*Centocinquanta euro all'anno.*"

"One hundred fifty euros a year," Sofia told him.

"That's like two hundred bucks," Augie said. "How much for a few days?"

Sofia translated, and the woman shook her head. "*Un anno è il minimo.*"

"One year is the minimum, Augie."

"Highway robbery."

Sofia leaned close. "Hon, we're out of options. Think of it in light of the value."

They completed the paperwork and the woman led them back to the vault, explaining that the bank would not open Augie's box unless he failed to renew the payment after a year. He felt better when they were back in the cab, the key in his pocket.

9:45 A.M.

When the taxi pulled in to Sofia's original hotel, she grabbed Augie's arm. The parking lot was full of blue and white *polizia* cars, along with a boxy white *ambulanza* with orange stripes.

"Avoid the front!" Augie said. "Pull in down there."

Sofia translated and the driver used a far entrance.

The back of the seat pressed against Augie's weapon as he slid out, slinging his empty leather bag over his shoulder. He and Sofia shaded their eyes against the piercing sun, watching the activity from one end of the parking lot. "I don't want to go in there," she said. "What if they're looking for me?"

"Why would they be? Someone's had a heart attack or something, that's all."

"Then why so many carabinieri? Somebody's exposed us, Augie. Better warn Roger."

"Not till we know what's going on. They can't have shut down the whole hotel. See if you can get to your room."

"Come with me."

Augie started to follow but stopped when his phone rang. Sofia didn't look back.

He didn't recognize the number. "This is Knox," he said.

"Augie, it's Roger. Don't go to Sofia's hotel."

"Just got here."

"Get out of there. It's all over the news. Fokinos was found dead in his room, twenty-two to the temple. They're looking for his traveling companion, the woman he checked in with. Sofia's picture is on TV. They'll trace her passport number and come straight here. I'm getting out. I'll meet you at—"

"Got to call you back, Rog."

"I don't have a ph—!"

Augie pocketed his phone and rushed inside, sprinting down a long corridor, ignoring the ringing in his pocket and afraid to call out Sofia's name.

He reached a perpendicular hallway, skidded to a stop and peeked left, then right, having no idea where her room was. At the next intersection he did the same. Far down the hall on the right Sofia had stopped in a corridor full of carabinieri. The cops had surrounded her and one was handcuffing her.

Augie reached for the Smith & Wesson and froze. What was he going to do, draw down on the *polizia* and rescue his fiancée? All things considered, she was safer with them for the moment. Augie didn't know whether he could forgive himself if he left Sofia behind, but if he admitted who he was he'd have little chance of talking his way out.

As he hurried back outside, Augie reminded himself that Sardinia still needed what only he had. Trouble was, Sardinia finally had access to the one bargaining chip that could make Augie give up the key to the safe-deposit box.

40

The Breaking Point

—————

FIRST-CENTURY ROME

—————

"I AM SO WEARY of darkness," Paul told Luke. "Your visits are of great encouragement, but nothing is so disheartening as being unable to see."

Luke had been in the dungeon only a few minutes when a loud scrape signaled the wood cover being dragged away from the hole. Primus leapt into the cell, and another guard handed him down a torch. "I am officially here to make sure your doctor is following protocol, Paul. But we all must whisper so I can show you what I found earlier today while you were asleep."

"I knew someone was here," Paul said, "but I could not muster the strength to even sit up. What were you working on?"

"Come and see."

Luke and Paul followed him until Paul reached the end of his chain.

"For many months I have had my eye on that block of tufa," Primus said. "See how the mortar has crumbled? Watch this." He knelt and worked the limestone this way and that until he was able to slide it away from the foundation. "It just needed coaxing. But now you have your own small storage area. In the morning, before anyone from the first watch has any reason to be down here, stow your extra coverings here and slide the stone all the way back in."

"I cannot imagine I have the strength," Paul said, slowly bending to get his fingers on the edge of the block. It slid out so quickly Luke had to catch him before he fell on his seat. "How did you do that, Primus?"

"A little ingenuity," the guard said. He lifted the end of the stone and pulled a thin, round dowel from beneath it. "I set several of these under the loose block. Just make sure these stay in place, and the heavy stone will move easily. When pressed flush with the wall it appears tight, yet there is room behind it."

"Splendid," Paul said.

"I just don't want any of the three of us to get in trouble again," the guard said.

That night as Luke picked up his reading, he couldn't help contrasting the frail old man in the dungeon with the fierce conscience of the Sanhedrin from thirty-five years before.

When I first heard the claims that the miracle worker from Galilee had risen from the dead, I was neither exercised nor enraged. I just roared with laughter. "His poor deluded minions just can't let this one go!" I cried, holding my belly as I swayed back and forth on my stool. "Some claim to have seen him, to have talked with him, to have eaten with him! I did not know ghosts had appetites! Well, where is he now?

Why does he not visit us? Why only those who knew him? They have no credibility. Say, sorcerer, show yourself to a skeptic. Convince someone."

For days I took great delight in making sport of the followers of Jesus, who seemed determined to keep his movement alive. I told Gamaliel, "You more than I have seen others who thrilled a sizable band of the gullible, only to have their causes dry up and blow away when they passed from the earth."

"It's true," Nasi said. "These things have a way of taking care of themselves."

Not many weeks hence, however, even I had to acknowledge that the band of disciples Jesus gathered had only grown since his crucifixion. That made no sense. Now there were rumors that these men were performing the same kinds of miracles Jesus had. As their numbers increased, so, it seemed, did their boldness. Not only did they go about brazenly preaching Jesus' gospel, but they also brought this heresy to the Temple Mount.

Soon I no longer found them amusing. They had grown to much more than a nuisance. They ignored our laws, flouted them, even disobeyed the direct orders of Caiaphas to stop preaching in the name of Jesus.

Some from our ranks—even priests—defected and became believers. On one day alone, thousands of Jerusalem citizens joined their numbers. Their leaders, the most visible an uneducated fisherman from Galilee named Peter, escaped from prison!

Was I jealous of their popularity and influence? Truly, I

was not. Was I worried about the influence they were having on my fellow Jews? Of course I was. But primarily I was livid over their refusal to obey the Sanhedrin. When their numbers began multiplying virtually every day, something had to be done. This movement had taken on a life of its own. Jesus had become more than a martyr. They did not apologize for claiming that he was the son of God, the Messiah, that he had risen from the dead, then appeared to dozens of them, and was transported into heaven before their very eyes.

This I could not abide. I scoured the law books and pleaded with Nathanael and other leaders of the Sanhedrin to allow me to enforce justice if they wouldn't. I would snuff out this blasphemous cult that had taken to sharing everything communally, meeting in private homes, and proclaiming a resurrected son of God.

I dragged them before the council and told Annas and Caiaphas that these men had flagrantly disobeyed their direct orders. Caiaphas leapt to his feet and said, "Did we not strictly command you not to teach in this name? And look, you have filled Jerusalem with your doctrine and intend to bring this man's blood on us!"

Peter said, "We ought to obey God rather than men. The God of our fathers raised up Jesus, whom you murdered by hanging on a tree. God has exalted Him to His right hand to be Prince and Savior, to give repentance to Israel and forgiveness of sins. And we are His witnesses to these things, and so also is the Holy Spirit whom God has given to those who obey Him."

That was all I needed to hear. These men were as worthy of death as their blasphemous leader had been. "You should kill them where they stand!" I said.

As soon as I saw Gamaliel get up, I knew he would thwart my plan with some weak, conciliatory appeal for reason. After he commanded that Peter and the other apostles be temporarily excused, he said, "Men of Israel, take heed to yourselves what you intend to do regarding these men. Keep away from these men and let them alone; for if this is of men, it will come to nothing; but if it is of God, you cannot overthrow it."

As usual, the other members of the Sanhedrin solemnly nodded. At least they called the apostles back in and beat them for disobeying. They were commanded again not to speak in the name of Jesus, but then they were set free.

This was a grave error. For days, in the temple and in houses all over Jerusalem, they continued to ignore the council's orders and preached Jesus as the Christ.

I reported to the Sanhedrin every such incident and worked tirelessly to rally support for taking drastic action against these people. The religious leaders of Jerusalem had to put a stop to this. They absolutely had to.

41

Téléphone à Trois

AUGIE RACED TO THE hotel cab stand, ready to run if he couldn't get one. He had long taught seminary students that becoming a person of faith was no guarantee things would always go well for you. He said silently, *Lord, Your Word says man is destined for trouble as surely as sparks fly upward, but You also promise You will be with me until the end. I just hope today isn't it. Tell me what to do.*

Augie wasn't from a culture comfortable with God speaking audibly to His people. He had always believed he should trust God fully and follow his own conscience. But right now he would have appreciated specifics.

When his turn came he dove into the back seat and said, "Piazza Sant'Ignazio."

The cabbie adjusted the mirror to look directly at Augie. "That is a *polizia* building. Lots of carabinieri right here."

"Quickly, please."

Augie's phone began chirping with texts from Roger. "out just in time. heard elevator while heading 2 stairs. cop cars in front. escaped out the side. pick me up?"

"stay put," Augie texted back. "back 2 u later."

"Sof w/u?"

"cops got her."

"where u?"

"art squad."

"avoid. danger."

"got 2 take chance. Later."

The Art Squad was housed in an ornate four-story salmon-colored stucco building bearing two flags below the third-floor windows and directly above the entrance. "Beautiful, no?" the driver said. "Almost three hundred years old. Protected landmark. Cannot deliver you to door. Those plants in concrete vases are actually barricades."

Augie got out across the street, where he found a shaded area with tables and chairs. Augie had calls he couldn't make in front of anyone anyway, and he couldn't just waltz into Art Squad headquarters. He set his empty bag on a wrought iron table and sat, careful not to look at the building as his face had to be known to authorities by now. He phoned Malfees Trikoupis.

"Dr. Knox!" the man exulted. "I was about to call you to arrange a meeting tonight. Good to hear your voice. Are you as excited as I am with Dimos's conclusions? We are both going to enjoy a huge—"

"So you haven't heard . . ."

"All I heard was good news. He called after midnight last night and—"

"Fokinos is dead, sir. And Sofia has been arrested."

Trikoupis voice lost its ebullience. "What are you telling me?"

"Fokinos was assassinated in his hotel room, so the carabinieri wanted to talk with the woman who had arrived with him from Greece."

"The man you are to meet with tonight can straighten this out right now."

"Is he highly placed enough to help with something this big?"

"Of course. I'll call and patch you in, and you'll see. But you must not speak. I guarantee she will be free very soon."

"Is this worth it, Mr. T.? Lying to your daughter, getting your employee killed . . ."

"I had nothing to do with that! But listen to me, Augie, the fewer people involved, the more value this project has to those of us who remain."

"Fokinos was here for you, sir, acting on your promise! His death isn't even a nuisance to you?"

Trikoupis suddenly sounded like himself again, hardly agitated despite that his employee had been murdered and his daughter taken into custody. "Well, it's both sad and an opportunity, August. Surely you can see that."

"But if Dimos could be eliminated, Sofia could too!"

"I won't let that happen. You'll see. Give me your number so I can link the call."

Oh, no, you don't.

"You don't need my number. I'll just stay on while you patch in your guy."

"You'll be impressed."

When the call was connected, Augie heard, "Malfees Trikoupis calling for Deputy Director Sardinia."

"Good morning, sir! He's out. Would you like the colonel?"

"No, I'll try Aldo's cell."

Within seconds Augie heard Sardinia's voice for the first time. It was clear he knew who was calling. "Hello, friend," he said.

"Can you talk, Aldo?"

"Not really. How are you?"

"None too pleased at the moment. My daughter will not be collateral damage if you have any continued interest in our agreement."

"You may rest assured of that."

"It sounds as if the only way to stay alive is to be indispensable to this project."

"I hope that's clear," Sardinia said.

"Just remember that I am both your buyer and seller. You don't want to handle that from a government office."

"Believe me, you are not in any danger."

"Prove that by releasing my daughter with dispatch."

"On my way there now. But until we take delivery, everything else is off the table."

"It won't be long, Aldo. The one with access to the merchandise will soon be family. And with one less person to cut in on the deal now, there will be more than enough to cover him. What are you doing about the South African?"

"The guide? It's just a matter of time. We almost had him today."

"And arresting him is not the goal, correct?"

The Art Squad deputy chief chuckled. "No, mere apprehension is not our aim."

When Sardinia hung up, Augie said, "Was that for my benefit, Mr. T., discussing the assassination of Roger Michaels? That's how you threaten me?"

"You're a prudent man, Augie. You heard what you needed to hear. I trust you realize that were Sofia not so fond of you . . . Look on the positive side—you and she will be set for life. Don't force me to do something that would break her heart."

"What if I don't know where the manuscript is?"

Trikoupis laughed. "Michaels would not have pleaded with you to come to Rome if not to confide in you."

"In case you're wrong, you might want to slow Sardinia down before he eliminates the last hope for finding the memoir."

"I am impressed, Augie. That's a creative maneuver to protect your friend. I wish I had a friend I cared about that much."

"I wish you had a daughter you cared about that much."

"Insults are beneath you. Now let me tell you what happens next. At eight this evening Deputy Director Sardinia will meet with you, and you will be as cooperative as possible. You know the reward, as well as the alternative. Will you do that for me? For Sofia?"

"It appears I have no choice."

"Now we're back to understanding each another. He will come to the Terrazzo."

"What?"

"You think he doesn't know where you're registered?"

Augie fought to keep his composure. The only thing keeping him alive was that Sardinia and Trikoupis believed he either had the ancient memoir or knew where it was.

"All right, but I do have one condition."

"This is not your meeting, Augie."

"Hear me out. I'll tell Mr. Sardinia everything I know, but only if you are also there."

"You want me in Rome? Impossible. I—"

Click.

42

The Stoning

I had long been an early riser, but now I began waking before dawn every day and rarely going to bed before midnight. I was filled with purpose. The acts of the Jesus followers flew in the face of everything I had ever been taught. These people were enemies of God, enemies of His law, blasphemers, deserving the ultimate punishment.

I hounded Nathanael daily until I wore him down, persuading him to personally seek a private audience for me with the high priest, Caiaphas. When it was granted, I pleaded with Caiaphas to extend to me the authority of the

Sanhedrin itself. "As long as these men proclaim a dead man the Messiah, I won't rest until they are brought to justice. What deliverer would be put to death in such a vile manner? You did right by having them beaten for disobedience, but it didn't stop them. Their blasphemy has escalated."

Caiaphas was strangely quiet, but I sensed he was impressed with my zeal. "I would have to discuss this with my father-in-law," he said, referring to the Roman-deposed Annas, whom everyone knew was the real high priest. "It would be most unusual to confer upon you authority above your station, but you have been so fervent in your service to this body that I sometimes consider you already a member. Tell me, are you aware that your views are shared by the Synagogue of Freedmen?"

I certainly was aware. Many of the Grecian Jews of that uniquely passionate congregation hailed from my home province of Cilicia, and I never let an opportunity pass without identifying myself as being a Roman citizen from Tarsus, so they knew well that we were fellow countrymen. Despite that these men were Greek, they considered me a compatriot.

"Frankly," I told Caiaphas, "I like the way those men think. They agree the council must take an unequivocal stand against these apostates to stop the daily increase in their number."

"The Freedmen are particularly incensed by the effectiveness of one of the new leaders," Caiaphas said. "You know of whom I speak?"

"Of course. The Freedmen have failed in their every

effort to shout down the one the rabble-rousers boast is full of faith and power."

"Stephen," Caiaphas said. "He is cunning and an effective speaker."

"Able to perform miracles, signs, and wonders, according to his cohorts."

"I thought the death of Jesus would put an end to this nonsense," Caiaphas said. "Now I wonder how much the life of this Stephen is worth to their cause."

"The Freedmen have all manner of evidence against him."

"We need more," Caiaphas said. "We need grounds to stone the man for gross impiety."

"Rome will not permit us to kill him," I said.

"How will they know whether that was our intention? Perhaps we can show that we afforded him every courtesy, allowed him to say whatever he wanted—as long as he respected our authority."

Allowing such a powerful speaker access to the ears of the council seemed risky, but I was for anything that might bring one of these men to face the wrath of the Sanhedrin. I told Caiaphas it was a brilliant idea. He asked me to come back the next morning to meet with him and his father-in-law, Annas.

I barely slept.

Annas was nothing like Gamaliel or even Caiaphas. Here was a man of action, eager to thumb his nose at Rome. Sure, in the past that had cost him his official title, but the joke was on them because, to this day, nothing happened within the Sanhedrin that Annas had not either instigated or at least approved.

"Saul," he said, "you are just the man we need to lead this effort. Work with the Freedmen, talk to every witness. Compile the evidence against Stephen and give us what we need to finally extinguish this dangerous movement."

In years past I might have reveled in this opportunity to shine in the eyes of the council, but by now my intellect and skills were well known. Already the toughest tasks often fell to me.

This time I would embrace duty for the purest of motives. No one felt as strongly as I did that this new sect was at enmity with Almighty God Himself. The fisherman Peter may have been their leader, but Stephen was quickly becoming their hero. The time had come to show him, and all who admired him, who really wielded the spiritual power in Jerusalem.

The Synagogue of Freedmen needed little encouragement to find men to swear that Stephen had decreed that the risen Jesus would destroy our temple and even change the customs passed down from Moses. They volunteered to testify that Stephen never ceased blaspheming against our holy place and the Law.

A few days later the Freedmen seized Stephen and brought him before the council. As the witnesses recited their serious charges, something very strange happened. Stephen's face began to glow like the midday sun! I couldn't take my eyes off him. Of what kind of sorcery was this man capable?

Caiaphas seemed transfixed, squinting into the strange visage of the accused. Annas whispered in his ear, and Caiaphas said, "This is your opportunity to tell us whether these charges are true."

Had not Annas and Caiaphas planned to defend themselves before Rome by allowing Stephen to speak for as long as he wished, I would not have been able to tolerate the length of his speech. It went on for so long that I began to circulate among the brethren, asking how they could put up with this impudence.

Stephen retold the story of Abraham and the covenant, then went on to describe Isaac, Jacob, the twelve patriarchs, the selling of Joseph into slavery, Moses, the burning bush, the commandments, and even up to King David.

"How dare he?" I said as I mingled among the council. "Will you have him lecture you on your own history?"

But it grew worse! After this long recitation, he insulted the Sanhedrin members. "You stiff-necked and uncircumcised in heart and ears!" he said. "You always resist the Holy Spirit; as your fathers did, so do you."

I leapt to my feet. "How dare he?" I cried. "For how much longer will you abide this?"

The Sanhedrin members scowled and pulled their robes about them, but Stephen would not stop. "Which of the prophets did your fathers not persecute? And they killed those who foretold the coming of the Just One, whom you have betrayed and murdered . . ."

"You are betrayers and murderers?" I shouted.

The members gnashed their teeth at Stephen and rose

up as one. As they rushed at him, he gazed up as if he could see something other than the ceiling. "Look!" he said. "I see the heavens open and the Son of Man standing at the right hand of God!"

"Blasphemer!" I screamed, and the council cried out, covering their ears, then surrounding Stephen and dragging him out. I ran ahead, leading them to a plain strewn with hundreds of rocks. "Stay away from any pit, and use no stones large enough to crush him! This must not look like an execution, but merely a punishment gone awry!"

As the men forced Stephen into an open area where he could not hide, I took their cloaks and pointed them to the piles of rocks. Nearly seventy men of all ages began throwing them at Stephen. It didn't take long for the weapons to find their mark. As first one, then another stone thudded into his belly and chest, he called out, "Lord Jesus, receive my spirit!"

He knelt and cried, "Lord, do not charge them with this sin."

Soon he lay in the dirt, a pool of blood under his head. When it was clear he was dead, I raised both fists, then began shaking hands with each of the men. We had done a righteous thing. It had been a great day.

That night I slept soundly for the first time in months.

43

Exposed

AUGIE KNEW EXACTLY WHAT Trikoupis would do. So eager to learn where the priceless memoir was, he would immediately call Sardinia and instruct him to get word to Sofia that her father would be joining them. Since Sofia no longer had a phone, and Augie was protecting his own number, having Sardinia tell his daughter would be the only way he could get word to Augie that he was honoring the demand to show up.

This was it. All the principals would be in place. And if Augie could talk him into it, Roger would be there too. He turned and faced the Art Squad headquarters and texted Roger, "b @ r suite 2nite @ 8."

"u suicidal?"

"I came here 4 u, Rog."

"2 keep me alive, not get me killed."

"if u trust me, b there."

"need 2 talk. will call."

"don't. busy till then."

Augie's phone rang. "I'm calling from a pay phone," Sofia said, "and I've got to hurry in case I'm being followed. I met Sardinia. Smooth and charming, not like the ones who started in on me. Right in the middle of questioning me he takes a call and tells me I'm free to go if I'll give you a message. 'Your wish has been granted.' Mean anything to you?"

"It does. Just tell me nobody hurt you."

"They just tried to intimidate me. For all I know they released me to be murdered."

"You know I never would have abandoned you—"

"No, I was afraid you'd follow me into their trap. Glad you didn't. Where did you go?"

Augie told her and said he planned to meet with Colonel Emmanuel as soon as he got off the phone, "while I know Sardinia is out of the office."

"Please don't, love," she said. "They'll arrest you on the spot."

"That's a risk I have to take. You just need to find somewhere to lie low until eight tonight and then meet Roger and me at the suite."

"No! They've been tracking us. They knew I'd switched hotels and that Roger is there. They've probably already found him."

"He got out just in time."

"Augie, please, just find out who Roger used for his new ID, get yourself a disguise and a forged passport, and get out of Italy. I'll try to meet you in the States."

"Sofia, do you trust me?"

"I'm not coming back to the hotel."

"You think I'd put you in harm's way for even one second?"

"No, but—"

"Then I'll see you at eight. Stay safe, I love you."

"Augie—"

As he stepped past the potted plants, Augie saw a sniper behind a fence on the roof. He was barking into a walkie-talkie. When Augie reached the entrance, he stood with his back to the wall, punching a number into his phone. A guard emerged. "*Stato prego il vostro business, sir. Non posso avere te vagabondaggio qui.*"

Augie covered his phone. "Sorry. English?"

"State your business please, sir. I can't have you loitering here."

"As soon as I finish this call, I'm coming inside."

"No more tours today."

"No tour. Business. Thanks for your patience."

He turned back to his phone.

"Augie, what the devil? It's four-thirty in the morning here!"

"Biff, listen, you know I'd never wake you if it wasn't crucial." Augie told him what he needed, which required Biff to immediately head to his own office at Dallas Seminary.

"You're gonna so owe me, Knox."

"Only my life. I know my phone has enough capacity, but how long for the download?"

"First I gotta see if it's there."

"Text me when you know."

"Want me to serve you breakfast too?"

"Seriously, Biff, you're the best."

"Who you tellin'? You got a charger with you, like I told you, right?"

"I do."

"How much battery life right now?"

"A little more than half."

"Charge it again as soon as you can."

The guard shadowed Augie as he approached the receptionist. "English?" he said. She nodded. "I need to see Colonel Emmanuel."

The woman checked her calendar. "I can see if he has any time next week."

"No, now."

"Without an appointment, I'm sorry."

"It's urgent. I know he'll want to—"

"Sir," the guard said, taking Augie's elbow. "Make an appointment or leave."

"I know he's in and will see me. Just tell him Dr. August A. Knox from Dallas, Texas, is here about the Klaudios Giordano murder."

The girl blanched and the guard produced handcuffs. "Call him," the guard said. "Hands behind your back. You're doing the right thing, giving yourself up."

"You don't have to cuff me."

"*No, Signore,*" the receptionist was saying, "*egli non sembra pericoloso.*" She covered the phone. "Dr. Knox, I told him you do not look dangerous, but he wants to know if you're armed."

"Yes, I am."

The guard tightened the cuffs, reached for his own sidearm, and pressed the button on his walkie-talkie. "*Hai bisogno di aiuto nella lobby prega, immediatamente!*"

"You don't need help," Augie said. "It's a nine millimeter under my shirt in back."

As the guard yanked it out, two other officers barged in with guns drawn. "Really," Augie said as the guard frisked him, "I'm harmless."

She sat back down. "Tell him he surrendered a handgun," the guard said.

"*Ha ceduto una pistola, colonnello . . .*" she said into the phone. "*Va bene, sì, Signore.*"

Ashen, voice shaky, the girl turned to the guard, "*Il colonnello dice di portarlo nella stanza sicura e lui sarà là voi in pochi minuti.*"

"Taking me to a holding cell?" Augie said.

"Just an interrogation room secured against surveillance. Looks like you got your appointment."

As the guard led him to an elevator, the receptionist's phone rang again. She said, "*E mi troverete nell'armadietto file sotto Knox?*"

"What was that about?" Augie said, as the guard hit the button for the fourth floor.

The man shrugged. "The colonel wants the Knox files."

"I'm on file already?"

When they reached the secure room, the guard nodded to a chair on the other side of a plain wood table. Augie said, "Could you get my phone and charger out of my pocket and plug it in?"

The guard shook his head.

Colonel Emmanuel showed up in a natty business suit. Carrying two file folders, one yellowed with age, he had the look of a man who had worked his way up through the ranks. He and the guard conversed in Italian, and Augie found Emmanuel surprisingly soft-spoken. As the guard was leaving, the colonel withdrew his own sidearm and traded it for the handcuff key.

Emmanuel delicately placed the folders on the table, along with a small recording device. Still standing, he flipped it on and said, "*Italiano o in inglese?*"

"Texan," Augie said.

Emmanuel did not appeared amused. His English was precise and formal, heavily accented. "I assume you will behave if I remove the manacles?"

"Promise."

The colonel stepped behind him and released the cuffs.

"Was that a Smith & Wesson you were carrying?" Augie said. "A nine millimeter?"

Emmanuel looked surprised. "A Beretta thirty-eight. Why?"

"Just curious. I'm new to all this stuff. Hey, I really need to charge my phone. Do you mind? I'll set it on silent."

The man narrowed his eyes as he took a seat across from Augie. Finally he nodded toward an outlet. Augie plugged in the phone, and as he sat back down, the director said, "You seem remarkably cheerful under the circumstances. Do you see the names on these files?" He turned them toward Augie.

"Knox and Knox. All right, you have my attention."

"And you have mine, Doctor. You told the receptionist you were from Dallas. Are you not actually from Arlington?"

"Yes, but most people only know the big city—"

"And your profession?"

"Professor at Arlington Theological Seminary."

Emmanuel pulled a photocopy from the newer file and turned it right side up for Augie. "Do you agree that this is a copy of your passport?"

"Of course."

Emmanuel put the older file on top. "Who is Dr. Edsel Knox?"

Augie recoiled. "That—that would be my father, sir."

"I wondered. How is he?"

"How is he? Not well, actually. Why do you ask?"

"I once met him."

"You *met* him?"

Emmanuel sat back and told how he, a young officer on one of his first cases, had been assigned the matter of a tourist in Dr. Knox's group who had found an ancient coin near a historic site and refused to surrender it to authorities. "Your father was most meticulous and honest. Were it not for him, the tourist could have easily left the country without being found out."

"That sounds like my father, all right."

"Which make this all the more surprising," Emmanuel said.

"This?"

"Your coming under suspicion for the theft of an antiquity, not to mention two homicides."

"And yet I voluntarily came to you, eager to tell you everything. I ask only that you hear my account."

Emmanuel offered a closed-mouth smile. "For the sake of your father. But you must understand that you will not be released unless you are cleared of some very serious charges. As we speak, my department is investigating you through Interpol and our own government, with the assistance of the FBI. In the meantime, in homage to your father's character, I offer you the courtesy of listening. But you realize that anything you say that does not align with what our investigation reveals will put you in further jeopardy."

Augie could see how Emmanuel ascended to his position. "That's fair. But I must inform you that by offering me this courtesy, you risk hearing things about your own squad that will surprise you."

Emmanuel looked skeptical. "Before we begin, I am required to ask: Do you wish to be represented by legal counsel?"

"No."

"You have the right to change your mind about that at any time, but meanwhile everything you tell me is on the record and may be used against you."

"Understood."

"Now, are you legally entitled to possess the weapon we confiscated?"

"I am not. And technically, you didn't confiscate it. I surrendered it, having carried it only in the belief that my life was in mortal danger."

Colonel Emmanuel rested his elbows on the table and steepled his fingers. "Tell me what you are doing in Italy, from the moment you decided to come, through your arrival, the procurement of the weapon, whom you saw, and what your business was. I will not interrupt you."

Augie nodded, knowing Emmanuel was offering him the rope with which he could hang himself.

"First, a question," Augie said. "Your recording device. May I ask its capacity?"

"Twelve hours. Do you expect to keep me that long, Doctor?"

"Oh, no. But you will see why I asked. If I can just check my cell, I'll be ready."

Emmanuel hesitated but finally shrugged. Augie peeked at his phone.

Don't respond till download is complete in less than an hour. Can't BELIEVE what you get yourself into. Promise me every detail.

Biff's contraption had worked from more than fifty-five hundred miles away and could provide the hammer to smash both a dirty carabiniere and a black marketer posing as a respected businessman.

But it could also cost Augie his life.

Emmanuel looked directly into Augie's eyes and indicated the floor was his.

"I am in Italy to help a friend. This past Wednesday, May 7, I was about to oversee a final exam for one of my classes at the seminary when Roger Michaels texted me to call him immediately and added that he was desperate. I first met Roger . . ."

For over an hour, Emmanuel barely moved, staring at Augie, probably assessing his body language. Augie was doing the same. He could tell that the colonel knew both Malfees Trikoupis and Dimos Fokinos.

When Augie quoted Fokinos's claim that his highly placed contact in the Art Squad played his boss like a fiddle, the chief pressed his lips together. Was he defensive, or did he simply find it impossible to believe the account?

Emmanuel's expression changed again when Augie recounted the phone conversation between Trikoupis and Sardinia. Augie wondered if he was trying to fathom the possibility that Sardinia really was a criminal.

As Augie came to the end of his story, Emmanuel stood. He had Augie repeat a couple of anecdotes, then said, "And you sincerely expect Deputy Director Sardinia and Malfees Trikoupis to actually meet you tonight?"

"I do."

"Thank you, Dr. Knox. I must say I was intrigued, if not entirely convinced. Let me check on what my staff has learned from Interpol and the FBI. I will also have the recording evaluated, so if you wish to amend any of your claims, now is the time."

"I stand by every word."

"If you need anything while I'm away—something to drink or to use the facilities—I can have someone escort you. Otherwise—"

"I'll be fine," Augie said, as Emmanuel gathered up the files and his recorder. "But there is one more thing."

"Yes?"

"I can prove that Dimos Fokinos actually said that about his inside man here at the Art Squad."

"You can prove it?"

"I can also prove I accurately represented what Sardinia said on the phone to Mr. Trikoupis."

"To prove hearsay, Dr. Knox, you would have to get the principals to admit they said what you claim."

"No, I recorded both those conversations."

The man shook his head as if trying to make sense of what he had heard. "You *recorded* them?"

Augie reached for his phone. "Would you like to hear?"

Emmanuel slowly returned to his seat and turned on his own recorder again, as Augie found the download listed on his screen.

There were street sounds, then a car door.

Just you?

Who'd you expect? Someone has to stay with the goods.

You find Sofia?

I wasn't looking for her. Were you?

"You recognize the other voice, sir?"

Emmanuel nodded, but his expression didn't change until the conversation turned to business.

You still don't trust me.

Why should I? I just met you.

I'm the guy who's going to make you rich.

Wait a second, friend. You and Trikoupis wouldn't have even known about this if I hadn't been dragged into it.

Don't be silly. This is the world we run in. We'd have found out sooner or later, and whoever had the prize would be looking for buyers with deep pockets.

Fact is, Dr. Knox, you need me. Until I authenticate it, your priceless find is just a rumor.

Emmanuel paled when Fokinos described the Japanese art dealer who only pretended to have turned over all the stolen Italian artifacts he claimed he had bought innocently.

By the time the recording got to Fokinos implicating Sardinia, Emmanuel stared at Augie's phone as if it smelled. He massaged his eyes, fingers trembling. He folded his hands in his lap and rested his chin on his chest as he listened to the phone call between Trikoupis and Sardinia.

Finally Emmanuel stood. "If I didn't know better, Dr. Knox, I would say these recordings were manufactured."

"But you do know better, don't you?"

"I will soon," the colonel said. "Give me a few minutes. I'll be right back."

44

House to House

FIRST-CENTURY JERUSALEM

FROM PAUL'S MEMOIR

Few outside the Sanhedrin knew my role in the execution of Stephen. I did not refer to it as murder then, as I do now, because even witnessing it from close enough to hear the horrid blows and the ripping of the flesh could not diminish my conviction that we had carried out the judgment of God Himself.

I knew the commandments; I knew the sin of putting another god before the God. The Jesus followers, who had begun calling themselves the people of The Way, had had the audacity to elevate Jesus to the position of a Christ, the Messiah. And despite his demise, they had now revered

Stephen—who seemed able to conjure the same miracles, yet who also proved merely mortal in the end.

Now would they worship their leader, the Galilean fisherman Peter, who may not have had the silver tongue of Stephen but was convincing enough to persuade thousands to become followers of The Way? Or would they revere Peter's brother Andrew, or the other James among them, one of the brothers of Jesus? Perhaps the new favorite would be young John, who apparently everyone agreed had been Jesus' favorite.

It mattered not to me, for while I had undertaken this assignment convinced I was an agent of God, it also served to raise my stature with Annas and Caiaphas and thus most of the rest of the council. I say most, because while Nathanael was proud of me, some—very few, in truth—agreed with the ever-timid Gamaliel who felt the Sanhedrin had overreacted in stoning Stephen to death.

Gamaliel tried to reason with me, to discourage such acts in the future. His counsel fell on deaf ears. He had lost my respect. I felt no need of his approval, as I had for so many years.

However, the death of Stephen did not have its intended effect on the people of The Way. Continuing to insist that Jesus had resurrected from the dead and could not be termed a martyr, they began calling Stephen the first martyr to the cause of Christ. Rather than cowering in fear of the same fate for themselves, some even expressed envy for the fact that Stephen had been privileged—imagine!—to have been persecuted this way for the sake of Jesus.

Stephen's violent death seemed to have discouraged no one from stepping up to replace him—not the young men of the sect nor even their mothers. Within days of his burial, dozens of devout believers seemed determined to take his place. Their new leaders were bolder, their proclamations louder, their resolve more intense. Even worse, they now began traveling to distant lands to expand the influence of their lies and subversion.

The daily tasks and assignments I had handled for Nathanael for years since leaving school—challenging and educational as they had been—held little interest for me anymore. I took personally the failure of the Freedmen and the Sanhedrin to hinder the astonishing growth of The Way. I had gotten a taste of blood, and I rather liked it. This, I told myself, was not violence for violence's sake, but the purest form of justice ever enforced. If the only way to stop the spread of apostasy was to arrest, imprison, or kill these people, that was what I must do.

Before a week had passed, Caiaphas—no doubt with the encouragement of his father-in-law—visited Nathanael's office one afternoon and asked that I join them. When I arrived he informed Nathanael that he was reassigning me. "Nathanael," he said, "I know if this were left up to you, you would never let him go."

"That is true," Nathanael said. "But he has earned whatever station you see fit for him, and I gladly confer him to your service."

The high priest said he wanted me as his special assistant, with all the power and authority of his office. "I want The Way driven from Jerusalem. Their teaching is illegal. Their assembling is illegal. Making known their beliefs is illegal. You have proven yourself able and committed."

"That I am," I said, eager to get started. "I will proudly bear your authority, but as for your power, I will need resources. Men, weapons, horses."

"Present me with a manifest," Caiaphas said, "and consider it done."

I immediately went to my office and began a list of the men and supplies I would need. I took to Caiaphas my request for ten men with horses, ropes, whips, and chains. These, he said, would be at my disposal by dawn the next day. Until late that night in my office, I formed a plan of attack. I knew from The Freedmen the homes in which the people of The Way congregated before going out to spread their false doctrine.

I confess I wondered whether I would get the best of the temple guards, or soldiers who currently had no assignment. Imagine how pleased I was the next morning when a complement of brawny horsemen arrived. Every one appeared about twice my size, yet they well understood who was in charge.

The next day and for several weeks after, I led my men on daily raids. We would begin before sunrise and quietly surround a house owned by one of Jesus' wealthy followers. Then we would storm in from every entrance, me leading the way through the front. We denounced them in the name of

God, whipped any who tried to flee or retaliate, then bound their hands and tethered them to our horses to be dragged off to prison.

As I reflect on those days of fervency I recall being infused with what I considered righteous anger, a godly hatred of these opponents of the Scriptures. My team and I were merciless, swift, and brutal. Fear in the eyes of my prisoners or pleading on the parts of mothers to not separate them from their children had no effect on me.

I had been born for this, schooled and trained for this. I felt uniquely equipped for the task.

The entire council was aware of the many prisoners I had delivered, and many congratulated me. Only Gamaliel seemed to take issue with the effort. He asked to see me one day, and I was certain even he would reluctantly praise me. He admitted he was impressed by the efficiency of my venture, but he asked kindly, "Does the nature of the work ever give you pause? Does it never bother you?"

I could have easily made myself look better in his eyes by saying, "Of course, no one really enjoys having to confront people so forcefully." But the fact was I did enjoy it. I was not a tyrant to gain power for its own sake. I was enforcing the will of God. What could be a higher calling?

I said, "Nasi Gamaliel, I feel alive, fulfilled, as if I am living life to the fullest, defending and glorifying the name of the Lord."

He looked at me sadly and conceded, "If the high priest, or more accurately his father-in-law, wishes to drive these people from the City of David, they could not have chosen a better man for the job."

I thanked him most sincerely. Naïvely—I realize now—I took his words as the highest personal compliment he had ever paid me. My goal was to do anything I could contrary to the name of Jesus of Nazareth. I cast my votes for the many death sentences decreed in Israel and even in foreign cities.

Learning that many of the people of The Way had scattered into Judea and Samaria and spread their influence as far as Damascus, I went again to Caiaphas, breathing threats and murder against them. I asked for a letter of introduction to the synagogues of Damascus. "Any disciples of Jesus I find there, whether men or women, I will bring to Jerusalem in chains."

This seemed to please the high priest. "Damascus is outside Roman law," he said. "So you will encounter no restrictions."

When he supplied me with the letters, I was thrilled to see they were signed by both him and Annas. With my band of enforcers, I traveled about 135 miles north of Jerusalem to the city that had so captured my attention as a child. Was this the culmination of that deep attraction? In those days I had been unable to imagine what possible role that city could play in my adult life. I was about to find out.

On horseback for the better part of four days, we traveled the way of the Sea of Galilee, crossing the Jordan River by bridge a few miles north of the Dead Sea. My excitement *built as we neared Kaukab, about twelve miles south of the great walled city of Damascus. This was the stretch of road on which my father and I, heading south when I was thirteen, had encountered heat so fierce we wondered if we would be able to continue.*

45

Bait

Georgio Emmanuel returned to the secure room. He was laden with file folders, Roger Michaels's nine millimeter, a bulging greasy sack, and two large paper cups.

"I have lost my appetite, Dr. Knox. But we are both going to need nourishment. There is much to do before eight o'clock."

"Before eight o'clock?"

Emmanuel set everything on the table and opened the sack, handing Augie a heavy, meat-laden sandwich and a cup of espresso. He set his own meal in front of him, sat, and crossed himself before digging in.

"You're a man of faith?" Augie said.

"With a name like Emmanuel, how could I escape?"

Augie breathed a prayer of thanks. With his first bite he realized how fear had camouflaged his hunger. "Very grateful for this, Colonel."

"I owe you thanks too, Dr. Knox, but you understand you have given me both a lawman's dream and his nightmare. All the clues I should have picked up on for months have fallen into place for me. Just now—as I was collecting the results of the investigations, conducting a *poligrafo* analysis of my recording of you, and finding a permit for your firearm— it struck me that I long ago placed my full trust in a colleague I apparently never really knew. It is as if a friend had died."

"I'm sorry."

Emmanuel took a huge bite of his sandwich and spoke around the bulge in his cheek. "Learning can be painful, but we must embrace the lessons." He dragged a napkin across his mouth and gulped his coffee. "You, however, appear to be exactly who you say you are. Except for a couple of traffic tickets as a young man, the only blemish on your record would be illegal possession of a firearm in a foreign country. However, this permit now grants you permission to carry it here. Fortunately, Mr. Michaels had registered it."

Hmm. His but not the one he left for me.

"You're giving the pistol back to me?"

"You might need it."

"I might?"

"This evening at eight."

"You want me to go through with the meeting?"

Emmanuel slid a sheet across the table. "Dr. Knox, the recorder I used for our interview has what my technical people call *estrema fedeltà*—extreme fidelity. It analyzes every nuance of your voice, even your breathing, evaluating with amazing accuracy your *veridicità versus inganno*—truthfulness versus deception. You exhibited virtually no deceptiveness. The men you recorded, however, tested highly decep- tive. They lied to you and to each other. Either would eliminate the other for a bigger portion of the spoils."

"I guess that's no surprise, sir."

"Call me Georgio. And the surprise will be on them tonight."

"I am not skilled in these things."

The colonel offered a sad smile. "Coming here without counsel made that clear. But you will do fine. And Mr. Michaels and your fian- cée can play important roles too."

"If they show up."

"I am as certain they will be there as you were that Mr. Trikoupis would come. He has already booked a flight."

"But as I told you, neither of my friends has a phone. I can text Roger, but unless Sofia calls me . . ."

"Perhaps you'll be able get a few moments alone with them before the meeting."

"Georgio, what if Mr. Sardinia sees me here?"

"He is hardly ever in the office, but, yes, we should go now." Pull- ing a tiny walkie-talkie from his pocket, he said, "*Ho bisogno di un auto con autista all'ingresso posteriore, per favore,*" then turned back to Augie, explaining that he had just asked for a car and driver at the back entrance.

"Where are we going, sir?"

"Follow me." Emmanuel led Augie down the back stairs. "It's way past time to look at Klaudios's message to Mr. Michaels. I don't know who else on the planet could have avoided the temptation this long."

They emerged into the afternoon sun, and Emmanuel whispered, "Do not mention Sardinia in front of the driver." They sat in the back seat of the unmarked sedan, and Emmanuel introduced him to the oper- ative behind the wheel. "Please tell him how to get to the bank."

Augie did, but added quietly to Emmanuel, "I'm still not sure we should open another man's mail."

"I do not share your hesitation, Dr. Knox. My priority is to see that no one else dies because of what has caused all this, this, ah, *loschi*. I'm trying to think of the closest English word . . ."

"Skullduggery," the driver said.

"Yes!" Georgio said. "Dr. Knox, it's time we take custody of the treasure. The world deserves the right to examine such an antiquity. And the document itself deserves the protection of the Republic of Italy. You understand that you could realize a significant reward if your efforts result in our regaining possession of the memoir."

Augie chuckled. "Never considered that, but I wouldn't turn it down." *How much could it be?* Maybe he would be able to pay back his mother, or put a dent in Rajiv Patel's school bill, or even get Sofia's diamond out of hock.

On the way, Emmanuel quizzed Augie about his hotel suite and took copious notes.

At the bank they were admitted to the vault, but when Augie slid out the large metal box he shot Emmanuel a look. "Feels too light," he said, setting it on a table under a ceiling light. When he raised the lid the bottom of the box reflected his own image.

"I was told no one else had access to this," Augie said, feeling his face flush. "I'm going to demand that the woman who rented me the box—"

"Wait," Georgio said, holding up a hand. "Slow down."

"She has to answer for—"

"Are you listening, my friend? Please, sit."

Augie plopped into a wood chair.

"Dr. Knox, in my profession anger leads to haste, and haste is the enemy of logic. Think this through. We both know who was given access to this box. Now put it back in place and let me do my job."

"The one place I was certain would be safe . . ."

Emmanuel put a finger to his lips and led Augie into the lobby. "Who waited on you?"

"Tall, dark hair, red dress," Augie whispered.

Georgio approached the woman with a smile, showing his badge. "*Solo il controllo per assicurarsi che il mio popolo era dato accesso a ciò che avevano bisogno di.*"

"*Sì, Signore. I documenti erano in ordine e abbiamo accordato il vostro ufficiale completa cooperazione.*"

"*Mille Grazie.*"

"All right, I'm confused," Augie said as he followed Emmanuel out to the car.

"Just keep smiling," the colonel said. "I told her I was just checking to make sure my people were given access to what they needed. She said yes, that my officer's search warrant was in order, so she extended him every courtesy."

"So that's it?" Augie said as they climbed into the car. "Your guy steals my stuff and you smile and say thank you?"

"I merely confirmed what I suspected. Your problem now is not the missing items. We know who has those. The problem arises only if they lead him to the artifact. Then everyone else becomes unnecessary."

"Roger, Sofia, and me."

"Even Mr. Trikoupis."

"Doesn't Sardinia need him to market the parchments?"

"He needed him for instant cash. But if Sardinia has sole access to the *merce*, the merchandise, he can market it directly through the Tombaroli. That takes more time, but he no longer has to split the profits with anyone."

"So tonight's meeting is off."

"Not necessarily. Our *schema* was going to be that you three had been persuaded—either by Trikoupis's threats or by the promise of big payoffs—to lead them to the merchandise."

"But now Sardinia has no need of us."

"But every person he thinks could implicate him will be at that meeting."

Augie cocked his head. "So once everybody's there, he sends in someone to assassinate all of us."

"And probably has the Tombaroli stage it to look like a murder-suicide, yes," Emmanuel said. "Your friend Mr. Michaels has already been implicated in the other two killings. With Rome's carabinieri closing in, Roger kills everyone, then himself, and the memoir remains hidden."

"Until it starts showing up on the black market, in pieces."

"Now you're starting to think like a carabiniere."

"But, Georgio, does that mean we're going to the meeting tonight merely as bait?"

"Actually, yes, but let's talk more back at headquarters." Emmanuel used his walkie-talkie to speak to his assistant. When they got to the office and headed up the back staircase, he said, "Sardinia left word he is working in the field this evening and will not be back in the office until tomorrow. I asked my assistant to invite four colleagues to join me in the interrogation room at three o'clock and to be prepared to remain on duty until at least midnight."

"Will four be enough?"

"No. Each has staff to direct."

Emmanuel suddenly appeared older than his years, shoulders slumped, gait less steady.

"This going to be a tough meeting, Georgio?"

The colonel hesitated as someone delivered four folding chairs that, along with the table, left little space for anything else in the interrogation room. "I must tell these people the hard truth about someone they have admired and respected for years. Be prepared to play your recordings, so there will be no question."

Augie sat while Emmanuel riffled through his notes. "I will be praying for you, Georgio."

Emmanuel's voice was raspy. "Thank you *sinceramente. Molto significa.*"

The four Art Squad operatives seemed to arrive as one, three men in their middle to late thirties and a young woman who looked Sofia's age. All wore sober, dark suits and expectant looks.

Emmanuel said, "*Telefoni cellulari di largo per favore,*" and they turned off their cell phones. "*Grazie per essere venuti.*"

One said, "*Abbiamo una scelta?*" and all laughed, even Emmanuel.

He turned to Augie. "I thanked them for coming and he asked if they had a choice."

Augie struggled to understand the Italian as Emmanuel summarized the story. When Georgio mentioned Aldo Sardinia's name in the same sentence with Klaudios Giordano and Dimos Fokinos *omicidio,* Augie read disbelief, then anger, on the agents' faces. He knew his part of the meeting was coming when Emmanuel referred to *prove incontrovertibili.*

The recordings sealed Sardinia's fate. As the agents scribbled in black leather notebooks, they could not hide their shock. A friend, a superior, had in an instant been revealed as the perpetrator of a crime that mocked their very department—*Comando Carabinieri per la Tutela del Patrimonio Culturale*, the first special police force in the world dedicated to combating art and antiquities crimes.

When Emmanuel finally dismissed the operatives, they filed past Augie, each saying some variation of "*Grazie mille per il vostro aiuto.*" Georgio told him they were thanking him for his assistance.

When it was just the two of them, Emmanuel said, "You won't see any of us until you need to." He looked at his watch. "Three and a half hours. Will you be hungry beforehand?"

"I couldn't eat."

"Me either, my friend," Georgio said. "You ready to do your part?"

"Do we really have to be there? Can't I just say we will be, and then you and your people arrest whoever Sardinia sends to kill us?"

"That's the plan. We have to apprehend the hired gun before he gets to you, then make sure he tells Sardinia the job is done. We have to be very careful, because they'll likely have a signal, one word to say all is well and another to say all is not well. Once Sardinia is convinced you all have been eliminated, he'll relax and we'll be able to arrest him easily. If he gets wind of a setup, he'll disappear."

"Georgio, I don't like any of this. Roger and Sofia and I should have pretended to play along, dangling the Klaudios letter until Sardinia and Trikoupis incriminated themselves . . ."

"But now Aldo has the contents of your deposit box, so we need to change to Plan B. Right now we are bugging your suite and setting up surveillance in the rooms on either side of yours—"

"Those rooms are occupied."

"They may have been. But those guests have been moved because of a suspected water leak. By the time you and Sofia and Roger get to your suite, we will have everything in place. You need to trust me, Dr. Knox. All of you will be safe. In any case, you are the theologian. I am just a layman. But I know the verse about laying aside every weight and sin and running with patience."

"Hebrews 12," Augie said. "One of my favorites: '. . . looking unto Jesus, the author and finisher of our faith, who for the joy that was set before Him endured the cross, despising the shame, and has sat down at the right hand of the throne of God.'"

"Amen," Emmanuel said, and for the second time since Augie met him, he crossed himself.

In the remaining time, Augie prayed for courage, for Sofia's safety, and for Roger's soul. All this would be worth it if Sardinia and Sofia's father were brought to justice, and Roger came to faith.

46

Eternal Reversal

FIRST-CENTURY JUDEA
FROM PAUL'S MEMOIR

On our way to Damascus, my mind drifted back more than twenty years to the journey with my father when, coming the other way on this very same route, we felt we had been cast into a fiery furnace like Shadrach, Meshach, and Abednego.

My men and I covered a little more than thirty miles a day, and I enjoyed getting better acquainted with them. Some had looked upon me with suspicion at first. I overheard one tell another he'd never before been commanded by a "small, bookish man."

But somehow I had won them over. Having a few days off from rousting infidels from their homes, we laughed and talked during stops for meals and lodging. Devout Jews, these

men were not taken with strong drink or inappropriate rev-
elry. Many were family men. Our fun consisted of wrestling
and running races. I was no match for these younger men
except that none could outrun me. They teased that speed
was my best defense.

At our last rest stop before our scheduled arrival in
Damascus, I sensed the men were impatient for action. They
boasted among themselves about how vigorously they would
represent Jerusalem and the council, should we find subver-
sives in the temples at Damascus. In short, they were ready.

As we remounted I pointed into the distance where the
road rose to a slight ridge. "Damascus will appear on the
horizon as we clear that incline, but don't be misled. It will
seem we have nearly arrived, but the city is still almost half
a day's journey from there." I turned to be sure everyone was
astride his horse. "Let's move out!"

I had caught the troops' excitement and had to remind
myself to slow my mount as the sun reached its apex. As we
neared the crest, I called out, "Stay alert, gentlemen!" to be
sure they were watching for the wall surrounding Damascus,
the very one I climbed as a thirteen-year-old.

Suddenly we were struck by a light so bright it made my
horse rear and emit a piercing whinny. I held fast to the reins
as I slid from his back. I found myself several feet off the
ground, my full weight hanging from those leather straps. I
had just enough presence of mind to let go so I wouldn't pull
him over backward and kill him.

As I fell I heard the other horses and men cry out as they
too crashed to the ground. I hit hard and the breath rushed

from my lungs. I lay there, eyes shut tight, face pressed into the dirt. Even that did no good against the sudden brilliance that radiated not just from above but also from all around me.

I heard men struggling to their feet and trying to calm their steeds. I fought to move but was rigid from fear. Suddenly a loud voice implored in Hebrew, "Saul, Saul, why are you persecuting Me?"

Astounded I could find utterance, I moaned, "Who are you, Lord?"

"I am Jesus of Nazareth, whom you are persecuting."

In that instant my world changed. I had believed with my entire being that Jesus had been an impostor and now was dead. There was no time to wonder, to question, to make sense of what was happening. Jesus was speaking to me. The light was the light of God, and it permeated my soul.

I said, "What shall I do, Lord?"

"Rise and stand, for I have appeared to you to make you a minister and a witness both of the things which you have seen and of the things which I will yet reveal to you. I will deliver you from the Jewish people, as well as from the Gentiles, to whom I now send you, to open their eyes, in order to turn them from darkness to light, and from the power of Satan to God, that they may receive forgiveness of sins. Now go into Damascus, and there you will be told all things which are appointed for you to do."

I struggled to my feet as the men came to my aid. "Did you see that?" I said.

"Yes! We were scared to death. The horses are still spooked."

"Did you hear the voice?"

"Yes, but we saw no one!"

"It spoke to me, the voice of God. I must get to Damascus with all haste, but I cannot see!"

Two led me by the hand and helped me remount my horse. "Hold on tight," one said. "We will lead him slowly."

Several hours later the sounds of the city told me we had arrived.

"Where should we take you, Saul?"

"To the home of Judas on the street called Straight."

For three days I stayed in Judas' home, but I had no hunger or thirst and remained blind. All I could do was pray, yet I hardly knew where to begin. It was true. Jesus was alive, and I had been the chief among sinners. Suddenly, in my mind's eye a man named Ananias stood before me, healing my eyes.

Soon a man by that name arrived and asked for me. I learned later he was devout according to the Law, having a good reputation among all the Jews in Damascus. He told me God had spoken to him too. "When He called my name, I said, 'Here I am, Lord.' And the Lord said, 'Arise and go to the street called Straight, and inquire at the house of Judas for one called Saul of Tarsus.'

"I said, 'Lord, I have heard from many about how much harm this Saul has done to Your saints in Jerusalem. And here he has authority from the chief priests to capture all *who call on Your name.' But the Lord said, 'Go, for he is a chosen vessel of Mine to bear My name before Gentiles, kings, and the children of Israel. For I will show him how many things he must suffer for My name's sake.'"*

Ananias laid his hands on me and said, "Brother Saul, the Lord Jesus, who appeared to you on the road, has sent me to restore your sight and fill you with the Holy Spirit."

Something like scales fell from my eyes, and I could see Ananias. He said, "The God of our fathers has chosen you that you should know His will, and see the Just One, and hear His voice. For you will be His witness to all men of what you have seen and heard. Arise and be baptized, and wash away your sins, calling on the name of the Lord."

As soon as I began to eat again, I was strengthened. I spent several days with the believers at Damascus, who immediately pressed me into preaching in the synagogues that Jesus is the Son of God. All who heard were amazed and said, "Is this not he who destroyed those who called on this name in Jerusalem, and has come here for that purpose, so that he might bring them bound to the chief priests?"

But I increased all the more in strength and confounded the Jews in Damascus, proving that Jesus is the Christ, the Messiah.

Many days later I got word of a plot by some Jews to kill me. Word had apparently gotten back to Jerusalem about my defection, and the orthodox in Damascus had been given permission to lie in wait for me. Hearing this, the people of The Way spirited me to the top of the wall one night. I remembered from my childhood that there was no way to scale the outsides of those walls. But they put me in a large basket and lowered me to the ground with ropes, and I escaped. I would never again complain of my small stature!

47

Beyond Understanding

ANY LINGERING DOUBT ABOUT Emmanuel's credibility was erased when he returned Roger's fully loaded nine millimeter along with a temporary license to conceal and carry it. Augie gave his secure cellphone number to Emmanuel, entrusting his life and those of his fiancée and his best friend into the man's hands.

They agreed Augie would take a cab to the Terrazzo, where he would remain in the lobby, visible enough for Trikoupis to spot him. He sat texting Roger, urging him to come, adding, "praying Sof will 2."

Roger shot back, "if she does, I will."

"holding u 2 that; stand by."

Finally Augie's phone rang, showing a local number he didn't recognize.

"You going through with this?" Sofia said.

"How soon can you get here?"

"I'm close, but I'm not coming."

"Just hear me out for two minutes before you decide."

"I've already decided."

"Nobody in the world loves you the way I do, and you can't give me two minutes?"

After a long silence, she said, "Two minutes."

Augie recounted everything that had happened to him, from learning that Emmanuel had met his father, to the recordings, the gun, the visit to the bank, and even Georgio quoting Scripture. He assured her the place would be crawling with undercover carabinieri.

"That took longer than two minutes," she said, "but it *is* incredible. Can't say it'll be easy for me, being there when my father realizes he's been had."

Augie immediately texted Roger, "Sof here soon; come now."

Roger arrived first and sat next to Augie, arms folded, beret pulled low, as he listened to Augie's summary. When Sofia got there, Augie reminded them that Plan A—appearing to play along before turning the tables— had been scrapped due to the safe-deposit box theft.

"Now I guess Plan B stands for bait," Roger muttered. "But whatever it takes . . ."

Augie's phone vibrated with a text from Emmanuel. "They in?"

"Look at this," Augie said, showing Sofia and Roger the message from the head of the Art Squad. "You think we're not being watched over?"

"Tell him we're in but nervous," Roger said.

Augie tapped it in and Emmanuel responded, "So am I. *Filippesi* 4:6–7."

"Philippians," Sofia said. "You have a Bible app on that thing?"

"Don't need one for those verses, babe. You'll recognize 'em: 'Be anxious for nothing, but in everything by prayer and supplication, with thanksgiving, let your requests be made known to God; and the peace of God, which surpasses all understanding, will guard your hearts and minds through Christ Jesus.'"

"Well, I'll be," Roger said. "Top cop sending Bible verses? That's got to be a first."

Sofia put a hand to her trembling lips and whispered through her fingers. "Peace right now *would* surpass all understanding."

Roger puffed his cheeks and exhaled loudly. "I heard that."

Augie said, "We're claiming that promise." He texted back, "u missed your calling, reverend."

"As soon as Trikoupis arrives, take him to your suite. Whoever Sardinia sent is likely watching, waiting till you're all up there. Don't worry, we won't let him get to you."

The three sat with their heads inches apart. "Only person we have to playact for is your dad," Augie said.

"He's going to prison for a long time, Sofia," Roger said. "You okay with that?"

"Guess who taught me that decisions have consequences?"

"I've heard that before!"

The three jerked around to see Trikoupis approaching. He carried a high-end leather attaché. *Just the right size*, Augie thought. Trikoupis beamed as he sat, throwing an arm around Sofia, who ignored him. "Mr. Michaels?" he said.

"That would be me," Roger said, hesitating before shaking Malfees's outstretched hand.

"I wouldn't have recognized you."

"Sort of the point," Roger said.

"Not after this evening! You'll no longer be on the run. And all of you will be set for life."

"Yeah, boy," Roger said.

The man removed his arm from Sofia's shoulder and patted his case. "The goods go in, the cashier's checks come out."

"Now we're talkin'," Augie said, forcing a smile.

Trikoupis raised a fist at him. "My boy."

Augie led the way to the elevator. When they entered the suite, Sofia's father looked at his watch and whispered, "We have fifteen minutes. He's never late."

Augie hung back to triple lock the door.

"Expecting someone other than my partner?" Trikoupis said.

Augie shook his head. "Can't be too careful."

"Don't be so jumpy. Meanwhile, how about a sneak preview?"

"I prefer to wait—"

"Just the first page then?"

Some partner. Didn't even tell you he'd stolen that.

"No."

Malfees Trikoupis scowled. "Enjoy imagining yourself in charge, Augie. It'll soon be time for you to deliver."

"Oh, I plan to. As you made clear, I have no choice."

Trikoupis grinned and patted Augie's shoulder.

At 7:55 p.m., as Augie and his future father-in-law joined Sofia and Roger at the table, his phone vibrated. A text from Emmanuel:

"Revert to Plan A! Acknowledge, please."

What was this? Now they *were* to keep playing along?

Augie texted back, "ok, what's up?"

"A.S. here. Careful."

Augie heard a knock at the door, and when Trikoupis rushed to open it, Augie quickly showed Sofia and Roger his phone.

Sofia's father breezed in with Sardinia. "Allow me to make the introductions!"

"No need," Sardinia said, smiling. "I met your beautiful daughter this morning—apologies again for our misunderstanding, and my sympathy on the loss of your friend."

"Thank you."

"And of course I know Mr. Michaels, though he looks a bit different from the last time I saw him. You'll be glad to hear the charade ends tonight."

It sure does, Augie thought.

"And you must be Dr. Knox! How nice to meet you."

Augie responded by pointing to the table. Everyone took a seat, Trikoupis to Sardinia's left, then Sofia, Augie facing Sardinia, and Roger on Sardinia's right.

"I like to get right down to business," Sardinia began. "Mr. Trikoupis is prepared to take immediate delivery and distribute compensation so we can all shake hands and be on our way. Miss Trikoupis, besides your two million euros, as a show of good faith I extricated you from an uncomfortable situation this morning as a courtesy to your father and in consideration of your fiancé having informed him of this find. Dr. Knox, I assume the finder's fee of one percent of total profits over the life of the antiquity is acceptable."

"It sure is."

"Well put. And Mr. Michaels, I assume you're aware that your two million is in lieu of my arresting you and tying you up in our judicial system for the rest of your natural life."

Roger nodded. "Getting my life back is almost as valuable to me as the money."

That brought a laugh from Sardinia. "*Almost!* Very good! Now then, if there's nothing else . . ."

Augie's phone vibrated and he peeked at another text from Emmanuel. "Hearing everything. Direct him to your 'representative' at the address below, but not until he gives you Giordano's letter."

"Dr. Knox?" Sardinia said, smiling. "We have agreed on terms. The ball, as they say, is in your court."

"I've got a problem," Augie said.

Sardinia's smile disappeared. "You understand negotiations are over."

"There's been a wrinkle."

"This is a straightforward deal with a lot of money going one direction. If this is some ploy—"

"Your plan was to go around us for the manuscript."

"I don't know what you—"

"You stole Klaudios Giordano's letter, hoping it would lead you to the original document and make us unnecessary."

"You're accusing me of—"

"You're the only person who had knowledge of both what it was and where it was, and the authority to take custody of it. But the letter must not have told you what you needed to know, did it? Because if it had, we wouldn't be here. We would have been as expendable as Klaudios and Dimos."

"What is it you want, Dr. Knox?"

"You said negotiations were over, Mr. Sardinia. But they're not, are they? I want the letter before I give you and Mr. Trikoupis what you came for."

Sardinia appeared to be thinking. "Two people died over this, so naturally you want to protect yourselves. I respect that. The letter is in my pocket. You're right that it proved meaningless to us, and it is a relief to know that you were able to decipher it. I am willing to surrender it as part of the transaction."

"And what guarantees do we have that we won't meet the same fate as the others?"

"You will have Mr. Trikoupis's money, Dr. Knox."

"Which guarantees our safety how?"

"It ensures your silence. What credibility would you have if you tried to expose me after being paid for your roles in the theft? Dr. Knox, my appreciation for you has risen. I assumed you were just a naïve professor dragged into this by a petrified friend."

"And now all you need to satisfy me is the return of a letter."

"At least tell me how you made sense of it, Doctor. It stymied several experts in code breaking. They gave me nothing more than I knew from a cursory glance. It's the first two lines from the first verse of an old Catholic hymn based on a twelfth-century poem by St. Bernard."

Augie tried to appear as if he had known this all along, and that it had told him where Klaudios had stashed the manuscript. "When I have it in my hands again, I'll tell you what I know."

Sardinia pulled an envelope from an inside jacket pocket and slid it across the table. Augie extracted the single sheet of white paper, on which was written in lavender marker:

> *Daily, daily sing to Mary,*
> *Sing, my soul, her praises due.*

"We know Klaudios traveled to Greece," Sardinia said. "But we had no idea where he might have hidden the memoir. There are so many potential clues in even a short biography of Bernard that we'd have been months trying to make sense of it. So humor me. How did this lead you to the manuscript?"

"I'm sorry. Did I say it did?"

"Something must have."

Roger said, "Maybe the old man just told me where to find it, and this was a red herring in case it ever fell into your hands."

"Clever, Mr. Michaels."

"Can we not lose sight of the fact that Klaudios was a friend of mine?" Roger said.

"Mine too," Augie said.

"His death is on you, sir," Roger said.

Sardinia appeared to suppress a smile. "Perhaps your check will assuage your grief."

"What about his family's?"

"Feel free to share your largesse with them."

Roger turned away, looking disgusted.

"Okay, Dr. Knox, can we get on with this?"

"You'd love to get rid of all of us, wouldn't you, Aldo? Mr. Trikoupis included."

"You have no idea."

"It's written all over you."

Malfees Trikoupis did a double take. "He'd be hard pressed to do without me."

"Once he has the goods, he doesn't even need you, sir," Augie said.

Sofia shook her head. "So it's okay with you, Dad, if he eliminates the three of us, me included, as long as he keeps you around?"

"Oh, honey, you know—"

"Yeah, Dad, I do."

Augie peeked again at his vibrating phone. Emmanuel: "Wrap this up."

"Just tell me what you gleaned from it, Doctor. I don't like puzzles I can't solve."

The word *puzzles* gave Augie an idea.

"No idea," Augie said. "This is the first I've seen Klaudios's letter."

"All right, fine! Let's have the manuscript and you all get paid."

"Were you under the impression I had it here?"

"To tell you the truth, I hoped I'd find it at the bank. So where is it?"

Augie jotted the address Emmanuel had texted him and handed it to Sardinia. "My representative is waiting for you."

"This is next door. What, the cafe? You're telling me someone's sitting at a cafe with a priceless antiquity? You *are* new to this game. All right, Malfees stays here, I call him when I have it in hand, and then he distributes the checks."

Augie laughed. "I'm not *that* new! What keeps you from disappearing and leaving Mr. T. holding the bag?"

"Ridiculous," Malfees said. "We're partners. He'd have to kill us all if he tried that." A look came over him, as if he finally understood Sardinia's plan. "We will all go."

As they headed to the elevator, Augie got another text from Emmanuel telling him where to send Sardinia. *Then get as far away from him and Trikoupis as possible.*

The cafe wasn't more than a hundred feet from the hotel. Whoever Emmanuel and his people worked with had succeeded in leaving empty an area near the bathrooms and the office. The five of them took a booth there and told the waitress to give them a few minutes.

Sardinia said, "Now what?"

"Knock twice on the manager's door," Augie said, nodding toward it.

"Classy. Hope he's got the thing packaged properly."

"You should worry more about whether our checks are good."

Sardinia approached the office, and when he raised his hand to knock, Augie said calmly, "Sofia, Roger, follow me, right now."

They slid out of the booth and headed for the entrance. Trikoupis hollered, "Where are you going? Aldo! It's a setup!"

Augie pushed open the door and held it for Sofia and Roger as he looked back. The manager's door burst open and Art Squad agents poured out. Some surrounded Trikoupis, still frozen in the booth, as Sardinia bolted toward a rear entrance, pulling his gun. He sprinted around to the front of the cafe and met Roger and Sofia as they emerged. Leveling his sidearm, he ordered them to kneel.

Augie watched from the door as a dozen more agents swarmed from every direction. "Everybody stand down!" Sardinia screamed. "I've got them! Hold your fire!" While he couldn't know he'd convicted himself on Augie's recordings and in the suite that had been wired for sound, he had to know he was almost out of options.

As Augie stepped out behind the kneeling pair, his hand on the butt of the nine millimeter at his back, Sardinia said, "You too, Knox! On the ground!" When Sardinia cocked his weapon, Roger and Sofia lunged at him. He took aim at Sofia, but Augie was too fast. From less than ten feet away the high velocity hollow point slug slammed into Sardinia's shoulder, and the back of his head hit the pavement.

In an instant carabinieri were atop him while others checked on Sofia and Roger and Augie. "We're trained not to shoot into a crowd," one said.

"Well, I wasn't trained, and he was about to kill my fiancée."

Augie felt a hand on his shoulder and turned to see Emmanuel. "Going to have to confiscate that Smith & Wesson for a while," he said.

"I've got a permit."

"Do you now?"

Sofia scrambled to Augie and wrapped her arms around his waist. "You hurt?" she said.

"No, I'm great."

"Me too, thanks to you."

Augie turned back to Georgio. "I'd hug you, Colonel, but I've got priorities."

"And taste. I've heard a lot about you, ma'am."

"As I have about you."

Roger, who had stayed on his hands and knees until Sardinia had been secured, joined them. "Looks like he'll survive to face charges."

"I don't expect it'll be much of a trial," Emmanuel said. "We've never given the prosecution as much as we've got on him and Trikoupis. We even found the original first page and the photocopies in the trunk of Sardinia's car. I almost feel sorry for him."

"Feel sorry for Augie," Roger said. "I drag him halfway around the world to save my tail and we're no closer to finding the original memoir than the day Klaudios hid it."

"Rest assured," Emmanuel said, "the Art Squad will never quit searching. And in the meantime, the first page can be authenticated and you can testify that the photocopies are of the real manuscript."

"No, no," Augie said. "Klaudios wasn't pulling Roger's chain. He wants us to find the memoir. The clues are in the letter. We just have to figure it out." He looked at his watch. "It's early afternoon in the States. I'm going to call somebody who might be able to help."

Augie dialed his father's hospital room.

48

The Unspeakable Gift

FIRST-CENTURY ROME
FROM PAUL'S MEMOIR

Though my ministry since the time of my miraculous conversion has consisted of preaching and writing in defense of the gospel of Christ, I confess it is difficult for me to put into words how I felt at that time. In the years since hearing the voice of Christ, I have daily strived to preach the gospel to all men, primarily Gentiles—for this is what I was called to do from the moment I became a believer. But in all that time, I have never witnessed another conversion like my own.

I know it is the Holy Spirit who is responsible, but I feel privileged to have played a part in enlightening many men and women. Yet to convert my own mind and heart,

God used none of the methods I have employed to per-suade people. I was dead in my trespasses and sins, so deeply entrenched that not only did I not see them as such, but I also thoroughly believed in my own righteousness. Though to that time I had never succeeded in developing the kind of relationship with God I had longed for, I could not have been more learned and devout and strict in obeying the laws of God.

It took a miracle to make the old things pass away and for all things to become new. There could have been no talking me into this. I went from a life of service to God characterized by persecuting people who believed Jesus was the Messiah, to being convinced by Christ Himself that He was indeed the Son of God. I traveled to Damascus as one person and arrived there as someone else entirely.

If it stunned and amazed people who knew me by repu-tation, imagine what it was like for me to barge into a syna-gogue one day to drag out the believers in Jesus, and the next day go there to proclaim that He was the Messiah.

When threats upon my life drove me from Damascus, I could not go back to my home. If I was a marked man in Damascus, I was a dead man in Jerusalem. It would have been a thrill to steal back there one night and inform the original disciples of Jesus that I had become one of them.

But why would they believe me? Even when I tried this, three years later, they were skeptical. I had to have others speak in my defense and then spend months earning their trust. And rightly so.

In the meantime, I realized God had used the threat

on my life to send me to Arabia, where He could best reveal His Son. During nearly three years there—which, for the first and only time I will reveal in detail following these thoughts—God Himself impressed upon me all the truths that would characterize my ministry. At one point while I was alone, meditating and enjoying that sweet fellowship with God the patriarchs had enjoyed—which had so eluded me when I was a zealous cleric—I was afforded a singular privilege so overwhelming that I dare not describe its details. All I will say is that I was supernaturally transported into the third heaven where I heard things I dare not utter.

I have come to believe that this miraculous journey was bestowed upon me because God, in His infinite wisdom, knew the trials I would later endure for His sake. He had called me to a life of endless work and self-sacrifice I might not have been able to survive, but for the memory of that gift.

I have often been persecuted and will ultimately give my life for the cause of Christ. Somehow God was preparing me for all this by a unique manifestation. I took with me a knowledge of the heavenlies that gave me confidence and assurance that what I was teaching was true and that I would return to that matchless realm when my days on earth ended.

I returned briefly to Damascus before finally returning to Jerusalem to meet with Peter for fifteen days. I saw none of the other apostles except James, the Lord's brother. Afterward I ministered in Syria and Cilicia. For years I was unknown by face to the churches of Judea which were in

Christ. They heard, "He who formerly persecuted us now preaches the faith which he once tried to destroy." And they praised God for my testimony.

Eventually Barnabas took me to the apostles and declared to them that I had seen the Lord and that He had spoken to me, and that I had preached fervently at Damascus in the name of Jesus. Finally I was able to minister with the disciples, speaking boldly in the name of the Lord Jesus and disputing the Hellenists, another faction of Jews who attempted to kill me. The brethren sent me to Tarsus again, and soon the churches throughout all Judea, Galilee, and Samaria walked in the fear of the Lord and in the comfort of the Holy Spirit.

The same zeal I had brought to my former life I now dedicated to the gospel of Christ, which I determined to proclaim for as long as the Lord Himself gave me breath. I am eager to recite here many details I have only summarized in many letters to the churches.

49

Solving the Riddle

"AUGUST!" HIS MOTHER SAID. "Edsel, it's Augustine!"

"I had an inkling when you shouted his name, Marie."

"Here, you can hold it yourself. Say hi!"

"Your mother's going to tell me every word to say, Augustine."

"Be nice, Dad. She's just excited."

"Don't I know it."

Augie was stunned to hear his father sounding much better. He seemed to be working to make each word understood, but he was making sense. "How're you feeling, Dad?"

"Like I've been in a coma. How's Rome? Have you seen Michaels?"

"Yes, I told you I was with him. Listen, Dad, are you up for a puzzle?"

"I'd love to do a crossword or an anagram again, but I can't hold a pen."

"A friend of mine hid something for Roger and me to find, and he left us a clue we can't figure out. Let Mom listen in and she can write this down for you." Augie heard his mother rustling to find pen and paper.

Augie described the plain white sheet and lavender ink, and then read the handwritten couplet. "It's from a poem from the—"

"I know," his father said. "St. Bernard in the 1100s. The thing's been made into a Catholic hymn."

Edsel Knox's prodigious mind never ceased to amaze Augie.

"Could be something simple if the author is the key," his father said. "He was known as Bernard of Clairvaux. French. He was an abbot, 'a doctor of the church' they called him at one point. He judged pope candidates once. Considered Pope Eugenius his best friend. Kind of a friend to Protestants now, because he was skeptical of the Immaculate Conception of Mary and an early proponent of justification. That help at all?"

"I'm scribbling, Dad. I don't know. Somehow we've got to narrow this down."

"I'll work on it."

"I appreciate it. You need a goal, something to shoot for? I'm going to ask Sofia to marry me in Texas in August."

"That's not the way these things go, Augustine. Her father will be paying for the wedding, so you just show up, I assume in Greece."

"But if we have it in Texas, I'd love to have you there."

"Who cares if I'm there?"

"I just told you who cares."

TUESDAY, MAY 13

The scandal exploded in the Italian press and swept the globe by late morning. Sofia's father's involvement seemed to shock all of Greece, and the prosecution laughed off his lawyer's attempt to plea bargain in exchange for testifying against Aldo Sardinia. The chief prosecutor told Emmanuel, "*Se avessi qualsiasi ulteriori prove contro Mr Sardinia, mi sentirei colpevole per l'eccesso*." ["If I had any more evidence against Mr. Sardinia, I would feel guilty about overkill."]

Sofia rushed home to be with her mother, who was desperate to defend herself against the vultures already circling their business. Augie had driven her to the airport at dawn and offered to fly with her, but Sofia insisted he stay and work with Emmanuel and Roger until they found Paul's memoir.

"Does your mother believe the charges, Sofia? Or will your dad convince her he was framed?"

"Too late for that. The first thing she said was, 'It's true, isn't it?' She told me she knew his reputation would come crashing down someday, because she was once in charge of his books."

Georgio Emmanuel said Malfees would wind up in an Italian prison. If that happened, Augie hoped to persuade Mrs. Trikoupis to move to the United States with her daughter, but all in good time.

Roger immediately moved back to his apartment and began letting his hair and beard grow again. He broadcast online notices to travel companies, letting them know he was back in business. The press hounded him for interviews, few of which he turned down.

Augie phoned Les Moore to let him know he would be at least a few days late for his summer-school assignment, expecting a threat or at least a lecture. But Les said, "You're all over the news here. It's as if you're our own Indiana Jones. Don't come back without the memoir!"

Augie laughed. "It won't likely ever leave Italy again, but I'll be back as soon as I can."

Augie talked to his parents at least once a day, careful not to push but eager to know whether his dad had made any progress on the puzzle. Meanwhile Augie worked with five analysts assigned to Emmanuel's office. They had been poring over Giordano's letter and generating lists of potential target cities suggested by every detail they could uncover about St. Bernard of Clairvaux.

Despite the colonel injecting himself into the effort, they had accomplished little. Italians were already clamoring for recovery of the artifact, and guesses to its nature ranged from the Holy Grail to the Ark of the Covenant.

FRIDAY, MAY 16, 10:05 A.M.

Colonel Emmanuel was giving a pep talk to Augie and the other analysts, urging them to concentrate on Greece, "because despite all the other possibilities raised by the Bernard connection, one thing we know for sure is that Giordano flew there and back the day after the heist."

Augie had forgotten to silence his phone, so when it rang he stepped into the hall.

"Mom, what time is it there?"

"Three in the morning," she said, "but your father insists on talking to you. He made me turn on the light and find my notes. He ignored the poem and kept asking about my other scribbles."

"Let me talk to Augustine!"

"All right, Edsel. Calm yourself. Here."

"Philippi," Augie's father said. "That's where you're going to find what you're looking for."

"How in the world did you figure that out?"

"The guy who wrote this, where's he from?"

"Here. He's Italian."

"Yet he wrote this in English. That's important. You said he wrote it in colored ink. Think that through and concentrate on the first two words, and you'll see it works only in English. Then it'll dawn on you."

"Just tell me, Dad. I've been working on this for days."

"Don't worry, you'll get it." *Click*.

Augie rushed back into Emmanuel's office. "Excuse me, Colonel, but forget the author. Focus on the fact that Klaudios wrote this in English and in colored ink. We're supposed to get Philippi out of that."

"Where in Philippi?"

"It's supposed to be obvious, but I have no idea."

A young woman at a laptop spoke as if thinking aloud. "Color. Lavender. Purple."

"That's it!" Augie shouted, smacking his head with both hands. "Give me an anagram for *Daily* . . ."

Georgio was the first to respond. "Lydia!"

Augie dropped into a chair. "The Apostle Paul met Lydia of Thyatira, the seller of purple-dyed cloth, at a riverside in Philippi. She became the first European and the first female convert to Christianity."

Georgio dismissed the others and told Augie, "If we can connect Klaudios to Philippi, we'll find the manuscript."

"Roger knew him better," Augie said, punching in his number.

As soon as Augie told him of his father's solution to the mystery, Roger said, "I know right where we're going to find the memoir. Remember that beautiful outdoor chapel in Philippi, with the little brook and the Baptistery of St. Lydia?"

"Sure."

"And the gorgeous little Greek Orthodox Church of St. Lydia on the grounds there—all kinds of original art on the walls?"

"Been there many times."

"Ever seen that wiry little guy, looks like he's two hundred years old, who hands out pamphlets in there?"

"Yeah, but he hardly says anything."

"That's him. You ready for this? He's some distant relative of Klaudios."

"Get out! I thought Klaudios's whole family was Catholic."

"I'm telling you, they squabble like brothers, but they're related. We find that guy—I'm trying to remember his name, it's got a z in it—and I guarantee we find the memoir."

"Tell Roger we'll pick him up," Georgio said. "We're going to pay a visit to Klaudios's widow, then the three of us will fly to Philippi."

Somehow Emmanuel talked his superiors into the use of a private jet and also put someone to work determining an appropriate reward for the two men responsible if Italy were to recover the most prized antiquity in history.

Just before noon, Mrs. Giordano confirmed that Yuri Zodiates, a caretaker at the Church of St. Lydia in Philippi, was Klaudios's uncle. "Most of the family shunned him, but Klaudios enjoyed him and saw him whenever he traveled to Philippi. You will find that he also does not believe Klaudios would ever steal."

On the way to the airport, Emmanuel said, "I didn't want to spoil her image of her husband. Down deep she must know. Still, Klaudios should have been charged, not murdered."

"Philippi is less than 150 kilometers from Thessaloniki," Augie said. "I'd hate to leave Sofia out of this when she's so close. No idea whether she'd leave her mother for a while . . ."

"It's all right with me," Georgio said. "She can pick us up at the airstrip in Alexandros and save us a few euros. She deserves to come."

A couple of hours later the three men greeted Sofia and followed her to a late-model Mercedes four-door.

As soon as they were on the road, headed toward the foot of Mount Orbelos, Georgio said, "*L'ironia non è perso su di me.*"

"No fair," Augie said. "Speak English."

Roger said, "He told her the irony was not lost on him. I'll bet we're closing the loop on all of this in Trikoupis's own car."

"It's true," Sofia said.

When they arrived and walked past the Baptistery of St. Lydia on their way to the church, they passed a busload of tourists leaving the outdoor chapel. Augie said, "I'll be right there," and stopped to examine trinkets offered by an elderly matron. He gave her three euros for an ichthus ring no thicker than a wire, then hurried to catch up.

The others were waiting at the stairs leading to a triple-arched entryway. They filed into the narthex, which featured a painting of *Hagios Paulos* (Saint Paul) holding that very church in one hand and a white Bible in the other. Next to a marble cabinet, which held candles for sale, sat a tiny priest in all black. He had tied back the long, straggly hair that protruded from a chimney pot-style hat, and he sported an untrimmed patchy white beard. He sat so still that he could have been a carving.

Roger knelt before him. "Remember me, Yuri?"

The old man blinked. "The voice," he breathed.

"Yes! You remember my voice! Imagine me with my bushy gray beard."

Finally Yuri focused and smiled. "Klaudios said you would come," he managed, crossing himself right to left. "Rest his soul. I will need help getting downstairs."

Yuri accepted Roger's outstretched hand and slowly pulled himself upright. The four followed him down a narrow staircase to a small office where he unlocked a cabinet to reveal a rough-hewn wooden box measuring about twenty-four by twenty inches. The initials *RM* had been penned atop it in lavender ink.

"Got to be sure this is it before we haul it out of here," Emmanuel said. "Mr. Zodiates, do you have a screwdriver or a hammer?"

Yuri rummaged through an old metal desk and found an oversize pair of scissors.

Roger hefted the box from the cabinet, and Emmanuel carefully used the scissors to work at the top pieces of wood. When he finally broke through, he gingerly lifted out the bubble-wrapped stack of about five hundred sheets of ancient parchment.

"Please," Augie said, "don't anyone touch them."

As if on cue, everyone pulled out their cell phones and began shooting pictures, even the old priest.

Finally Georgio said, "This isn't standard operating procedure, but shouldn't someone pray?"

The five of them held hands and Augie said, "Father, we are overcome. We feel unworthy, yet blessed beyond measure. When we think of the man who penned these pages and what he endured for Your sake, we are reminded of what Your Son endured for us. We say with the Apostle Paul himself, who wrote to the believers in this very city: 'Have this mind among yourselves, which is yours in Christ Jesus, who, though He was in the form of God, did not count equality with God a thing to be grasped, but made Himself nothing, taking the form of a servant, being born in the likeness of men.

"'And being found in human form, He humbled Himself by becoming obedient to the point of death, even death on a cross. Therefore God has highly exalted Him and bestowed on Him the name that is above every name, so that at the name of Jesus every knee should bow, in heaven and on earth and under the earth, and every tongue confess that Jesus Christ is Lord, to the glory of God the Father.'

"Thank You in the name of Jesus the Christ, our Lord and our Redeemer. Amen."

As they made their way back to the car, Roger—tears streaming— carried the box. On the flight back Georgio used a satellite phone to announce to his superiors the procurement of the memoir. They arranged a press conference for the following morning. There Roger officially presented to Italy the most valuable antiquity ever discovered.

Roger and Augie received checks for two hundred fifty thousand euros each. "Depending on how soon you cash this," Roger told Augie, "it should net you somewhere between three hundred thirty and three hundred fifty thousand dollars."

50

The Spectacle

FIRST-CENTURY ROME

BY LATE SPRING LUKE had succeeded at both his most glorious assignment—helping Paul complete his personal memoir—and his most odious: keeping his dearest friend alive only so he could be put to death.

As Luke had pored over the hundreds of pages covering many events he had personally witnessed, he discovered insights that continued to amaze him. His friend was the most cogent thinker he had ever met. Paul had a way of ferreting truth from every anecdote. And whatever God had taught him, especially during the three years of solitude following his conversion, manifested itself in ideas easily understood by any reader.

That was why Luke insisted—much to Paul's dismay—that every word of the memoir, even the very last pages that brought the story fully up to date, be written in Paul's own hand. The old man insisted that no one would care. "They will know these are my thoughts and that you, my friend, served as my amanuensis at the end."

"I'm not going to do it," Luke said. "This is an important document the brethren will cherish all the more because it is your own."

"But my hand is unsteady, my writing sloppy!"

"All the more meaningful and unquestionably authentic."

And so Luke lugged sections of the manuscript back and forth with him every night. He had additions and deletions to suggest, but the actual writing was done by the old evangelist himself. Luke interviewed Paul, urging him to write every detail he could remember from his earliest days with Jesus' disciples.

When it was finished, Luke was filled with pride. Paul, naturally, thought it "a mess. Whatever import or gravity it carries in the beginning will be lost on the reader in the end due to the distraction of ink blotches and the illegibility of an ancient man's hand."

Paul's execution was scheduled for three days hence, so that evening Luke brought the complete memoir with him—an unwieldy stack of parchments wrapped in a bag. Equipped with plenty of oil for his lamp, he and Paul went over the last few portions page by page. "I remain opposed to the handwriting," Paul said.

"And you must know by now that I have stopped listening."

"Or caring."

"Don't you dare say that," Luke said, suddenly overcome. "Not in jest, not in anger, not even to make a point. It is too close to the end for you to even imply such a thing."

Paul rose, opening his arms to Luke. "Forgive me, my friend. You know how I exaggerate."

As the doctor embraced Paul and drew him near, he longed for him to enjoy the glorified body promised him in paradise. Paul had nearly wasted completely away. Luke didn't know how the man could stand or walk, let alone be led miles out of Rome on the Ostian Road for his execution.

"I will never be able to thank you, Luke, not this side of eternity. I will watch and wait for you there, and perhaps in that beautiful dominion I will have the capacity to tell you all you have meant to me."

"Stop!" Luke said. "I will miss you as if a part of me has died."

"I *am* a part of you, my friend, for we are closer than brothers. We are united in Christ."

Luke heard the scrape of the wood as the covering over the hole was pulled away. He was relieved when it was Primus who descended.

"Hide the manuscript," he whispered urgently. "The execution has been moved up to tomorrow. They are coming now to move you to a cell above ground tonight."

"You must take the parchments," Paul said. "We cannot risk their being found with either of us."

"I have nowhere to hide them, Paul," Primus said. "I remain under suspicion. I had long before arranged for my day off to coincide with your execution—"

"Bless you."

"But when it was changed, I told them I wanted my day off changed too. My superiors are demanding to know why tomorrow is so important to me."

Luke heard voices above. "They are here already!"

"Give me the manuscript," Primus said.

Luke quickly stacked the pages in the cloth sack. "What will you do with it?"

"Hide it in the wall for now. I'll slip in here as soon as I can and take it home so you can have it."

As the guards above positioned themselves to drop into the dungeon, Primus quickly slid out the block of tufa, set the sack into the opening, and pushed the stone back. To Luke it didn't appear as flush as the day before, but no one seemed to notice. Paul beamed when his manacle was removed, but he looked unsteady as three men pulled him to his feet and then up through the opening.

Luke followed him to a holding cell about a tenth the size of the dungeon, but torches both warmed Paul and offered him light. He immediately began to preach to the guards. When one tried to shout him down, he said, "Come now, friend. Surely you can grant a condemned man the opportunity to practice for tomorrow when I will address all who come for the spectacle."

Most executions of Roman citizens were done without fanfare. The condemned was dragged outside the city, and wherever it seemed convenient, a swordsman would quickly do the deed.

The procession scheduled to leave the prison at eleven the next morning, however, would be accompanied by throngs. For weeks the emperor had daily sent tributes throughout the capital to announce the event, assuring citizens they would not be disappointed. "Nero has caught the snake by its head, and this will be no ordinary execution!" they said. The strongest man in Nero's army would behead the man with a five-foot sword.

Paul was to be bound and prodded along the route to where a small hillside provided natural seating and a clear view. Even people who had not heard what was to happen would be attracted by the sheer pageantry of Nero's men in full dress.

Luke arrived at dawn and found his friend sitting with his eyes closed, quietly praying. "Did Primus bring you the parchments?" Paul said.

"He did not. He said the dungeon was full all night. Apparently it is being prepared for the next prisoner."

"Prepared?" Paul said with a sad smile. "New draperies and bed coverings? Perhaps a bowl of fruit as a welcoming gift? Wait, I know! A fresh coat of slime."

"Whatever they're doing, Primus will get down there as soon as he can. But Paul, I have bad news."

Paul grinned. "Oh, Luke! What could be bad news on the day I am to die?"

"I'm just so sorry. But there is no time to get word to Timothy or Mark. They had planned to arrive two days from now, and when they do . . ."

"I will be gone. Tell them I knew of their intentions. I cherish knowing I will see you all again."

Luke looked up, alarmed to see men lowering bricks and mortar through the hole. When he noticed Gaius, he asked what was going on.

"They noticed cracks between some of the blocks," he said. "Rather than replace them, they're reinforcing the walls with a new layer of bricks all the way around. New bench. New chain. New everything. The dungeon will be about a foot narrower on all four sides."

Luke hurried out to find Primus, who had just arrived in civilian clothes. "You must get down there before they seal the manuscript away forever!"

Primus rushed inside and dropped into the dungeon. He returned quickly, looking grave. "It's already done," he told Luke. "That block has been thoroughly covered."

Luke closed his eyes. "We cannot tell Paul. All that work for naught. What a loss!"

"You can recreate it, Luke!" Primus said. "You have a good memory, and you know how he expressed himself."

Luke knew he could never produce anything like the original. Only dread over what was happening to his friend kept him from obsessing over the loss of the memoir. When he returned to Paul, the old man said, "You have kept your promise to spare me for this day. Just tell me again that you will not let the parchments fall into the wrong hands."

Luke studied the expectant eyes. "I will do everything in my power."

"I know you will."

Half an hour before the procession set out, the clamor of the troops and the crowds reached inside the prison. Luke couldn't hide his distaste for the fanfare.

"You hear a celebration you cannot enjoy," Paul said. "I hear an excited crowd. If only I can capture their attention, then I can engage their minds and, I pray, win their hearts."

Ever the optimist, Luke thought. He tried to pray for the success of Paul's efforts, but his eyes filled and his throat constricted.

"Say your good-byes, Doctor," Gaius said as he arrived with the executioner. "You will not see Paul again, except from a distance."

Luke's face contorted as he turned to his old friend. "Godspeed to you," he whispered, lips trembling. "I pray it will be quick and painless and that you will awaken in heaven."

"Oh, dear Luke! You need not request that last, as it is certain. Pray I will be allowed to preach, and then that the sword is swift."

"I love you, Paul."

"You have proved that in countless ways, my friend. Do not despair. Encourage the brethren, console the downhearted, but above all continue to spread the good news: Jesus Christ, the same yesterday, today, and forever."

"Time's up," Gaius said. "Doctor, please step out. Paul, this is Quintus."

Luke embraced Paul fiercely, certain the man would never have endured this long without the extra rations he had brought him daily. What a travesty that Nero should turn his death to sport.

Luke stepped outside the cage as the huge soldier went in and sat next to Paul. The physician was shocked at the softness of the executioner's voice and the gentleness of his manner. It was as if he truly wanted to be of help to Paul.

"The walk will be difficult," he began. "Unfortunately the horsemen have been told not to impede the people, should they want to get to you. They will throw things and some will try to strike you. Just keep moving. Now, as for the deathblow itself, I want you to know that I have done this many times and know how you can make it the easiest on yourself. As you kneel, you may find it hard to remain still, but you must. I will not torture you by delaying. The blade is so heavy that even I find it hard to lift, and it has been sharpened to its maximum. If you do not flinch or duck, I will end it with a single blow. I want you to know, sir, that I have no interest in making this more difficult for you than it needs to be."

"How very kind."

"Any questions for me?"

"Just one request. I will be preaching when I am kneeling before you. I do not expect you to wait long for me to finish, but if I am in the middle of a point, would you allow me to complete it?"

"I've never been asked that before, but yes, if I can I will. I must say, most of the men I have talked with in your situation have been too distraught to even speak, let alone discuss arrangements."

The death walk was worse than Luke feared. Thousands had been drawn to it as Nero gloated over besting one of his greatest adversaries, claiming Paul had been the mastermind behind the arson that had destroyed so much of Rome.

Paul was pushed, poked, jabbed with sticks, pelted with rocks, and shouted down all along the route. Luke could not understand where he found the strength to remain upright. He could only assume the man had been living for this day for so long that he was determined not to spoil it by collapsing.

Luke prayed that the crowd would become still when the procession reached the killing ground, but he was stunned when his prayer was answered. As the people found their places on the hillside, they actually shushed one another. Perhaps they simply didn't want to miss Paul's demise, but for whatever reason, during the several minutes it took for them to find places to sit, the only sound was the nickering and stamping of horses.

Paul was forced to kneel on flat, dusty ground. It pained Luke to watch as Paul, hands and feet still bound, came down hard and tumbled onto his side. He thrashed trying to get up until Quintus reached under his arm with one hand and pulled him to his knees.

The soldier ceremoniously pulled the monstrous sword from its sheath and held it aloft so the long blade gleamed in the sun. The crowd cried out, but when he lowered it they fell silent again.

Seemingly to everyone's surprise, Quintus stalled. He faced Paul, set the tip of the blade in the ground, and rested his hands on the hilt. Paul thanked him, lifted his head, and began.

At first Luke could not believe the vigorous quality of his voice. It was as if the Paul of twenty years before had reappeared. Preaching from his knees, hands behind his back, he mustered the strength to proclaim loudly enough for everyone to hear:

"Despite my circumstance, I kneel before you today thanking God Himself for the unspeakable privilege of declaring to you the gospel of His Son, Jesus Christ. I deliver to you that which I also received: that Christ died for our sins according to the Scriptures, and that He was buried, and that He rose again the third day. I am the least of the apostles, not worthy because I persecuted the church of God. But by the mercy of God, His grace toward me was not in vain.

"I am not ashamed of the gospel of Christ, for it is the power of God, granting salvation to everyone who believes.

"Now to Him who is able to also save you from your trespasses and sins, according to the gospel and the preaching of Jesus Christ, according to the revelation of the mystery kept secret since the world began but now made manifest, and by the prophetic Scriptures made known to all nations, according to the commandment of the everlasting God, for obedience to the faith—to God, alone wise, be glory through Jesus Christ forever."

Paul looked directly at Quintus, bowed his head, and remained perfectly still. The big man deliberately lifted the massive sword, spread his feet, and unleashed a mighty swing so fast that Luke heard the whoosh before the gruesome thud that sliced Paul asunder.

The crowd gasped as Paul's body fell to the dirt.

The crowd remained quiet as it began to dissipate. Luke had no destination and little will to carry on. He was soon overtaken by Primus, who put a hand on his shoulder.

"The world may never again see such a man," Luke managed, his cheeks and beard wet.

"He has a worthy successor, Doctor."

"No, no. I am not worthy to be mentioned in the same breath."

"But you are able to explain his message, are you not?"

"That I plan to continue to do."

"Then don't leave Rome because your friend is gone."

"I'm afraid I will be called to the churches, friend."

"Not until you have finished teaching me what Paul began."

"Have you counted the cost?"

"I just saw the cost," Primus said.

"Then I am at your service."

Epilogue

PRESENT-DAY TEXAS

IN AUGUST, WHEN AUGIE and Sofia were married in the chapel at Arlington Theological Seminary, Roger Michaels both gave away the bride and served as best man, slipping Augie the wedding band—the wire ring he'd bought in Philippi.

Biff Dyer and Rajiv Patel stood as groomsmen.

The mother of the bride—soon to move to America—was escorted down the aisle by Colonel Emmanuel, whose wife had also accompanied him.

The father of the bride was represented by a handwritten card mailed from Rebbibia Prison in Rome. Sofia later translated for Augie: "Perhaps with the passage of time you will come to believe the sincerity of my deepest regrets. Regardless whether you can ever forgive me, I wish you and August only the best. Love, your father."

The mother of the groom walked the aisle pushing a wheelchair, in which her husband sat in an ill-fitting tuxedo. At the reception, he and Dr. Les Moore would offer the first two toasts.

The elder Knoxes' wedding gift was to trade Augie the family home for his small house.

With his bride's approval, Augie Knox donated $100,000 to Arlington Theological Seminary, and an alcove in the library was named for his father and fashioned to house the first exquisite replicas of the Memoir of St. Paul the Apostle—scheduled to be delivered and displayed with great fanfare before the Christmas holidays.

Meanwhile, during every spare moment—rare due to Augie's teaching load, his father's rapid decline, and his new marriage—he immersed himself in poring over the photocopies of original parchments of Paul. It proved painstaking as he carefully parsed every sentence and jotted copious notes. It wasn't uncommon for him to spend several hours late at night working his way through only half a dozen or so pages.

Several hundred pages in, Augie reached a couple of lines that thrilled him with anticipation. Referring to his exile to Arabia, Paul had written: *During nearly three years there—which, for the first and only time I will reveal in detail following these thoughts—God Himself impressed upon me all the truths that would characterize my ministry.*

And later, referring to his missionary journeys, Paul had added: *I am eager to recite here many details I have only summarized in many letters to the churches.*

Augie had to force himself not to skip ahead. It took all the fortitude he could muster to continue combing through the narrative in the sequence Paul had penned it.

A month later, Augie neared the end of the photocopies and still had not reached the accounts Paul had foreshadowed. Then came news of Augie's father's death.

For the funeral of Dr. Edsel Knox, Roger Michaels and Georgio Emmanuel again made the trip from Rome. When the officiating pastor opened the floor for personal tributes, only a handful were offered. But the last two to stand at the microphone were Augie and Roger.

Augie began his remarks, "Six months ago I would not have anticipated the tears I shed today . . ."

Roger began his, "Six months ago I was not a believer . . ."

While he consoled his mother, helped her settle the estate, and prepared
for the exchange of houses, Augie put on hold the rich task of his thorough reading of the priceless memoir and writing his commentary on it.

When he finally got back to the photocopies his alarm became
dread over how few pages remained without Paul having covered Arabia
and the later details he had promised. Augie finally reached the last page
one night during the wee hours and slumped in his chair. He went back
to the passages that promised more and now studied not just the words
but also the handwriting.

The section immediately following the mention of adding more had
clearly been written later by a much older Paul. It didn't seem possible
he would have left out such important content. Augie paced in the darkness, finally mounting the stairs and sitting on the edge of his and Sofia's
bed. He sighed.

"What is it, love?" she slurred.

"Sorry, babe. I didn't mean to—"

"Tell me, Augie."

"What time is it in Rome?"

She squinted at the clock. "Almost two here means just before nine
in the morning there. Why?"

He reached for the phone. "I've got to call Georgio."

Sofia sat up. "Augie—"

When Augie reached the head of the Italian Art Squad, Georgio immediately said, "It's wonderful to hear from you, Dr. Knox, but more importantly, how is my favorite adopted daughter?"

"She's right here, and she's fine. And fond of you, sir."

"It's after midnight there, Augie. Is there a problem?"

Augie told him what he had found. "I'm hoping Klaudios just skipped those pages when he was copying them. How many original pages are there?"

"Five hundred and four."

Augie groaned. "That's how many photocopies I have, Georgio. The memoir is incomplete."

"You think Klaudios held some back?"

"I have no idea who did this or when. All I know is that pages are missing."

THE END

Acknowledgments

Dr. James S. MacDonald is a Bible teacher nonpareil. Access to his inexhaustible mind and research was a treasure, as is his friendship.

Thanks also to Dr. Laurie Norris, then of James's Harvest Bible Chapel staff and now on the faculty of the Moody Bible Institute of Chicago, who so ably provided every detail I needed.

Dr. Charlie Dyer was always at the ready with a generous response to any question about the Holy Land.

Chuck and Krissie Cilano helped with the Italian. If it's right, it's because of them. If it's wrong, that's on me.

I'm grateful to the following for their input on the New Testament: Dr. Wallace A. Alcorn, Joe Buonassissi, Dr. Michael Easley, Dr. Gene Getz, and Dr. Grant Osborne.

Jeana Ledbetter, editorial vice president at Worthy Publishing, has been steadfast in her support and encouragement.

Thanks to Worthy CEO Byron Williamson for green-lighting the project and believing in me. His entire team has proved a delight.

The skill of my editor, the legendary Phyllis Grann, is reflected on every page, and her cheerleading made the task a treat.

More than three hundred people came alongside from the announcement of this project and agreed to pray for and encourage me. I cannot think of this novel without a deep sense of connection to that team, too numerous to list here but wholly appreciated nonetheless.

Lynn and Debbie Kaupp and Trisha Priebe bear loads daily that would otherwise rob me of the time necessary to frolic in the land of make-believe.

My agent, David Vigliano, has become a dear friend and champion, a welcome voice on the phone, and a generous host in the Big Apple.

I could not be a writer, and certainly not a novelist, without my wife, Dianna. It would take another book as long as this one to list all she does for me.

Jerry B. Jenkins's novels have sold more than 70 million copies, including the phenomenal mega-bestselling Left Behind series. Twenty of his books have reached the *New York Times* Best Sellers List, including seven that debuted at number one, and also the *USA Today*, *Publishers Weekly*, and *Wall Street Journal* bestseller lists. Jenkins has been featured on the cover of *Newsweek* magazine. He and his wife, Dianna, live in Colorado.

WORTHY
PUBLISHING

IF YOU ENJOYED THIS BOOK, WILL YOU CONSIDER
SHARING THE MESSAGE WITH OTHERS?

- Mention the book in a Facebook post, Twitter update,
  Pinterest pin, or blog post.

- Recommend this book to those in your small group,
  book club, workplace, and classes.

- Head over to facebook.com/jerry.b.jenkins, "LIKE" the
  page, and post a comment as to what you enjoyed the most.

- Tweet "I recommend reading #ISaul by @JerryBJenkins
  // @worthypub"

- Pick up a copy for someone you know who would be
  challenged and encouraged by this message.

- Write a review on amazon.com, bn.com, goodreads.com,
  or cbd.com.

You can subscribe to Worthy Publishing's newsletter at
worthypublishing.com.

**WORTHY PUBLISHING
FACEBOOK PAGE**

**WORTHY PUBLISHING
WEBSITE**